Civil War Settlers

Civil War Settlers is the first comprehensive analysis of Scandinavian Americans and their participation in the US Civil War. Based on thousands of sources in multiple languages, Anders Bo Rasmussen brings the untold story of Scandinavian American immigrants to life by focusing on their lived community experience and positioning it within the larger context of western settler colonialism. Associating American citizenship with liberty and equality, Scandinavian immigrants openly opposed slavery and were among the most enthusiastic foreign-born supporters of the early Republican Party. However, the malleable concept of citizenship was used by immigrants to resist draft service, and support a white man's republic through territorial expansion on American Indian land and, in part, into the Caribbean. Consequently, Scandinavian immigrants after emancipation proved to be reactionary Republicans, not abolitionists. This unique approach to the Civil War sheds new light on how whiteness and access to territory formed an integral part of American immigration history.

Anders Bo Rasmussen is Associate Professor of American History at the University of Southern Denmark. He is the recipient of the Carlsberg Foundation Monograph Fellowship, a former Fulbright scholar at New York University, and has explored the Scandinavian Civil War experience across the United States for more than a decade.

FIGURE 0.1 Norwegian-born artist Ole Balling's most famous painting "Grant and His Generals" from 1865. Photo by National Portrait Gallery, Smithsonian Institution via Getty Images.

Civil War Settlers

Scandinavians, Citizenship, and American Empire,
1848–1870

ANDERS BO RASMUSSEN

University of Southern Denmark

CAMBRIDGE
UNIVERSITY PRESS

CAMBRIDGE
UNIVERSITY PRESS

University Printing House, Cambridge CB2 8BS, United Kingdom

One Liberty Plaza, 20th Floor, New York, NY 10006, USA

477 Williamstown Road, Port Melbourne, VIC 3207, Australia

314–321, 3rd Floor, Plot 3, Splendor Forum, Jasola District Centre,
New Delhi – 110025, India

103 Penang Road, #05–06/07, Visioncrest Commercial, Singapore 238467

Cambridge University Press is part of the University of Cambridge.

It furthers the University's mission by disseminating knowledge in the pursuit of
education, learning, and research at the highest international levels of excellence.

www.cambridge.org
Information on this title: www.cambridge.org/9781108845564
DOI: 10.1017/9781108980135

© Anders Bo Rasmussen 2022

First published 2022

A catalogue record for this publication is available from the British Library.

ISBN 978-1-108-84556-4 Hardback

Cambridge University Press has no responsibility for the persistence or accuracy of
URLs for external or third-party internet websites referred to in this publication
and does not guarantee that any content on such websites is, or will remain,
accurate or appropriate.

Contents

Contents

Figures

Acknowledgments

By the banks of the Yazoo and Mississippi rivers, the ironclad USS *Cairo* sits protected by a constructed roof that naturally leads the eyes upward toward the Vicksburg National Military Park Visitor Center. Together with two friends, Rasmus Nielsen and Erik Hardick, I visited Vicksburg in December 2002, and there I found the database of Civil War soldier names that sparked this project. During my visit, I noticed many Scandinavian names that have been with me since, and in the process I met countless people who helped bring their stories to life.

After a decade of intermittent research, both helped and hindered by graduate school, the spring of 2013 proved a key turning point, as Eric Foner generously facilitated a visiting scholar experience at Columbia University that, with the help of Kevin Coyne, enabled me to finish a long-form story on the Scandinavian Civil War experience. Later that same year, April Holm organized a wonderful Civil War Conference at the University of Mississippi together with the ebullient John Neff. The conference introduced me to a number of great scholars, among them David J. Gerleman and J. David Hacker, who graciously shared some of their research with me, and Jim Downs, who co-organized the SHA conference in 2016 and kindly trusted me to chair a panel. The SHA conference, in turn, allowed me to meet Susannah Ural and her former editor Deborah "Debbie" Gershenowitz. For years, Debbie supported the book and eventually recommended it to her successor at Cambridge University Press, Cecelia Cancellaro. Aided by their excellent editorial assistants Rachel Blaifelder and Victoria Phillips, Debbie and Cecelia expertly guided the project through the publication stages. To all I am grateful.

Also among the people that deserve the most gratitude are Stephen Kantrowitz and Pernille Ipsen, who shared their insight on both sides of the Atlantic on several occasions. Steve and Pernille at one point opened their Wisconsin home, with a book-filled basement, for an entire summer, which allowed for one of the most productive immersion experiences of this project. Moreover, since Pernille is a Danish-born immigrant in the United States, and Steve a former Fulbright Professor at my home university, we have regularly met in Denmark. Thus, in Copenhagen, over a breakfast bowl of *gröd* (porridge) several years back, Steve in his sharp-witted way laid out some important connections between Scandinavian-born immigrants' Old World ideology and New World experiences that have helped guide this project since.

A few years earlier, Julie Allen worked tirelessly to provide a visiting scholar opportunity in Madison during the Wisconsin winter, which proved to be another memorable experience of exploration, inspiration, and snow shoveling (thank you to Terri Regner, who let me stay at her house in exchange for clearing the driveway).

Inspiration and guidance also characterized my experience in Professor Martha Hodes' graduate seminar in 2016 when I spent a year as a Fulbright scholar at New York University. On top of everything, Professor Hodes found time to offer crucial encouragement and continued inspiration. Also during my Fulbright year, Robert Boynton and Ted Conover, along with their talented students, provided a host of opportunities for stimulating storytelling, social experiences, and friendship. In addition, Karen V. Hansen kindly invited me to a warm and inspiring family dinner in New York City when I first arrived. Andrew Hartman, another former Fulbright scholar in Denmark, also opened up his home. Visits to the Hartman household in Illinois were convenient excuses for great conversation and an occasional high-quality beer. Andrew also introduced me to Andrew Zimmerman, who generously took time to talk transnational Civil War issues over lunch by the National Archives. In similar impressive form, Steven Hahn shared his thoughts on the Civil War and American empire over a cup of coffee at the Huntington Library.

Lastly, on the American academic side, thank you to Michael Douma, a kind of long-lost scholarly twin, who – as siblings do when they first learn of each other's existence – got in touch out of nowhere in late 2013, after realizing we were both working on colonization and the West Indies. Together with Rob Faith, some of the most interesting discoveries related to citizenship and American empire in this book can be traced back to this collaboration.

In addition, several Americans – some Scandinavian descendants, others passionate librarians, and still others generous people offering a couch or a meal – have helped make this book much richer (and better illustrated). In no particular order they are: Steve Sayre, Roger and Leah Johnson, Anne Winslow, Laura Sadovnikoff, Helene Leaf, Georgia Kestol, and Ordelle Hill, who generously shared private family collections of Swedish, Norwegian, and Danish Civil War–era immigrants. Moreover, Scott Cantwell Meeker, Lynette Brenzel, Louis Garcia, the passionate Diane Maurer–led volunteers at the Norwegian American Genealogical Center in Madison, and Vesterheim Museum's Jennifer Kovarik also deserve thanks. John Mark Nielsen activated his enormous Danish-American network when I first started the research process, and Jill Seaholm, Susanne Titus, and Lisa Huntsha (as well as Amanda Hadzidedic) at Augustana College did the same on the Swedish-American side. Among archivists, Germain Bienvenu at Louisiana State University Libraries as well as Lee Grady, Simone Munson, Lisa Marine, Jenny Barth, and all the good people at the Wisconsin Historical Society – including Dee Grimsrud, now retired – are unparalleled, enthusiastic, and helpful. In Northfield, Minnesota, Norwegian-American archivists Kristell Benson, Christina Warner, Jeff Suave, and Amy Boxrud made sure I had an excellent and productive visit – one that even concluded with me seeing my first-ever bald eagle.

Among the many other hospitable Americans who have opened their homes to me during many research trips are Paul Supple in Texas, Lowell and Marilyn Kramme in Iowa, and John and Shawn Berry, my Maryland host-parents in 1994–5 as well as my hosts during several subsequent visits to the National Archives. At Ohio University, Phyllis Field pointed me to the rich Fritz Rasmussen material in Wisconsin and, together with Marvin Fletcher, sharpened my (under)graduate thinking in 2002–3.

At the University of Southern Denmark, before and now, I give thanks to superb teachers and scholars such as David Nye, Clara Juncker, Thomas Ærvold Bjerre, Tom Buk-Swienty, and Peter Bro, as well as other wonderful colleagues, students, and librarians. As an example, Rasmus Glenthøj alerted me to Hobsbawm's writing on the threshold principle, and Morten Ottosen along with Michael Bregnsbo helped me

understand the 1848 revolutions in Scandinavia more deeply while Kasper
Grotle Rasmussen explained key French phrases and Niels Bjerre-Poulsen
bought me valuable writing time by editing a special issue of *American
Studies in Scandinavia*. Thanks especially though to Jørn Brøndal, who
has mentored the project from the very beginning read countless drafts,
and expertly organized a Scandinavian encounters network that included
Dag Blanck and Gunlög Fur, whose scholarship continues to inspire. I also
benefited from the assistance of Torben Grøngaard Jeppesen at Odense
City Museums who generously shared his work and included me in several
enlightening discussions, as well as a behind-the-scenes visit to Ellis Island,
during the year I worked within his organization.

The book was aided as well by Morten Michaelsen, who found elegant
phrases for tricky translations, and experienced researchers, museum
workers, and illustrators such as Leif Ernst, Knud Aundorf, Jan Ingar
Hansen, Michael Bach, Lisbeth Pedersen, Bendt Nielsen, and Mads Findal
Andreasen. Also thank you to the host of genealogists in DIS-Odense (not
least H. C. and Steen who taught me gothic handwriting) and Birgit
Christensen, who helped read what I could not at key stages of this
project.

Importantly, this project would not have been possible without the
financial support of the Danish American Heritage Society, the Swenson
Center, the University of Wisconsin – Friends of the Library, the Iowa
State Historical Society, the Fulbright Program and Marie Mønsted, the
Danish Council for Independent Research – Humanities, the University of
Southern Denmark, The Carlsberg Foundation, Den Fynske Bladfond,
Zetland, and not least *Informations Forlag* (including editors Jacob
Maagaard and Jakob Moll).

Finally, thank you to my family, both immediate and extended. To Erin
and Henry, who read and reread chapters; to Kristine, who organized
writing retreats; to my parents, who bought me my first Civil War books;
and to Zia, a literal light in the world.

A few sections of this book, here rewritten and recontextualized, appeared previously in:

Rasmussen, Anders Bo. "'On Liberty and Equality': Race and Reconstruction among Scandinavian Immigrants, 1864–1868." In *Nordic Whiteness and Migration to the USA: A Hierarchy of Colour*, edited by Jana Sverdluck and Terje Joranger. New York: Routledge, 2020.

Douma, Michael J., Anders Bo Rasmussen, and Robert O. Faith. "The Impressment of Foreign-Born Soldiers in the Union Army." *Journal of American Ethnic History* 38, no. 3 (2019): 76–106.

Rasmussen, Anders Bo. "The Spoils of the Victors: Captain Ferdinand Winslow and the 1863 Curtis Court of Inquiry." *Annals of Iowa* 76, no. 2 (2017): 161–179.

Rasmussen, Anders Bo. "'The States' Readmission Puts an End to All Civil and Political Questions': Scandinavian Immigrants and Debates over Racial Equality during the Impeachment of President Andrew Johnson." *Swedish-American Historical Quarterly* 68, no. 4 (2017): 202–217.

Rasmussen, Anders Bo. "'Drawn Together in a Blood Brotherhood': Civic Nationalism amongst Scandinavian Immigrants in the American Civil War Crucible." *American Studies in Scandinavia* 48, no. 2 (2016): 7–31.

Douma, Michael J., and Anders Bo Rasmussen. "The Danish St Croix Project: Revisiting the Lincoln Colonization Program with Foreign-Language Sources." *American Nineteenth Century History* 15, no. 3 (2014): 311–342.

Rasmussen, Anders Bo. *I krig for Lincoln* [*To War for Lincoln*]. Copenhagen: Informations Forlag, 2014.

Introduction

The Problem and the Method

Abraham Lincoln's first annual message to Congress was conveyed with excitement on the front pages of the Scandinavian-American press.[1] Questions surrounding civil war, military service, and slavery set the agenda for *Emigranten* (the Emigrant) and *Hemlandet* (the Homeland), and their intimate connection to issues of citizenship and American empire were revealed by the president's words on December 3, 1861.[2]

"Fellow Citizens of the Senate and House of Representatives," the president began.[3] Due to the "factious domestic division," the United States was exposed to a "disrespect abroad."[4] One strong nation, Lincoln explained, would ensure a more "durable peace" and "reliable commerce" than would that "same nation broken into hostile fragments."[5] Now that Civil War was upon the United States, however, the president recommended Congress' consideration of a series of wartime legislation.[6]

Mindful of avoiding the term "slavery," Lincoln explicitly addressed the fate of enslaved people. As "the legal claims of certain persons to the labor and services of certain other persons" had "become forfeited" due to the Confiscation Act of August 8, 1861, formerly enslaved people in the

---

[1] "Præsidentens Budskab [The President's Message]," *Emigranten*, December 9, 1861; "Presidentens Budskap [The President's Message]," *Hemlandet*, December 11, 1861.

[2] "Washington," *Emigranten*, December 2, 1861; "The Proceedings of Congress," *New York Times*, December 4, 1861.

[3] Abraham Lincoln, "First Annual Message" (online by Gerhard Peters and John T. Woolley, The American Presidency Project, www.presidency.ucsb.edu/documents/first-annual-message-9, 1861).

[4] Ibid.   [5] Ibid.   [6] Ibid.

insurgent states would have "to be provided for in some way," Lincoln specified.[7]

To this end, the president proposed that steps toward colonization – the settlement of Black Americans outside the nation's borders – be taken.[8] It "may be well to consider, too," Lincoln added, "whether the free colored people already in the United States could not, so far as individuals may desire, be included in such colonization."[9] To realize colonization plans, acquisition of territory and "appropriation of money" would be neces- sary: "If it be said that the only legitimate object of acquiring territory is to furnish homes for white men, this measure effects that object, for the emigration of colored men leaves additional room for white men remain- ing or coming here."[10]

Lincoln's First Message to Congress, arguing for acquisition of land and funding to remove people of African descent to "a climate congenial to them," revealed important aspects of his administration's ideas about white citizenship and empire through expansion. Lincoln's renewed call for colonization built on political ideas stretching back decades, despite Black people's opposition and search for alternatives.[11]

In a developing American empire, "ruled in the interests of white people," nonwhites were, as Steven Hahn reminds us, forced to "leave or submit."[12] Debates over colonization and acquisition of territory therefore became closely related "intellectually and politically, as well as chronologically."[13] The white supremacist ideology underpinning colonization also justified territorial expansion on the North American continent.[14]

---

[7] Ibid.

[8] Ibid. For a discussion of colonization, see Eric Foner, "Lincoln and Colonization," in *Our Lincoln*, ed. Eric Foner (New York: W. W. Norton, 2008), 136. Also Sebastian N. Page, *Black Resettlement and the American Civil War* (Cambridge, MA: Cambridge University Press, 2021), 1–9.

[9] Lincoln, "First Annual Message."   [10] Ibid.

[11] Manisha Sinha, *The Slave's Cause: A History of Abolition* (New Haven, CT: Yale University Press, 2016), 163–171; Marie Tyler-McGraw, *An African Republic: Black and White Virginians in the Making of Liberia* (Chapel Hill: University of North Carolina Press, 2007), 64.

[12] Steven Hahn, *A Nation without Borders: The United States and Its World in an Age of Civil Wars, 1830–1910* (New York: Viking, 2016), 45.

[13] Ibid. Also Natalie Joy, "The Indian's Cause: Abolitionists and Native American Rights," *Journal of the Civil War Era* 8, no. 2 (2018): 215–216. According to Joy, the anti-slavery movement drew important inspiration from opposition to dispossession of American Indians.

[14] Foner, "Lincoln and Colonization," 137; Michael J. Douma and Anders Bo Rasmussen, "The Danish St Croix Project: Revisiting the Lincoln Colonization Program with Foreign-Language Sources," *American Nineteenth Century History* 15, no. 3 (2014):

Lincoln's call for territorial acquisition to ensure "one strong nation" was an idea widely shared among intellectuals and politicians in the nineteenth century and one clearly expressed by influential German-born economist Friedrich List, who was shaped "in a profound way" by his experience in the United States between 1825 and 1830.[15]

List emphasized the need to secure "a large population and an extensive territory endowed with manifold natural resources," due to the belief that expansion was needed to establish a healthy nation (and, one might add, empire).[16] The perceived importance of population growth and territorial expansion – what Eric Hobsbawm has called the *threshold principle* – helped guide policy in the mid-nineteenth-century United States as well as in Europe.[17] According to Hobsbawm, nations had to engage in *Grossstaatenbildung* (large state building) or at least maintain a threshold of a "sufficient size" in order to preserve their "historical justification."[18] The alternative, a descent into *Kleinstaaterei* (a "system of mini-states"), was seen as a sure path to foreign domination or annihilation.[19]

8–10; Stephen Kantrowitz, "White Supremacy, Settler Colonialism, and the Two Citizenships of the Fourteenth Amendment," *Journal of the Civil War Era* 10, no. 1 (2020): 32, 39–40. As Kantrowitz notes, "the history of settler-colonialism has unfolded in close and complicated relationship with the history of white supremacy with regard to African Americans. The histories are not the same, but they cannot be disentangled from each other."

[15] Gregor Thum, "Seapower and Frontier Settlement: Friedrich List's American Vision for Germany," in *German and United States Colonialism in a Connected World: Entangled Empires*, ed. Janne Lahti (Palgrave Macmillan, 2021), 18; Eric J. Hobsbawm, *Nations and Nationalism since 1780: Programme, Myth, Reality* (Cambridge: Cambridge University Press, 1992), 29; William Notz, "Frederick List in America," *American Economic Review* 16, no. 2 (1926): 260.

[16] Quoted in Hobsbawm, *Nations and Nationalism since 1780: Programme, Myth, Reality*, 30–32. My definition of "empire" is inspired by Paul Frymer, who points out that building an expanding nineteenth-century "American empire" was "a project of population control and settlement" with land policy as a central instrument, based on the premise that being American "meant to be white." See Paul Frymer, *Building an American Empire: The Era of Territorial and Political Expansion* (Princeton, NJ: Princeton University Press, 2017), 11, 21–22.

[17] Lincoln, "First Annual Message," 31; Hobsbawm, *Nations and Nationalism since 1780: Programme, Myth, Reality*; Rasmus Glenthøj, "Pan-Scandinavism and the Threshold Principle?," in *A History of the European Restorations: Governments, States and Monarchy*, ed. Michael Broers and Ambrogio Caiani (Bloomsbury Academic, 2019). I am grateful to my colleague Rasmus Glenthøj for sharing his ideas on Hobsbawm and "the threshold principle" with me.

[18] Hobsbawm, *Nations and Nationalism since 1780: Programme, Myth, Reality*, 30–35.

[19] Ibid.

The importance of a large population had been pointed out at least since Adam Smith's 1776 claim that the "most decisive mark of the prosperity of any country is the increase of the number of its inhabitants."[20] As an example, J. David Hacker's argument that "eighteenth- and nineteenth-century political observers equated rapid population growth with economic and political strength" was clearly expressed in the 1850 US census.[21] The census pointed to an increase in the US population (over five million "whites" between 1840 and 1850) and directly compared its numbers to European powers such as the more populated Great Britain (less than one million people added between 1841 and 1851).[22]

Additionally, the republic's "territorial extent" was now "three times as large as the whole of France, Britain, Austria, Prussia, Spain, Portugal, Belgium, Holland, and Denmark, together" and was "of equal extent with the Roman empire, or that of Alexander."[23]

Indeed, ideas of territorial and population expansion, in Hobsbawm's words, "seemed too obvious to require argument" for nineteenth-century policymakers.[24] Still, in his first annual message to Congress, Lincoln expressed pride in the nation's population growth and concluded his address with the prediction that some Americans alive in 1861 would "live to see" the Union "contain 250,000,000" (if it could be preserved).[25]

In the decades leading up to the Civil War, several ascending and established American politicians either directly or indirectly articulated their belief in the threshold principle.[26] In an 1844 speech entitled "Elements of Empire in America," William Seward, the future Republican secretary of state, laid out the themes of nonwhite subjugation

---

[20] James R. Otteson, ed., *Adam Smith: Selected Philosophical Writings* (Exeter: Imprint Academic, 2004), 119.

[21] J. David Hacker, "New Estimates of Census Coverage in the United States, 1850–1930," *Social Science History* 37, no. 1 (2013): 75.

[22] *The Seventh Census of the United States: 1850* (Washington, DC: Robert Armstrong, Public Printer, 1853), xxxi–xxxiv.

[23] Ibid., xxix; Torben Grøngaard Jeppesen, *Danske i USA 1850–2000. En Demografisk, Social Og Kulturgeografisk Undersøgelse Af De Danske Immigranter Og Deres Efterkommere* [*Danes in the United States 1850–2000: A Demographic, Social and Cultural Geographic Study of the Danish Immigrants and Their Descendants*] (Odense: Syddansk Universitetsforlag, 2005), 67.

[24] Hobsbawm, *Nations and Nationalism since 1780: Programme, Myth, Reality,* 30; Glenthøj, "Pan-Scandinavism and the Threshold Principle?," 4.

[25] Lincoln, "First Annual Message."

[26] Hobsbawm, *Nations and Nationalism since 1780: Programme, Myth, Reality,* 29.

and expansion when he argued that "expansive territory inseparably belongs to the idea of National Greatness."[27] The following year, James K. Polk took office with an Inaugural Address celebrating the new states "admitted," the territories created, the population expanded, and the "title of numerous Indian tribes to vast tracts of land" extinguished.[28]

Moreover, in his first Senate speech in 1850, Seward expressed the view that white Europeans, what he called "the ruling homogeneous family planted at first on the Atlantic shore," was destined to spread "itself westward" through continued population growth.[29] Speaking in Saint Paul, Minnesota, an increasingly attractive locality for Scandinavian immigrants, a decade later Seward explicitly mentioned American expansion north, west, and south as part of a crosscontinent national project and reiterated the idea that "this is the land for the white man."[30] Seward, along with Wisconsin Senator James Doolittle, who spoke of "the great national policy which is to control this continent," also welcomed annexation of Cuba if slavery was abolished.[31]

As it turned out, the deep-seated belief in continued territorial expansion, and the underlying issue of slavery, was a central cause of the Civil War.[32]

[27] Quoted in Richard H. Immerman, *Empire for Liberty: A History of American Imperialism from Benjamin Franklin to Paul Wolfowitz* (Princeton, NJ: Princeton University Press, 2012), 8–11, 106. Immerman notes, "Even as they annihilated or forcibly relocated Native Americans, executed foreign nationals, and conquered territories," Americans generally perceived empire positively. See also Frymer, *Building an American Empire: the Era of Territorial and Political Expansion*, 12–15.

[28] James K. Polk, "Inaugural Address" (online by Gerhard Peters and John T. Woolley, The American Presidency Project, www.presidency.ucsb.edu/documents/inaugural-address-3 0, 1845).

[29] Quoted in Immerman, *Empire for Liberty: A History of American Imperialism from Benjamin Franklin to Paul Wolfowitz*, 112. Seward also expressed the view that the "African race" and "the aborigines, savage and civilized" were incapable of assimilation and thus articulated his and many white contemporaries' view of territorial and population expansion.

[30] George E. Baker, ed., *The Works of William H. Seward*, vol. 4 (Boston, MA: Houghton, Mifflin and Company, 1884), 333–334. Seward's speech made such an impression on Swedish-born Hans Mattson that he explicitly mentioned it in his memoirs thirty years later. See Hans Mattson, *Reminiscences: The Story of an Emigrant* (Saint Paul, MN: D. D. Merrill Company, 1891), 56.

[31] Quoted in Gregory P. Downs, *The Second American Revolution: The Civil War–Era Struggle over Cuba and the Rebirth of the American Republic* (Chapel Hill, NC: University of North Carolina Press, 2019), 87. For leading Republican politicians' support of colonization, see Page, *Black Resettlement and the American Civil War, 104-114*

[32] James Oakes, *Freedom National: The Destruction of Slavery in the United States, 1861–1865* (New York: W. W. Norton, 2013), 78–80; Steven E. Woodworth, *Manifest Destinies: America's Westward Expansion and the Road to Civil War* (New York: Knopf, 2010), 341–358. See also James M. McPherson, "'Two Irreconcilable

Fiercely opposed to slavery's expansion but willing to accept slavery's temporary survival inside a "cordon" of freedom, leading Republican politicians in the Civil War era supported an expanding white man's republic.[33]

Still, when South Carolina's leaders voted to secede from the Union on December 20, 1860, their decision threatened an American decline toward *Kleinstaaterei*.[34] Such fears were articulated by Seward on January 12, 1861, when he warned the Senate of a looming "momenteous and disastrous revolution" that imperiled an "empire" that had grown to "thirty-three parts" and "no less than thirty million inhabitants."[35] Seward's trepidations proved prescient as other states soon followed South Carolina's lead. By February 1861, representatives from seven southern states were meeting in Montgomery, Alabama, to form a new nation, and two months later four more joined the Confederate States of America.

Peoples'? Ethnic Nationalism in the Confederacy," in *The Civil War as Global Conflict: Transnational Meanings of the American Civil War*, ed. David T. Gleeson and Simon Lewis (Columbia: University of South Carolina Press, 2014), 89; Stephen Kantrowitz, *More Than Freedom: Fighting for Black Citizenship in a White Republic, 1829–1889* (New York: Penguin Press, 2012), 176–180. See also Charles B. Dew, *Apostles of Disunion: Southern Secession Commissioners and the Causes of the Civil War* (Charlottesville: University Press of Virginia, 2001), 14–15. In a speech to the Confederate Congress on April 29, 1861, President Jefferson Davis emphasized the Republican Party's threatening position regarding slaveowners' access to the territories as a central reason why "the people of the Southern States were driven by the conduct of the North to the adoption of some course of action to avert the danger with which they were openly menaced." Also, in his so-called "Cornerstone Speech," Confederate vice president Alexander Stephens in March 1861 described the issue of slavery as the "immediate cause" of secession. See Alexander H. Stephens, "'Corner-Stone' Speech, March 21, 1861," in Brooks D. Simpson, Stephen W. Sears, and Aaron Sheehan-Dean, eds., *The Civil War: The First Year Told by Those Who Lived It* (New York: Library of America, 2011), 226.

[33] Oakes, *Freedom National: The Destruction of Slavery in the United States, 1861–1865*, 42. George Julian, Owen Lovejoy, and Richard Yates, among other Republican politicians, supported homestead legislation in the 1850s. See Eric Foner, *Free Soil, Free Labor, Free Men: The Ideology of the Republican Party before the Civil War* (New York: Oxford University Press, 1995), 29, 236. See also Roy P. Basler, ed., *Collected Works of Abraham Lincoln*, vol. 4 (New Brunswick, NJ: Rutgers University Press, 1953), 203. See as well Hahn, *A Nation without Borders: The United States and Its World in an Age of Civil Wars, 1830–1910*, 196–197, 284.

[34] Lincoln, "First Annual Message."

[35] John C. Rives, ed., *The Congressional Globe: Containing the Debates and Proceedings of the Second Session of the Thirty-Sixth Congress* (Washington, DC: Congressional Globe Office, 1861), 39; Kantrowitz, "White Supremacy, Settler Colonialism, and the Two Citizenships of the Fourteenth Amendment," 39–40.

If states could break away from the Union this easily, then the possibility existed that, in Steven Hahn's words, "the United States might unravel in a variety of ways and leave the North American continent awash in potentially rivalrous states and confederations."[36]

Scandinavian-born men and women, even if unfamiliar with List's work or Republican oratory, proved receptive to ideas of territorial and (white) population expansion based on free labor, as they generally associated American citizenship with the liberty and equality embodied in landownership but downplayed the violence toward American Indians involved in landtaking.

Consequently, the two main strands of Hobsbawm's threshold principle – the need to attract "a large population and an extensive territory" – coupled with an exploration of citizenship's malleable meaning to Scandinavian immigrants constitute the foundation for the following chapters.[37]

By analyzing eastern political decision-making and western settlement experience – meaning the chronological, intellectual, and political connections between national policies of an American imperial project and their concrete ramifications at the local level – this book details the lived community experience and worldview among Scandinavian-American immigrants.

These transnational connections are significant in order to understand Civil War–era politics at both the ideological and social levels, and the story that unfolds therefore heeds recent calls to combine "microhistorical work in the archives [with] macro-historical frameworks."[38] As an example, foreign-born immigrants resisting military service in their communities took up so much energy in the American Department of State that Ella Lonn later wondered how Secretary of State Seward "had time to attend to any other duties"?[39]

---

[36] Hahn, *A Nation without Borders: The United States and Its World in an Age of Civil Wars, 1830–1910*, 228.

[37] Hobsbawm, *Nations and Nationalism since 1780: Programme, Myth, Reality*, 30.

[38] Jo Guldi and David Armitage, *The History Manifesto* (Cambridge: Cambridge University Press, 2014), 121. See also Susannah J. Ural, ed., *Civil War Citizens: Race, Ethnicity and Identity in America's Bloodiest Conflict* (New York: New York University Press, 2010), 1–8. Also David T. Gleeson and Simon Lewis, "Introduction," in *The Civil War as Global Conflict: Transnational Meanings of the American Civil War*, ed. David T. Gleeson and Simon Lewis (Columbia: University of South Carolina Press, 2014).

[39] Ella Lonn, *Foreigners in the Union Army and Navy* (Baton Rouge: Louisiana State University Press, 1951), 469–70.

Civil War Settlers thus contributes to American nineteenth-century historiography along transnational, ethnic, and racial dimensions. First, the book nuances the immigrant populations' role in the Republican Party's Civil War–era coalition. In the existing literature, German and Irish immigrants have taken center stage due to their larger share of the population. However, their experience and at least partial attraction to the Democratic Party does not generally represent European immigrants because of differences in religious background, language, settlement patterns, and Old World history.[40]

Second, despite more than 20 percent of the Union army claiming foreign-born roots, the ethnic aspect of the Civil War has only recently attracted wider scholarly attention.[41] The scrutiny of

[40] See for example Susannah Ural Bruce, *The Harp and The Eagle: Irish-American Volunteers and the Union Army, 1861–1865* (New York: New York University Press, 2006), 47; Walter D. Kamphoefner and Wolfgang Helbich, eds., *Germans in the Civil War: The Letters They Wrote Home* (Chapel Hill: University of North Carolina Press, 2006), 12. Though leading clergymen of the Norwegian Synod, inspired by the German Missouri Synod, argued that slavery was sanctioned by the Bible, their congregations were largely anti-slavery during the Civil War. Brynjar Haraldsø, *Slaveridebatten i Den Norske Synode: En Undersøkelse Av Slaveridebatten i Den Norske Synode i USA i 1860-Årene Med Særlig Vekt På Debattens Kirkelig-Teologiske Aspekter* [*The Slavery Debate in the Norwegian Synod: A Study of the Slavery Debate in the Norwegian Synod in the United States During the 1860s Emphasizing the Debate's Church-Theological Aspects*] (Oslo: Solum Forlag, 1988), 68–71.

[41] For a valuable overview of the "imperial" trajectory in Civil War–era studies of immigration, see Alison Clark Efford, "Civil War–Era Immigration and the Imperial United States," *Journal of the Civil War Era* 10, no. 2 (2020): 233–253. Other recent studies of Civil War era immigration include Paul Quigley, ed., *The Civil War and the Transformation of American Citizenship* (Baton Rouge: Louisiana State University, 2018); Ryan W. Keating, *Shades of Green: Irish Regiments, American Soldiers, and Local Communities in the Civil War Era* (Fordham University Press, 2017); Kristen Layne Anderson, *Abolitionizing Missouri: German Immigrants and Racial Ideology in Nineteenth-Century America* (Baton Rouge: Louisiana State University Press, 2016); David T. Gleeson and Simon Lewis, eds., *The Civil War as Global Conflict: The Transnational Meanings of the American Civil War* (Columbia: University of South Carolina Press, 2014); Alison Clark Efford, *German Immigrants, Race, and Citizenship in the Civil War Era* (Washington, DC: Cambridge University Press, 2013); Don H. Doyle, *Cause of All Nations: An International History of the American Civil War* (New York: Basic Books, 2013); David Armitage et al., "Interchange: Nationalism and Internationalism in the Era of the Civil War," *Journal of American History* 98, no. 2 (2011): 455–489; Ural, *Civil War Citizens: Race, Ethnicity and Identity in America's Bloodiest Conflict*; Christian G. Samito, *Becoming American under Fire: Irish Americans, African Americans, and the Politics of Citizenship During the Civil War Era* (Ithaca, NY: Cornell University Press, 2009); Bruce, *The Harp and The Eagle: Irish-American Volunteers and the Union Army, 1861–1865*; Dean Mahin, *The Blessed Place of Freedom: Europeans in Civil War America* (Washington, DC: Brassey's Incorporated,

Scandinavian-American immigrants' ideology adds to a growing body of research examining the evolving definitions of American citizenship and the way citizenship was used to construct, challenge, or maintain racial hierarchies and political power in the Civil War era.

Third, this book contributes to the English-language scholarship of Scandinavian-American immigration where Norwegian, Swedish, and Danish writers have frequently sought to accentuate narrow ethnic and national contributions to American history, not least in terms of patriotism and civic contributions, despite significant evidence of necessary pan-Scandinavian cultural and political cooperation in the years surrounding the Civil War.[42] This study recalibrates those claims to show that many Scandinavian-born immigrants, often publicly embracing a common Scandinavian identity, were reluctant to accept the citizenship duty of military service and after emancipation remained reluctant to embrace equal citizen rights for freedpeople.[43]

Lastly, the Scandinavian scholarly contribution to American historiography has mainly been focused inwardly on the Scandinavian communities, while immigrants' encounters with other ethnic groups have taken a back seat. As Gunlög Fur has pointed out, "settlement and [Indian] removal is rarely discussed in the same context, and in most immigration history, these processes remain unconnected."[44] Building on Fur and other contemporary Scandinavian American historians, this study redirects the historiographical focus in order to emphasize Scandinavian

---

2002); William Burton, *Melting Pot Soldiers – The Union's Ethnic Regiments*, 2nd ed. (New York: Fordham University Press, 1998).

[42] For a discussion of ethnic categories ascribed to Scandinavian-Americans and the reason they must be studied collectively in the Civil War era, see Jørn Brøndal and Dag Blanck, "The Concept of Being Scandinavian-American," *American Studies in Scandinavia* 34, no. 2 (2002): 4–13; Anders Bo Rasmussen, "'Drawn Together in a Blood Brotherhood': Civic Nationalism amongst Scandinavian Immigrants in the American Civil War Crucible," *American Studies in Scandinavia* 48, no. 2 (2016): 8–13.

[43] See for example, Waldemar Ager, *Oberst Heg Og Hans Gutter [Colonel Heg and His Boys]* (Eau Claire, WI: Fremad Publishing Company, 1916); Theodore C. Blegen, ed., *The Civil War Letters of Colonel Hans Christian Heg* (Northfield, MN: Norwegian-American Historical Association, 1936); Nels Hokanson, *Swedish Immigrants in Lincoln's Time*, reprint ed., Scandinavians in America (New York: Arno Press, 1979); Peter Sørensen Vig, *Danske i Krig i Og for Amerika [Danes Fighting in and for America]* (Omaha, NE: Axel H. Andersen, 1917).

[44] Gunlög Fur, "Indians and Immigrants – Entangled Histories," *Journal of American Ethnic History* 33, no. 3 (2014): 55–56.

collaboration, encounters, and entanglements with other ethnic groups as these interactions became increasingly important in the Civil War era.[45]

Thus, inspired by Gregory P. Downs and Kate Masur's effort to investigate "precisely how the changes that rippled out from the Civil War did – and did not – echo in people's lives and communities," the book is guided by the following questions:[46]

- How did Old World ideology, not least related to territory and population, inform Scandinavian immigrants' attempt to navigate life in the New World?
- Why did Scandinavian immigrants overwhelmingly support the Republican Party between 1860 and 1868 when Irish and German immigrants, among other ethnic groups, did not?
- How did implicit and explicit American definitions of citizenship impact perceptions of ethnic identity and belonging among Scandinavian immigrants?

Methodologically, *Civil War Settlers* adapts the German and Italian schools of microhistory (focusing on community studies and marginal individuals, respectively) based on the premise that "microscopic observation will reveal factors previously unobserved."[47]

The following chapters provide a "thick description" of New Denmark, a small immigrant community in Wisconsin's Brown County, by utilizing a previously untapped wealth of letters, diaries, and memoirs, which are bolstered by census data, pension records, and draft rolls.[48]

---

[45] The Civil War, for example, forced people of many different backgrounds to serve together or at the very least contemplate serving together. See Rasmussen, "'Drawn Together in a Blood Brotherhood': Civic Nationalism amongst Scandinavian Immigrants in the American Civil War Crucible."

[46] Gregory P. Downs and Kate Masur, "Echoes of War: Rethinking Post–Civil War Governance and Politics," in *The World the Civil War Made*, ed. Gregory P. Downs and Kate Masur (Chapel Hill: University of North Carolina Press, 2015), 3.

[47] Giovanni Levi, "On Microhistory," in *New Perspectives on Historical Writing*, ed. Peter Burke (Cambridge: Polity Press, 1991), 97. See also, for example, Hans Medick, "Weaving and Surviving in Laichingen, 1650–1900: Micro-History as History and as Research Experience," in *Agrarian Studies: Synthetic Work at the Cutting Edge*, ed. James C. Scott and Nina Bhatt (New Haven, CT: Yale University Press, 2001). See as well Carlo Ginzburg, *The Cheese and the Worms: The Cosmos of a Sixteenth-Century Miller* (New York: Penguin Books, 1982).

[48] This approach, a combination of letters and diaries with census data and draft rolls, allows for what Hans Medick has called the possibility of pursuing "a qualitative life-history approach as well as a quantitative analysis" of community relations. See Medick, "Weaving and Surviving in Laichingen, 1650–1900: Micro-History as History and as Research Experience," 288. Also Levi, "On Microhistory," 98. Levi stresses the

New Denmark was not "representative" or "typical," since, as Stephen Kantrowitz rightly notes, "no community was," but it did play an import-ant part in the Scandinavian-American chain migration that picked up speed by the 1840s with Wisconsin as a central hub.[49] Along with slightly older and slightly bigger Scandinavian immigrant communities in Wisconsin such as Muskego and New Upsala, New Denmark served as an important early link between Old World Scandinavia and the United States. Moreover, the lack of attention paid to New Denmark and its inhabitants by historians is in and of itself methodologically important. As Carlo Ginzburg argued in his now famous *The Cheese and the Worms*, through deep engagement with a "modest individual who is himself lacking in significance" it is possible to "trace, as in a microcosm, the characteristics of an entire social stratum in a specific historical period."[50] Accordingly, the centrality of historical actors' own "point of view" is here accentuated and their words and behavior illuminated.[51]

Furthermore, the researcher's role in the constructed narrative is laid bare in microhistorical writing in order to allow the reader to follow the researcher's narrowing of the interpretive range based on the available information while weighing the impact of structural factors in relation to individual agency.[52] Central to this understanding of historical writing is the conviction that it is impossible to reproduce exactly "what really

importance of identifying "a series of signifying events or facts which would otherwise be evanescent" through "microscopic analysis."

[49] Kantrowitz, *More Than Freedom: Fighting for Black Citizenship in a White Republic, 1829–1889*, 7.

[50] Ginzburg, *The Cheese and the Worms: The Cosmos of a Sixteenth-Century Miller*, xx. See also Medick, "Weaving and Surviving in Laichingen, 1650–1900: Micro-History as History and as Research Experience," 283–287. In Medick's words, the reduction of the analytical scale can achieve "new insights into the constitution of historical structures." See also Lawrence Stone, "The Revival of Narrative: Reflections on a New Old History," *Past & Present* 85 (1979): 19.

[51] Clifford Geertz, "'From the Native's Point of View': On the Nature of Anthropological Understanding," *Bulletin of the American Academy of Arts and Sciences* 28, no. 1 (1974): 28–30. Carlo Ginzburg, "Checking the Evidence: The Judge and the Historian," *Critical Inquiry* 18, no. 1 (1991): 90. As Ginzburg notes, "the hypotheses, the doubts, the uncertainties, ... [become] part of the narration; the search for truth [becomes] part of the exposition of the (necessarily incomplete) truth attained." See "Microhistory: Two or Three Things That I Know About It," *Critical Inquiry* 20, no. 1 (1993): 24.

[52] Levi, "On Microhistory," 94–95. As Levi has pointed out, "all social action is seen to be the result of an individual's constant negotiation, manipulation, choices and decisions in the face of a normative reality which, though pervasive, nevertheless offers many possi-bilities for personal interpretations and freedoms. The question is, therefore, how to define the margins – however narrow they may be – of the freedom granted an individual by the interstices and contradictions of the normative systems which govern him."

happened," yet it is possible to construct convincing historical narratives "in search of meaning" through microhistorical methodology.[53] To achieve this end, scholars of microhistory, in Giovanni Levi's words, take the "highly specific and individual" as a starting point to analyze how a word, a concept, or an event was perceived in order to establish "its meaning in the light of its own specific context."[54]

In sum, by reducing the analytical scale to a relatively small group of Scandinavian-born men and women, focusing on seemingly marginal communities and individuals, highlighting their point of view in their own words, and placing the interpretations in a contemporary historio-graphical context, certain historical explanations, presented in the pages that follow, gain credence over others.[55]

In Part I, *Civil War Settlers* details the impact of the 1848 revolution in Europe and North America in terms of renewed ideas about liberty, struggles over territory, and Caribbean emancipation. Additionally, the importance of Old World colonial culture, religion, and scientific racism are highlighted as keys to unlocking Scandinavian-born men and women's perception of citizenship and empire in the New World. Scandinavian immigrants' understanding of American citizenship rights was often articulated as liberty and equality, which led to widespread opposition to slavery, but this understanding of citizenship paradoxically did often

---

[53] Ibid., 99. On the impossibility of reproducing "what really happened" and the importance of using "narrative as a means of illuminating structures," see, for example, Peter Burke, "History of Events and the Revival of Narrative," in *New Perspectives on Historical Writing* (University Park: Pennsylvania State University Press, 2001), 290–293.

[54] Levi, "On Microhistory," 110; Geertz, "'From the Native's Point of View': On the Nature of Anthropological Understanding," 44–45.

[55] See Edward Muir and Guido Ruggiero, "Afterword: Crime and the Writing of History," in *History from Crime*, ed. Edward Muir and Guido Ruggiero (Baltimore: Johns Hopkins University Press, 1994), 232–235. Spatial and temporal factors derived from surviving histor-ical documents "define a range of possibilities," according to Muir and Ruggiero, and some texts a "more narrow range than others." It is therefore logically impossible, for example, to claim that Thomas Jefferson's presidency, which ended in 1809, was meaningfully influenced by Abraham Lincoln (who was born on February 12, 1809). See also Ginzburg, *The Cheese and the Worms: The Cosmos of a Sixteenth-Century Miller*, xii; Carlo Ginzburg and Anna Davin, "Morelli, Freud and Sherlock Holmes: Clues and Scientific Method," *History Workshop* 9 (1980): 7–10. See as well Ginzburg, "Microhistory: Two or Three Things That I Know About It," 32. Ginzburg notes: "All phases through which research unfolds are *constructed* and not *given*: the identification of the object and its importance; the elaboration of the categories through which it is analyzed; the criteria of proof; the stylistic and narrative form by which the results are transmitted to the reader." Also Alun Munslow, *Narrative and History* (New York: Palgrave Macmillan, 2007), 5–6.

not include nonwhites. Scandinavian immigrants, not least the Scandinavian elite, perceiving themselves as superior to other ethnic groups, directly and indirectly supported an American imperial project defined by territorial expansion and conflict with nonwhite and, to an extent, non-Protestant peoples.[56]

Furthermore, Part I delves into the question of why Scandinavian immigrants' understanding of American citizenship led them almost unanimously to support the Republican Party by 1860. As the Republican Party, partially prompted by its interest in German-born voters, retreated somewhat from nativist policies and built a coalition on homestead advocacy, free labor ideology, and anti-slavery, Scandinavian immigrants increasingly embraced the party's platform.

At a time when Scandinavian-American civic participation grew through involvement in local, statewide, and national elections, Norwegians, Swedes, and Danes embraced the possibilities of American equality and pointed to these democratic opportunities as departures from Old World monarchical and religious practice. Economic equality and free labor ideology, which in the Scandinavian view meant an opportunity to improve one's social standing through landownership and hard work, were some of the key pull factors associated with American citizenship.

As the antebellum era came to a close, Scandinavian immigrants' Old World experience and New World settlement patterns in rural enclaves built around strands of Lutheran religion, separated Norwegian, Swedish, and Danish immigrants from many Irish and German settlers to such an extent that the Scandinavians – whether the issue was landownership, access to credit, or ties to a political spoils system – came to see themselves in opposition to and in competition with these larger, more urban and Catholic ethnic groups, many of whom supported the Democratic Party.[57]

Part II details the Scandinavian immigrant experience during the Civil War and argues that Scandinavian ethnic leaders successfully constructed a public pan-Scandinavian ethnic identity to spur military mobilization in late 1861. When the Norwegian, Swedish, and Danish immigrants initially went to war, many rhetorically did so "for God and Country" – an invocation adapted from the Old World rallying cry "For God, King, and

---

[56] Jon Gjerde, "'Here in America There Is Neither King nor Tyrant': European Encounters with Race, 'Freedom,' and Their European Pasts," *Journal of the Early Republic* 19, no. 4 (1999): 675. See also Fur, "Indians and Immigrants – Entangled Histories."

[57] Efford, *German Immigrants, Race, and Citizenship in the Civil War Era*, 11. Efford demonstrates that the Republican Party alienated German immigrants in Wisconsin, but this was not the case with the numerically smaller group of Scandinavian immigrants.

Country" – and over time benefited economically and politically from such service. Several Scandinavian-born officers became political leaders after the war, and several enlisted specifically to make sure German and Irish immigrants did not profit disproportionately in terms of political office-holding after the war.

Moreover, this part of the book explores the fierce religious and ideological debate within the Scandinavian-American church over slavery's sinfulness. In this religious and political controversy, Old World currents of white superiority revealed themselves among the state church–affiliated clergy and, from their congregation members' standpoint, came dangerously close to pro-slavery paternalist arguments (e.g. rejection of the nation's egalitarian principles) used by Southern planters.[58] Part II demonstrates the nuances along class lines of Scandinavians' commitment to a white man's republic, as the majority of Scandinavian immigrants openly opposed slavery and empathized with the enslaved, but a larger share of the well-educated immigrants openly opposed racial equality. Still, they all, consciously or unconsciously, participated in, and often supported, a settler colonialist project which, in Patrick Wolfe's words, was predicated on "access to territory."[59]

Additionally, underscoring the ideological, rhetorical, and chronological connection between colonization and Indian removal, the intense colonization negotiations initiated by the Danish government and in revised form consummated in 1862 occurred simultaneously with Scandinavian immigrants increasingly settling on former Dakota land in Minnesota. The subsequent 1862 US–Dakota War left lasting imprints on Scandinavian immigrants' perceptions of American Indians in Minnesota and, broadly speaking, strengthened the commitment to landtaking and opposition to indigenous people's citizenship rights.[60] Underlining the centrality of racism to both colonization and Indian dispossession

---

[58] Hahn, *A Nation without Borders: The United States and Its World in an Age of Civil Wars, 1830–1910*, 68–69. "Slavery's defenders commenced to reject the egalitarianism that the Declaration of Independence had enshrined."

[59] Patrick Wolfe, "Settler Colonialism and the Elimination of the Native," *Journal of Genocide Research* 8, no. 4 (2006): 387–388; Karen V. Hansen, *Encounter on the Great Plains: Scandinavian Settlers and Dispossession of Dakota Indians, 1890–1930* (Oxford: Oxford University Press, 2013), 2–7; Kantrowitz, "White Supremacy, Settler Colonialism, and the Two Citizenships of the Fourteenth Amendment," 31.

[60] En Minnesotabo, "Minnesota D. 21. Aug 1862," *Hemlandet*, August 27, 1862. For an English-language example of the same perspective, see "Matters in Minnesota," *Green Bay Advocate*, October 9, 1862.

schemes, Scandinavian-born men by 1862 referred to both enslaved Africans and American Indians as "savages."[61]

Lastly, despite later hagiographic ethnic accounts, enlistment enthusiasm was low among Scandinavian immigrants, not least the Danes and Swedes; even in 1861 and by 1862, the pan-Scandinavianism on display through the earlier formation of purely ethnic Scandinavian military units was challenged by Norwegian, Swedish, and Danish immigrants' reluctance to volunteer for military service. The draft resistance exposed fault lines between the Scandinavian elite and their countrymen without formal education, as the latter's draft resistance complicated ethnic leaders' aspirations for later political gain.

For many Scandinavian-born farmers, the coercive Old World state, from which they had fled, found a new form in New World draft legislation and spurred widespread forms of resistance such as renouncing interest in American citizenship in Scandinavian enclaves. This draft resistance has generally been overlooked historiographically, but a close examination of rural Wisconsin enclaves nuances James McPherson's statement that "virtually all those who denounced and resisted the militia draft were Democrats" and, building on Tyler Anbinder, shows concretely how "immigrants employed" citizenship, or lack thereof, as a means to obtain exemptions from the draft.[62]

Part III analyzes the post–Civil War era along two main strands: on the one hand, the American government's interest in imperial expansion into the Caribbean through the purchase of the Danish West Indies; and on the other hand, Scandinavian immigrants' engagement with contiguous expansion and debates over universal citizenship.

This final part of the book shows the Homestead Act's centrality to Scandinavian immigrants' economic aspirations after the Civil War and demonstrates the continued discrepancy between their egalitarian idealism and a racial reality centered on whiteness. Scandinavian immigrants' enthusiasm for landownership opportunities did not extend to enthusiasm

---

[61] Lincoln, "First Annual Message"; James Mitchell, *Report on Colonization and Emigration Made to the Secretary of the Interior by the Agent of Emigration* (Washington, DC: Government Printing Office, 1862), 8. Also Hahn, *A Nation without Borders: The United States and Its World in an Age of Civil Wars, 1830–1910*, 45.

[62] See, for example, James M. McPherson, *Battle Cry of Freedom: The Civil War Era* (New York: Oxford University Press, 1988), 493; Tyler Anbinder, "Which Poor Man's Fight? Immigrants and the Federal Conscription of 1863," *Civil War History* 52, no. 4 (2006): 352; Vig, *Danske i Krig i Og for Amerika* [*Danes Fighting in and for America*], 185–197; also Ager, *Oberst Heg Og Hans Gutter* [*Colonel Heg and His Boys*], 223–261.

for freedpeople's economic opportunities or regard for indigenous peoples' landholding rights.

Emancipation highlighted the issue of equal rights for the formerly enslaved, and in the Scandinavian communities these debates revealed well-educated immigrants' reservations about freedpeople's potential for full and equal citizenship. Using the impeachment trial of President Andrew Johnson as a pretext, the Scandinavian elite publicly started to abandon reconstruction no later than 1868 to focus their collective political energy on issues of more evident self-interest such as economic growth, agricultural opportunities, and industrial development. In the process, Scandinavian Civil War veterans and community leaders underscored the importance of a white complementary identity, meaning "the dual loyalties to nation and subgroup," by exhibiting greater solidarity with recently arrived Old World countrymen than they did with recently emancipated fellow Black citizens.[63]

On women's citizenship rights, Scandinavian-born men continued to perceive of themselves as the main economic and practical decision-makers even as the women in Midwestern settlements at times during the war were elevated to being heads of their households. Moreover, the Scandinavian-American press, often emphasizing women's subordinate role, ran letters ridiculing the emerging post-war women's movement and left little room inside or outside the home for Scandinavian women's social or political aspirations, including voting, which was deemed central to Scandinavian immigrant men's understanding of citizenship.

Lastly, the attempted purchase of the Danish West Indies, initiated by the Lincoln administration in 1865 but rejected by the Senate in 1870, is here explained in the context of domestic American reconstruction politics, which led to a lack of political will in Congress to fund the transaction. Political conflict between the Johnson administration and Congress, centered on freedpeople, clearly outweighed any personal relationships, however strong, that Danish diplomats had built in the United States.

As an example of the threshold principle's importance, the widening asymmetrical power relationship between the United States, stepping more forcefully onto the global political scene, and Denmark, a declining international power following the loss of territory at the hands of Prussia and Austria in the Second Schleswig War of 1864,

[63] Jon Gjerde, *The Minds of the West: Ethnocultural Evolution in the Rural Middle West 1830–1917* (Chapel Hill: University of North Carolina Press, 1997), 59.

allowed the Senate to ignore an agreed-upon treaty with international impunity.

This last part of *Civil War Settlers* thereby details the chronology of continued American attempts at territorial and population growth, while the Danish fear of falling under a crucial threshold, or being incorporated into the German Confederation, is shown to be an important variable in the ongoing negotiations between Denmark and the United States.[64]

The early American attempts to build a *Grossstaat* through war with Mexico and the Danish fear of descending into *Kleinstaaterei* by losing German-speaking territory through revolutionary violence can, in important respects, be traced to 1848, which is where this study begins.

---

[64] Torben Grøngaard Jeppesen, *Dannebrog På Den Amerikanske Prærie* [*Dannebrog on the American Prairie*] (Odense: Odense University Press, 2000), 10.

PART I

SETTLERS

I

1848

The revolutions of 1848 set Europe ablaze. The flames erupted in Paris on February 22 and soon spread north, south, east, and west. In short order, the fiery revolutions leapt from France into the Caribbean Sea and onto the American mainland.[1]

The 1848 revolutions impacted American domestic and foreign policy as they increased the need for agricultural labor in the West Indies, elevated fear of abolition among southern slaveholders, and brought disappointed European revolutionaries to seek new opportunities across the Atlantic.[2] Importantly, the European revolutions of 1848 resulted in slavery's abolition in both the French and Danish West Indies and served as a striking example of the transnational ties between Europe and the New World.

On February 25, 1848, the French provisional government "declared a republic and also emancipation with indemnity" on the slaveholding

[1] Robert E. May, *Slavery, Race, and Conquest in the Tropics* (New York: Cambridge University Press, 2013), 61.

[2] Rebecca Hartkopf Schloss, *Sweet Liberty: The Final Days of Slavery in Martinique* (Philadelphia: University of Pennsylvania Press, 2009), 152–165. While British anti-slavery debates led to the British Emancipation Act of 1833 (coincidentally the same year the American Anti-Slavery Society was formed), slaveholders in the French and Danish West Indies successfully stalled similar measures through their continued influence on Old World politics. When Danish King Christian VIII, on July 28, 1847, finally decided to abolish slavery, it was with the provision that emancipation would only come to fruition after a twelve-year transition period for enslaved people born before the edict took effect. See Niklas Thode Jensen, Gunvor Simonsen, and Poul Erik Olsen, "Reform Eller Revolution 1803–48 [Reform or Revolution 1803–48]," in *Vestindien: St. Croix, St. Thomas Og St. Jan*, ed. Poul Erik Olsen (Copenhagen: Gads Forlag, 2017), 270–279. See also Stephen Kantrowitz, *More Than Freedom: Fighting for Black Citizenship in a White Republic, 1829–1889* (New York: Penguin Press, 2012), 54–58.

islands of Guadeloupe and Martinique, in part due to fears of slave revolts such as the one that led to Haitian independence in 1804.[3] As Rebecca Schloss has shown, events in the West Indies soon overtook political decisions on the mainland about the practical transition to free labor.

[O]n May 22 more than twenty thousand enslaved workers crowded the streets of Saint Pierre, Martinique demanding their freedom. Shortly afterward, the island's governor proclaimed emancipation and initiated a new chapter in the complex interplay of race, class, and gender in the French Atlantic.[4]

By July 1848 the French West Indian unrest, and ensuing emancipation, served as partial inspiration for an uprising on the neighboring island of St. Croix in the Danish West Indies (see Figure 1.1).[5] Thus, Governor

FIGURE 1.1 French depictions of abolition in the West Indies, such as this one by artist François-Auguste Biard, mirrored those in Denmark and underscored the pervasive Old World colonial mindset. Photo by Photo12/Universal Images Group via Getty Images.

---

[3] Schloss, *Sweet Liberty: The Final Days of Slavery in Martinique*, 227. See also Steven Hahn, *A Nation without Borders: The United States and Its World in an Age of Civil Wars, 1830–1910* (New York: Viking, 2016), 14.

[4] Schloss, *Sweet Liberty: The Final Days of Slavery in Martinique*, 227.

[5] For a description of the conditions that led to emancipation in the Danish West Indies, see Jensen, Simonsen, and Olsen, "Reform Eller Revolution 1803–48 [Reform or Revolution 1803–48]."

Peter von Scholten concluded that the islands' enslaved population would wait no longer for freedom. A widespread but generally peaceful uprising on St. Croix in July settled the matter.[6]

Von Scholten's emancipation had not been authorized by King Frederik VII, however, and the governor was promptly replaced by councillor of state Peter Hansen, who was tasked with reorganizing labor relations between a planter class who felt betrayed by the Danish government's failure to ensure the twelve-year transition period promised them in 1847 and the newly freed laborers who demanded better work conditions.[7] From Governor Hansen's perspective, retaining control of the labor force was the main objective, and, following the lead of larger European powers, not least Great Britain and France, Danish officials by the late 1850s looked to amend American colonization policy to augment the islands' labor force.[8]

During the early 1860s, colonization in the United States was legally directed toward Liberia, but – in no small part due to Danish diplomats – the policy was reoriented to also include the Caribbean.[9] Moreover, slavery's abolition in the Danish and French West Indies sparked fear, as well as jubilation, in the United States.[10] In the immediate aftermath of emancipation in the West Indies, southern slaveholders peered somewhat fearfully toward the Caribbean emancipation initiatives.[11] In New York, Frederick Douglass, abolitionist and editor of the *North Star* after his escape from slavery, remarked optimistically in 1848 that the revolution initiated in Europe

---

[6] Ibid., 271–281.

[7] Vilhelm Birch, "Memorandum," in *Collection 1175. Koloniernes centralbestyrelse kolonialkontoret. 1855–1918 Immigration af arbejdere. Immigration af arbejdere fra Afrika 1855–1859 mm. Box 909* (Copenhagen: Rigsarkivet 1860).

[8] Ibid. See also Sebastian N. Page, *Black Resettlement and the American Civil War* (Cambridge: Cambridge University Press, 2021), 189–193.

[9] Secretary, "Monday 18 Augt 1862. Meeting at Governmenthouse According to Invitation of His Excellency." See also Hunter Miller, ed., *Treaties and Other International Acts of the United States of America* (Washington, DC: Government Printing Office, 1948).

[10] May, *Slavery, Race, and Conquest in the Tropics*, 61. May notes that it was "unsettling to Cuban planters and southern slave owners that a revolutionary régime in France in 1848 ended slavery in all of France's overseas possessions – including Guadeloupe and Martinique in the West Indies – and that some antislavery northerners vocally supported emancipation in Cuba."

[11] Daniel Walker Howe, *What Hath God Wrought: The Transformation of America, 1815–1848* (Oxford: Oxford University Press, 2007), 792–794. According to Howe, news of "an uprising in Paris," one that Americans learned "had broken out – appropriately, they thought – on the twenty-second of February, George Washington's birthday," reached New York on March 18, 1848, where it also became clear that the revolution had led to slavery's abolition in the French West Indies.

flashed "with lightning speed from heart to heart, from land to land," until it would eventually traverse the entire globe (see Figure 1.2).[12]

Yet by 1851 it was clear that American abolitionists would have to bide their time, as most nations on the European mainland had reverted back to their prerevolution roles in an uneasy equilibrium of monarchical and imperial power balanced mainly between Russia, France, Great Britain, Austria, and the German states.[13]

On the European mainland, underlying social issues and overarching political structures tied population groups together across borders. Uprisings in Frankfurt in 1833, Paris in 1839, and Kraków in 1846

FIGURE 1.2 An 1848 portrait of *North Star* editor Frederick Douglass, who saw great abolitionist potential in the European revolutions. Image by Fotosearch/ Stringer/Archive Photos via Getty Images.

[12] Quoted in Benjamin Fagan, "*The North Star* and the Atlantic 1848," *African American Review* 47, no. 1 (2014): 56.

[13] As Jonathan Sperber has noted, "In the end, the mid-century revolutions were defeated by soldiers loyal to the monarchical authority to the tsar, the Austrian emperor, the king of Prussia, the king of the Two Sicilies, and the soon to be emperor Louis-Napoleon Bonaparte. Ties of religious and dynastic loyalty, of civilian and military authority, and of reliance on the state for prosperity had proven stronger than the divided and mutually quarreling forces of nationalism, social and economic discontent, and of aspiration towards the realization of popular sovereignty and civic freedom." See Jonathan Sperber, *The European Revolutions, 1848–1851* (Cambridge: Cambridge University Press, 1994), 271.

attested to the widespread political, social, and economic discontent across Europe.[14] In Wolfram Siemann's words, lack of political participation, the urge for national self-determination, a crisis of "pre-industrial craft trades," and failed harvests resulting in famine were key driving forces behind uprisings in the spring of 1848.[15] As a result, revolutionary sentiment among nationalist and politically marginalized groups within Scandinavia, France, Italy, Poland, and Germany sparked uprisings across the continent that simultaneously strengthened and challenged nationalistic ideas within existing borders. In Northern Europe, along Denmark's southern regions, embers that had smoldered for years suddenly burst into flames and led to a civil war within the kingdom that revealed tangible divisions along political, ideological, social, ethnic, national, separatist, and dynastic lines.[16]

Despite his personal resistance to democratic reform, King Christian VIII had prepared an eventual transition from absolutism to constitutional monarchy before his death on January 20, 1848. This political move toward at least nominal democracy based on a moderately liberal constitution was accepted by the new king, Frederik VII, in the so-called January rescript of January 28, 1848, the commitment to which was strengthened and reiterated after a sizable but peaceful demonstration by an estimated 20,000 people in Copenhagen on March 21, 1848.[17]

In Sweden and Norway, the European revolutions fueled protests in Stockholm and a popular Norwegian movement led by revolutionary Marcus Thrane, but the relatively well-functioning political system in

---

[14] Morten Nordhagen Ottosen, "Folkenes Vår: De Europeiske Revolusjonene 1848–1851 [The People's Spring: The European Revolutions 1848–1851]," in *Demokratiet: Historien Og Ideerne*, ed. Raino Malnes and Dag Einar Thorsen, pp. 218–233 (Oslo: Dreyers Forlag, 2014), 222.

[15] Wolfram Siemann, *The German Revolution of 1848–49*, trans. Christiane Banerji (New York: St. Martin's Press, 1998), 45–46.

[16] Michael Bregnsbo, "Danmark 1848 – Systemskifte Og Borgerkrig [Denmark 1848 – Political Change and Civil War]," *Fortid og Nutid* (1998): 255–257, 66. As Bregnsbo notes, the succession of Danish monarchs between 1665 and 1834 held absolute legislative, executive, and judicial power. See also Rasmus Glenthøj, *1864: Sønner Af De Slagne* [1864: Descendants of the Defeated] (Copenhagen: Gads Forlag, 2014), 176–179.

[17] Bregnsbo, "Danmark 1848 – Systemskifte Og Borgerkrig [Denmark 1848 – Political Change and Civil War]," 262–268. See also Hans Vammen, "Anmeldelse Af Betænkninger Fra Christian VIII's Tid Om Styrelsen Af Det Danske Monarki [Review of Deliberations from Christian VIII's Reign on Ruling the Danish Monarchy]," *Historisk Tidsskrift* 13, no. 2 (1975): 365–366.

Norway (based on the Eidsvoll Constitution of 1814), coupled with an eventual crackdown by the authorities on Thrane "for conspiracy against the state" in July 1851, prevented the movement, which at its height attracted close to 30,000 followers, from gaining even wider traction during these years.[18]

Despite the largely peaceful political responses to grassroots dissent, King Frederik VII's decision to move toward constitutional monarchy left a power vacuum within the Danish kingdom. Danish- and German-speaking nationalists both seized this European revolutionary moment, hoping to shape the Danish kingdom's future according to their own interests.[19]

On Denmark's southern border, the key point of contention was the status of Schleswig and Holstein.[20] Since the so-called Ribe Treaty of 1460, the duchies Schleswig and Holstein had been united, based on an understanding that they would remain forever undivided ("up ewig Ungedeelt").[21] Hereafter, the Danish monarch became the Count of Holstein and also incorporated the duchy of Schleswig under Danish rule.

The rise of nationalist sentiment among Danish speakers throughout the 1840s, concretized in a political faction called "nationalliberale" (national liberals), led to calls for the consolidation of the Danish

---

[18] Ottosen, "Folkenes Vår: De Europeiske Revolusjonene 1848–1851 [The People's Spring: The European Revolutions 1848–1851]," 230. By 1850, the population in Norway was approximately 1.4 million, in Sweden 3.5 million, and in Denmark 1.4 million. See Åke Holmberg, *Skandinavismen i Sverige, Vid 1800-Talets Mitt* [Scandinavianism in Sweden, by the Middle of the 1800s] (Göteborg: Elanders, 1946), 46; Torben Grøngaard Jeppesen, *Danske i USA 1850–2000. En Demografisk, Social Og Kulturgeografisk Undersøgelse Af De Danske Immigranter Og Deres Efterkommere* [Danes in the United States 1850–2000. A Demographic, Social and Cultural Geographic Study of The Danish Immigrants and Their Descendants] (Odense: University Press of Southern Denmark, 2005), 67. Marcus Thrane emigrated to the United States in 1863 and became a newspaper editor in Chicago after the American Civil War. See Theodore C. Blegen, *Norwegian Migration to America 1825–1860* (Northfield, MN: The Norwegian-American Historical Association, 1931), 323–328. Also Jørn Brøndal, *Ethnic Leadership and Midwestern Politics: Scandinavian Americans and the Progressive Movement in Wisconsin, 1890–1914* (Chicago: University of Illinois Press, 2004), 17, 109–111.

[19] Bregnsbo, "Danmark 1848 – Systemskifte Og Borgerkrig [Denmark 1848 – Political Change and Civil War]," 262. The spring of 1848 was characterized by unrest within the Danish Kingdom exemplified by strikes among smallholders and agricultural workers, but legislation benefiting the lower strata of Danish society in March 1848 alleviated some of the tension in the Danish-speaking regions.

[20] Siemann, *The German Revolution of 1848–49*, 46.   [21] Ibid., 46–47.

kingdom more clearly along cultural and linguistic lines, by dividing Schleswig from German-speaking Holstein along Ejderen, a river running east–west toward the important seaport of Kiel.[22] Conversely, the population within the Danish kingdom's borders who identified as German took the revolution in France as a touchstone for their own nationalist claims. On March 18, 1848, less than a month after the revolution's outbreak in Paris, German-speaking residents of Schleswig-Holstein demanded that the duchies remain undivided with the aim to break away from Denmark. The Danish king dismissed the German-speaking Schleswig-Holsteiners' petition and instead made statements about incorporating Schleswig without Holstein directly under Danish rule. The irreconcilable positions led to German separatists seizing a Danish fortress in Schleswig-Holstein on March 24, 1848, and forming a "provisional state government."[23]

This civil war, now known as the First Schleswig War, lasted from 1848 to 1850.[24] In accordance with the threshold principle, the national liberals feared that Denmark would become a mini-state, if it lost part of Schleswig and all of Holstein, and therefore started to explore Scandinavian alliances.[25] Pan-Scandinavian sentiment was especially strong among the younger Scandinavian intelligentsia, in spite of the relatively modest 387 Swedes and Norwegians (several of whom would eventually end up in the American Civil War) who volunteered to fight against German separatists.[26] The spirit of

---

[22] Glenthøj, "Pan-Scandinavism and the Threshold Principle?," in *A History of the European Restorations*: Governments, States and Monarchy, edited by Michael Broers and Ambrogio Caiani, pp. 245–255 (London: Bloomsbury Academic, 2019), 10–11.

[23] Siemann, *The German Revolution of 1848–49*, 60.

[24] For Danish nationalists, grassroots political organizing, enthusiasm for military enlistment, and popular songs such as "Dengang jeg drog afsted" (When I Set Out), emphasizing the importance of the king, the Fatherland, the flag (called Dannebrog) and the Danish language, reflected increased national awareness. See Inge Adriansen and Jens Ole Christensen, *Første Slesvigske Krig 1848–1851: Forhistorie, Forløb Og Følger [First Schleswig War 1848–1851: Causes, Course, and Consequences]* (Sønderborg: Sønderborg Slot, 2015), 25.

[25] Glenthøj, "Pan-Scandinavism and the Threshold Principle?," 10–11. Even with Schleswig and Holstein, Denmark's territorial size, excluding the colonial "possession" of Greenland, was less than 1 percent of the United States in 1850. See Jeppesen, *Danske i USA 1850–2000. En Demografisk, Social Og Kulturgeografisk Undersøgelse Af De Danske Immigranter Og Deres Efterkommere* [Danes in the United States 1850–2000: A Demographic, Social and Cultural Geographic Study of The Danish Immigrants and Their Descendants], 67.

[26] Rasmus Glenthøj and Morten Nordhagen Ottesen, *Union Eller Undergang: Kampen for Et Forenet Skandinavien [Union or Ruin: The Struggle for a United Scandinavia]*

pan-Scandinavianism, however, was concretized at the political level when Sweden, prompted by King Oscar, sent 4,500 troops to defend Denmark's monarchical rule against the German-speaking rebels, with the promise of up to 15,000 troops in all if the Danish mainland were to be invaded (safeguarded by the provision that Sweden would then have to be part of a broader international coalition led by Great Britain and Russia).[27]

Yet the pan-Scandinavian enthusiasm proved to have notable diplomatic (and nationalist) limitations when confronted with the complexity of high-level European politics. In just one of numerous factors complicating the First Schleswig War, Denmark and Sweden had been on opposite sides for parts of the Napoleonic Wars, and the peace conference of 1814 in Kiel forced Denmark to cede Norway (which had been part of the Danish Kingdom since 1380) to Sweden.[28]

Thus, despite several ambitious attempts, a pan-Scandinavian state incorporating northern Schleswig but excising the German-speaking regions found little concrete backing among more experienced Scandinavian power brokers, not least Danish conservative leaders who

(Copenhagen: Gads Forlag, 2021), 228–230. Among the Norwegian and Swedish volunteers who later served in the Civil War were Ole Balling and Hans Mattson. See O. P. Hansen Balling, *Erindringer Fra Et Langt Liv* [Memories from a Long Life] (Kristiania: S. & Jul Sørensens Bogtrykkeri, 1905), 28–35; see also Mattson, *Reminiscences: The Story of an Emigrant* (Saint Paul, MN: D. D. Merrill Company, 1891), 11–12.

[27] Glenthøj, *1864: Sønner Af De Slagne* [1864: Descendants of the Defeated], 206–09. See also Adriansen and Christensen, *Første Slesvigske Krig 1848–1851: Forhistorie, Forløb Og Følger* [First Schleswig War 1848–1851: Causes, Course, and Consequences], 19. See also Sven Dalhoff-Nielsen, *Nordiske Frivillige* [Nordic Volunteers] (Graasten: Nordisk Institut, 1944), 33. See also "Af Et Brev Fra Frivillig Og Underofficer Hansen Balling [From a Letter by Volunteer and Junior Officer Hansen Balling]," *Den Norske Rigstidende*, June 14, 1848. The Danish navy, including conscripts, numbered 22,413, and the standing army numbered 24,282 but could be augmented by citizens who were eligible to be called into service as part of the reserve until the age of forty-five. Counting the Swedish contingent held in reserve, the Danish army was augmented by more than 10 percent by troops from Sweden and Norway. See Generalstaben [General Staff], *Den Dansk-Tydske Krig i Aarene 1848–1850* [*The Danish-German War between 1848 and 1850*] (Copenhagen: J. H. Schultz's Bogtrykkeri, 1867), 41–42; Klaus Bjørn, *1848: Borgerkrig Og Revolution* [1848: Civil War and Revolution] (Copenhagen: Gyldendal, 1998), 194–195.

[28] Rasmus Glenthøj, "Adskillelsen: Hvorfor Denmark Og Norge Blev Skilt i 1814 [The Partition: Why Denmark and Norway Were Separated in 1814]," in *Mellem Brødre: Dansk-Norsk Samliv i 600 År* [*Between Brothers: Danish-Norwegian Coexistence over 600 Years*], edited by Rasmus Glenthøj, pp. 92–107 (Copenhagen: Gads Forlag, 2016), 92.

insisted on keeping the entire state together to maintain the territory and population already under Danish rule.[29]

Additionally, there was a strong sense among Europe's great powers, especially Great Britain and Russia, that German control of the important Schleswig harbor of Kiel was undesirable as it would help German *Grossstaatenbildung*.[30] Consequently, Russia and Great Britain worked actively to curtail the armed conflict and protect Danish territorial sovereignty in the name of stability (as opposed to revolution or disruption of the international trade). Thus, through the great powers' intervention, the pre-1848 borders were eventually reestablished.[31]

Across Europe, the lack of revolutionary result caused thousands of disappointed "Forty-Eighters" to seek freedom and liberty elsewhere – and many in the United States.[32] Even in Scandinavia, where the 1848 revolutions had prompted King Frederik VII to sign *grundloven* (the Constitution), the effect for people with little economic or political power was negligible. Consequently, a steady emigration from Scandinavia started picking up speed, especially from rural areas.

Additionally, decisions to emigrate were likely accelerated among the German-speaking population in Schleswig and Holstein by the Danish government's determination to impose strict language requirements and banish revolutionary leaders such as Hans Reimer Claussen and Theodore

---

[29] Glenthøj, "Pan-Scandinavism and the Threshold Principle?," 9–13.

[30] Great Britain and Russia, in 1721 and 1773 respectively, had guaranteed the Danish king's right to Schleswig. For a discussion of the converging British, Russian, and Austrian interests in the peace negotiations that eventually prevented a partition along lines of ethnicity, culture, and language in Schleswig and Holstein, see Bjørn, *1848: Borgerkrig Og Revolution* [1848: Civil War and Revolution], 123–134, 95, 249–251.

[31] Ibid., 123–134, 92–94. For a timeline over major events in the First Schleswig War, see Adriansen and Christensen, *Første Slesvigske Krig 1848–1851: Forhistorie, Forløb Og Følger* [First Schleswig War 1848–1851: Causes, Course, and Consequences], 42–43. German-speaking troops won a battle around the town of Schleswig on April 23 and subsequently were ordered north across the border between Schleswig and the Danish mainland of Jutland. By August 26, 1848, in no small part due to international pressure, Prussia accepted a seven-month ceasefire, buying the Danish government precious time to find an acceptable domestic solution to the crisis so closely tied to events outside the kingdom's realm. See Glenthøj, *1864: Sønner Af De Slagne* [1864: Descendants of the Defeated], 204–209.

[32] Andrew Zimmermann, "From the Rhine to the Mississippi," *Journal of the Civil War Era* 5, no. 1 (2015): 9. Zimmermann notes about the failed revolution in Baden that "Those who survived the Prussian siege soon joined their comrades in Switzerland, where more than eleven thousand German refugees fled after the revolution."

Olshausen, both of whom eventually ended up in America.[33] When Claussen arrived in Davenport, Iowa, he apparently found a welcoming community of a "large number of his closest countrymen, the Schleswig-Holsteiners."[34]

Other German-speaking subjects living within Danish borders struck out for Wisconsin, as was the case for August Hauer, who arrived with his family in what became New Denmark (and who, according to one account, "was a mortal enemy" of everything associated with the Danish state for decades afterward).[35]

The exact number of German-speaking Forty-Eighters who emigrated for political reasons after the First Schleswig War is difficult to ascertain, but the legacy of the 1848 revolutions in terms of political rights, economic opportunity, and abolition of slavery continued to impact American and Scandinavian society in the years afterward.[36]

Whether settling in Iowa, Wisconsin, Illinois, or Minnesota – or, for a few, even Missouri, Louisiana, or Texas – the German, Danish, Swedish, and Norwegian Forty-Eighters who emigrated in the wake of the revolutions generally found some common ground in their interpretation of equality and liberty. Despite Old World divisions, these Northern European immigrants' experience with class divisions would continue to shape their engagement with issues of social mobility and equality in America. At the very center of such discussions was the importance of owning land.[37]

---

[33] Thomas P. Christensen, "A German Forty-Eighter in Iowa," *Annals of Iowa* 26, no. 4 (1945): 247.

[34] Ibid.

[35] Fritz W. Rasmussen, "Den 17. Mandag [November]," in *Fritz William Rasmussen Papers. Diaries, 1856–1876. Green Bay Mss 4. Box 8* (Wisconsin Historical Society, 1862).

[36] Zimmermann, "From the Rhine to the Mississippi," 4.

[37] Gunlög Fur, "Indians and Immigrants – Entangled Histories," Journal of American Ethnic History 33, no. 3 (2014): 55–76, 61. In her study of Scandinavians' entangled histories with Native Americans in the Midwest, Fur notes on the importance of land that "concurrent histories begin there, and the significance of land cannot be overstated."

2

Exodus

It was still dark when Claus Clausen shook his mother's hand for the last time. Prompted by Norwegian settlers in Wisconsin, the twenty-two-year-old aspiring pastor was leaving Denmark for the relative unknown of America along with his twenty-seven-year-old wife Martha.[1] In time, Claus Clausen would become one of the most prominent Scandinavian anti-slavery pastors in America and chaplain of a celebrated Scandinavian Civil War unit (see Figure 2.1). Yet, this early spring morning, April 10, 1843, Claus and Martha Clausen were part of a mass-migration vanguard that in less than a century would lead more than two million fellow Scandinavians to the United States.[2]

Since the 1830s, *Amerikafeber* (America fever) had spread slowly across Scandinavia and was now beginning to reach even remote villages. Like an invisible hand, the "contagion" crept from Norway through Sweden and into Denmark.[3] Poets and cultural icons such as Denmark's

---

[1] Rasmus Andersen, *Pastor Claus Laurits Clausen – Banebryder for Den Norske Og Danske Kirke i Amerika. Første Skandinavisk Feltpræst.* [*Pastor Claus Laurits Clausen: Trailblazer for the Norwegian and Danish Church in America. First Scandinavian Chaplain*] (Blair, NE: Danish Lutheran Publishing House, 1921), 27–30; Anders Bo Rasmussen, *I Krig for Lincoln* [*To War for Lincoln*] (Copenhagen: Informations Forlag, 2014), 25–29.

[2] Andersen, *Pastor Claus Laurits Clausen – Banebryder for Den Norske Og Danske Kirke i Amerika. Første Skandinavisk Feltpræst.* [*Pastor Claus Laurits Clausen: Trailblazer for the Norwegian and Danish Church in America. First Scandinavian Chaplain*], 235–236. See also Gunlög Fur, "Indians and Immigrants – Entangled Histories," *Journal of American History* 33, no. 3 (2014): 55–76, 55.

[3] The earliest nineteenth-century example of Scandinavian migration was a group of fifty-two Norwegians who arrived in New York in 1825, emigrating in large part because of

FIGURE 2.1 Claus L. Clausen photographed on the island of Langeland during a visit to Denmark after the Civil War. Courtesy Vesterheim Norwegian-American Museum Archives.

Hans Christian Andersen, Sweden's Fredrika Bremer, and Norway's Henrik Wergeland (at least initially) helped spread this fervor for America and tied it closely to a mental image of an economic dreamland

religious reasons, but it would be more than a decade before a sizable party left Scandinavia for America again. In the subsequent years, partially spurred by emigration pamphlets, migration to the United States slowly but surely picked up. See Jørn Brøndal, *Ethnic Leadership and Midwestern Politics: Scandinavian Americans and the Progressive Movement in Wisconsin, 1890–1914* (Chicago: University of Illinois Press, 2004), 16–17. Also Andrew Nilsen Rygg, *Norwegians in New York 1825–1925* (New York: Norwegian News Company, 1941), 1–6; see also Rasmussen, *I Krig for Lincoln* [*To War for Lincoln*], 25–29.

across the Atlantic.[4] In America, according to Andersen, horses' hoofs were covered in silver and fields bloomed with money.

> Der går solen aldrig ned [there the sun never sets],
> stegt er hver kastanje [every chestnut roasted],
> der er alting kærlighed [there everything is love],
> kilderne champagne [in champagne toasted][5]

Together, Andersen and Bremer, who knew each other well, helped disseminate a New World image closely associated with upward social mobility, and Scandinavian literature regularly portrayed the United States as an El Dorado. Yet, perhaps not surprisingly, prospective Scandinavian emigrants needed more tangible advice before making life-changing decisions associated with emigration. Thus, when seemingly reliable pamphlets appeared just a few years after Andersen's song lyrics, so did Scandinavian communities start to appear across the Atlantic.

The first published pamphlet based on concrete experience in the United States was Ole Rynning's *True Account of America* from 1838, which sparked the migration imagination in several Norwegian villages. Rynning described abundant land, wildlife, and relatively cheap agricultural opportunities. Especially the idea of ample American government land was attractive for many Scandinavian smallholders who often found it impossible to amass more than a few acres in their Old World villages due to the nobility's vast landholdings.[6]

Rynning's account, written in the winter of 1837–8, "had a considerable effect upon the emigration," noted the late Norwegian-American historian Theodore C. Blegen.[7] Unfortunately, Rynning's pioneer group of Norwegians settled in a swampy region of Iroquois County, Illinois, and by 1838 many had succumbed to malarial fever and other

---

[4] Sven H. Rossel, "The Image of the United States in Danish Literature: A Survey with Scandinavian Perspectives," in *Images of America in Scandinavia*, ed. Poul Houe and Sven Hakon Rossel, pp. 1–23 (Amsterdam: Rodopi, 1998), 8–11, 15. Rossel notes that "the romantic poet Henrik Wergeland, George Washington and Benjamin Franklin were heroes who had perfected the ideal of humanity in the land of liberty," but by the 1840s he was warning against emigration to the United States. See also Norman L. Willey, "Wergeland and Emigration to America," *Scandinavian Studies and Notes* 16, no. 4 (1940): 121–127.

[5] Rossel, "The Image of the United States in Danish Literature: A Survey with Scandinavian Perspectives," 3.

[6] Theodore C. Blegen, ed., *Ole Rynning's True Account of America* (Minneapolis, MN: Norwegian-American Historical Society, 1921), 81–82. See also Richard N. Current, *The History of Wisconsin. Volume II. The Civil War Era, 1848–1873* (Madison: State Historical Society of Wisconsin, 1976), 54.

[7] Blegen, *Ole Rynning's True Account of America*, 16.

illnesses – Rynning among them.[8] Yet Ansten Nattestad, one of Rynning's fellow community members, carried his manuscript back in the spring of 1838 along with several "America letters." Upon Nattestad's return to family and friends in Norway, he was besieged by prospective emigrants, one of whom noted:

> Hardly any other Norwegian publication has been purchased and read with such avidity as this Rynning's *Account of America*. People traveled long distances to hear "news" from the land of wonders, and many who before were scarcely able to read began in earnest to practice in the "America-book," making such progress that they were soon able to spell their way forward and acquire most of the contents.[9]

Another writer noted, "It is said that wherever Ole Rynning's book was read anywhere in Norway, people listened as attentively as if they were in church."[10] One of the emigration parties that left Norway shortly after the publication of Rynning's book, and Nattestad's visit, was a group from Telemarken who established their colony in eastern Wisconsin and by 1841 needed a spiritual guide. The settlement leaders, a young emigrant named Sören Bache among them, wrote family and friends back in Norway to find the right person. Bache's father, Tollef, helped convince Claus Clausen, who had traveled through Norway in the summer of 1841, that Muskego, Wisconsin, would be the best locality to do religious work. Letters from Sören Bache helped cement the agreement.[11]

On October 6, 1842, Sören Bache wrote Clausen from Muskego, a Norwegian settlement about 20 miles south of Milwaukee, to ease any concern about "his material well-being"; he assured Clausen that the land "is very good and rich and bears all sorts of grains without being fertilized. There is still plenty of government land to be had at $1.25 per acre. ... I believe that anyone who is not too emotionally bound to his native place will be happy in America."[12]

Bache's letter to Clausen underscored the importance of landownership as a means to social uplift among Scandinavian immigrants, and Rynning's original account reflected these concerns by treating the "quality of the land" in one of his first and most thorough chapters.[13]

---

[8] Ibid., 9–15.   [9] Quoted in ibid., 17.   [10] Ibid., 15–17.

[11] Andersen, *Pastor Claus Laurits Clausen – Banebryder for Den Norske Og Danske Kirke i Amerika. Første Skandinavisk Feltpræst* [*Pastor Claus Laurits Clausen: Trailblazer for the Norwegian and Danish Church in America. First Scandinavian Chaplain*], 13–16.

[12] Clarence A. Clausen and Andreas Elviken, eds., *The Chronicle of Old Muskego: The Diary of Søren Bache, 1839–1847* (Northfield, MN: Norwegian-American Historical Association, 1951), 91.

[13] Blegen, *Ole Rynning's True Account of America*, 40–46.

While the decision to emigrate from Scandinavia could have multiple individual causes, economic opportunity, political rights, and religious freedom were the most significant factors pulling Scandinavian immigrants toward the United States in the Civil War era. The lack of land in the Old World was the most important circumstance pushing poorer immigrants out of Norway, Sweden, and Denmark in the years leading up to the Civil War, and the letters and emigration pamphlets that appeared in Scandinavia in the 1840s sparked ideas about American institutions that powerfully informed Scandinavian immigrants' imaginations about the meaning of American citizenship.[14]

To afford the dream of emigration to, and landownership in, America, a number of prospective Norwegian, Swedish, and Danish farmers started selling off their possessions during the 1840s.[15] For Claus Clausen, the allure of "a safe income for the future" played an important part in his decision to emigrate, but there was also a strong religious component to his choice.[16] In this, Clausen was far from alone. As Theodore Blegen argued in 1921, "religious motives" played a larger part "than has usually been recognized in connection with the emigration after 1825," and, for several Norwegians, Swedes, and Danes in the earliest settlements, the Scandinavian state churches' conservatism was a contributing factor to emigration.[17]

Clausen was deeply influenced by Nikolai F. S. Grundtvig, who spearheaded the revivalist movement known as Grundtvigianism and was

---

[14] Torben Grøngaard Jeppesen, *Danske i USA 1850–2000. En Demografisk, Social Og Kulturgeografisk Undersøgelse Af De Danske Immigranter Og Deres Efterkommere* [*Danes in the United States 1850–2000. A Demographic, Social and Cultural Geographic Study of The Danish Immigrants and Their Descendants*] (Odense: University Press of Southern Denmark, 2005), 29–30.

[15] See, for example, Andreas Frederiksen, "Wilmington Ill, Den 28 Juli 1850," in *Afskrift af 22 breve til Frederik Nielsen, Herlev DK fra A.F. Wilmington Ill. og West Denmark og Neenah Wisc. (1847–1872)* (Det Danske Udvandrerarkiv, 1850). See also Johannes Romwall, "Håkabo Okt. 16 1863," in *Sven August Johnson Papers, 1831–1921. SSIRC Mss P:9* (Augustana College, 1863). For a description of social conditions in Denmark in the 1840s, see Asger Th. Simonsen, *Husmandskår Og Husmandspolitik i 1840erne* [*Smallholder Conditions and Smallholder Politics in the 1840s*] (Copenhagen: Landbohistorisk Selskab, 1977), 16–19.

[16] Clausen and Elviken, *The Chronicle of Old Muskego: The Diary of Søren Bache, 1839–1847*, 91.

[17] Blegen, *Ole Rynning's True Account of America*, 16.

censored by the Danish state church between 1826 and 1837 for his writings.[18] By 1843, however, Grundtvig had been accepted back into the state church, resumed preaching, and become an increasingly influential pastor of international renown.[19] Additionally, Clausen had been introduced to the teachings of Hans Nielsen Hauge, a layman preacher who led a religious protest against the Norwegian state church and was jailed for his views between 1804 and 1814.[20] It was followers of Hans Hauge in Muskego who enticed Claus Clausen to emigrate with the promise of a denomination – as well as official ordination – in Wisconsin.[21]

Thus, the Clausen family members said their final goodbyes at 4 a.m. in a little Danish hamlet.[22] "We wished them [to] live well in peace of the lord until we all are reunited at the lamb's throne and they wished us the same under many tears," wrote Clausen in his diary.[23]

A friend drove the couple to the town of Slagelse, 63 miles (and a twelve-hour carriage ride) outside of Copenhagen, where they arrived half an hour before the horse-drawn stagecoach left for the Danish capital. Claus and Martha Clausen decided to remain in Copenhagen for a week

[18] On Claus Clausen's deep knowledge of Grundtvig's abolitionist writings, see Andersen, *Pastor Claus Laurits Clausen – Banebryder for Den Norske Og Danske Kirke i Amerika. Første Skandinavisk Feltpræst* [*Pastor Claus Laurits Clausen: Trailblazer for the Norwegian and Danish Church in America. First Scandinavian Chaplain*], 61.

[19] For a discussion of Grundtvig's perspective on Christianity and the Danish state church, see Julie Allen, *Danish, but Not Lutheran: The Impact of Mormonism on Danish Cultural Identity, 1850–1920* (Salt Lake City: University of Utah Press, 2017), 96–99.

[20] Eugene F. Fevold, "The Norwegian Immigrant and His Church," *Norwegian-American Studies* 23 (1967): 3–16.

[21] Andersen, *Pastor Claus Laurits Clausen – Banebryder for Den Norske Og Danske Kirke i Amerika. Første Skandinavisk Feltpræst* [*Pastor Claus Laurits Clausen: Trailblazer for the Norwegian and Danish Church in America. First Scandinavian Chaplain*], 13–16. See also Blegen, *Ole Rynning's True Account of America*, 86. Rynning wrote about the multitude of religious strands in the United States: "Catholics, Protestants, Lutherans, Calvinists, Presbyterians, Baptists, Quakers, Methodists, and many others." And while there were also "various sects among the Norwegians," he wrote, they did not "yet have ministers and churches."

[22] Clausen and Elviken, *The Chronicle of Old Muskego: The Diary of Søren Bache, 1839–1847*, 88–90.

[23] Claus L. Clausen, "Dagbog [Diary]," in *Clausen, Claus L. (1820–1892). P59* (Northfield, MN: Norwegian-American Historical Association, 1843). See also Andersen, *Pastor Claus Laurits Clausen – Banebryder for Den Norske Og Danske Kirke i Amerika. Første Skandinavisk Feltpræst* [*Pastor Claus Laurits Clausen: Trailblazer for the Norwegian and Danish Church in America. First Scandinavian Chaplain*], 39.

over Easter, where the couple, according to Clausen's diary entries, had the pleasure of attending several sermons by Grundtvig at an important political moment in the Danish anti-slavery cause.[24]

Since 1839, Grundtvig had been one of three founding members of the Danish anti-slavery committee (the other two being Professor Christian N. David and Jean-Antoine Raffard of the French Reformed Church of Copenhagen), a society formed in the immediate aftermath of a visit from the British and Foreign Anti-Slavery Society.[25] The society's secretary, George W. Alexander, met with several dignitaries when he visited Scandinavia in September 1839 to advocate abolition of slavery on the islands of the Danish West Indies and Swedish St. Barthelémy, and he subsequently reported back that he deemed Grundtvig, along with David and Raffard, "among the best friends of the Cause of negro freedom."[26]

Notably, none of the three founding members of the Danish anti-slavery committee were uncritical members of the Danish political and religious "establishment." Both Grundtvig and David (the latter an economics professor of Jewish descent) had experienced censorship of their writings, and Raffard's role in the French Reformed Church by definition set him apart from the Danish establishment clergy. The three founding anti-slavery committee members were therefore somewhat removed from more conservative societal institutions. The members of the committee advocated the importance of belief in a common humanity and the immediate abolition of slavery, but they also regularly expressed a sense of moral superiority in relation to people of African descent.[27]

After the three members' first meeting, Grundtvig was asked to write a statement about the views and aims of the committee. Grundtvig denounced slavery and expressed empathy with "our unhappy fellow human beings, who are sold as commodities and are treated – be it harshly or in a lenient way – as domestic animals," but he also claimed that "the slaves on our west-indian islands usually are treated in a milder way than are the majority of others."[28] Grundtvig's statement was never published,

---

[24] K. E. Bugge, "Grundtvig and the Abolition of Slavery," *Grundtvig-Studier* 56, no. 1 (2005): 171–172.

[25] Ibid., 161–163. [26] Ibid.

[27] For American examples of the same sense of racial superiority within the abolitionist movement, see Stephen Kantrowitz, *More Than Freedom: Fighting for Black Citizenship in a White Republic, 1829–1889* (New York: Penguin Press, 2012), 58–64.

[28] Quoted in Bugge, "Grundtvig and the Abolition of Slavery," 165.

but the document's ideological underpinnings – slavery's immorality, infused with supposed superior Scandinavian morality in dealing with slavery – were not uncommon among educated Scandinavians and found their way to the public through C. N. David's writings in late 1839.[29]

After praising the Danish monarch for being the first European regent to abolish the slave trade in 1792, David informed Danish readers that the native inhabitants of the African Gold Coast, despite the supposed civilizing influence from Europeans, had over time only become more unenlightened, more sinful, and more bestial because of the slave trade.[30] Though the Danish slave trade ban did not take effect until 1803, the decree served as the source of countless claims of moral superiority by Scandinavian authors in subsequent debates over slavery.[31] As Pernille Ipsen has succinctly pointed out, "the discourse that helped abolish the slave trade also helped produce racial difference" as the better-educated Scandinavians in the Civil War era came of age in a slaveholding nation where subjugation of Africans, justified in part through science and culture, was an extension of the power and labor dynamics within the Danish and Swedish kingdoms.[32]

In Denmark, "the period of Atlantic slavery," as Ipsen has demonstrated, was marked "by an ever-deepening linkage of slavery and

---

[29] A decade later, American congressman Thaddeus Stevens mirrored David's viewpoint when he noted that "slavery always degrades labor." Quoted in Keri Leigh Merritt, *Masterless Men: Poor Whites and Slavery in the Antebellum South* (Cambridge: Cambridge University Press, 2017), 110.

[30] Christian N. David, "Om Slavehandel [On the Slave Trade]," *Fædrelandet*, September 28, 1839. Given the fact that the Danish monarch had imposed strict censorship on the press to eliminate revolutionary ideas from the public sphere, it was noteworthy that David's anti-slavery notions appeared in print without censure. The explanation, as Knud Bugge has suggested, may have been Grundtvig and Raffard's close ties to Princess Caroline Amalie (Grundtvig sermonized at the court, and Raffard helped the princess distribute food and supplies to the needy). K. E. Bugge, *Grundtvig Og Slavesagen [Grundtvig and the Slavery Cause]* (Aarhus: Aarhus Universitetsforlag, 2003), 39–71, 202. See also Bugge, "Grundtvig and the Abolition of Slavery," 161–164.

[31] David, "Om Slavehandel [On the Slave Trade]." See also Pernille Ipsen and Gunlög Fur, "Scandinavian Colonialism: Introduction," *Itenerario* 33, no. 2 (2009): 7–16, 11. For example, in 1828, the famous Danish poet Adam Oehlenschläger in a tribute to the royal family wrongfully claimed that Denmark had been the first country in the world to abolish slavery; see Bugge, *Grundtvig Og Slavesagen [Grundtvig and the Slavery Cause]*, 33–34.

[32] Pernille Ipsen, *Daughters of the Trade: Atlantic Slavers and Interracial Marriage on the Gold Coast* (University of Pennsylvania Press: Philadelphia, 2015), 155.

blackness," a process that "happened not only on European slave ships, but in European art, literature, and travel accounts and in every corner of the Atlantic touched or affected by the Atlantic slave trade and plantation system."[33]

These texts about Africa and Africans became part of a transnational flow of ideas that framed Black people as undesirable and inferior in an attempt to rationalize Danish slavery. As an example of perceived African inferiority, a Danish governor of the slavetrading post Christiansborg on Africa's west coast in 1726 dismissed the idea of his men bringing their local African wives back to Copenhagen, "as the general opinion in Denmark was [not] in favor of Africans."[34]

The same was true in the Swedish kingdom, where cultural images and scientific texts legitimizing African inferiority circulated with increased frequency in the eighteenth century. While Benjamin Franklin, in his by now well-known classification from 1751, lumped Swedes together with "the Spanish, the Italians, the French, and the Russians" as people with a "swarthy complexion," lower than white English people and slightly above "black or tawny" people, Scandinavian researchers more clearly demarcated themselves from Africans in culture and so-called science.[35]

Swedish scientist Carl von Linné (Linneaus), for example, in 1735 created a typology where he distinguished Europeans from Indians, Asians, and Africans. In his *Systema Naturae*, Linneaus situated human beings at top of the animal kingdom, and at the "pinnacle of his human kingdom reigned *H. sapiens europaeus*: 'Very smart, inventive. Covered by tight clothing. Ruled by law.'"[36] At the other end of Linneaus' typology were Africans, a group the Swedish scientist described as "sluggish, lazy ... crafty, slow, careless. Covered by grease. Ruled by caprice."[37]

---

[33] Ibid., 100.   [34] Ibid., 94.

[35] Quoted in Peter Kolchin, "Whiteness Studies: The New History of Race in America," *Journal of American History* 89, no. 1 (2002): 154–173, 158. For examples of "romantic" and "scientific" hierarchies based on whiteness, see also Jørn Brøndal, "'The Fairest among the So-Called White Races': Portrayals of Scandinavian Americans in the Filiopietistic and Nativist Literature of the Late Nineteenth and Early Twentieth Centuries," *Journal of American Ethnic History* 33, no. 3 (2014): 6–9.

[36] Quoted in Ibram X. Kendi, *Stamped from the Beginning: The Definitive History of Racist Ideas in America* (New York: Nation Books, 2016), 82. For a discussion emphasizing the nuances of Linneaus' work on race, see Stefan Müller-Wille, "Race and History: Comments from an Epistemological Point of View," *Science, Technology, & Human Values* 39, no. 4 (2014): 600–602.

[37] Quoted in Kendi, *Stamped from the Beginning: The Definitive History of Racist Ideas in America*, 82. See also Erika K. Jackson, *Scandinavians in Chicago: The Origins of White Privilege in Moderne America* (Urbana: University of Illinois Press, 2019), 60–61.

Linneaus' student, Peter Kalm, while expressing regret at enslaved Americans' subordinate position, also wrote about the enslaved kept in "their heathen darkness" in 1756.[38]

Building on Linneaus' and Kalm's work, German anthropologist Johann Friedrich Blumenbach in 1776 differentiated between races on account of the shape of the skull while Olof Erik Bergius, who had been an official in the Swedish West Indian colony St. Barthélemy, in 1819 published a book where he clearly demarcated Black and white people. The former was destined for servitude and would gain "bildung" (edification or enlightenment) through interaction with the white people who were destined to rule.[39] Additionally, Anders Retzius, a prominent Swedish scientist who was a member of the Royal Swedish Academy and in 1842 "introduced the cephalic index" linking race to skull size, knew and corresponded with German-born scientist Lorenz Oken, who in 1807 created a racial hierarchy based on senses (Black people who were associated with "touch" at the bottom and white people associated with "vision" at the top of Oken's five races) and was inducted into the prestigious Swedish society in 1832.[40]

---

[38] Pehr Kalm, *En Resa Til Norra America* [*Travels to North America*] (Stockholm: Lars Salvii, 1756), 476–485. See also Frank Shuffelton, "Circumstantial Accounts, Dangerous Art: Recognizing African-American Culture Intravelers' Narratives," *Eighteenth-Century Studies* 27, no. 4 (1994): 591–594.

[39] Ale Pålsson, *Our Side of the Water: Political Culture in the Swedish Colony of St Barthélemy 1800–1825* (Stockholm: Stockholm University, Faculty of Humanities, Department of History, 2016), 27–28, http://su.diva-portal.org/smash/record.jsf?pid=diva2%3A967510&dswid=-7542. For a discussion of "romantic" and "scientific" racism in the 1800s, see Brøndal, "'The Fairest among the So-Called White Races': Portrayals of Scandinavian Americans in the Filiopietistic and Nativist Literature of the Late Nineteenth and Early Twentieth Centuries." See also O. E. Bergius, *Om Westindien* [*About The West Indies*] (Stockholm: A. Gadelius, 1819), 30–31.

[40] On the cephalic index, see Alan Mann, "The Origins of American Physical Anthropology in Philadelphia," *Yearbook of Physical Anthropology* 52 (2009): 160. See also David Howes, ed., *The Sixth Sense Reader* (New York: Berg, 2009), 10. See also Olaf Breidbach and Michael T. Ghiselin, "Lorenz Oken and 'Naturphilosophie' in Jena, Paris and London," *History and Philosophy of the Life Sciences* 27, no. 2 (2002): 227. See also David Howes, "The Expanding Field of Sensory Studies," www.sensorystudies.org/sensorial-investigations/the-expanding-field-of-sensory-studies/. As David Howes has noted, "Oken's ascending scale of 'sensory perfection' in 'Man' (with the European eye-man at the apex) was not based on any intrinsic propensities of the peoples concerned, but rather dependent on the typologies of the Western social imaginary." On the connection between Retzius and Oken, I am grateful to Anne Miche de Malleray of the Royal Swedish Academy of Sciences for providing this information in an e-mail dated November 29, 2018.

Retzius also corresponded often with Samuel George Morton, the founder of American physical anthropology, "about their mutual interest in craniometry."[41] Morton's views were influential and his "measures of cranial capacity placed Europeans on top with the largest capacities, Africans at the bottom and Asians in between."[42] While Retzius early in his career criticized phrenology – later recognized as a pseudo-science based on skull measurements – Morton in his book *Crania Americana* included a section on phrenology's relationship to anthropology and helped legitimize perceptions of Black inferiority.[43]

While it is difficult to ascertain the extent to which culturally infused ideas of race and scientific racism impacted the general Scandinavian population, there are important examples of the cultural, social, and political elite being familiar with scientific explanations and the storytelling used, directly and indirectly, to undergird slavery in both the Old and the New World.

Among the prominent Scandinavians to demonstrate interest in, and knowledge of, the scientific currents of the day – and their ramifications in terms of race relations – was renowned Swedish writer Fredrika Bremer. During her travels around the United States between 1849 and 1851, Bremer, who was greatly interested in educational matters and regularly commented on issues of race, described Linneaus and Benjamin Franklin (along with Isaac Newton), as "heroes of natural sciences."[44] Bremer also expressed interest in phrenology and wrote favorably about the relocation of the formerly enslaved from America to Africa. While the connection between Bremer's admiration of Linneaus, belief in phrenology, and support for colonization are not in themselves a direct link between Old World racial ideology and its expression in the New World, they do help explain Bremer's admission that "I can not divest my mind of the idea that

---

[41] Mann, "The Origins of American Physical Anthropology in Philadelphia," 160–161.

[42] Ibid.

[43] Ibid. See also Steven Hahn, *A Nation without Borders: The United States and Its World in an Age of Civil Wars, 1830–1910* (New York: Viking, 2016), 67. According to Hahn, defenders of slavery in the United States "eagerly embraced the racialist thought that had penetrated more and more of the Atlantic world since the last third of the eighteenth century." Additionally, as Alan Levine has noted, Samuel Morton's influence and arguments were "amplified" by immigrant scholars such as English-born George R. Gliddon and Swiss-born Jean Louis Rodolphe Agassiz. See Alan Levine, "Scientific Racism in Antebellum America," in *The Political Thought of the Civil War*, ed. Alan Levine, Thomas W. Merrill, and James R. Stoner Jr. (Lawrence: University Press of Kansas, 2018), 98.

[44] Fredrika Bremer, *The Homes of the New World: Impressions of America* (New York: Harper & Brothers, 1853), 20.

they [negro slaves] are, and must remain, inferior as regards intellectual capacity."[45]

Bremer published her thoughts on race relations in the United States in 1853, but, as we have seen, expressions of racial hierarchies were prevalent among the Europeans engaged with Atlantic World slavery decades earlier. Moreover, despite the physical distance between Denmark, Western Africa, and the Caribbean, there was no denying slavery's larger societal impact in Scandinavia and its positive economic impact on Nordic maritime cities in the years leading up to 1849. Both in terms of the material wealth that slavery created and in terms of its cultural imprint, slavery directly and indirectly impacted life in major Scandinavian cities and, as Pernille Ipsen has argued, infused life in a city like Copenhagen with a sense of "colonial haunting."[46]

In Denmark, Hans Christian Andersen's play *Mulatten* (The Mulatto), which was set in the French West Indies, debuted on the Royal Danish Theater's stage in Copenhagen in 1840. At this time, the Danish abolitionist movement was still in its infancy, but the play – and the success it enjoyed – indicated Andersen's awareness of slavery's impact on Europe's slaveholding nations while simultaneously revealing some of the racial stereotypes that helped legitimize slavery from a white European perspective.[47]

By consciously situating his play on Martinique, Andersen likely helped his elite Copenhagen audience maintain the perception that Danish colonial slavery was qualitatively different from French colonial slavery, an argument that fit into Grundtvig's view of "benign" Danish slave rule,

---

[45] Ibid., 20, 351. In a previous paragraph, Bremer prefaced her assessment of Black people's intellectual capacity by expressing support for colonization: "much is done in Georgia for the instruction of the negro slaves in Christianity for their emancipation, and their colonization at Liberia, on the coast of Africa." See also Rossel, "The Image of the United States in Danish Literature: A Survey with Scandinavian Perspectives," 10. Also Jørn Brøndal, "An Early American Dilemma? Scandinavian Travel Writers' Reflections on the Founding Ideals of the United States and the Condition of African Americans, Ca. 1850–1900," in *Les Constitutions: Des Révolutions À L'épreuve Du Temps Aux Etats-Unis Et En Europe* [*Constitutions: On-Going Revolutions in Europe and the United States*], ed. Marie-Elisabeth Baudoin and Marie Bolton (Paris, 2016), 143–144, 55.

[46] Pernille Ipsen, "'Plant Ikke Upas-Træet Om Vor Bolig': Colonial Haunting, Race, and Interracial Marriage in Hans Christian Andersen's *Mulatten* (1840)," *Scandinavian Studies* 88, no. 2 (2016): 130–132. See also Ipsen, *Daughters of the Trade: Atlantic Slavers and Interracial Marriage on the Gold Coast*, 99–104.

[47] H. C. Andersen, *Mulatten* [*The Mulatto*] (Copenhagen: Bianco Luno's Bogtrykkeri, 1840), 29.

while avoiding having his play comment explicitly on contemporary monarchical politics, in which the royal court along with Danish merchants for years had been intimately tied to the colonial goods flowing from the West Indies.[48]

Moreover, Andersen understood the racial stereotypes that would make his play legible and perhaps even credible to an elite Scandinavian audience. Playing on fears of slave uprisings, Andersen made the half-naked former slave Paléme a central part of his play. Describing plans for a future slave rebellion, Paléme appeared in the first scene of Andersen's second act, sipping rum from a coconut (which he in Andersen's imagination had been nursed on), before proclaiming "in blood and fire everything shall perish."[49]

Slaves, or former slaves, of African descent – half-naked, and perhaps by implication closer to nature, hard-drinking, and vengeful – were part of the stereotypes that helped maintain legal measures to keep the enslaved population and freedpeople under control and part of the stereotypes that shaped attitudes toward Africans in Europe in the decades leading up to the Civil War.[50]

By being somewhat removed from the influence of the Danish state church and the political establishment, Grundtvig, David, and Raffard were able to set themselves apart from more "establishment" ideas of slavery and race relations in their concrete and active efforts to abolish slavery. In this small abolitionist circle, Grundtvig played an important part, and Claus Clausen on his way to America in April 1843 received concrete anti-slavery inspiration from the pastor that he considered "the North's spiritual high priest" as he

---

[48] Ipsen, "'Plant Ikke Upas-Træet Om Vor Bolig': Colonial Haunting, Race, and Interracial Marriage in Hans Christian Andersen's *Mulatten* (1840)."

[49] Andersen, *Mulatten* [*The Mulatto*], 29.

[50] Even while working at the forefront of the small Danish abolitionist movement and trying to refute charges of slaves being "rude," "immoral," and "devoid of all religion," in an address read by Professor C. N. David to Danish politicians in 1844 the anti-slavery activists seemed to acknowledge the existence of a racial hierarchy. On behalf of the Danish anti-slavery committee, David did allow that the present generation of slaves may well be "as rude and morally corrupt" as they were represented to be, but he blamed the slaveowners for this condition before calling for immediate abolition (yet steeping the call in paternalist discourse): "It is obvious that freedom, to a certain extent at least, must be given before it can be enjoyed. A child will not learn to walk by being continually held in leading strings." See C. N. David et al., "Denmark – Proceedings in the States," *British and Foreign Anti-Slavery Reporter*, January 8, 1845. Also Ipsen, *Daughters of the Trade: Atlantic Slavers and Interracial Marriage on the Gold Coast*, 175.

attended several of Grundtvig's Easter sermons together with his wife Martha.[51]

On Maundy Thursday, April 13, 1843, at a time when he had been working actively for slavery's abolition for four years, Grundtvig preached on his belief in a common humanity.

[Humankind, originating from the same set of parents, was considered] as children of one blood as Christianity otherwise could not be extended to all people under the heavens, for wherever it comes to black or white ... it follows that all of mankind both can and shall be of one blood.[52]

Grundtvig's Protestant Christian ideas, and his earlier expressed view of slavery's sinfulness, were part of the ideological inspiration that Clausen carried with him to America – ideas with important implications for discussions of citizenship. If one followed Grundtvig's conviction that slavery was sinful and "all of mankind of one blood," then people "black or white" would deserve equal rights. Grundtvig's ideas about Christianity and slavery – and his history of state-church criticism – would therefore continue to play a part in Claus Clausen's own anti-slavery struggle in the New World well into the 1860s. While Claus Clausen initially devoted himself to religious matters in America, it became increasingly clear, as more Scandinavian immigrants arrived in the region, that this Danish "disciple" of Grundtvig was more forceful in his denunciation of slavery's sinfulness than his state church–affiliated colleagues but also served as one of many individual examples connecting ideas of landownership, liberty, and colonialism.

[51] Andersen, *Pastor Claus Laurits Clausen – Banebryder for Den Norske Og Danske Kirke i Amerika. Første Skandinavisk Feltpræst. [Pastor Claus Laurits Clausen: Trailblazer for the Norwegian and Danish Church in America. First Scandinavian Chaplain]*, 40–41, 61. Clausen wrote, "That he is called the North's spiritual high priest is rather high [praise] but not [a] wholly incorrect designation." See also Johannes W. C. Dietrichson, *Pastor J. W. C. Dietrichsons Reise Blandt De Norske Emigranter i "De Forenede Nordamerikanske Fristater." Paany Udgiven Af Rasmus B. Anderson* (Madison: Amerika's Bogtrykkeri, 1896), 27.

[52] Jette Holm and Elisabeth A. Glenthøj, eds., *Grundtvig: Prædikener i Vartov, 1842–43* [*Grundtvig: Sermons in Vartov, 1842–43*], vol. 5 (Copenhagen: Forlaget Vartov, 2007), 170–178. See also Sebastian N. Page, *Black Resettlement and the American Civil War* (Cambridge: Cambridge University Press, 2021), 3.

3

Old and New World Liberty

A "very severe epidemic" raged through Muskego during the winter months of 1844.[1] According to Sören Bache, somewhere between seventy and eighty men, women, and children were carried "to their graves," and Claus Clausen's role in the community was thus highlighted in tragic fashion as he conducted more than fifty funerals in a community of 600 people within his first five months in the United States.[2]

The heartbreak led several immigrants to send what Bache described as "ill-considered letters" to family and friends back in Norway portraying life in the United States unfavorably and complicating the early settlers' hopes of creating a steadily growing and thriving community in Wisconsin. To counteract the negative stories, the Muskego settlement leaders jointly wrote an open letter which appeared in the Norwegian *Morgenbladet* (Morning Paper) on April 1, 1845. According to the settlers' religiously infused worldview, the current hardship was God's will,

---

[1] Clarence A. Clausen and Andreas Elviken, eds., *The Chronicle of Old Muskego: The Diary of Søren Bache, 1839–1847* (Northfield, MN: Norwegian-American Historical Association, 1951), 141. The epidemic may well have been cholera, as Rasmus B. Anderson describes recurring outbreaks in the late 1840s and early 1850s; see Rasmus B. Anderson, *The First Chapter of Norwegian Migration, Its Causes and Results*, second ed. (Madison: Published by the author, 1896), 274.

[2] Albert O. Barton, "The Most Historic Norwegian Colony," *Wisconsin Magazine of History* 21, no. 2 (1937): 134. See also Enok Mortensen, *The Danish Lutheran Church in America* (Philadelphia, PA: Board of Publication, Lutheran Church in America, 1967), 30. Also Johannes W. C. Dietrichson, *Pastor J. W. C. Dietrichsons Reise Blandt De Norske Emigranter i "De Forenede Nordamerikanske Fristater." Paany Udgiven Af Rasmus B. Anderson [Pastor J. W. C. Dietrichson's Travels among the Norwegian Emigrants in "the United North American States." Reprinted by Rasmus B. Anderson]* (Madison, WI: Amerika's Bogtrykkeri, 1896).

but the Lord also gave reason for optimism:[3] "God has made it more convenient to produce human food in America than perhaps in any other nation in the world," the authors noted.[4] Moreover, foundational American ideas set the New World apart from Scandinavia. "We make no pretense about acquiring riches, but we are subjects under a liberal government in a bountiful country where freedom and equality rules in religious and civic matters."[5]

Liberal government, freedom of religion, equality in societal matters: such ideas had resonated in Scandinavian communities for years and would continue to do so for decades. To Scandinavian immigrants, the concepts of liberty and equality, closely tied to ideas of American citizenship and prospect of landownership, were simple and alluring at a time when Old World opportunities seemed increasingly precarious due to population growth (which kept wages down), large landholding estates, emerging industrialization, and few opportunities for political influence to alter socio-economic conditions.[6]

Thus, America's relatively cheap and seemingly abundant land, secular ethnic newspapers free of censorship, freedom to support non–state-church pastors, and concrete civic participation through voting or eventually running for office, were significant factors for Scandinavians contemplating emigration in the antebellum era.[7]

---

[3] Setlementet Muskigo, "Beretning Fra Nordamerika [Account from North America]," *Morgenbladet*, April 1, 1845.

[4] Ibid.   [5] Ibid.

[6] Torben Grøngaard Jeppesen, *Danske i USA 1850–2000. En Demografisk, Social Og Kulturgeografisk Undersøgelse Af De Danske Immigranter Og Deres Efterkommere [Danes in the United States 1850–2000. A Demographic, Social and Cultural Geographic Study of the Danish Immigrants and Their Descendants]* (Odense: University Press of Southern Denmark, 2005), 28–30. Even by the 1860s and 1870s, as Jørn Brøndal has noted, "only an estimated 52.4 percent of Danish males above the age of twenty could vote in parliamentary elections, and then only for the lower house, *Folketinget*, along with just 38.1 percent of their Norwegian, and, after the introduction of the bicameral *Riksdag* in 1866, a bare 20.4 percent of their Swedish brethren. Women, of course, were denied suffrage." See Jørn Brøndal, *Ethnic Leadership and Midwestern Politics: Scandinavian Americans and the Progressive Movement in Wisconsin, 1890–1914* (Chicago: University of Illinois Press, 2004), 32.

[7] Brøndal, *Ethnic Leadership and Midwestern Politics: Scandinavian Americans and the Progressive Movement in Wisconsin, 1890–1914*, 18. In his study of Danish emigration after 1868, Kristian Hvidt also points to the primacy of economic explanations, while acknowledging political and religious grievances as secondary factors; see Kristian Hvidt, *Flugten Til Amerika, Eller Drivkræfter i Masseudvandringen Fra Danmark 1868–1914 [Flight to America or Driving Forces in the Mass Emigration from Denmark 1868–1914]* (Aarhus: Universitetsforlaget i Aarhus, 1971), 263–264.

"Everything is designed to maintain the natural liberty and equality of men," Ole Rynning had written in his *True Account of America* from 1838.[8] In Rynning's text, the allure of "liberty and equality" and the accompanying opportunities were central, but the author also made clear that important regional differences guided economic prospects. American democratic ideals were undermined by "the disgraceful slave traffic."[9] Slavery, according to Rynning, constituted a "vile contrast" in a country which could otherwise rightfully be proud of its foundational values.[10] Rynning's subtitle specifically indicated that he wrote for "peasants and commoners," and the Norwegian author thus described conditions in the South in terms legible to readers who had likely never seen nonwhite people outside of Norway.[11] In the South, Rynning wrote, "a race of black people with wooly hair on the head called negroes" suffered from their masters' violence, and slavery was driving a wedge between the North and the South, which could likely soon lead to "a separation between the northern and southern states, or else bloody civil disputes."[12]

Rynning's argument for settling in the Midwest rested partly on morality, but there was an implicit economic argument about immigrant prospects in the North as opposed to the South as well. As Ole Rasmussen Dahl later noted in a letter to his brother in Norway, the American experience had shown that "a free laborer" could never sustain himself "among slaves."[13] Dahl's description was somewhat hyperbolic, but opportunities for economic uplift, as Keri Leigh Merritt has demonstrated, were indeed scarcer in the South, as "wage rates were lower in areas where slavery thrived."[14] Where New England farm laborers in 1850 "could expect to earn $12.98 per month," similar work in Georgia would yield $9.03 and even less in South and North Carolina.[15]

Other Scandinavian travel writers, whether recommending Wisconsin, Missouri, Louisiana, or even Texas, also grappled with the difference between North and South, but all connected landownership to a sense

---

[8] Theodore C. Blegen, *Ole Rynning's True Account of America* (Minneapolis, MN: Norwegian-American Historical Society, 1921), 87. Blegen's translation.

[9] Ibid., 48. Blegen's translation.   [10] Ibid. Blegen's translation.

[11] Ibid., 25, 61. Blegen's translation.

[12] Ibid., 47–50, 88. "The slave trade is still permitted in Missouri; but it is strictly forbidden and despised in Indiana, Illinois, and Wisconsin Territory." Blegen's translation.

[13] Olaf Yderstad, "Et Amerikabrev Fra 1863," *Årsskrift for Nordmøre historielag* (1931): 30.

[14] Keri Leigh Merritt, *Masterless Men: Poor Whites and Slavery in the Antebellum South* (Cambridge: Cambridge University Press, 2017), 73.

[15] Ibid.

of liberty uniquely attainable in America.[16] In a lengthy guidebook and letters to Norwegian newspapers, Johan Reymert Reiersen, for example, explicitly argued for landownership as a natural and religious right for civilized, white people such as Scandinavians.[17] In Reiersen's view, "the red man" was monopolizing more land than consistent with humankind's general welfare, and he therefore supported "civilized" settlers taking land from "barbarians" until the nation was linked from coast to coast.[18]

The paradox between landownership as a natural right for humankind, in Reiersen's view equated with civilized, white people, and American Indians' lack of right to the land they inhabited was maintained by most Scandinavian writers through a belief in white superiority. While Reiersen admitted that "negro slavery exists in Texas," he did not reflect on its economic implications for immigrants but mainly presented slavery as a source of regional conflict over expansion and political power: "Liberty seems absorbed with the mother's milk and appears as indispensible for every citizen of the United States as the air he breathes," Reiersen claimed.[19] In this manner, Norwegian, Swedish, and Danish settlers, along with other European immigrants, were able to take advantage of American citizenship, enter into politics, and in the process, according to Jon Gjerde, "became among the most vociferous advocates of a *herrenvolk* republic."[20] Racial ideology and economic opportunity were closely linked to land claims.

---

[16] Blegen, *Ole Rynning's True Account of America*, 56 57. After Ole Rynning's death, a slightly revised 1839 version of his book appeared. In this edition, based on recommendations from the early Norwegian immigrant Kleng Peerson, Norwegian immigrants were introduced to the slave state Missouri as a fruitful future home.

[17] A letter by Reiersen dated March 19, 1844, published in *Christianssandsposten* and *Morgenbladet* back in Norway in July 1844, did not mention human bondage in a single word. Johan Reymert Reiersen, "Cincinnatti, Ohio Den 19de Marts 1844," in *J. R. Reierson Papers. P0325* (Northfield, MN: Norwegian-American Historical Association, 1844).

[18] Reierson, *Veiviser for Norske Emigranter Til De Forenede Nordamerikanske Stater Og Texas [Guide for Norwegian Emigrants to the North American States and Texas]* (Christiania: G. Reiersens Forlag, 1844), 135. As Stephen Kantrowitz has shown, such arguments were also part of the American political mainstream after the Civil War. See Kantrowitz, "White Supremacy, Settler Colonialism, and the Two Citizenships of the Fourteenth Amendment," 44.

[19] Reiersen, *Veiviser for Norske Emigranter Til De Forenede Nordamerikanske Stater Og Texas [Guide for Norwegian Emigrants to the North American States and Texas]*, 134, 49. On American people, Reiersen argued that they recognized "no moral right for any class of individuals to monopolize the soil" and "halt the progress of industry, civilization, and Christianity."

[20] Jon Gjerde, "'Here in America There Is Neither King nor Tyrant': European Encounters with Race, 'Freedom,' and Their European Pasts," *Journal of the Early Republic* 19, no. 4 (1999): 673–690.

In his guidebook, Reierson – articulating central elements of the threshold principle – expressed admiration for the United States' ability to grow both population and territory without succumbing to the small-state rivalries that had often characterized the European continent. "[The country] has maintained its political unity, multiplied its population, expanded its trade to all corners of the world, continued its system of domestic improvements and opened a wide, almost limitless field for individual enterprise," Reiersen marveled.[21] Hence, prospective Scandinavian immigrants in the 1840s had a choice between the newly admitted nonslaveholding states in the Midwest, the slaveholding state of Missouri, which was popular among German immigrants, and the deep South.[22]

For Claus and Matha Clausen, the choice rested on personal relationships, religion, and economic prospects. The couple arrived in Muskego, an important Scandinavian social hub and stepping stone, on August 8, 1843.[23] After receiving his ordination, Clausen preached first on colony leader Even Heg's farm, known as "Heg hotel," and later in a log church before relocating in 1846 to accommodate Johannes W. C. Dietrichson, an "official representative of the Church of Norway."[24]

Claus and Martha Clausen moved to Rock Prairie in the southern part of Wisconsin in 1845. The couple, who had lost a newborn son in the spring of 1844, welcomed another son into the world in the spring of 1846, but shortly thereafter tragedy struck again.[25] Martha Clausen, "well and cheerful" when Claus Clausen left to visit a neighboring

---

[21] Reiersen, *Veiviser for Norske Emigranter Til De Forenede Nordamerikanske Stater Og Texas [Guide for Norwegian Emigrants to the North American States and Texas]*, 125. Also William Notz, "Frederick List in America," American Economic Review 16, no. 2 (1926): 265.

[22] When the 1850 census was taken, 44,352 German-born immigrants lived in Missouri; see Jeppesen, *Danske i USA 1850–2000. En Demografisk, Social Og Kulturgeografisk Undersøgelse Af De Danske Immigranter Og Deres Efterkommere [Danes in the United States 1850–2000. A Demographic, Social and Cultural Geographic Study of the Danish Immigrants and Their Descendants]*, 86. For southern Democrats' support for the annexation of Texas, see Kevin Waite, "Jefferson Davis and Proslavery Visions of Empire in the Far West," Journal of the Civil War Era 6, no. 4 (2016): 545.

[23] Barton, "The Most Historic Norwegian Colony," 131–134. According to Barton, Muskego served as a "gateway through which hundreds of immigrants passed in their westward quest for homes."

[24] Mortensen, *The Danish Lutheran Church in America*, 31.

[25] Rasmus Andersen, *Pastor Claus Laurits Clausen – Banebryder for Den Norske Og Danske Kirke i Amerika. Første Skandinavisk Feltpræst. [Pastor Claus Laurits Clausen: Trailblazer for the Norwegian and Danish Church in America. First Scandinavian Chaplain]* (Blair, NE: Danish Lutheran Publishing House, 1921), 93–94.

congregation on November 7, became critically ill with pneumonia, and her husband only barely made it back for a final goodbye early on Sunday, November 15.[26] In a letter dated December 7, 1846, demonstrating the close transnational ties maintained even three years into their migration, Claus Clausen described the heartbreak to Martha's brother in Denmark, and the relatives stayed in touch subsequently.[27] Less than a year after Martha's death, her brother and other community members from the island of Langeland wrote to Claus Clausen asking him to elaborate on conditions in America and perhaps nuance some of the ideas about liberty and equality appearing in Old World emigration pamphlets.[28]

The prospective emigrants' inspiration came from at least two sources published in 1847. Laurits J. Fribert's ninety-six-page *Haandbog for Emigranter til Amerikas Vest* (Handbook for Emigrants to America's West) served as a source for a shorter, widely circulated, second pamphlet, published by Rasmus Sörensen in Denmark later that same year.[29]

During his time in the United States, Fribert, who settled among Swedish immigrants in Wisconsin in 1843, researched American citizenship requirements that he, based on the 1802 naturalization act, explained as the ability to demonstrate "good moral character" and adhere to the "principles of the Constitution."[30] Fribert clearly did not have to worry about his skin color and instead emphasized the importance of immigrants renouncing any "hereditary title" and

[26] Ibid., 94–100. See also Mathilde Rasmussen, *Martha Rasmussen* (Little Library of Lutheran Biography, 1945), 22.

[27] Jeppesen, *Danske i USA 1850–2000. En Demografisk, Social Og Kulturgeografisk Undersøgelse Af De Danske Immigranter Og Deres Efterkommere [Danes in the United States 1850–2000. A Demographic, Social and Cultural Geographic Study of The Danish Immigrants and Their Descendants]*, 230. See also Peter Sørensen Vig, *Danske i Amerika [Danes in America]*, 2 vols., vol. 1 (Minneapolis, MN: C. Rasmussen Company, 1907), 259. As the chain migration initiated from Martha's place of birth to Wisconsin after her death demonstrates, Clausen's letters "were eagerly read" back home.

[28] C. L. Clausen, "Luther Valley, Rock County, Beloet-Post-Office, Wisconsin Territory, North-Amerika, Den 6. Septbr. 1847," *Fyns Stifts*, November 26 (Friday morning), 1847. Martha Clausen's brother, Peder Rasmussen, wrote to Claus Clausen on June 30, 1847, with nine specific questions (the first about the quality of land) and received an answer on September 6 which was then published in November.

[29] William J. Orr, "Rasmus Sørensen and the Beginning of Danish Settlement in Wisconsin," *Wisconsin Magazine of History* 65, no. 3 (1982): 200.

[30] L. J. Fribert, *Haandbog for Emigranter Til Amerikas Vest [Handbook for Emigrants to America's West]* (Christiania [Oslo]: Forlaget af Johan Dahl, 1847), 95–96; Pia Viscor, "Danish Immigration to Racine County, Wisconsin: A Case Study of the Pull Effect in Nineteenth-Century Migration," *The Bridge* 31, no. 2 (2008): 13.

concluded by detailing the differences between state citizenship and national citizenship:

Only according to the above-mentioned conditions can complete American citizenship be attained according to the laws of Congress, but this does not prevent individual states from conferring citizenship in said state on less strict conditions ... In Wisconsin, which is a territory and not yet a state, and therefore cannot make its own provisions in this regard, the above-mentioned general laws of the United States apply.[31]

Fribert's notes on emigration and citizenship sparked Sörensen's pamphlet which also offered its own ideas of citizenship's rights and duties.[32] Sörensen recognized the discontent among landless laborers and tied these to much larger European discussions in the years leading up to the 1848 revolutions.[33] According to Sörensen, Scandinavian farm workers faced many of the same issues that had led to "the large English, German, and France emigrations to America."[34]

In a three-page introduction, Sörensen argued that "the fatherland" had to provide material goods necessary for sustenance for all or risk seeing its younger generations emigrate. If all that was left for landless children, after their parents' estate had been settled, were the duties associated with subjecthood of a Scandinavian monarch and none of the basic economic rights, a house and land to obtain sustenance from, then everyone – king, country, and prospective emigrant – were better off by letting young people explore opportunities across the Atlantic. The highest expression of one's affection for the fatherland, even higher than nationality, language, faith, and self-sacrifice in wartime, was the love of

[31] Fribert, *Haandbog for Emigranter Til Amerikas Vest* [*Handbook for Emigrants to America's West*], 196.
[32] Rasmus Sørensen, *Om De Udvandrede Nordmaends Tilstand i Nordamerika: Og Hvorfor Det Vilde Vaere Gavnligt, Om Endeel Danske Bønder Og Handvaerker Udvandrede Ligeledes, Og Bosatte Sig Sammesteds* [*On the Condition of Emigrated Norwegians in North America: And Why it Would be Beneficial if Some Danish Peasants and Artisans Emigrated and Settled There as Well*] (Copenhagen: Niskenske Bogtrykkeri, 1847), 4.
[33] Morten Nordhagen Ottosen, "Folkenes Vår: De Europeiske Revolusjonene 1848–1851 [The People's Spring: The European Revolutions 1848–1851]," in *Demokratiet: Historien Og Ideerne*, edited by Raino Malnes and Dag Einar Thorsen (Oslo: Dreyers Forlag, 2014), 222; Sørensen, *Om De Udvandrede Nordmaends Tilstand i Nordamerika: Og Hvorfor Det Vilde Vaere Gavnligt, Om Endeel Danske Bønder Og Handvaerker Udvandrede Ligeledes, Og Bosatte Sig Sammesteds*, 3.
[34] Sørensen, *Om De Udvandrede Nordmaends Tilstand i Nordamerika: Og Hvorfor Det Vilde Vaere Gavnligt, Om Endeel Danske Bønder Og Handvaerker Udvandrede Ligeledes, Og Bosatte Sig Sammesteds*, 3.

fellow man, Sörensen proclaimed.[35] This love had to be expressed by "allowing and affording one's neighbor the same worldly goods as one, under similar circumstances, would want allowed and afforded by him."[36]

Fribert and Sörensen both had concrete experience with the small Danish islands where Clausen and his wife had lived before emigrating and therefore knew firsthand about the recurring issues regarding lack of land availability. Their writings therefore resonated with a wide swath of smallholders.[37]

Rasmus Sörensen's publication "inspired several" members from Martha Clausen's childhood community to travel to "this Canaan's land," and as a consequence her brother wrote to Claus Clausen asking about conditions in America.[38] Perhaps still grieving, Clausen's response was gloomy. "Seldom have I seen more misleading nonsense," the widowed husband replied in response to the emigration pamphlets.[39] Clausen was upset that Fribert and Sörensen, in his view, had provided too rosy a picture with their information on travel costs, harvest yields, and disease.[40] The Danish-born pastor worried that these descriptions now roused the America fever in Scandinavia and might "entice people to injudiciously initiate such an important step as emigration."[41] Not all which "glistens in America" is gold, warned Clausen.[42]

Clausen went on to offer advice on climate, land, and emigration practicalities in such detail that his response took up the majority of two newspaper issues. Toward the end of his letter, Clausen did concede,

---

[35] Ibid., 1–3.   [36] Ibid.

[37] Viscor, "Danish Immigration to Racine County, Wisconsin: A Case Study of the Pull Effect in Nineteenth-Century Migration," 12–14.

[38] "Mr. Editor," Martha's brother wrote to the local newspaper after having heard from his brother-in-law, "In the year 1843, Mr. C. L. Clausen travelled ... to North America and settled in the territory of Wisconsin among Norwegian emigrants, where he [Clausen], who had received seminary training, was hired as pastor and teacher for several parishes. Through his continual travels in the district he has gained a quite exact knowledge of the countryside's character and the people's condition." See C. L. Clausen, "Luther Valley, Rock County, Beloet-Post-Office, Wisconsin Territory, North-Amerika, Den 6. Septbr. 1847," *Fyns Stifts*, November 26 (Friday morning), 1847.

[39] Ibid. See also Orr, "Rasmus Sörensen and the Beginning of Danish Settlement in Wisconsin," 201.

[40] Clausen, "Luther Valley, Rock County, Beloet-Post-Office, Wisconsin Territory, North-Amerika, Den 6. Septbr. 1847." See also Orr, "Rasmus Sörensen and the Beginning of Danish Settlement in Wisconsin," 201.

[41] Clausen, "Luther Valley, Rock County, Beloet-Post-Office, Wisconsin Territory, North-Amerika, Den 6. Septbr. 1847."

[42] Ibid.

however, that there was no shortage of "good laws or sufficient civic order and safety for the quiet, honest, and diligent citizen in all things regarding his worldly welfare."[43]

Clausen's letter was revealing as it demonstrated Scandinavian emigrants' concern with landownership and the Danish-born pastor's concrete knowledge of these concerns.[44] Additionally, Clausen, albeit without reflecting on whiteness's importance, equated productive citizenship in the United States with honesty and hard work that in turn could lead to socioeconomic progress for younger Scandinavian men and women.[45] The latter point was also made by Danish-born Peter C. Lütken of Racine, Wisconsin, when he in March 1847 wrote a piece on the connection between landownership and freedom that was published in a trade journal in Denmark the following year.

The truth remains that the soil here rewards its faithful cultivator and that one in all essentials enjoys the full fruit of one's labor; for taxes do not oppress, and if a man is here in possession of his property free of debt, then no one on earth can be more independent and more free than him.[46]

Liberty and equality were recurrent themes, both implicitly and explicitly, in the emigration literature. Fribert, for example, in a section titled "Everyone should go to Wisconsin" pointed out that because of slavery, with its important implications for labor relations and pay, it was "not as honorable to work for the white man, whom many wealthy men will not regard higher than a black man."[47] In short, economic concerns, landownership, and the institution of slavery remained the most important reasons for settling north of the Mason–Dixon line. Settlement patterns

[43] C. L. Clausen, "Slutningen Af Brevet Fra Nordamerika; See Morgenavisen! [The Conclusion of the Letter from North America; See the Morning Edition!]," *Fyens Stifts*, November 26 (Friday evening), 1847.
[44] Ibid.
[45] Clausen, "Luther Valley, Rock County, Beloet-Post-Office, Wisconsin Territory, North-Amerika, Den 6. Septbr. 1847."
[46] P. C. Lütken, "Noticer Vedkommende Agerdyrkningsvæsenet Og Landboforholdene i Territoriet Wiscounsin i Nord-Amerika [Notices Regarding Agriculture and Farming in the Wisconsin Territory in North America]," *Tidsskrift for Landoekonomie* 9 (1848): 427.
[47] Fribert, *Haandbog for Emigranter Til Amerikas Vest [Handbook for Emigrants to America's West]*, 10. Fribert warned against settling in the South, where a prospective immigrant – on top of difficulties in the labor market – might encounter a climate "way too hot for a Scandinavian," as well as yellow fever, poisonous snakes, and alligators. On Southern fear of immigrant influence, see Merritt, *Masterless Men: Poor Whites and Slavery in the Antebellum South*, 73–75, 191.

reflected the emigration pamphlets' advice. When the 1850 census was taken, only 202 Scandinavian-born immigrants were counted in Texas and just 247 in Missouri, while 12,516 Scandinavian-born immigrants lived in Wisconsin and Illinois.[48]

In the Midwest, emigrants found the added security of living among fellow Scandinavians, and, starting in the late 1840s, thousands of young, white, Protestant Scandinavians (their average age was around thirty) pursued the promise of equality through landownership close to the Great Lakes.[49] Yet, Midwestern landownership, as most Scandinavian-born immigrants at least tacitly admitted, was predicated on the fact that the "Indian hordes" through "deceit and force" had been removed.[50]

*　*　*

The first newspaper published in Wisconsin by Scandinavian immigrants was *Nordlyset* (The Northern Light).[51] In the inaugural issue on July 29, 1847, *Nordlyset*'s editors emphasized their attempted neutrality in political and religious matters and stated the newspaper's aim as elevating "ourselves, in regards to our nationality, among our surroundings," by enlightening and guiding its readership in order to achieve equality at the level of fellow citizens. The first step to achieving political enlightenment among the Scandinavian readers was a translation of the Declaration of

[48] Theodore C. Blegen, "Cleng Peerson and Norwegian Immigration," *Mississippi Valley Historical Review* 7, no. 4 (1921): 321. According to Blegen, most Norwegian immigrants who were attracted to Missouri by Peerson soon after moved to Iowa, where 611 Scandianian-born immigrants lived by 1850. See also Jeppesen, *Danske i USA 1850–2000. En Demografisk, Social Og Kulturgeografisk Undersøgelse Af De Danske Immigranter Og Deres Efterkommere* [*Danes in the United States 1850–2000. A Demographic, Social and Cultural Geographic Study of the Danish Immigrants and Their Descendants*], 86.

[49] Fribert, *Haandbog for Emigranter Til Amerikas Vest* [*Handbook for Emigrants to America's West*], 13. "Where men of the three Scandinavian nations come together, they always regard each other as countrymen and help each other as brothers and the harmony and good faith that is not being worked on between the three kingdoms has already been realized in America that also in this respect is hastening ahead of Europe." See also Jeppesen, *Danske i USA 1850–2000. En Demografisk, Social Og Kulturgeografisk Undersøgelse Af De Danske Immigranter Og Deres Efterkommere* [*Danes in the United States 1850–2000. A Demographic, Social and Cultural Geographic Study of the Danish Immigrants and Their Descendants*], 130.

[50] Dietrichson, *Pastor J. W. C. Dietrichsons Reise Blandt De Norske Emigranter i "De Forenede Nordamerikanske Fristater." Paany Udgiven Af Rasmus B. Anderson*, 25.

[51] Barton, "The Most Historic Norwegian Colony," 134–135. The printing shop for *Nordlyset* was located on Even Heg's farm in Muskego and thus underscored the community's importance in defining early Scandinavian notions of American citizenship.

Independence.[52] From a Scandinavian immigrant perspective, the Declaration of Independence, the Constitution, and the Bill of Rights provided the vision and legal foundation to ensure economic opportunities in the New World. Thus, in addition to the implicit and explicit recognition of citizenship's importance, it was pointed out, again and again, in the pamphlets and letters flowing back to Scandinavia that "the United States has no king."[53]

When adopted on February 1, 1848, the first two sections of Wisconsin's State Constitution echoed the Declaration of Independence and specifically outlawed slavery as well as "involuntary servitude." Moreover, in section 14, feudal tenures were prohibited, and section 15 specifically ensured that "no distinction shall ever be made by law between resident aliens and citizens, in reference to the possession, enjoyment or descent of property."[54]

Thus, with the Wisconsin Constitution in hand, immigrants in the early Scandinavian enclaves could distance themselves from Old World feudalism and pursue their dream of landownership, confident in its legality and ties to ideals of liberty and equality.[55] As such, Scandinavian immigrants were quickly able to enjoy the fruits of American citizenship, and in the process they generally supported an

---

[52] "Til Vore Landsmænd [To Our Countrymen]," *Nordlyset*, July 29, 1847. See also "Den Enstemmige Erklæring Af De Tretten Forenede Stater Af America [The Unanimous Declaration of the Thirteen United States of America]," *Nordlyset*, July 29, 1847.

[53] Gjerde, "'Here in America There Is Neither King nor Tyrant': European Encounters with Race, 'Freedom,' and Their European Pasts," 682. As Jon Gjerde has noted, "Americans in the mid-nineteenth century celebrated the many ways in which their Republic improved upon the tired systems of the old European States. As they invented an American nationality that allegedly reflected these advancements, they stressed the conviction that their nation was structured according to abstract notions of freedom, equality, and self-government." See *The Minds of the West: Ethnocultural Evolution in the Rural Middle West 1830–1917*, 54–55. See also Linda K. Kerber, "The Meanings of Citizenship," *Journal of American History* 84, no. 3 (1997): 841. See also Blegen, *Ole Rynning's True Account of America*, 87.

[54] Wisconsin Constitutional Convention, *Constitution of the State of Wisconsin* (Madison: Beriah Brown, 1848), online facsimile at www.wisconsinhistory.org/turningpoints/search .asp?id=1627.

[55] Barton, "The Most Historic Norwegian Colony," 129. See also Torben Grøngaard Jeppesen, *Dannebrog På Den Amerikanske Prærie [Dannebrog on the American Prairie]* (Odense: Odense University Press, 2000), 41. Lastly, see Fritz W. Rasmussen, "History of the Town of New Denmark, Brown County, Wisconsin! Both Politically and Privately," in *Fritz William Rasmussen Papers. Correspondence, 1834–1942. Green Bay Mss 4. Box no. 1* (Wisconsin Historical Society, 1876).

expansion of American territory, especially if the population therein was mainly white.[56]

In the midst of the American war against Mexico between 1846 and 1848, *Nordlyset*, under Norwegian-born editor James D. Reymert, initially expressed support for manifest destiny by declaring that "a strong United States was probably destined to annex the enemy's territory."[57] Under its second editor, Even Heg, however, *Nordlyset* nuanced its position on territorial expansion based on ethnic considerations and on March 10, 1848, deemed it inadvisable to annex any further territory from Mexico as this would mean incorporating additional "half-civilized inhabitants" into the United States.[58] The same hesitation to annex Cuba, based on a sense "that a people of mixed blood, mainly Negro and Spanish, could not readily be assimilated," was expressed by American politicians and the Norwegian immigrant papers in the 1850s and appeared again in the following decade.[59]

Heg's quote, and the sentiments expressed in subsequent ethnic newspapers, underscored the importance of whiteness among Scandinavian immigrants. Importantly, both Reymert and Heg – by settling in Wisconsin, on land formerly occupied by Native people – were actively partaking in the expansion of American boundaries.

In the Midwest, as Stephen Kantrowitz has shown, "Wisconsin's 1848 constitution" and those of other Midwestern states encouraged the dissolution of American Indians' collective affiliation, and white settlers, whether in Wisconsin, Kansas, Michigan, or elsewhere, "quickly abetted outright dispossession, aided by unequal tax policies and official tolerance of white squatting."[60]

---

[56] Gjerde, "'Here in America There Is Neither King nor Tyrant': European Encounters with Race, 'Freedom,' and Their European Pasts," 674. Gjerde rightly points out that "there are shadings of freedom and unfreedom, white and nonwhite that clearly complicate the story," but Scandinavian-born immigrants generally expressed a sense of freedom soon after arrival.

[57] Quoted in Arlow William Andersen, *The Immigrant Takes His Stand: The Norwegian-American Press and Public Affairs, 1847–1872* (Northfield, MN: Norwegian-American Historical Association, 1953), 34.

[58] Quoted in ibid.

[59] Frymer, *Building an American Empire: The Era of Territorial and Political Expansion*, 210–212. See also Andersen, *The Immigrant Takes His Stand: The Norwegian-American Press and Public Affairs, 1847–1872*, 39.

[60] Stephen Kantrowitz, "'Not Quite Constitutionalized': The Meaning of 'Civilization' and the Limits of Native American Citizenship," in *The World the Civil War Made*, ed. Gregory P. Downs and Kate Masur (Chapel Hill: University of North Carolina Press, 2015), 77–78.

As Scandinavian editors started to voice their opinion on American public matters for their fellow countrymen in the ethnic press, it became increasingly clear that they, along with other European immigrants, were solid supporters of a "white man's republic."[61]

Andreas Frederiksen Herslev, who arrived in the United States in 1847 and adopted the name Andrew Frederickson, wrote home in 1849 and assessed the Mexican War's consequences. According to Frederickson, the American military, based on volunteerism, tied into broader societal ideals where "the poor" had greater opportunity for equality and could "attain justice more or less as well as the rich."[62] Still, some were more equal than others based on skin color, as exemplified by Frederickson's ideas about land and the opportunities war service could provide.

Around the time Casper and I arrived, the government issued posters that able-bodied soldiers could receive 7 dollars a month and 160 acres of land which could be surveyed anywhere in the United States where there were unsold sections.[63]

After the war, Frederickson bought two land warrants from Mexican War veterans and used the certificates to claim what he termed "free land" in Brown County, Wisconsin.[64] As was the case with Frederickson, Scandinavian immigrants often did not reflect explicitly on their role in the American expansion through land acquisition. Scandinavian immigrants did, however, often arrive in the United States with preconceived notions of American Indians partly due to literary texts. As Gunlög Fur has noted, James Fenimore Cooper's "books were translated into Swedish

---

[61] See Gjerde, "'Here in America There Is Neither King nor Tyrant': European Encounters with Race, 'Freedom,' and Their European Pasts," 690.

[62] Andreas Frederiksen, "Milvaukii Wisconsin Den 24de November 1849," in *Afskrift af 22 breve til Frederik Nielsen, Herlev DK fra A.F.Wilmington Ill. og West Denmark og Neenah Wisc. (1847–1872)* (Aalborg: Det Danske Udvandrerarkiv, 1849). Also "Wilmington Ill, Den 28 Juli 1850."

[63] "Milvaukii Wisconsin Den 24de November 1849."

[64] Ibid. See also Red., "Et Par Ord Om De Norskes Representation i Legislaturen [A Few Words on the the Norwegians' Representation in the Legislature]," *Emigranten*, October 15, 1852. See also Howe, *What Hath God Wrought: The Transformation of America, 1815–1848* (Oxford: Oxford University Press, 2007), 809–810. As Howe notes, "counting Texas, Oregon, California, and New Mexico, James K. Polk extended the domain of the United States more than any other president even Thomas Jefferson or Andrew Johnson (who acquired Alaska)," but in the process also brought land into the United States that had previously belonged to Mexican subjects or indigenous nations. "The state of California placed heavy burdens of legal proof on the owners of Mexican land grants to validate their titles, in violation of the spirit if not the letter of the Treaty of Guadalupe Hidalgo ... California did not recognize Mexican Americans as citizens until a decision by the state supreme court in 1870."

and, already published in the 1820s, they became readily available for a reading audience to such an extent that Fredrika Bremer regarded him as one of 'the first to make us in Sweden somewhat at home in America.'"[65]

In 1847, Norwegian-born lawyer Ole Munch Räder, observing a forest fire in the Mississippi Valley, wondered if the local indigenous warriors would interpret the smoke as a "huge peace pipe of their great father in Washington or as war signals and spirits of revenge from the land of their fathers which they had to leave in disgrace to give place to the 'pale faces.'"[66] Räder quickly added, "This expression by the way, I use only out of respect for Cooper's novels; it is claimed that no Indian has ever called the whites by such a name," but in the darkness the Norwegian traveller could not help his mind from wandering and imagining an encounter with an Indian "fully equipped with tomahawk and other paraphernalia, and of course on the watch for someone to scalp."[67]

Back in Wisconsin, Räder encountered bands of Pottawatomie returning from Green Bay, "where they had received the annual payment provided for in their treaty with the United States government," and described their "features and their clothing" as somewhat akin to "our Lapps, although they were taller, more dignified, and also more cleanly" than the indigenous people living in northern Sweden, Norway, and Finland to which he compared them.[68]

Still, the problem with the American Indians, according to Räder, was that they had "lost their old reputation for honesty," which was part of the reason that people "generally despise and hate the Indians." People in the western part of the United States, which Räder considered Wisconsin part of, "find it a great nuisance that the Indians never seem to accustom themselves to the fact that the country no longer belongs to them."[69]

Such tropes of American Indian presence and practice echoed regularly among Scandinavian-American writers. In 1845, the residents of Muskego praised the pioneers who "fought wild animals and Indians," and Räder, while acknowledging that American Indians were subjected to "injustice" and that the laws passed for their protection were "never

[65] Fur, "Indians and Immigrants – Entangled Histories," 59–60.

[66] Gunnar Malmin, ed., *America in the Forties: The Letters of Ole Munch Ræder* (Minneapolis: University of Minnesota Press, 1929), 133.

[67] Ibid. See also Betty Bergland, "Norwegian Immigrants and 'Indianerne' in the Landtaking, 1838–1862," *Norwegian-American Studies* 35 (2000): 331–333.

[68] Malmin, *America in the Forties: The Letters of Ole Munch Ræder*, 142.

[69] Ibid., 143–145.

enforced," nevertheless took it for granted that their Midwestern removal was just a matter of time.[70]

Describing a treaty between the Chippewa and local Indian commissioners in August 1847, Räder wrote: "It is specified in the treaty that certain lands west of Wisconsin are to be abandoned in favor of a new territory, Minnesota, which is to be established there. To begin with, the Winnebago are to be placed there."[71]

In a different example, Hans Mattson depicted his first encounters with "Sioux Indians" positively but also wrote about a "war dance" that "in lurid savageness" exceeded anything he ever saw.[72] Moreover, Mattson's countryman, Pastor Gustaf Unonius, who had founded the Swedish Pine Lake settlement in Wisconsin, described the Winnebago tribe as "the wildest and most hostile tribe of all the tribes that are still in this area."[73] Unonius' description was one of several that pointed to American Indians as uncivilized and thereby unfit for a place in American society. Within a decade, however, Scandinavian immigrants also settled in Minnesota and shortly thereafter on American Indian land in the Dakota territory. Thereby, Scandinavian immigrants often embraced the notion of independence, through fruitful contributions as land cultivators not wholly unlike Jefferson's ideal of an economically and morally independent yeoman farmer, while maintaining support for a sizeable nation-state predicated on territorial expansion and Indian removal.[74]

The Scandinavian definition of citizenship, closely tied to the dream of landownership, was fueled throughout Scandinavia by Räder, Rynning, Fribert, and Rasmus Sörensen's descriptions of American liberty in the antebellum era.

[70] Muskigo, "Beretning Fra Nordamerika [Account from North America]." See also Malmin, *America in the Forties: The Letters of Ole Munch Ræder*, 146–147.

[71] *America in the Forties: The Letters of Ole Munch Ræder*, 146–147.

[72] Hans Mattson, *Reminiscences: The Story of an Emigrant* (Saint Paul, MN: D. D. Merrill Company, 1891), 43.

[73] Gustaf Unonius, *Minnen Från En Sjuttonårig Vistelse i Nordvestra Amerika I-II* [*Memories from a Seventeen-Year-Long Stay in the American Northwest I–II*] (Uppsala, 1862), 188.

[74] Reiersen, *Veiviser for Norske Emigranter Til De Forenede Nordamerikanske Stater Og Texas* [*Guide for Norwegian Emigrants to the North American States and Texas*], 135. Also Lisi Krall, "Thomas Jefferson's Agrarian Vision and the Changing Nature of Property," *Journal of Economic Issues* 36, no. 1 (2002): 131–132. See also Henry Nash Smith, *Virgin Land: The American West as Symbol and Myth*, first Vintage ed. (New York: Vintage Books, 1957), 144–145. Smith notes that Jefferson "saw the cultivator of the earth, the husbandman who tilled his own acres, as the rock upon which the American republic must stand."

While emigration pamphlets and America letters were secondary to political and economic conditions on the ground, they did, however, effectively juxtapose Old and New World conditions and opened new opportunities and concrete roadmaps to families seeking a new life across the Atlantic.[75] The "America fever" brought on by the emigration pamphlets and social conditions set off a chain migration to Wisconsin, where ideas of free soil and free labor soon became powerful political rallying cries among Scandinavian immigrants.[76] After 1847, first hundreds then thousands of Norwegians, Swedes, and Danes poured into the Midwest. By 1860, a total of 72,576 Scandinavians lived in the United States, with almost a third claiming Wisconsin as their home.[77]

---

[75] Sörensen's writings also inspired emigrants in the northern part of Denmark. See, for example, Celius Christiansen, *En Pioneers Historie (Erindringer Fra Krigen Mellem Nord- Og Sydstaterne)* [*A Pioneer's Story: Memoirs from the War between North and South*] (Aalborg: Eget forlag, 1909), 5. Christiansen, along with two brothers, emigrated to America in 1853 and cited Rasmus Sörensen's writings as the direct cause due its portrayal of brighter prospects across the Atlantic.

[76] The way some of the first settlers in Wisconsin from Langeland, the island where Claus Clausen's wife was born, remembered it, Rasmus Sörensen had indeed served as one of the key inspirational sources for emigration. Fritz W. Rasmussen, "New Denmark, Brown Co. Wis. January 3rd, 1900," in *Fritz William Rasmussen Papers, 1834–1942. Green Bay Mss 4. Box 1* (Green Bay: Wisconsin Historical Society, 1900).

[77] Jeppesen, *Danske i USA 1850–2000. En Demografisk, Social Og Kulturgeografisk Undersøgelse Af De Danske Immigranter Og Deres Efterkommere* [*Danes in the United States 1850–2000. A Demographic, Social and Cultural Geographic Study of The Danish Immigrants and Their Descendants*], 131.

4

Republican Reign

It was late August 1847 when Fritz Rasmussen's parents left the island of Lolland along with their six children. Fritz's father, Edward, decided to emigrate to America in pursuit of "liberty and equality," which he found sorely lacking in Denmark.[1] The year before, one of the Lolland's social reform leaders, C. L. Christensen, had also emigrated to America, and the reason was believed to be the Danish authorities' harsh treatment of dissidents who advocated on behalf of smallholders and peasants.[2]

By 1847, Fritz Rasmussen's father was also engaged in political activity in opposition to the Danish authorities to such a degree that both political necessity and economic opportunity prompted his decision.[3] On Lolland, where the Rasmussen family resided, land shortage was acute. In one county, Maribo Amt, 87 percent of all land belonged to properties larger

[1] Fritz W. Rasmussen, "Record! Of Skandinavians, Who Have Been Settled and Lived in the Town of New Denmark," in *Fritz William Rasmussen Papers. Diaries, 1857–1876. Green Bay Mss 4. Box 8* (Wisconsin Historical Society, 1880); "February 1883. Sunday the 18th. 11 Oclock A.M.," in *Fritz William Rasmussen Papers, 1834–1942. Green Bay Mss 4. Box 2* (Wisconsin Historical Society, 1883).
[2] Erik Helmer Pedersen, *Drømmen Om America* [*The Dream of America*], Politikens Danmarkshistorie (Copenhagen: Politikens Forlag, 1985), 56–59.
[3] Rasmussen, "February 1883. Sunday the 18th. 11 Oclock A.M." For a discussion of reasons for emigration, see, for example, Kristian Hvidt, *Flugten Til Amerika, Eller Drivkræfter i Masseudvandringen Fra Danmark 1868–1914* [*Flight to America or Driving Forces in the Mass Emigration from Denmark 1868–1914*] (Aarhus: Universitetsforlaget i Aarhus, 1971), 263–270. Also Jørn Brøndal, *Ethnic Leadership and Midwestern Politics: Scandinavian Americans and the Progressive Movement in Wisconsin, 1890–1914* (Chicago: University of Illinois Press, 2004), 16–17.

than 4.4 acres.[4] It was therefore no coincidence that Fritz Rasmussen, looking back from the vantage point of 1883, used the language of the oppressed and stressed the importance of *emancipation*:

> He [Father], I afterwards came to understand, had to leave the Country, like many others, as a political refugee – : on account of his writings & doings, for and among the communalities, in regard to a more & thorough emancipation of the people generally, from the oppressive Sovereignty of the nobility.[5]

Edward Rasmussen's family emigrated on August 27, 1847, two months after Martha Clausen's brother had written to Claus Clausen to ask about emigrant prospects in Wisconsin, but the family did not see Clausen's cautionary letter.[6] Where Claus Clausen had been guaranteed employment at arrival, the Rasmussen family's future was from the outset more precarious.

In Fritz Rasmussen's account, the family stopped briefly in Hamburg (then a sovereign state in the German confederation), boarded the ship *Washington*, and arrived in New York City on October 26. From New York the family travelled to Albany where the recently constructed Erie Canal originated. A few weeks later they boarded the *Atlantic* in Buffalo to be transported over the Great Lakes to Wisconsin (see Figure 4.1). Only later did they realize their good fortune. One of the next ships that went west over Lake Erie and Lake Huron was *Phoenix*, a modern steamer named after the bird in Egyptian mythology. But in contrast to the legend, *Phoenix* never rose from the ashes in November 1847. Instead, hundreds of Dutch emigrants lost their lives in the flames or icy water on their way to a new Midwestern home.[7] "We were spared the suffering and catastrophe," remembered Fritz Rasmussen.[8]

While the Rasmussen family's ship made it unscathed over the lakes, the family did not. Nine-month-old Henry died of disease shortly before

---

[4] Asger Th. Simonsen, *Husmandskår Og Husmandspolitik i 1840erne [Smallholder Conditions and Smallholder Politics in the 1840s]* (Copenhagen: Landbohistorisk Selskab, 1977).

[5] Rasmussen, "February 1883. Sunday the 18th. 11 Oclock A.M."

[6] "Record! Of Skandinavians, Who Have Been Settled and Lived in the Town of New Denmark."

[7] William O. Van Eyck, "The Story of the Propeller Phoenix," *Wisconsin Magazine of History* 7, no. 3 (1924): 282–284; Anders Bo Rasmussen, *I Krig for Lincoln [To War for Lincoln]* (Copenhagen, Informations Forlag, 2014), 33–34.

[8] Rasmussen, "Record! Of Skandinavians, Who Have Been Settled and Lived in the Town of New Denmark," Memorandum.

FIGURE 4.1 Fritz Rasmussen, born on the island of Langeland, emigrated with his family to Wisconsin in 1847 and eventually settled in New Denmark. Courtesy Wisconsin Historical Society.

they reached Milwaukee on a "cold, bleak" November day, and disease was ever-present. On the snow-covered wharf in eastern Wisconsin, survival more than enjoyment of liberty, equality, and champagne-filled springs was the main concern.[9] "No money and could not speak [the language] and no countrymen: Father sick unto death – and so my youngest sister and youngest Brother. This was

[9] The same observation was made by John Matteson when he arrived in New Denmark. "[John] Matteson found his soggy berth [in New Denmark] to be 'much different from the songs of praise we had heard about America in the old country ... about her magnificent forests teeming with unsurpassed wildlife, her crystal-clear springs, majestic waterfalls, and so on.'" Quoted in Frederick Hale, "The Americanization of a Danish Immigrant in Wisconsin 1847–1872," *Wisconsin Magazine of History* 64, no. 3 (1981): 208.

a landing, opposite the gloriously golden and happy anticipation when leaving," remembered Rasmussen.[10] But an older Danish sailor, in the United States known as Johnson, "solicited help and finally by evening got us carted off into town and sheltered in a small, poorly furnished tavern or restaurant, kept by a young German and his wife," recounted Rasmussen.[11]

At the German couple's place, the family regained their strength somewhat. With the help of fellow Scandinavian immigrants, they – after a brief stay at the local poor house – slowly regained their collective footing. Their fourteen-year-old son Fritz was sent away to work for a newly arrived Norwegian shoemaker, and shortly thereafter a sizable group of approximately fifty Danish immigrants, inspired by Rasmus Sörensen's emigration pamphlets and Claus Clausen's letters, arrived.[12] By June 1848, the newcomers had established a settlement, which was later named New Denmark.[13]

For six years, Fritz Rasmussen worked odd jobs in Wisconsin away from the small immigrant town, but in 1854 he returned, bought land, and soon started to keep meticulous records of major and minor events in New Denmark – not least land transactions.[14] In his thousands of surviving diary pages, Rasmussen on several occasions mentioned his acquisition of Section 24, N.E. ¼, S.E. ¼ in New Denmark, and the pride thus exhibited in landownership was in no small part tied to his family's Old World experience.[15]

Looking back later in life, Fritz Rasmussen reflected on his experiences in New Denmark in contrast to the Old World despite the hardship also encountered in Wisconsin: "We have come to this

---

[10] Fritz W. Rasmussen, "FWR Milwaukee," in *Fritz William Rasmussen Papers. Correspondence, 1834–1942. Green Bay Mss 4. Box no. 1* (Green Bay: Wisconsin Historical Society, 1847).

[11] "Record! Of Skandinavians, Who Have Been Settled and Lived in the Town of New Denmark."

[12] "FWR Milwaukee."

[13] "New Denmark, Brown Co. Wis. January 3rd, 1900." See also Peter Sørensen Vig, *Danske i Amerika* [*Danes in America*], 2 vols., vol. 1 (Minneapolis, MN: C. Rasmussen Company, 1907), 258–262. See as well William J. Orr, "Rasmus Sørensen and the Beginning of Danish Settlement in Wisconsin," *Wisconsin Magazine of History* 65, no. 3 (1982): 195–210.

[14] Fritz W. Rasmussen, "Dagbog of F. W. Rasmussen. New Denmark, Brown Co. State of Wis [June 5]," in *Fritz William Rasmussen Papers. Diaries, 1856–1876. Box 8. Green Bay Mss 4* (Green Bay: Wisconsin Historical Society, 1859).

[15] "Record! Of Skandinavians, Who Have Been Settled and Lived in the Town of New Denmark."

Country, where we are as free, previledged [sic] and no distinction – as to 'Liberty and Equality' of person – as the Nobles – so called – are in the lands where we came from."[16]

This idea – Old World nobility whose disproportional political power and landownership "restrained" the hard-working, honest, common man from achieving liberty and establishing his "pedigree" – defined Fritz Rasmussen's worldview and, as we have seen, recurred regularly among early Northern European laborers.[17] While Rasmussen, consciously or unconsciously, benefited from his skin color and religion in terms of landownership and employment opportunities, his views on New World citizenship were not unlike those of the German forty-eighters, who, as Allison Efford Clark has shown, proposed "a nationalism based on residence, not race or even culture, and a form of citizenship grounded in universal manhood suffrage."[18]

Still, this ability to enjoy the fruits of one's own labor, earning one's own bread through one's own sweat, was a key pull factor to Scandinavian immigrants and one made possible, in part, by whiteness.[19] When Catharina Jonsdatter Rüd, a Swedish immigrant maid making $2 a week and living in Moline, Illinois, wrote home in March 1856, she celebrated America and the individual liberty she experienced as a white woman:

Here the servant can come and go as it pleases her, because every white person is free and if a servant gets a hard employer then she can quit whenever she likes and even keep her salary for the period she has worked ... A woman's situation is as you can imagine much easier here than in Sweden and I Catherine feel much calmer, happier and more satisfied here than I used to do when I attended school in Nässjö. Everything in this country [seems praiseworthy] – to describe all benefits would take a lifetime![20]

Rüd underlined the word "white" and thereby proved herself aware, as Jon Gjerde has pointed out, that she enjoyed "freedoms that did not exist

[16] Ibid.
[17] Ibid. See also Andrew Zimmermann, "From the Rhine to the Mississippi," *Journal of the Civil War Era* 5, no. 1 (2015): 9.
[18] Alison Clark Efford, *German Immigrants, Race, and Citizenship in the Civil War Era* (Washington, DC: Cambridge University Press, 2013), 32.
[19] Fritz W. Rasmussen, "Den 31. Søndag. Paaske [The 31st Sunday. Easter]," in *Fritz Wiliam Rasmussen Papers. Diaries, 1861, June–1883, June. Box No. 2. Green Bay Mss 4* (Green Bay: Wisconsin Historical Society, 1861).
[20] Quoted in Werner Sollors, "How Americans Became White: Three Examples," in *Multiamerica: Essays on Cultural Wars and Cultural Peace*, ed. Ishmael Reed (New York:Penguin Books, 1998), 4.

in Sweden or for nonwhite people in the United States."[21] Since enslaved people in the United States were denied the fruits of their labor, Scandinavian-born laborers generally opposed slavery, with its parallels to the forced labor and serfdom which had been common in Denmark and Norway up until 1788. Unequal power and labor dynamics continued to exist in various guises in Scandinavia subsequently, and the Norwegian, Swedish, and Danish immigrants therefore arrived in the United States with suspicion of slavery's extension or its beneficiaries' political powers in the New World.

Thus, by the mid-1850s, the Republican Party's ideology, what Eric Foner has termed *free soil, free labor,* and *free men,* meaning wage earners' opportunity to become "free men" through landownership, aptly described a large swath of Scandinavian immigrants' economic and social priorities and, by extension, their attraction to the Republican Party in the years surrounding the Civil War.[22]

The issue of free soil was of central concern to Norwegians, Swedes, and Danes in the Midwest. With its importance for economic uplift and perceptions of liberty, land availability, in areas where slavery did not impact labor relations, played a significant part in shaping economic, legal, and moral positions in the Scandinavian-American immigrant community.

Yet, well-read Scandinavian immigrants such as Even Heg and his fellow early editors of *Nordlyset,* who had advocated legislation to prevent slavery from spreading into the territories between 1848 and 1850, in line with the Free Soil party's platform, rarely extended their argument to advocate for nonwhite people.[23] In this regard, Norwegians, Swedes, and Danes were far from alone. As Henry Nash Smith observed more than sixty years ago, "the farmers of the Northwest were not as a group pro-Negro. Free-soil for them meant keeping Negroes, whether slave or free, out of the territories altogether. It did not imply a humanitarian regard for the oppressed black man."[24]

---

[21] Gjerde, "'Here in America There Is Neither King nor Tyrant': European Encounters with Race, 'Freedom,' and Their European Pasts," *Journal of the Early Republic* 19, no. 4 (1999): 387.

[22] Eric Foner, *Free Soil, Free Labor, Free Men: The Ideology of the Republican Party before the Civil War* (New York: Oxford University Press, 1995), 8–10, 83–87.

[23] Arlow William Andersen, *The Immigrant Takes His Stand: The Norwegian-American Press and Public Affairs, 1847–1872* (Northfield, MN: Norwegian-American Historical Association, 1953), 60; Theodore C. Blegen, "Colonel Hans Christian Heg," *Wisconsin Magazine of History* 4, no. 2 (1920): 144.

[24] Henry Nash Smith, *Virgin Land: The American West as Symbol and Myth,* First Vintage ed. (New York: Vintage Books, 1957), 193.

Smith might as well have added lack of humanitarian regard for American Indians. In their dismissal of Native peoples' rights, Scandinavian immigrants, not least the better educated ethnic elite, differed from the central actors of the abolitionist movement who explicitly connected Indian dispossession to slavery's extension.[25] In short, Scandinavian immigrants, over time, showed themselves to be passionate Republicans but not abolitionists.

During the late 1840s and early 1850s, with the Democratic Party, the Free Soil Party, and the Whigs all vying for the Scandinavian vote, it was not evident that these newly arrived immigrants would eventually side with what became the Republican Party's platform, but it was clear that the majority of Scandinavians were primarily interested in free land and less in nonwhite free men despite their professed love of liberty and equality.[26]

Despite his Old World abolitionist inspiration, Claus Clausen in 1852 attempted to find a golden mean politically as the first editor of *Emigranten*.[27] Clausen saw *Emigranten*'s mission in the New World as mobilizing its Scandinavian readership politically, not least in support of liberty and economic opportunity, and in the process he loosely aligned the newspaper with the Democratic Party while relegating discussions of nonwhite people in America to the margins.[28]

In an opening editorial, written both in English and Danish, Clausen stressed the importance of embracing assimilation, which underlined the advantages enjoyed by the paper's mainly Protestant, literate, and white readership who were generally shielded from nativist critique.

We sincerely believe that the truest interest of our people in this Country is, to become AMERICANIZED – if we may use that word – in language and customs, as soon as possible and be one people with the Americans. In this way alone can

---

[25] Natalie Joy, "The Indian's Cause: Abolitionists and Native American Rights," *Journal of the Civil War Era* 8, no. 2 (2018): 233. For example, abolitionists involved in the antislavery Liberty Party in 1845 argued that "the forcible relocation of southern Indians could be traced to the Slave Power's efforts (with northern participation) to obtain fertile land for the expansion of slavery."

[26] Blegen, "Colonel Hans Christian Heg," 147. Blegen writes, in his somewhat uncritical portrait of the Norwegian immigrant leader, "[In Hans] Heg there is evident a deep faith in American ideals, in democracy, equality, and human freedom. A champion of such principles, Heg was put forward in 1852 as a Free-soil candidate for the state legislature."

[27] Claus L. Clausen, "Et Par Ord Til Læserne [A Few Words to the Readers]," *Emigranten*, January 30, 1852; Theodore C. Blegen, *Norwegian Migration to America: The American Transition* (New York: Haskell House Publishers, 1940), 308–317.

[28] Claus L. Clausen, "To Our American Friends," *Emigranten*, January 30, 1852.

they fulfill their destination, and contribute their part to the final development of the character of this great nation.[29]

This openness (and ability) to Americanize, based on both individual and broader public interest, made Scandinavian immigrants more politically acceptable to Yankee Americans otherwise attracted to nativist ideas well into the 1850s and slowly provided political prospects for Scandinavian candidates as well.[30] Emphasizing the political rights and opportunities associated with American citizenship, Clausen, in an editorial dated February 13, 1852, underlined the importance of "schools, churches, and other civilizing influences" necessary for achieving political influence in America and warned his readership against wandering "out into the wilderness as soon as the land is acquired from the Indians."[31] Focusing solely on land development might lead to missed political opportunities, Clausen warned.[32]

During the presidential election campaign of 1852, *Emigranten*, under the editorship of Clausen's successor, Charles M. Reese, explicitly supported the Democratic candidate Franklin Pierce at the national level but encouraged the paper's readership to support Scandinavian candidates in local elections for the state legislature regardless of political party.[33]

One such candidate was Hans Heg, the twenty-two-year-old son of Even Heg. Hans Heg ran for the Wisconsin State legislature on a Free Soil platform out of Racine in 1852 but – partly due to the fact that Scandinavian immigrants still made up less than 10 percent of

---

[29] Ibid.

[30] Foner, *Free Soil, Free Labor, Free Men: The Ideology of the Republican Party before the Civil War*, 228–230.

[31] Quoted in Harold M. Tolo, "The Political Position of Emigranten in the Election of 1852: A Documentary Article," *Norwegian-American Studies* 8 (1934): 98.

[32] Clausen wrote: "For my part, I fear that if some farm work is to be done on election day, [Norwegians] will fail to go to the polls even though the work could easily be postponed. It is a sad situation; it indicates that the Norwegian-American has no conception of what it means to be an American citizen. ... Let us try to create a little political instinct in ourselves! Let us read and listen and I am sure you will more than stand your ground also in political colloquia of the future." Clausen quoted in ibid., 106.

[33] Clausen, "Et Par Ord Til Læserne [A Few Words to the Readers]"; Blegen, *Norwegian Migration to America: The American Transition*, 308–317. See also Foner, *Free Soil, Free Labor, Free Men: The Ideology of the Republican Party before the Civil War*, 124–128. On Scandinavian editors such as Claus L. Clausen and Chales M. Reese walking a middle editorial ground on abolitionism, see Andersen, *The Immigrant Takes His Stand: The Norwegian-American Press and Public Affairs, 1847–1872*, 62.

Wisconsin's foreign-born population in 1850 – lost narrowly to a Democratic candidate.[34]

Yet, as the Whig and Free Soil Party morphed into the new Republican Party in the wake of the 1854 Kansas–Nebraska Act, the new political alliance, based on a strong commitment to free labor ideology, free soil, and, in time, a strong anti-slavery platform, increasingly appealed to Scandinavian immigrants.[35] By November 3, 1854, *Emigranten*, now edited by Norwegian-born Knud J. Fleischer, stated the paper's position as being firmly in support of the Republican Party:[36]

The November 7 election day is upon us!
Then it will become apparent if wrong shall conquer right, good conquer evil, if slavery shall be expanded and supported, liberty suppressed and curtailed! The Republican Party fighting for liberty and right has risen up to fight the "Democratic" Party's friends, the defenders of slavery. Norsemen, you would not [want] the advance of slavery![37]

Emigranten conveniently ignored any lingering Republican nativist sentiment left over from the locally successful Know-Nothing party in the 1854 elections and tried to shift readers' focus.[38] By the summer of 1855, Fleischer was urging "Norwegians to work for the Republican platform,"

[34] J. A. Johnson, *Det Skandinaviske Regiments Historie* [*The Scandinavian Regiment's History*] (La Crosse: Fædrelandet og Emigrantens Trykkeri, 1869), 104; Blegen, "Colonel Hans Christian Heg," 147; Jeppesen, *Danske i USA 1850–2000. En Demografisk, Social Og Kulturgeografisk Undersøgelse Af De Danske Immigranter Og Deres Efterkommere* [*Danes in the United States 1850–2000. A Demographic, Social and Cultural Geographic Study of The Danish Immigrants and Their Descendants*] (Odense: University Press of Southern Denmark, 2005), 86; "Wisconsin-Affærer. Hans Christian Heg [Wisconsin Affairs. Hans Christian Heg]," *Emigranten*, September 12, 1859.

[35] Foner, *Free Soil, Free Labor, Free Men: The Ideology of the Republican Party before the Civil War*, 124–128.

[36] Blaine Hansen, "The Norwegians of Luther Valley," *Wisconsin Magazine of History* 28, no. 4 (1945): 428.

[37] "Til Norske Vælgere i Dane County. Washburn! Washburn!! [To Norwegian Voters in Dane County. Washburn! Washburn!!]," *Emigranten*, November 3, 1854.

[38] McPherson, *Battle Cry of Freedom: The Civil War Era* (New York: Oxford University Press, 1988), 135–144. McPherson points out that the 1854–1855 election ended the two-party system consisting of Whigs and Democrats. "Most estimates [of the newly elected Congress] counted somewhere in the neighborhood of 105 Republican congressmen, 80 democrats and 50 Americans [nativists] … Of the Republicans (not all of whom yet acknowledged that label), perhaps two-thirds had at least a nominal connection with Know-Nothingism." See also Rasmussen, "'Drawn Together in a Blood Brotherhood': Civic Nationalism Amongst Scandinavian Immigrants in the American Civil War Crucible," *American Studies in Scandinavia* 48, no. 2 (2016): 7–31. On the Republican Party and nativism, see Foner, *Free Soil, Free Labor, Free Men: The Ideology of the Republican Party before the Civil War*, 226–60.

as in his opinion there "prevailed a vicious alliance of antiforeign Know-Nothing enthusiasts and unrighteous 'slavocrats'" in the Democratic Party's ranks.[39]

Thus, *Emigranten*, which had for its first two years maintained an affiliation with the Democratic Party, as evidenced by Reese's endorsement of Pierce in the 1852 election, adjusted its position based on the debate over free soil and, by extension, nonwhite free men, in part due to the impact slavery had on labor relations. From 1855, with the Republican Party gaining strength on the ground in Wisconsin, *Emigranten* aligned itself clearly with the anti-slavery party and urged Scandinavian immigrants to do the same.[40]

By 1855, even openly Democratic newspapers such as *Den Norske Amerikaner* (The Norwegian American) made anti-slavery arguments. *Den Norske Amerikaner* pointed out that slavery had been "the main theme" in American politics since 1850, and in a front-page piece titled "Negerslaveriet og fremtiden" ("Negro Slavery and the Future") the editor argued that the conflict between slavery and freedom had the potential to break the United States into pieces.[41] Expansion of slavery into the territories, it was argued, "would paralyze all political power in the northern states and make them a sort of commercial appendix to the all-commanding slave oligarchy" where free labor was subjugated in relation to "a profitable and advantegous monopoly."[42] Perhaps worst of all, slavery's sinfulness was being ignored in the South, and when Northerners pointed this out, "they point to their slaveholding clergy and slaveholding churches, with their prayers, awakenings, and the entire mechanism of a hypocritical religion."[43]

Starting with the Republican Party's grassroots organizational activity in 1854 and supported by amplified anti-slavery advocacy in the Scandinavian press in 1855, the Scandinavian immigrant community became increasingly aware of slavery's economic and moral implications on life in America. If the future United States could only be built on free

[39] Andersen, *The Immigrant Takes His Stand: The Norwegian-American Press and Public Affairs, 1847–1872*, 63.
[40] Carl Hansen, "Pressen Til Borgerkrigens Slutning [The Press until the Civil War's End]," in *Norsk-Amerikanernes Festskrift 1914*, ed. Johannes B. Wist (Decorah: The Symra Company, 1914), 39. Carl Hansen claimed that *Emigranten* in the subsequent years "had an impact that can hardly be exaggerated" and noted the role of *Fædrelandet*, which was first published in 1864, as another key culture-carrying news outlet.
[41] "Negerslaveriet Og Fremtiden [Negro Slavery and the Future]," *Den Norske Amerikaner*, February 28, 1855.
[42] Ibid.   [43] Ibid.

soil, free labor, and free (but not necessarily equal) men, then Scandinavian-born agricultural laborers were willing to support the Republican Party's political project in ever-increasing numbers.

When the Republican Party's foot soldiers started to fan out over the Midwest to influence local, state, and national elections, they also helped shape opinions in Scandinavian immigrant enclaves. Andrew Fredrickson in 1861 remembered the middle of the 1850s as a politically formative period, where "the Republican Party, of which I am part," was created.[44] Also, Celius Christiansen in his memoirs specifically remembered an 1854 visit to New Denmark by a representative of the Republican Party which he – along with Harriet Beecher Stowe's bestselling novel *Uncle Tom's Cabin* and a bribe of two dollars to vote for De Pere as Brown County's county seat – credited with cementing his anti-slavery views in support of the Republican Party.[45]

With the help of Norwegian leaders such as Hans Heg (see Figure 4.2), *Emigranten*'s agenda-setting ability on behalf of the Republican Party, and the canvassing and bribery experienced by immigrants such as Celius Christiansen, Scandinavian immigrants were slowly but surely primed through political campaigns and editorials to support the Republican Party.[46] On July 11, 1856, Scandinavian anti-slavery sentiment was concretely tied to support for the Republican Party when a broadside from the Republican state central committee was distributed by *Emigranten* in Norwegian. "The Union's current political battle is the conflict between liberty and serfdom," read the proclamation's first paragraph, in language that closely mirrored the phrases used by Scandinavian immigrants themselves.[47]

The Central Committee's plea for Republican presidential candidate John C. Fremont went on to emphasize the fact that it was not trying to

[44] Andreas Frederiksen, "Denmark. Brown Co. Wisc. Den 16. Februar 1861," in *Afskrift af 22 breve til Frederik Nielsen, Herlev DK fra A.F.Wilmington Ill. og West Denmark og Neenah Wisc. (1847–1872)* (Det danske udvandrerarkiv, 1861). See also Hale, "The Americanization of a Danish Immigrant in Wisconsin 1847–1872," 211.

[45] Christiansen, *En Pioneers Historie (Erindringer Fra Krigen Mellem Nord- Og Sydstaterne) [A Pioneer's Story: Memoirs from the War between North and South]* (Aalborg: Eget forlag, 1909), 15–32.

[46] Blegen, "Colonel Hans Christian Heg," 148. On attempts to counter claims of the Republican Party's ties to nativist movements, Blegen writes: "Many Germans and Scandinavians at this time believed that the Republican party was tainted with Know Nothingism, and Heg's place on the Republican ticket in Wisconsin was undoubtedly a Republican bid for the Scandinavian vote."

[47] Edward Ilsley, "Fra Den Republikanske Stats-Central-Committee [From the Republican State Central Committee]," *Emigranten*, July 11, 1856.

FIGURE 4.2 Hans Heg was among the most successful early Scandinavian immigrants. His leadership ability and political savvy earned him the position of colonel when the Civil War broke out. Image by The History Collection/ Alamy Stock Photo.

influence "the Scandinavians or other adopted citizens to do anything other than what any good and informed Christian would recognize as right" and additionally distanced the party from the "despised Know-Nothingers." In conclusion, the Republican committee added, "everyone who in his heart hates slavery will vote for Fremont."[48] In other words,

---

[48] Ibid. See also Blegen, *Norwegian Migration to America: The American Transition*, 317.

any anti-slavery, pro-free labor, enlightened Christian immigrant could safely support the Republican Party going into the 1856 election.

The link between religion and anti-slavery sentiment was an important one. The abolitionist movement had long and deep ties to religious factions, such as the Quakers and Puritans, arguing, as did Grundtvig and Claus Clausen among others, for a common humanity.[49] On June 10, 1857, *Nordstjernen* (The North Star), a newly established "National Democratic Paper" within the Scandinavian-American public sphere explicitly linked free soil, popular sovereignty, and religion in its opening editorial but implicitly admitted the difficulty of defending "popular sovereignty" and the resulting violence in western territories to a Scandinavian audience.[50] While admitting that bands of bandits, who "happened to vote the Democratic ticket," had crossed into Kansas and committed violent acts against settlers, *Nordstjernen*'s editor attempted to shift the responsibility to abolitionist agitators.

Who was it that eagerly seized this opportunity for political gain? Who collected money, arms, ammunition and people to send to Kansas and keep up the Civil War? The "Republicans"! . . . Men like Horace Greeley, Henry Ward Beecher and thousands of others of the same mold, who overtly preached insurrection through the press and from the pulpit.[51]

Beecher's importance in the anti-slavery struggle was not lost on Scandinavians residing in or visiting the New York area. As early as 1850, Fredrika Bremer heard Beecher preach on his opposition to the Fugitive Slave Act and described the chapel as "full to overflowing." He is "much esteemed and beloved," as well as "highly gifted," noted Bremer.[52]

Since 1847, Henry Ward Beecher had placed his Brooklyn-based Plymouth Church on the national map with his fight against slavery and, according to at least one study, used the church as a hub for the Underground Railroad and a stage for anti-slavery events (see Figure 4.3).[53] Among the several Scandinavian immigrants who regularly

---

[49] Manisha Sinha, *The Slave's Cause: A History of Abolition* (New Haven, CT: Yale University Press, 2016), 15–17.

[50] "Til Vore Læsere, Gamle og Nye [To Our Readers, Old and New]." *Nordstjernen*, June 10, 1857.

[51] Ibid.

[52] Fredrika Bremer, *The Homes of the New World: Impressions of America* (New York: Harper & Brothers, 1853), 553–554, 615. During an earlier visit in March 1850, Bremer described Beecher as "full of life and energy" and preaching "with riveting effect."

[53] Frank Decker, "Working as a Team: Henry Ward Beecher and the Plymouth Congregation in the Anti-Slavery Cause," *International Congregational Journal* 8, no. 2

FIGURE 4.3 Henry Ward Beecher, here photographed with his famous sister Harriet after the Civil War, made a strong impression on Scandinavian congregationists and visitors to Plymouth Church. Photo by Sepia Times/ Universal Images Group via Getty Images.

(2009): 38. See also Wayne Shaw, "The Plymouth Pulpit: Henry Ward Beecher's Slave Auction Block," *American Transcendental Quarterly*, no. 14 (2000): 335–337; Jonathan Earle, "Beecher's Bibles and Broadswords: Paving the Way for the Civil War in the West, 1854–1859," in *Empire and Liberty: The Civil War and the West*, ed. Virginia Scharff (Oakland: University of California Press, 2015), 52.

attended Beecher's sermons was Danish-born Ferdinand Winslöw, who on December 14, 1856, braved heavy rain en route to Plymouth Church to witness what he would describe to a Midwestern audience the following day as "Henry Ward Beechers Prædikener Om Negerne i Amerika" (Henry Ward Beecher's Sermons on the Negros in America).[54]

However, when Winslöw published his Beecher-based musings in the pages of *Kirkelig Maanedstidende* (Church Monthly) in March 1857, the powerful, conservative, well-educated Scandinavian clergy was in the process of distancing itself from revivalist interpretations of Lutheranism and aligning itself more closely with pro-slavery interpretations of the Bible.

Claus Clausen had started *Kirkelig Maanedstidende* together with his Norwegian-born colleagues Adolph Carl Preus and Hans Andreas Stub in 1851, but few members of the Scandinavian religious elite held positions as close to abolitionism as him. Consequently, collaboration on religious matters was not frictionless.[55]

The Norwegian synod's clergymen, many of whom were closely affiliated with the Norwegian state church, underscored their theological conservatism when they conducted a Midwestern search to establish collaboration with a larger Lutheran synod for future Scandinavian clergymen's education. To achieve this goal, two pastors appointed by a synod committee to study theological seminars between 1852 and 1857 settled for an affiliation with the German-led Concordia College in the slave state Missouri, instead of Buffalo or Columbus in the north.[56]

Given the Norwegian synod's decision to establish a partnership with the conservative German Missouri Synod, where an August 1856 article in the church's periodical *Lehre und Wehre* (Teaching and Guidance)

---

[54] Ferdinand S. Winslow, "Henry Ward Beechers Prædikener Om Negerne i Amerika [Henry Ward Beecher's Sermons on the Negros in America]," in *Kirkelig Maanedstidende* [*Church Monthly*], ed. Kirkens præster i Amerika (Inmansville, WI: Den Skandinaviske Presseforening, 1857).

[55] Brynjar Haraldsø, *Slaveridebatten i Den Norske Synode: En Undersøkelse Av Slaveridebatten i Den Norske Synode i USA i 1860-Årene Med Særlig Vekt På Debattens Kirkelig-Teologiske Aspekter* [*The Slavery Debate in the Norwegian Synod: A Study of the Slavery Debate in the Norwegian Synod in the United States During the 1860 Emphasizing the Debate's Church-Theological Aspects*] (Oslo: Solum Forlag, 1988), 39. See also Hansen, "Pressen Til Borgerkrigens Slutning [The Press until the Civil War's End]," 15–16. The Press Association's founding meeting was held on March 10, 1852, and admitted James D. Reymert, the first editor of *Nordlyset* in 1847, who later became active in Democratic politics and journalism. Additionally, the Scandinavian Press Association's first board of managers included, among others, Clausen, Gustav Fredrik Dietrichson, and A. C. Preus.

[56] Ibid., 40.

"concluded that slavery and Christianity were not in any way incompatible," it may seem surprising that Winslöw's depiction of Beecher's anti-slavery sermons were published in the official outlet for the Norwegian Synod in 1857.[57]

Winslöw's timing is part of the answer. Anti-slavery contributions stopped appearing in *Kirkelig Maanedstidende* after the first Norwegian students left for Concordia College in St. Louis in the summer of 1858. Yet, outside the Norwegian Synod, the revivalism and anti-slavery of Henry Ward Beecher clearly inspired Scandinavians like Winslöw who felt compelled to disseminate the Plymouth Church preacher's ideas about slavery and sin, which seemed closer in spirit to the Scandinavian revivalist factions than the Scandinavian state churches, to a wider Scandinavian audience in the Midwest.

"One of the most brilliant personalities in this country is undoubtedly Henry Ward Beecher, admired by his friends, hated and slandered by his enemies," Winslöw wrote. To the Danish immigrant, Beecher was "the forceful giant of truth in these times of confusion."[58]

Yet, one of the "truths" that Beecher promoted was the idea of a social hierarchy based on typologies of race. The distance between Lorenz Oken's "five races of man" – or Carl Linneaus' *Systema Naturae* with Europeans on top of a racial hierarchy – and Beecher's sermon this Sunday was negligible.[59] In Beecher's sermon one found the savage yet noble Indian, too "proud to be subdued to Slavery," fleeing before civilization

---

[57] Quoted in Kristen Layne Anderson, *Abolitionizing Missouri: German Immigrants and Racial Ideology in Nineteenth-Century America* (Baton Rouge: Louisiana State University Press, 2016), 77–78.

[58] Winslow, "Henry Ward Beechers Prædikener Om Negerne i Amerika [Henry Ward Beecher's Sermons on the Negros in America]"; "Africa among Us: Sketch of Two Sermons by Rev. Henry Ward Beecher, at His Church, Yesterday, on the African Race in America," *New York Times*, December 15, 1856.

[59] David Howes, *The Sixth Sense Reader* (New York: Berg, 2009), 10; Stefan Müller-Wille, "Race and History: Comments from an Epistemological Point of View," *Science, Technology & Human Values* 39, no. 4 (2014): 600–602; "Africa among Us: Sketch of Two Sermons by Rev. Henry Ward Beecher, at His Church, Yesterday, on the African Race in America." After singing two hymns and reading the notices, one of which concerned a fair to raise money for "fugitives from slavery," Beecher, according to the *New York Times*, started his sermon on slavery with musings on westward expansion. "This Continent, said the preacher, presented a most curious spectacle of mixed peoples. Here were the original people – the Indians – too haughty and proud to be subdued to Slavery. They are crumbling away. Civilization carries hell on its outer edge, and burns up everything it first touches. The whole Indian race retreats to the westward, following the path of the sun; they will soon imitate its example, and go down, but into a night that knows no morning."

but destined for destruction, as well as the unattractive, uneducated slave who needed white Anglo-Saxon Protestant help to attain social uplift. The substance of Beecher's sermon was significant because of the influence the preacher had on American religious culture and, by extension, the countless congregationists attending and disseminating his sermons.[60]

While Beecher emphasized that "African people are not stupid," that "for music, oratory, gentility, for physical learning and the fine arts, they have a genius just as truly as we have not," and that colonization was a hypocritical pipedream, it was clear that the Plymouth Church preacher did not consider African-Americans his equals. "We are the great Anglo-Saxon people," said Beecher. "We boast that the African was brought here from his own wretched home to learn the truths that are brought to light in the Bible, but when he is here we pass laws forbidding him to learn to read it." He added:

The whole nation is guilty. But the thing cannot go on; either Slavery will kill out Christianity, or Christianity will abolish Slavery ... Emancipation is only a question of time, not of fact. Society must lift up these dregs, or they will eat out the bottom and all fall through ... Society can't carry our Slavery in its bosom. Slaves, without culture, will rock down our civilization – with culture they will free themselves.[61]

The means to cultural uplift was education, according to Beecher, and toward the end of the service a collection was made to benefit a school for young Black women. Among the school's original benefactors was Henry Ward Beecher's older sister Harriet, the famed abolitionist author.[62] Yet Beecher's view of "Africa among us" clearly demonstrated the limits of abolitionist sentiment, even among individuals who were considered central to, or at least active in, the movement. As such, Beecher's sermon

---

[60] Clifford E. Clark Jr., "The Changing Nature of Protestantism in Mid-Nineteenth Century America: Henry Ward Beecher's Seven Lectures to Young Men," *Journal of American History* 57, no. 4 (1971): 833. As Clifford E. Clark Jr. has argued, "because of his immense popularity, Henry Ward Beecher exerted a strong influence on the religious outlook of his day. Through his extensive activities as newspaper editor, lyceum lecturer, and preacher, he spoke to thousands of Americans and helped shape their views on a variety of religious and social questions."

[61] "Africa among Us: Sketch of Two Sermons by Rev. Henry Ward Beecher, at His Church, Yesterday, on the African Race in America." See also Clark Jr., "The Changing Nature of Protestantism in Mid-Nineteenth Century America: Henry Ward Beecher's Seven Lectures to Young Men."

[62] Winslow, "Henry Ward Beechers Prædikener Om Negerne i Amerika [Henry Ward Beecher's Sermons on the Negros in America]"; Debby Applegate, *The Most Famous Man in America: The Biography of Henry Ward Beecher* (New York: Doubleday, 2006), 262–372.

reflected Stephen Kantrowitz's point that "open advocacy of interracial sociability as a means of improving society was rare even among committed white abolitionists."[63]

Nonetheless, Beecher's notion of the thrifty, beautiful European immigrants and Anglo-Saxon Americans, who, despite their original sin, could get ahead in society if they worked hard and played by the rules, appealed to Scandinavian immigrants like Winslöw and his Scandinavian social circle. Winslöw's older brother, Wilhelm, later recalled:

In the beginning of 1857 my younger brother Ferdinand invited me to come and stay with him in the United States. A year and a half was spent on that visit, which proved of great importance to me in more than one respect. I shall here only mention that I became highly influenced by the preaching and theological views of Henry Ward Beecher.[64]

Furthermore, Ferdinand Winslöw's brother-in-law, Christian Thomsen Christensen, practiced what Beecher preached in the aftermath of the 1856 sermon. Christensen and his family joined Plymouth Church in July 1857, and, though they temporarily "dissolved" their connection in December 1857, they renewed their membership and played a prominent part in the church after the Civil War.[65] Other people in the Scandinavian network listened to Beecher's sermons, as evidenced by the church's prominence in several travelogues from America before and after the Civil War.[66]

The Scandinavian connection to Beecher's revivalist church and the connection between his anti-slavery views based on white Protestant

---

[63] Kantrowitz, *More Than Freedom: Fighting for Black Citizenship in a White Republic, 1829–1889* (New York: Penguin Press, 2012), 60–64.

[64] Wilhelm Winsløw, "Reports and Letters. The Rev. Wilhelm Winslow," in *The New Church Messenger* (Brooklyn: Swedenborg Press, 1885), 292. Also Marcus Thrane expressed admiration of Henry Ward Beecher's sermons. See Marcus Thrane, "Program [Program]," *Marcus Thrane's Norske Amerikaner*, May 25, 1866.

[65] Christian Thomsen Christensen corresponded with Beecher and volunteered in Plymouth Church after the Civil War, for example as president of the Church Work Committee. "Plymouth Church Membership 1847–1901" (Plymouth Church, 1857). See also Clark Jr., "The Changing Nature of Protestantism in Mid-Nineteenth Century America: Henry Ward Beecher's Seven Lectures to Young Men," 845. See also Henry Ward Beecher, "My Dear Mr. Christensen," in *Papers of Christian T. Christensen, 1862–1906* (Huntington Library, Art Collections & Botanical Gardens, 1877); "Plymouth Church and Foreign Missions," *Brooklyn Daily Eagle*, December 4, 1892.

[66] Bremer, *The Homes of the New World: Impressions of America*, 553–554, 615. Also Robert Watt, *Hinsides Atlanterhavet: Skildringer Fra Amerika [Beyond the Atlantic: Accounts from America]*, 3 vols., vol. 2 (Copenhagen: P. Bloch, 1872), 234–245; "General Christensen to Give up Business," *Brooklyn Daily Eagle*, March 25, 1900.

superiority were important because Winslöw worked consciously to establish a link between Beecher's ideas and the Scandinavian Midwestern communities by disseminating the December 1856 sermon to *Kirkelig Maanedstidende*'s readers.

In Beecher's sermons, religion intersected with politics. Henry Ward Beecher's brand of Protestantism, known as "the gospel of love" or "the gospel of success," focused on individual agency (e.g. "his belief that anyone could become successful if only he worked at it"), while maintaining some belief in "original sin," and his humorous, populist preaching style – what Mark Twain later termed the ability to discharge "rockets of poetry" and explode "mines of eloquence" – attracted thousands every Sunday.[67]

Importantly, Beecher's views on slavery and social mobility and his notions of white superiority to some extent inspired and closely mirrored well-educated Scandinavian immigrants' thinking, helping undergird their "free soil" opposition to slavery as well as their rationale for participation in American territorial expansion.[68] Moreover, Beecher's gospel of success served as an argument for free labor ideology – the call for Christianity to abolish slavery was an argument in support of "free men" – yet a notion of white, Protestant superiority held the sermon's two strands together.

This was part of the reason Winslöw described Beecher as "a giant of truth," excitedly relaying his sermon, and it was part of the reason Beecher continued to inspire. Beecher helped legitimize Scandinavian immigrants' rationale for claiming and owning land in the Midwest and their attempt to achieve upward social mobility through hard work in a free labor economy. Moreover, due to the constant influx of immigrants from the East Coast to Scandinavian settlements in the Midwest, as well as the fact that Norwegian immigrants had travelled from Muskego, Wisconsin, to New York as early as 1852 to help their newly arrived countrymen, Winslöw and his brother-in-law Christian Thomsen Christensen were well-known in the larger Scandinavian settlements out west.[69] Claus

---

[67] Applegate, *The Most Famous Man in America: The Biography of Henry Ward Beecher*, 181, 372. See also Clifford E. Clark Jr., "The Changing Nature of Protestantism in Mid-Nineteenth Century America: Henry Ward Beecher's Seven Lectures to Young Men," 832–836.

[68] Ferd. S. Winslow, "Brooklyn. 11th Septbr. 1856. Religion Og Politik [Brooklyn. September 11, 1856. Religion and Politics]," in *Kirkelig Maanedstidende*, ed. Kirkens Præster i Amerika (Inmansville: Den Skandinaviske Presseforening, 1856).

[69] Ferd S. Winslow, "Det Skandinaviske Selskab i New-York [The Scandinavian Association in New York]," *Emigranten*, January 30, 1857.

Clausen, for example, later in life described both Christensen and Winslöw as friends, and vice versa.[70]

Whether it was in Beecher's church in Brooklyn or in more primitive Midwestern places of worship, numerous early Norwegian, Swedish, and Danish immigrants availed themselves of this opportunity to explore religion outside the Scandinavian state churches. As we have seen, the early Norwegian immigrants of Muskego, Wisconsin, transplanted parts of the Haugean movement to American soil; the early Swedish settlement in New Sweden, Iowa, converted to Methodism; and importantly a large proportion of Danish immigrants to the United States who did not settle in the Midwest came on tickets paid by the Mormon Church en route to Utah.[71]

Claus Clausen also increasingly linked religion and anti-slavery agitation in the more secular public sphere and initially found an ideological ally in Norwegian-born Carl Fredrik Solberg, who took over *Emigranten* on April 17, 1857 (see Figure 4.4).[72] Solberg gladly carried on the paper's position on "the slavery and public land issues," which had been in place since Fleischer's editorship.[73]

Almost simultaneously with *Emigranten*'s editorial change, prominent Scandinavian-born men founded the Scandinavian Democratic Press Association and a few months later launched "a National Democratic"

[70] Writing a letter on behalf of Claus L. Clausen in 1872, Christian T. Christensen noted: "I have known him intimately for a number of years past, and esteem him highly"; see C. T. Christensen, "Danish Consulate and Legation, Pro. Tem. New York April 4th 1872," in *Papers of Claus Clausen. RG 15. Box 1. Correspondence 1871–1876* (Luther College Archives, 1872). Also Rasmus Andersen, *Pastor Claus Laurits Clausen – Banebryder for Den Norske Og Danske Kirke i Amerika. Første Skandinavisk Feltpræst. [Pastor Claus Laurits Clausen: Trailblazer for the Norwegian and Danish Church in America. First Scandinavian Chaplain]* (Blair, NW: Danish Lutheran Publishing House, 1921), 128. On Clausen's relationship with Ferdinand and Wilhelm Winslöw, Andersen writes: "He [Ferdinand] and his brother Wilhelm Winslow stood as Clausen's friends through the years." On Norwegians from Muskego, see Hansen, "Pressen Til Borgerkrigens Slutning [The Press until the Civil War's End]," 25.

[71] See, for example, Eugene F. Fevold, "The Norwegian Immigrant and His Church," *Norwegian-American Studies* 23 (1967), 3–16. Also Earl D. Check and Emeroy Johnson (translator), "Civil War Letters to New Sweden, Iowa," *Swedish-American Historical Quarterly* 36, no. 1 (1985); Enok Mortensen, *The Danish Lutheran Church in America*; Allen, *Danish, but Not Lutheran: The Impact of Mormonism on Danish Cultural Identity, 1850–1920* (Philadelphia: Board of Publication, Lutheran Church in America, 1967).

[72] Harold M. Tolo, "The Political Position of Emigranten in the Election of 1852: A Documentary Article," *Norwegian-American Studies* 8 (1934): 94–95.

[73] Blegen, *Norwegian Migration to America: The American Transition*, 318.

FIGURE 4.4 As editor of *Emigranten*, Carl Fredrik Solberg was one of the most influential Scandinavian-American voices in the Civil War era. Courtesy Vesterheim Norwegian-American Museum Archives.

competitor to *Emigranten*.[74] *Nordstjernen* (The North Star), which succeeded *Den Norske Amerikaner*, published its first issue on June 10, 1857,

[74] Andersen, *The Immigrant Takes His Stand: The Norwegian-American Press and Public Affairs, 1847–1872*, 12–13, 65. See also Hansen, "Pressen Til Borgerkrigens Slutning [The Press until the Civil War's End]," 26. The Scandinavian Democratic Press Association, according to Hansen, was established on April 1851 by prominent Scandinavian-born Democrats. Among the organization's founders were Gabriel Björnson, who served in the Wisconsin Assembly in 1851, Charles Reese, and J. D. Reymert (who had previously been part of the leadership behind *Emigranten*), and it was supported by prominent Norwegian farmers in Dane County. Also R. M. Rashford, ed., *The Legislative Manual of the State of Wisconsin* (Madison, WI: E. B. Bolens State Printer, 1877), 158.

but quickly ran into trouble based on its position regarding slavery.[75] Before 1854, the Democratic Party's insistence on individual freedom and support of immigrant causes seemed to hold some sway over a Scandinavian audience averse to interference from the government or clergy based on their Old World experience, but increasingly the question of slavery, exacerbated by Democratic leader Stephen Douglas' advocacy of "popular sovereignty" in Kansas, proved difficult for Democratic newspaper editors to defend. The issue of free soil, with its underlying premise that American Indians had no right to the land, was an issue of utmost importance for Scandinavian immigrants: in tying discussions of free soil to discussions of free men, not least the moral issue of free non-white men, *Emigranten* gained an upper hand in the competition.[76]

Not even Charles M. Reese, a skillful writer and editor who "was not without a following" and who found employment with Democratic news-papers after his departure from *Emigranten*, could gloss over the increas-ing political differences on the issue of slavery, and the Scandinavian editors' position on human bondage proved to be the key to the success, or lack thereof, of *Nordstjernen* in competition with *Emigranten*.[77]

When Solberg recounted the competition between the two papers later in life, he noted that *Nordstjernen* failed "to make much headway among the Norwegians" and emphasized the Republican Party's increasing appeal to immigrants advocating free soil and anti-slavery politics.[78]

When the *Emigranten* plant was moved to Madison I was made editor of the paper, and when the new Norwegian paper [*Nordstjernen*] was started I became at once one of the targets of its abuse. We had it hot back and forth, but I felt that I had the better of it as our paper was on the right side of public questions.[79]

While it is difficult to determine the exact ideological leanings in Scandinavian communities at the ground level, subscription numbers and scattered diary references indicate that *Emigranten*, as a loyal

---

[75] Andersen, *The Immigrant Takes His Stand: The Norwegian-American Press and Public Affairs, 1847–1872*, 24–25, 65-68. See also Hansen, "Pressen Til Borgerkrigens Slutning [The Press until the Civil War's End]," 26.

[76] Andersen, *The Immigrant Takes His Stand: The Norwegian-American Press and Public Affairs, 1847–1872*, 68. Andersen argues "that Solberg, through *Emigranten*, represented majority opinion among the Norwegians on this issue [slavery]."

[77] "Til Vore Læsere, Gamle Og Nye [To Our Readers, Old and New]." See also Andersen, *The Immigrant Takes His Stand: The Norwegian-American Press and Public Affairs, 1847–1872*, 20.

[78] Blegen, *Norwegian Migration to America: The American Transition*, 318.

[79] Albert O. Barton, "Reminiscences of a Pioneer Editor," *NAHA Studies and Records* 1 (1926).

supporter of the Republican Party, was far more attractive than *Nordstjernen.* By early 1854, *Emigranten's* self-proclaimed subscription list counted between 500 and 600 names, and its overall readership, due to newspapers being shared in the settlements, was likely higher.[80] In contrast, no issues of *Nordlyset* were published between October and December of 1857, and in subsequent editions complaints over the newspaper's financial state appeared regularly, while *Emigraten's* weekly issues arrived steadily in Scandinavian enclaves and helped build a Scandinavian Republican electorate during the same time span.[81]

In addition to the issue of free soil, Reese and Solberg sparred over the issue of Black people's ability to vote in Wisconsin when the question was debated in the summer and fall of 1857. On November 3, 1857, a referendum was held in Wisconsin on the issue of "Suffrage for African Americans," meaning African-American men over twenty-one years of age, and Solberg's editorials in the weeks and months leading up to the election argued for Black people's right to vote while also explicitly stating that *Emigranten's* editors distinguished between the Republican Party's policy and abolitionist policy.[82]

According to the editor, it was *Emigranten's* position that everyone should "be free and have equal rights." The Scandinavian newspaper opposed slavery's expansion but would not interfere with slavery where it already existed. "Abolitionists we have never been," the editor stated. Yet, "when a free Negro settles in Wisconsin, he should enjoy his share of civil rights."[83]

Conversely, Reese warned *Nordstjernen's* readers that the result would be "a black governor and a black legislature in Wisconsin! ... Would not

---

[80] Andersen, *The Immigrant Takes His Stand: The Norwegian-American Press and Public Affairs, 1847–1872,* 12–13, 61. According to Andersen, *Emigranten* was more "representative of Norwegian-American opinion in the 1850s" with its "antislavery Democratic" program until 1854 when it switched to support the Republican Party. On subscription list numbers, based on then-editor Charles M. Reese, see Hansen, "Pressen Til Borgerkrigens Slutning [The Press until the Civil War's End]," 24. See also Blegen, *Norwegian Migration to America: The American Transition,* 317–319.

[81] Hansen, "Pressen Til Borgerkrigens Slutning [The Press until the Civil War's End]," 28.

[82] "Bør Negerne Have Stemmeret i Wisconsin?," *Emigranten,* August 12, 1857; "Tale Af Carl Schurz, Republikansk Candidat for Lieutenant Governor, Holdet i Madison Den 16. Oktober 1857 [Speech by Carl Schurz, Republican Candidate for Lieutenant Governor, Held in Madison October 16, 1857]," *Emigranten,* October 23, 1857.

[83] Andersen, *The Immigrant Takes His Stand: The Norwegian-American Press and Public Affairs, 1847–1872,* 65; "Bør Negerne Have Stemmeret i Wisconsin?," *Emigranten,* August 12, 1857.

our Black Republican friends then rejoice? Then there would be not freedom and equality, but first the Negro and after him the white man."[84]

While Solberg likely was ahead of the Scandinavian public opinion on this issue – and also later changed his editorial stance – Solberg's editorship does indicate the increased focus on anti-slavery issues within the Republican Party. Moreover, the Scandinavian electorate in Wisconsin seemed to be increasingly following Solberg's arguments.[85]

Thus, when Solberg later in life remembered that he got the better of *Nordstjernen*, it had much to do with the Republican Party's appeal to Scandinavians based on free soil and free labor policies.[86] In a September 12, 1859, profile of Hans Heg, likely written by Solberg, the Norwegian-born politician's successful rise from farmer to businessman and candidate for statewide office with broad-based ethnic support was emphasized along with his long-standing "opposition to the spread of slavery."[87]

Thus, Abraham Lincoln's speeches in Cincinnati and Milwaukee in September 1859, building on his argument for the primacy of free labor stretching back to the mid-1840s, likely resonated powerfully in the Scandinavian-American community. Social mobility, what Abraham Lincoln on September 17, 1859, called, "improvement in condition" in a free country, was "the great principle for which the government was really formed."[88]

A few weeks later, at the Wisconsin State Fair in Milwaukee, Lincoln elaborating on these free labor thoughts. "Men, with their families – wives, sons and daughters – work for themselves, on their farms in their houses and in their shops," he said, "taking the whole product to themselves, and asking no favors of capital on the one hand, nor of hirelings or slaves on the other."[89] Free labor, Lincoln argued, led workers to reap

---

[84] Quoted in Andersen, *The Immigrant Takes His Stand: The Norwegian-American Press and Public Affairs, 1847–1872*, 66–67.

[85] Hansen, "Pressen Til Borgerkrigens Slutning [The Press until the Civil War's End]," 31.

[86] Barton, "Reminiscences of a Pioneer Editor."

[87] "Wisconsin-Affærer. Hans Christian Heg [Wisconsin Affairs. Hans Christian Heg]."

[88] Eric Foner, *The Fiery Trial: Abraham Lincoln and American Slavery* (New York: W. W. Norton & Company, 2010), 113–115. See also Roy P. Basler, ed., *Collected Works of Abraham Lincoln*, vol. 3 (New Brunswick, NJ: Rutgers University Press, 1953), 438–463.

[89] Quoted in Foner, *The Fiery Trial: Abraham Lincoln and American Slavery*, 113–115. According to Foner, by the time Lincoln gave his speech in 1859 he had embraced the market revolution and "advised farmers to abandon traditional ways in favor of new methods of plowing and crop rotation and new fertilizers, seeds, and agricultural machinery." See also Basler, *Collected Works of Abraham Lincoln*, vol. 3, 438–463.

"the fruit of labor" and thereby gain the opportunity for economic improvement.[90] On July 2, 1860, in one of the few editorials in *Emigranten* signed directly by Solberg himself, he clearly laid out his and his newspaper's reasons for supporting Abraham Lincoln in the important upcoming presidential election. The Democratic Party's political decay and despotism, after decades in power, played a part, but anti-slavery attitudes, pro-homestead sentiment, and opposition to non-contigious empire were issues at the top of the list.

"Emigranten" will work actively in this electoral campaign and be in "the thicket of the fight" for Lincoln and Hamlin, for the freeing the territories, for the Homestead Bill's adoption, for the Cuba Bill's rejection, for a moderate toll's adoption to protect interests in the northern and western states etc.[91]

For a few months, Solberg even lowered *Emigranten*'s subscription price to 50 cents annually compared to $2 during the previous presidential election campaign and thereby indicated the importance he placed on influencing Scandinavian popular opinion in the coming months.[92] The ties between *Emigranten* and anti-slavery advocacy was made even clearer in August 1860, when Solberg's good friend, Hans Heg, serving as prison commissioner, decided to shield abolitionist editor Sherman Booth from arrest by the authorities at the Wisconsin State Prison.[93]

Booth had gained national fame in March 1854 when he gathered a crowd to free runaway slave Joshua Glover in Racine and afterward became a prominent voice in the anti-slavery struggle.[94] "We send greetings to the free states of the Union, that, in the state of Wisconsin, the fugitive slave Law is repealed!" Booth wrote in his newspaper the *Milwaukee Free Democrat*.[95] Yet, in a prolonged back-and-forth legal toggle, Booth was by March 7, 1859, unanimously found guilty of

---

[90] Foner, *The Fiery Trial: Abraham Lincoln and American Slavery*, 113.

[91] Solberg, "Emigranten under Præsidentvalgkampen [The Emigrant During the Presidential Election]." For discussions of Cuban annexation, see "Annexation of Cuba Made Easy," *New York Times*, December 13, 1860.

[92] Ibid.

[93] Royal M. Bryant, "State of Wisconsin, County of Dodge [August 21]," in *Hans Christian Heg Letters, 1840, 1861–1863* (Wisconsin Historical Society, 1860). See also Hans C. Heg, "Booth Flygtet – Breve Fra Hans C. Heg [Booth Escaped – Letters from Hans C. Heg]," *Emigranten*, August 13, 1860.

[94] Diane S. Butler, "The Public Life and Private Affairs of Sherman M. Booth," *Wisconsin Magazine of History* 82, no. 3 (1999): 168. Butler points out that Booth also at this time had gained national infamy "by seducing, and possibly raping, a fourteen-year-old girl."

[95] Quoted in ibid., 178.

violating the Fugitive Slave Act by the United States Supreme Court led by Chief Justice Roger B. Taney.[96]

Accordingly, federal authorities arrested Booth on March 1, 1860 and placed him in the federal custom house in Milwaukee. Booth remained confined in Milwaukee until August 1, when ten of his political allies broke him free and ushered him to the state penitentiary in Waupun, where he received lodging under Heg's supervision.

On August 2, 1860, a US marshal arrived at the Waupun prison looking to apprehend Booth, with a letter from a federal marshal, John H. Lewis, asking Heg to assist in Booth's arrest. The Norwegian-born prison commissioner, however, replied that his men "currently were employed in a better and more honorable way."[97] By August 3, Heg instead invited Marshal Garlick in to arrest Booth in person, but Booth threatened to shoot anyone who tried to arrest him.[98] When later deposed, witnesses remembered Garlick saying, "The men that talk so much about shooting are not the ones to shoot."[99] When Garlick, however, asked Heg what he thought about the situation, he received the following answer:

Mr. H. replied that he did not know what Booth would do, but if he was in Booth's place and had been houn[d]ed round for the last six years, the very first man that should make an attempt to arrest me I would shoot him down as I would a dog. Mr. Garlick asked H. if he had anything against him as a man. Heg replied I have nothing against you Garlick as a man, but I think you ought to be in better business than serving as the tool for the slave catchers.[100]

Heg's remarks, and Booth's threat of violence, made the federal marshal leave the prison; with the aid of abolitionist allies, Booth continued to escape federal agents for two more months before he was finally arrested in Berlin, Wisconsin, on October 8, 1860. Because of Heg's role in what turned out to be Booth's initial escape, the Scandinavian prison commissioner, who held larger political aspirations, was afforded considerable statewide attention, as he relayed his version of events in English-language and Norwegian-language newspapers.[101]

---

[96] Ibid., 182–189. Heg, "Booth Flygtet – Breve Fra Hans C. Heg [Booth Escaped – Letters from Hans C. Heg]."

[97] Hans C. Heg, "Booth Flygtet – Breve Fra Hans C. Heg [Booth Escaped – Letters from Hans C. Heg]."

[98] "Booth Flygtet – Breve Fra Hans C. Heg [Booth Escaped – Letters from Hans C. Heg]."

[99] Bryant, "State of Wisconsin, County of Dodge [August 21]."   [100] Ibid.

[101] Barton, "Reminiscences of a Pioneer Editor."

To Scandinavian readers, at least the way it was remembered, the episode added to Heg's anti-slavery credentials and solidified his position as a Scandinavian political leader. The event was important to *Emigranten*, and likely to its readers, because it was a Norwegian-born immigrant taking an overt stand against the Fugitive Slave Act, and in that context it mattered less that Booth's personal popularity in the pages of *Emigranten* was negligible due to his sexual assault of a fourteen-year-old girl the year before.[102]

Emigranten's increasingly firm anti-slavery position seemingly resonated with Scandinavian newspaper readers to a much greater extent than was the case with the rival *Nordstjernen*. Between 1858 and September 1860, *Nordstjernen* was edited by the politically ambitious Danish-born immigrant Hans Borchsenius, but it failed to find an effective counter to *Emigranten*'s popularity, since the Democratic Party seemed increasingly pro-slavery from the Scandinavian readers' perspective.[103] When Borchsenius was nominated by the Democratic Party on September 19, 1860, to run for county clerk, he passed the editorial duties over to his employee Jacob Seeman. In his first editorial on October 10, Seeman drew upon the Democratic Party's long history and central position in American politics as an appeal to Scandinavian readers. Seeman simultaneously expressed pride in and support for the threshold principle's main strands of population growth and territorial expansion, which likely had a broad appeal among a Scandinavian readership.

I pay tribute to democratic principles and support the Democratic Party because the Union under Democratic rule has grown from 13 to 33 states, has increased its population from close to 4 million to 30 million people and now is regarded one of the mightiest and proudest empires on earth in terms of trade, sea power, agriculture, arts and sciences.[104]

According to Seeman, the Democrats had always been the immigrant's friend, and it was therefore imperative that the "abolitionizing" Republican Party's "wrong, deplorable, and treasonous teachings,"

---

[102] Butler, "The Public Life and Private Affairs of Sherman M. Booth," 168, 82–89. *Emigranten* noted that Booth had "lost his good name" in a "scandalous trial" the previous year before describing events related to his escape from authorities in August of 1860. Heg, "Booth Flygtet – Breve Fra Hans C. Heg [Booth Escaped – Letters from Hans C. Heg]."

[103] Andersen, *The Immigrant Takes His Stand: The Norwegian-American Press and Public Affairs, 1847–1872*, 68.

[104] Jacob Seemann, "Til 'Nordstjernens' Læsere [To the *North Star*'s Readers]," *Nordstjernen*, October 10, 1860.

were given a more "conservative, honest and truthful quality," as only the Democratic Party could, or the result could be the deathknell of the Union.[105] Nevertheless, Seeman's editorial would prove to be the last ever published in *Nordstjernen*. Shortly after the October 10 issue, Borchsenius sold the newspaper to Solberg. In a letter to subscribers in January 1861, distributed through *Emigraten*, the former editor detailed the reasons why and lamented the fact that there was no longer room for "two political papers with opposite views."[106]

Two years as editor of a Democratic newspaper had disabused Borchsenius of the notion that Scandinavian immigrants, "under the circumstances, due to little interest in reading or more correctly little interest in subscribing to political papers," were willing to support a newspaper in competition with the Republican Party's anti-slavery platform. According to Borchsenius, a newspaper needed between 1,500 and 2,000 subscribers to survive, and "the highest number" he had been "able to achieve at 'Nordstjernen'" had been between 800 and 900, and out of that number there had always "been a few hundred that did not pay."[107]

Consequently, Borchsenius sold his list of subscribers to Solberg to get out of debt. *Emigranten*'s subscription list, which, according to Reese, in early 1854 had counted between 500 and 600, had grown sizably under K. J. Fleischer's and later Solberg's editorship. When Fleischer handed the editorial reins to Solberg in April 1857, he expressed satisfaction that the subscription list now numbered between 1,300 and 1,400 names.[108] Moreover, Solberg, in an editorial published on December 7, 1863, put the subscription number at 2,700.[109] This positive development in subscribers, if the editors' own numbers can indeed be trusted, corresponds with Theodore Blegen's assessment. Solberg, according to Blegen, "expanded the paper in size, varied its contents, increased its interest and value as a literary magazine, reached out to all parts of the Northwest for Scandinavian Americans, and built up its circulation until, in Civil War times, it had nearly four thousand subscribers."[110]

---

[105] Ibid.

[106] Hans Borchsenius, "Cirkulære Til Nordstjernens Abonnenter [Circular to the *North Star*'s Subscribers]," *Emigranten*, January 7, 1861.

[107] Ibid.   [108] Solberg, "Til Emigrantens Læsere [To the *Emigrant*'s Readership]."

[109] "Emigranten for Aaret 1864 [The *Emigrant* for the Year 1864]," ibid., December 7, 1863.

[110] Blegen, *Norwegian Migration to America: The American Transition*, 318. Blegen's estimate of close to 4,000 subscribers is based on Solberg's recollection later in life,

Solberg's claims that *Emigranten*'s position was on the "right side of public questions" and therefore decisive in his competition with *Nordstjernen* found support in the writings of the enterprising Reese, who, by September 22, 1860, now on his fourth newspaper editorship, wrote for a newly established and, as it turned out, short-lived "Republican campaign paper," *Folkebladet,*

The struggle this fall will be simply between Freedom and Slavery, and where is the man in the North who can for a moment be undecided as to which side to take? We for one have bid a long farewell to the so-called Democracy and shall hereafter be found battling for Freedom, Free Speech, and Free Territory![111]

Folkebladet was published out of Chicago, which was also the home of the much more established and influential Swedish-language newspaper *Hemlandet*. Edited by Swedish-born Pastor Tuve N. Hasselquist (see Figure 4.5), who emigrated in 1852 in part due to his criticism of the Swedish state church, *Hemlandet* had catered to Illinois' growing Swedish-born population since 1855.[112] For years, *Hemlandet* touted anti-slavery viewpoints to its readership; though it had fewer than 1,000 subscribers, it, according to the estimate of biographer Oscar Fritiof Ander, probably had several thousand readers.[113]

"Perhaps the most effective testimony to Hasselquist's influence in forming the political opinion of the Swedes is found in the success of *Hemlandet* over its competitors, *Svenska Republikanen* and *Minnesota Posten*," notes Ander, who adds, "Swedes were Democratic in 1852, but voted Republican in 1856, and since that time they remained so faithful to the principles of that party that all attempts made after 1860 to start at Democratic newspaper were doomed to fail because of lack of support."[114]

when he stated: "During the war I built up a circulation of nearly four thousand for *Emigranten*." See also Barton, "Reminiscences of a Pioneer Editor." Also Borchsenius, "Cirkulære Til Nordstjernens Abonnenter [Circular to the *North Star*'s Subscribers]."

[111] Andersen, *The Immigrant Takes His Stand: The Norwegian-American Press and Public Affairs, 1847–1872*, 69.

[112] Dag Blanck, *The Creation of an Ethnic Identity: Being Swedish American in the Augustana Synod, 1860–1917* (Carbondale: Southern Illinois University Press, 2006), 27–28, 39.

[113] Blegen, *Norwegian Migration to America: The American Transition*, 318.

[114] Oscar Fritiof Ander, *T. N. Hasselquist: The Career and Influence of a Swedish-American Clergyman, Journalist and Educator* (Rock Island, IL: Augustana Historical Society, 1931), 159–160.

FIGURE 4.5 Tuve N. Hasselquist was a towering figure among early Swedish-American immigrants and through his editorship of *Hemlandet* served as an opinion leader in Scandinavian communities. Courtesy of the Library of Congress.

Consequently, the solidly Republican *Hemlandet* and *Emigranten* were by 1860 the only surviving secular Scandinavian newspapers in Illinois and Wisconsin, since they were the only ones that could be sustained through Scandinavian-born subscribers.

In trying to explain why Scandinavian immigrants chose so clearly to support the Republican Party, editor Knud Langeland, who by 1867 published the newspaper *Skandinaven* (The Scandinavian) out of Chicago, offered this explanation: "The Scandinavian people in America joined the Republican party en masse because it was founded upon the eternal truth: 'Equality before the law for all citizens of the land without regard to religion, place of birth, or color of skin.'"[115]

[115] Quoted in Arlow W. Andersen, "Knud Langeland: Pioneer Editor," *Norwegian-American Studies* 14 (1944). Arlow W. Anderson, "Knud Langeland: Pioneer Editor," *Norwegian-American Studies* 14 (1944).

While this Scandinavian hagiography necessarily needs to be context-ualized by their implicit and explicit support for and benefit from their white, Lutheran background, the extent to which Scandinavian immigrants in Wisconsin, Illinois, and Minnesota backed the Republican Party before, during, and after the Civil War is noteworthy.[116] Thus, the elections of 1860 provided a litmus test for the political power of ethnicity in relation to the Republican platform's focus on free soil, free labor, and free men among Scandinavian immigrants. The settlement of New Denmark was just one of many examples.

On a beautiful Tuesday morning, November 6, Fritz Rasmussen awoke in New Denmark and observed frost still visible in areas shaded by the trees as he went down to the local schoolhouse to vote.[117] The Danish immigrant cast his vote for Abraham Lincoln and followed the election proceedings for some time thereafter before returning home to butcher pigs.[118] Rasmussen thereby took the political advice of *Emigranten*, but the same was not the case among all New Denmark's residents. New Denmark, like the rest of the United States, was split in two. The town's eligible voters gave Stephen Douglas forty-three votes, while Abraham Lincoln received thirty-seven. According to the 1860 census, New Denmark counted 424 inhabitants, including 139 with Scandinavian heritage, while the rest were mainly Irish or German-speaking.[119] Despite the community's ethnic differences, every-day life was relatively frictionless, but the presidential election of 1860 revealed political differences tied to Scandinavian immigrants' notions of ethnicity, the politics of class, and the racially charged notions of citizen-ship. As such, the election of 1860 foreshadowed future conflict zones surrounding the Scandinavian community.

---

[116] Hans Borchsenius, "Et Par Ord Om Valgene [A Few Words on the Elections]," *Emigranten*, October 27, 1862; Peter Sørensen Vig, *Danske i Krig i Og for Amerika* [*Danes Fighting in and for America*] (Omaha, NE: Axel H. Andersen, 1917). Being politically and economically savvy, and perhaps genuinely influenced by the course of events in 1860 and 1861, *Nordstjernen*'s former Democratic editors, Hans Borchsenius and Charles M. Reese, had by 1862 both volunteered for the Union Army and publicly proclaimed their support for the Republican Party's Union and anti-slavery platform.

[117] Fritz W. Rasmussen, "November 1860. Den 7de. [November 1860. The 7th]," in *State Historical Society of Wisconsin Archives Division. Rasmussen, Fritz. Additions, 1860–1919. Gren Bay Mss 4. Box 9* (Wisconsin Historical Society, 1860), 51–52; Rasmussen, *I Krig for Lincoln [To War for Lincoln]*.

[118] Rasmussen, "November 1860. Den 7de. [November 1860. The 7th]."

[119] Joseph C. G. Kennedy, ed., *Population of the United States in 1860* (Washington, DC: Government Printing Office, 1864), 533. The number of Scandinavian residents is gathered from www.ancestry.com.

While immigrants generally had to reside at least two years within the United States to be able to apply for citizenship and vote in elections, Wisconsin's State Constitution of 1848 specified that "white persons of foreign birth who have declared their intention to become citizens conformably to the laws of the United States" were eligible to vote.[120] Thus, together with his brother Jens (James), Fritz Rasmussen declared his intention to become a citizen of the United States on March 29, 1860, with the aim of getting a local position of trust in the New Denmark town election in April.[121] While Rasmussen failed to win local office in April, his declaration of intent made it possible for him to help elect the next president of the United States. As November 1860 drew nearer, New Denmark residents followed political events with increasing interest and, based on Rasmussen's diary entries, tracked local news closely.[122]

Despite Wisconsin being lauded as the possible birthplace of the Republican Party, Brown County was not a Republican stronghold.[123] The local newspaper, *Green Bay Advocate*, was edited by Charles D. Robinson, a Democrat who had served as Wisconsin's secretary of state between 1852 and 1854; Robinson strongly supported Stephen Douglas in the presidential campaign of 1860.[124]

Leading up to the election, Robinson on a weekly basis lauded Douglas and, on October 19, in an attempt to build up and Democratic groundswell enthusiasm, passionately described a Douglas campaign event in Fond du Lac where he estimated a crowd of 15,000 to be "entirely in bounds."[125] Robinson did not report the substance of Douglas' speech, but, in the week leading up to the election, the editor was much clearer about the fact that slavery was the most important election issue, and he laid out what was at stake to his readership. The *Green Bay Advocate* urged a vote for Stephen Douglas to ensure that slaves were kept in

[120] Wisconsin Constitutional Convention, *Constitution of the State of Wisconsin* (Madison, WI: Beriah Brown, 1848), 4.

[121] Fritz W. Rasmussen, "Den 31. Løverdag [March]," in *Fritz William Rasmussen Papers. Diaries, 1856–1876. Green Bay Mss 4. Box 8* (Wisconisn Historical Society, 1860).

[122] Ibid.; Rasmussen, "November 1860. Den 7de. [November 1860. The 7th]."

[123] "Brown County Election Returns," *Green Bay Advocate*, November 16, 1860. In the 1860 presidential election, Stephen Douglas received 1,272 votes to Abraham Lincoln's 874 votes in Brown County.

[124] For Charles D. Robinson's political career, see William J. Anderson and William A. Anderson, eds., *The Wisconsin Blue Book* (Madison, WI: Democrat Priting Company, 1929), 144. Also Harold Holzer, *Lincoln and the Power of the Press: The War for Public Opinion* (New York: Simon & Schuster Paperbacks, 2015), 518–519.

[125] Charles D. Robinson, "The Douglas Gathering at Fond Du Lac," *Green Bay Advocate*, October 19, 1860.

bondage, as abolition, "if the Republican platform is properly inter-preted," would mean equality for Black people, increased competition in the labor market, and a potential threat to white women.[126] "To the People of Brown County," Robinson wrote:

Large numbers of pamphlets in the French and Holland languages, have been put in circulation by Republicans in this county, so utterly untrue in their statements, and so odious in all respects, that it is important something should be said to expose them, although the time is so short before election, and the means of printing in those languages so limited.[127]

Conversely, *Emigranten*, which also circulated in New Denmark, encour-aged support at the ballot box for "freedom and equality," which, from the editor's perspective, was personified by Abraham Lincoln and Hannibal Hamlin.[128] Thus, to Scandinavian voters in New Denmark, there was a clear choice between Abraham Lincoln (advocated by *Emigranten*) and Stephen Douglas (supported by the *Green Bay Advocate*) ahead of the November 6 election.

Since the Democratic Party at its June 1860 convention had split into a Northern (Douglas) and Southern faction (John C. Breckinridge), the Republican Party's chances seemed promising by November.[129] Hence, it was a confident *Emigranten* editor who penned his last editorial on the eve of the electoral contest. Solberg predicted a resounding Republican vic-tory in the North and Midwest and projected Wisconsin to be called for Lincoln at margins even greater than would be the case in Minnesota and Iowa.[130]

[126] "To the People of Brown County," *Green Bay Advocate*, November 1, 1860.

[127] Ibid.

[128] See "National Replication Nomination," *Emigranten*, September 24, 1860. One of New Denmark's founders, Frederik Hjort, subscribed to *Emigranten* in 1860, and Fritz Rasmussen described his neighbor Lars Andersen paying a subscription to *Emigranten* in 1863 as well. See "Indbetalt På Emigr. [Paid to Emigranten]," *Emigranten*, January 7, 1861. Also Fritz W. Rasmussen, "Thursday December 31," in *Fritz William Rasmussen Papers. Diaries, 1857–1876; Account Books, 1856–1909; "Record of Skandinavians Who Have Been Settled and Lived in the Town of New Denmark, Brown County, Wisconsin." Box no. 8* (Wisconsin Historical Society, 1863).

[129] Foner, *Free Soil, Free Labor, Free Men: The Ideology of the Republican Party before the Civil War*, 307–308. Also James M. McPherson, *Abraham Lincoln* (New York: Oxford University Press, 2009), 26. Regarding the political complexity of the 1860 election, McPherson adds, "a remnant of Whigs, mostly from the border states," in an attempt to avert disunion, established the Constitutional Union party.

[130] "Præsidentvalget [The Presidential Election]," *Emigranten*, November 5, 1860. On Wisconsin's congressional districts, which were apportioned and expanded from three to six in 1861, see the Chief Clerks of the Senate and Assembly in the Year 1863, *The*

Moreover, alluding to the importance of ethnicity in politics, Solberg criticized his countryman James D. Reymert for accepting a Democratic congressional nomination. "In the Second District our sly countryman Reymert has attempted to lead 5,000 Norwegian Lincoln-men astray against their better judgement in a manner that is a poor example to follow," *Emigranten*'s editor wrote.[131] Solberg feared that Reymert's Norwegian origin could lead Scandinavian voters to abandon Lincoln and the Republicans at the national and state levels in favor of a fellow countryman regardless of his political views. However, Solberg's fear proved unfounded. In Wisconsin, Abraham Lincoln won a clear victory with a majority of over 20,000 votes, and Scandinavian-born immigrants largely supported the Republican Party.[132]

In New Denmark, for example, Lincoln performed better than in the rest of Brown County, and it is likely that a sizable chunk of the Lincoln vote came from the Scandinavian residents. As we have seen, Fritz and Jens Rasmussen, along with their brother-in-law Celius Christiansen and Andrew Frederickson, supported the Republican Party.[133] Additionally, New Denmark resident Frederik Hjort was on the list of paying subscribers to the solidly Republican *Emigranten*.[134] As such, Hjort, and the neighbors he shared the newspaper with, could read Solberg's assessment of the election on November 10, where he rejoiced that

Wisconsin has elected all three Republican candidates – Potter, Hanchett and Sloan – for Congress with large majorities. Our friend Reimert, to the credit of

---

Legislative Manual of the State of Wisconsin (Madison: Atwood & Rublee, 1863), 131. Also L. D. H. Crane, *A Manual of Customs, Precedents and Forms, in the Use in the Assembly of Wisconsin* (Madison, WI: E. A. Calkins & Co., 1861), 42.

[131] "Præsidentvalget [The Presidential Election]."

[132] "Brown County Election Returns." See also "Valgene Tirsdagen Den 6te November – Et Tusinde Hurraer for Lincoln Og Hamlin [The Elections Tuesday November 6 – A Thousand Hurrahs for Lincoln and Hamlin]," *Emigranten*, November 12, 1860.

[133] Christiansen, *En Pioneers Historie (Erindringer Fra Krigen Mellem Nord Og Sydstaterne) [A Pioneer's Story: Memoirs from the War between North and South]*, 15–17. For Christiansen's naturalization information, I have used www.fold3.com. James took out his naturalization papers together with Fritz and later served in the Wisconsin Legislature for the Republican Party while Hjort was on the list of paying subscribers to the solidly Republican *Emigranten*. James E. Heg, ed., *The Blue Book of the State of Wisconsin* (Madison, WI: Democrat Printing Co., 1885), 159, 427. See as well Frederiksen, "Denmark. Brown Co. Wisc. Den 16. Februar 1861." See also Hale, "The Americanization of a Danish Immigrant in Wisconsin 1847–1872," 205–211. According to Hale, "like many other Scandinavian-Americans, he [Frederikson] declared his allegiance to the Union and supported the infant Republican party."

[134] "Indbetalt På Emigr. [Paid to Emigranten]."

the Norwegian part of the population, did not succeed in leading the Norwegian Lincoln-men away from their duty and obtain their votes. Here and there he has received up to half a dozen votes more than his party in a Norwegian township, that is all, and several places he lags behind.[135]

The election returns published by Solberg the following week seemed to validate his point about there being little Scandinavian support for an ethnic Democratic candidate. In the Norwegian townships of Perry, Springdale, and Vermont, which were located in a district won by both James D. Reymert at the congressional level and Douglas at the presidential level, there was no significant ethnic boost in votes, and the same was the case in the Republican-leaning township of Pleasant Springs, where the numbers 119 for Lincoln and seventy-five for Douglas were exactly the same as the numbers for Luther Hanchett and Reymert. All told, Reymert lost by more than 500 votes (4,797–4,210) to the Republican Hanchett in Dane County.[136]

Notably a small handful of Democratic candidates at the local county clerk level – Hans Borchsenius, Ole Heg, and Farmer Risum – all lost also, while John A. Johnsen, a Republican, won in Dane County.[137] On the topic of slavery's extension, Scandinavian immigrants likely disagreed with their Irish- and German-born counterparts. As Frederick Luebke has argued, "Lutheran and Catholic Germans in rural areas remained loyal to the Democracy in 1860, while other Protestants and the freethinking liberals were attracted to Republicanism. Irish Catholics were uniformly Democratic despite intraparty problems."[138]

Lincoln, in the the words of James McPherson, "carried every free state except New Jersey, whose electoral votes he divided with Douglas, and thereby won the election despite garnering slightly less than 40 percent of the popular votes."[139] Among the states that decided the 1860 election was Illinois.[140] On election day in Rockford, Illinois, the Swedish

---

[135] "Valgene Tirsdagen Den 6te November – Et Tusinde Hurraer for Lincoln Og Hamlin [The Elections Tuesday November 6 – A Thousand Hurrahs for Lincoln and Hamlin]."
[136] "Official Statement of Votes Cast at The Election in Dane County, November 6, 1860," *Emigranten*, November 19, 1860.
[137] "Valgene Tirsdagen Den 6te November – Et Tusinde Hurraer for Lincoln Og Hamlin [The Elections Tuesday November 6 – A Thousand Hurrahs for Lincoln and Hamlin]."
[138] Frederick C. Luebke, ed., *Ethnic Voters and the Election of Lincoln* (Lincoln: University of Nebraska Press, 1971), xxviii.
[139] McPherson, *Abraham Lincoln*, 26.
[140] Foner, *Free Soil, Free Labor, Free Men: The Ideology of the Republican Party before the Civil War*, 216. The election of 1860, Foner points out, "hinged on the states Frémont had failed to carry – New Jersey, Pennsylvania, Indiana, and Illinois."

immigrants in town, according to *Hemlandet*'s correspondent, unanimously gathered in front of the Swedish church and marched to the courthouse while cheering "hurrah" under the American and Swedish flags, "the true Republican ballot making up their only weapon," and met up with an estimated 100 members of "The Young Men's Republican Legion" voting for the first time.[141]

According to the letter-writer, every single Swede in town voted Republican and cheered in front of the courthouse, while a group of Irish immigrants left the area, remarking that "had any other nation dared to show up with their national flag it would surely have been torn apart."[142] In Red Wing, Minnesota, Swedish-born Hans Mattson remembered leading several meetings in a Republican club before the election and later posited that Scandinavians "almost to a man" were "in favor of liberty to all men" and therefore "joined the Republican party, which had just been organized for the purpose of restricting slavery."[143]

The Scandinavian vote was not decisive for the outcome of the presidential election of 1860, though ethnic scholars subsequently tried to emphasize its importance. Still, the votes that were cast by Norwegian, Swedish, and Danish immigrants did support the Republican Party with seemingly significant margins.[144]

Additionally, in Iowa, ethnically German forty-eighters such as Hans Reimer Claussen and Theodor Olshausen, who had fled Denmark after the First Schleswig War, supported the Republican Party by 1860; in the predominantly Scandinavian township of Cedar in Mitchell County, only 1.4 percent of the inhabitants voted for a Democratic candidate.[145]

In Illinois, Danish-born Ferdinand Winslöw described, on February 12, 1861, going to Springfield with the German-born Republican politician Francis Hoffman to see Lincoln. Here Winslöw was introduced to

---

[141] H., "Rockford, Ill. D. 10 Nov. 1860," *Hemlandet*, November 14, 1860.   [142] Ibid.

[143] Mattson, *Reminiscences: The Story of an Emigrant* (Saint Paul, MN: D. D. Merrill Company, 1891), 56–57.

[144] As an example of trying to prove Swedish immigrants' outsize influence on the 1860 election, see Hokanson, *Swedish Immigrants in Lincoln's Time* (New York: Arno Press, 1979), 27. According to Hokanson, "the outcome of the presidential election of 1860 hung on a very small margin. Lincoln could not have been elected without the support of the Germans and the Swedes."

[145] Thomas P. Christensen, "A German Forty-Eighter in Iowa," Annals of Iowa 26, no. 4 (1945): 248–249; George H. Daniels, "Immigrant Vote in the 1860 Election: The Case of Iowa," in *Ethnic Voters and the Election of Lincoln*, ed. Frederick C. Luebke (Lincoln: University of Nebraska Press, 1971), 126–127. See as well Walter D. Kamphoefner and Wolfgang Helbich, *Germans in the Civil War: The Letters They Wrote Home* (Chapel Hill: University of North Carolina Press, 2006), 4, 12.

Lincoln, shook his hand, and listened to the "impressive and tender" farewell address that the newly elected president gave before leaving for the White House.[146]

"I know I cried when the cars started bearing him along with his destiny and that of over thirty millions [sic] men, whose fates he was going to shape," Winslöw wrote to his wife, adding: "It was a solemn moment for me, but I have an unshaken confidence in his ability, firmness and honesty."[147]

By February 1861, Lincoln's ability to shape the country's fate was already being severely tested. Writing from New York on February 5, 1861, Denmark's acting consul general, Harald Döllner, assessed the situation in no uncertain terms. "Sir," Döllner wrote to the Minister of Foreign Affairs, C. C. Hall, "the Union of the states is virtually dissolved."[148] South Carolina, Alabama, Mississippi, Florida, Georgia, and Louisiana had broken away, and delegates were now gathered in Alabama to "form a Southern confederacy."[149] One week later, utilizing the language of the threshold principle, Döllner added that "the State of Texas, an empire within itself according to size and resources, has seceded from the Union."[150]

Two months later, Civil War broke out, and diplomatic tension ran high. In the conflict's early phase, when the loyalties of several states were still in question, American fear of foreign powers' interference was palpable. The latent or explicit fear of *Kleinstaaterei* thus hung over the State Department and left little room for error or compromise, especially in the border states.[151]

---

[146] Ferdinand S. Winslöw, "Chicago, February 12th, 1861" (transcribed letter in possession of Laura Sadovnikoff, 1861). In the evening Hoffman and Winslow dined with Carl Schurz, William Ogden, and Jonathan Scammon who all had ties to Lincoln and the Republican Party.

[147] Ibid.

[148] H[arald] Dollner, "Consulate General of Denmark. New York, 5th February 1861," in *Collection 0002. Udenrigsministeriet. 1848–1972. Depecher. Washington 1861–1862 mm. Box 155* (Copenhagen: Rigsarkivet, 1861).

[149] Ibid.

[150] H[arald] Dollner, "New York, 12th Febr. 1861," in *Collection 0002. Udenrigsministeriet. 1848–1972. Depecher. Washington 1861–1862 mm. Box 155* (Rigsarkivet, 1861).

[151] Given the political pressure generated by Civil War, it is perhaps not surprising that the Swedish consul in New York on October 22, 1861, acknowledged receipt of a letter from Secretary of State Seward telling the Swedish-Norwegian government to replace their vice-consuls in Norfolk and Baltimore respectively as they, according to the Americans, had "allowed themselves to be made mediums of private treasonable correspondence." See Claudius Habicht, "New York 22d Octobr 1861," in *M-60. Notes from the Swedish*

In Scandinavian enclaves across the Midwest, the Civil War simultaneously forced Norwegians, Swedes, and Danes to articulate in even clearer terms their understanding of American citizenship. Accordingly, Scandinavian immigrants' notions of liberty and equality in relation to upward social mobility, their notions of political competition with Irish and German immigrants, and at the highest possible level their notion of universal values in relation to the the Declaration of Independence's egalitarian ideal were put to the test when civil war broke out on April 12, 1861.[152]

Legation in the U.S. to Dept. of State, 1813–1906. Roll T3 (National Archives at College Park, 1861).

[152] On the Declaration of Independence and "the nation's implied promise to those who had been denied the rights espoused in its founding documents," see Edna Greene Medford, *Lincoln and Emancipation* (Carbondale: Southern Illinois University Press, 2015), 21, 111–112. On the the Declaration of Independence and continued belief in white superiority, see, for example, Hahn, *A Nation without Borders: The United States and Its World in an Age of Civil Wars, 1830–1910* (New York: Viking, 2016), 67–68.

PART II

CITIZENS

5

For God and Country

What Walt Whitman called the "volcanic upheaval of the nation, after that firing on the flag at Charleston" prompted a meeting in New York's Scandinavian Society in April 1861.[1] The meeting helped organize the first Scandinavian company in the Civil War and incorporate it into the First New York Infantry Regiment.[2] Company recruits elected Norwegian-born Ole Balling as captain, Danish-born Christian Christensen as first lieutenant, and Swedish-born Alfred Fredberg as second lieutenant. Both Balling and Fredberg had experience from the First Schleswig War in 1848, and Christian Christensen, the Scandinavian Society's president and the recruitment meeting organizer, seemed a natural selection, since he was "well-known among all Scandinavians in America" (see Figure 5.1).[3]

With the Scandinavian Society's host J. A. Jansen "chosen as First Sergeant," the company's leadership, representing the three Scandinavian countries, reflected the general composition of the unit. "The company now consists of approximately 80 Scandinavians evenly divided between the

---

[1] Brooks D. Simpson, Stephen W. Sears, and Aaron Sheehan-Dean, eds., *The Civil War: The First Year Told by Those Who Lived It* (New York: Library of America, 2011), 336. Ole Balling, on the other hand, wrote of drums, trumpets, and "immense crowds" in New York City after the war's outbreak. See O. P. Hansen Balling, *Erindringer Fra Et Langt Liv* [*Memories from a Long Life*] (Kristiania, S. & Jul Sørensens Bogtrykkeri, 1905), 66.

[2] "Skandinavisk Militær-Kompagni Fra New York [Scandinavian Military Company from New York]," *Emigranten*, August 12, 1861. Original article in "Skandinaverne i Nordamerika [The Scandinavians in North America]," *Dagbladet*, July 2, 1861.

[3] "Skandinavisk Militær-Kompagni Fra New York [Scandinavian Military Company from New York]."

FIGURE 5.1 Christian Christensen, president of the Scandinavian Society in New York and Civil War officer, photographed in New York early in the war. Courtesy Sayre Family Private Collection.

three countries," the unit's librarian reported back to the Copenhagen paper *Dagbladet* (The Daily).[4]

Before embarking for Newport News in Virginia on May 26, 1861, the company received a battle flag from the Swedish ladies in New York and a drum from a local Danish-born attorney, while also participating in a parade down Broadway with the rest of the First New York Regiment.[5] Shortly after arriving in camp by Fort Monroe, the First New York, along with several other New York regiments, saw action at the battle of Big

[4] Ibid.   [5] Ibid.

Bethel. The June 10 engagement ended in a Union defeat; it also prompted several letters to New York newspapers and family members back home.[6] In a letter to his mom, Danish-born Wilhelm Wermuth stressed that he had thus far escaped unscathed, but he also admitted, "I have been near our Lord a few times, I was in a pitched battle on June 10 and a man fell close to me."[7] About the war's larger implications, Wermuth added: "Now we await a big battle by Washington which will presumably settle the fate of the blacks."[8]

The topic of slavery was also important in public statements about enlistment, though reality, perhaps not surprisingly, proved more complex. In a letter dated August 22, the Scandinavian company's librarian recounted the battle of Big Bethel in *Dagbladet* and attempted to put the soldiers' motivation into words. According to the Scandinavian-born letter writer, the men greatly desired to "meet the enemy in open battle," since they had volunteered not out of "ambition or greed or other ignoble motives, but to defend and assert freedom and all human beings' equal entitlement thereto, regardless of how the skin color varies."[9]

With this statement, *Dagbladet*'s correspondent articulated support for equality and freedom as universal values worth risking one's life for, values that Scandinavian immigrants had also equated with the essence of American citizenship, and Wermuth's letter in addition demonstrated awareness that the war directly or indirectly revolved around the issue of slavery.

Though they privately expressed more pragmatic reasons for enlisting, these early Scandinavian volunteers *may* have been more idealistic in their motivations for war service than was the case for recruits who joined later in the war. According to James McPherson, this was the case for many Anglo-American soldiers, and it was certainly the way Scandinavian Civil

---

[6] See also "News from Fortress Monroe: Additional Particulars of the Fight at Big Bethel," *New York Herald*, June 14, 1861. Also John V. Quarstein, *Big Bethel: The First Battle* (Charleston, NC: History Press, 2011). On the minor role played by the First New York Regiment, see Colonel William H. Allen, "Official Report of Colonel Allen, First Regiment N. Y. V.," *New York Herald*, June 16, 1861.

[7] Wilhelm Wermuth, "Newport News 24 Sept 1861," in *Håndskriftsafdelingen. Ny Kongelig Samling 2719. II. Folio. Karl Larsen's Collection, Unused Material. Wilhelm Adolf Leopold Wermuth, USA (Soldat, guldgraver, mine-ejer)* (Copenhagen: Det Kongelige Bibliotek, 1861).

[8] Ibid.

[9] "Camp Butler, Newport News (Virginia) Den 22de August," *Dagbladet*, September 13, 1861.

War soldiers wanted their service to be remembered.[10] In several publications, Scandinavian immigrants later described themselves as having volunteered in greater proportion than did any other ethnic group in the United States.[11] The claim likely has some merit among Norwegian-Americans, who often came to America with less social and economic capital than their Swedish and Danish counterparts and settled in closer-knit rural ethnic enclaves where they likely experienced greater pressure to enlist.[12] There is, however, also ample evidence of contemporary

[10] James M. McPherson, *For Cause and Comrades: Why Men Fought in the Civil War* (New York: Oxford University Press, 1997), 5–6, 102–103.

[11] J. A. Johnson, ed., *Det Skandinaviske Regiments Historie [The Scandinavian Regiment's History]* (La Crosse: Fædrelandet og Emigrantens Trykkeri, 1869); Peter Sørensen Vig, *Danske i Krig i Og for Amerika [Danes Fighting in and for America]*,2 vols., vol. 1 (Minneapolis, MN: C. Rasmussen Company, 1907).

[12] According to the 1860 census, 5,624,065 men were of military age on the eve of the Civil War and close to 4.7 million military-age men were available for the Union Army outside of the Confederate States, but loyal Southerners, especially in the Upper South, also fought for the Union Army. According to James McPherson, it is "generally accepted" that 2.1 million men fought for the Union, and one might therefore approximate that close to 45 percent of all military-age men (2,100,000 out of 4,700,000) outside of the Confederacy served in the military. Based on census superintendent Joseph C. G. Kennedy's observation that immigrants usually arrived at an age eligible for military service in the "newly settled States of the West," and the "proportion of 'fighting men'" was generally greater there "than in the Atlantic States," one would expect close to 10,000 Norwegians, slightly more than 4,000 Swedes, and 2,000 Danes to have been eligible for military service. See Joseph C. G. Kennedy, ed., *Population of the United States in 1860* (Washington, DC: Government Printing Office, 1864), xvii; James M. McPherson, *Battle Cry of Freedom: The Civil War Era* (New York: Oxford University Press, 1988), 306–307. Extensive research by Norwegian-American volunteer researcher Jerry Rosholt has unearthed "at least 6,500 Civil War Union soldiers" born in Norway, which would mean that 65 percent of the military-age Norwegians residing in the United States in 1860 served in the army (based on no additional immigration between 1860 and 1865 and based on 22 percent military-age men, which is likely a low estimate as 56.4 percent of Norwegians emigrants were men). Yet, Rosholt at times counts soldiers born outside of Norway, and the census counts may be low given that some immigrants arrived in Canada before travelling to the Midwest. See Jerry Rosholt, *Ole Goes to War: Men from Norway Who Fought in America's Civil War* (Decorah: Vesterheim Norwegian-American Museum, 2003), 20. On the difficulty of using census counts and potential for miscalculations as well a description of Scandinavian settlement patterns, see Torben Grøngaard Jeppesen, *Danske i USA 1850–2000. En Demografisk, Social Og Kulturgeografisk Undersøgelse Af De Danske Immigranter Og Deres Efterkommere [Danes in the United States 1850–2000: A Demographic, Social and Cultural Geographic Study of the Danish Immigrants and Their Descendants]*, Odense: University Press of Southern Denmark, 2005), 43, 123–138; Torben Grøngaard Jeppesen, *Skandinaviske Efterkommere i USA [Scandinavian Descendants in America]* (Odense: Odense Bys Museer, 2010), 14–26. For Swedish soldiers, Roger Kvist arrives at slightly above 18 percent of Swedish immigrants living in Illinois, Wisconsin, Minnesota, and Iowa serving in the Union Army (2,178 service-members out of 11,786

resistance to military service among Scandinavian-born immigrants. In other words, Norwegian, Swedish, and Danish immigrants entered the military based on a complex set of motivations that was often as much about economic and political opportunity (and social perceptions of honor) as it was about love for the adopted country or anti-slavery sentiment.[13]

In New York's Scandinavian company, the early Norwegian, Swedish, and Danish volunteers did indeed publicly claim to be fighting out of idealism, and part of the reason may well have been the fact that the soldiers quickly were exposed to concrete discussions of slavery and abolition. The Union forces at Fortress Monroe were commanded by Benjamin Butler, who since May 23, 1861, had afforded runaway slaves protection within Union lines (see Figure 5.2).[14]

As Eric Foner explains, Butler claimed to be drawing on international law when designating the runaways as "contrabands," and by May 27, 1861, at least fifty local runaways "including a three-month-old infant" had sought refuge "at what blacks now called the 'freedom fort.'"[15] Thus, Scandinavian soldiers stationed around Fortress Monroe experienced first-hand the centrality of slavery to the Civil War, yet the company's two highest-ranking officers seemingly volunteered for less idealistic reasons than defending "all human beings' equal entitlement" to freedom.[16] Captain Balling (see Figure 5.3) admitted in his memoirs that he had no interest in the political questions of the day and also indicated that First Lieutenant Christensen joined the military mainly for economic

---

Swedes listed in the 1860 census) and thereby slightly more than 50 percent of military-age men. Roger Kvist, *For Adoptivlandets Och Mänsklighetens Sak: Svenskarna i Illinois Och Det Amerikanska Inbördeskriget* [*For Adopted Country and Humanity's Sake: The Swedes in Illinois and the American Civil War*] (Umeå: Norrlands universitetsförlag, 2003), 101–102. No concrete studies of Danish Civil War enlistment have been published, but thorough research by writer Leif Ernst has uncovered at least 800 names, less than 10 percent of the 9,956 Danish immigrants counted in the 1860 census but approximately 40 percent of military-age men; see Leif Ernst, e-mail to author, May 25, 2011. For the importance of recruiting and pressure at the local level, see Steven E. Woodworth, ed., *The Loyal, True, and Brave: America's Civil War Soldiers* (Wilmington, DE: Scholarly Resources Inc., 2002), 16–23.

[13] In an unpublished MA thesis, Petter Drevsland's reading of close to 100 letters from Norwegian-born soldiers also leads him to conclude that economic concerns often were among the primary factors in enlistment. See Petter Strøm Drevland, "Norwegian Immigrants in the American Civil War: Reasons for Enlistment According to the America Letters" (MA thesis: Universitetet i Oslo, 2013), 53–54.

[14] Eric Foner, *The Fiery Trial: Abraham Lincoln and American Slavery* (New York: W. W. Norton & Company, 2010), 169.

[15] Ibid., 170.   [16] "Camp Butler, Newport News (Virginia) Den 22de August."

FIGURE 5.2 Drawing by Ole Balling depicting Federal troops engaging with a blockade runner near Fort Monroe in September 1861. Courtesy of the Library of Congress.

reasons.[17] Christensen never wrote concretely about his motivation for enlisting, noting only that "Company I of 1st New York Volunteers was formed in the Scandinavian Society of New York, of which I was then (in the spring of 1861) president."[18]

Christensen's brother-in-law, Ferdinand Winslöw, however, in a private account written to his wife Wilhemina in the fall of 1861, suggested that the first lieutenant's incentive for military service was mainly economic.[19] "Christensen had to admit of all the debts that

[17] Balling, *Erindringer Fra Et Langt Liv* [*Memories from a Long Life*], 65–67.

[18] The famous Danish journalist Henrik Cavling later described Christian Christensen and other New York Scandinavians as having been carried along by "general enthusiasm for war." See Henrik Cavling, *Fra Amerika*, vol. II (Copenhagen: Gyldendalske Boghandels Forlag, 1897), 106. Balling, *Erindringer Fra Et Langt Liv* [*Memories from a Long Life*], 67. See also McPherson, *For Cause and Comrades: Why Men Fought in the Civil War*, viii. Also Anders Bo Rasmussen, "'I Long to Hear from You': The Hardship of Civil War Soldiering on Danish Immigrant Families," *The Bridge* 37, no. 1 (2014): 17–19.

[19] Henrik Cavling, *Det Danske Vestindien* [*The Danish West Indies*] (Copenhagen: Det Reitzelske Forlag, 1894), 148. See also Ferdinand Sophus Winsløw, "October 24 1861

FIGURE 5.3   A self-portrait of the colorful painter and officer Ole Balling after the Civil War. Courtesy of Marinemuseet in Norway.

bothered him," wrote Winslöw in October 1861, and Balling years later wrote that Christensen had confided in him: "My house went bankrupt yesterday, I am in dire straits and I do not know what I tomorrow shall give my family to live off of."[20]

Balling's reference to Christensen's "house" probably had to do with the Danish immigrant's position at a brokerage firm on Wall Street. According to Christensen's personal papers, he worked for Pepoon, Nazro & Co. on 82 Wall Street until the Civil War's outbreak in April 1861 but never afterward. Based on Winslöw's letter to his wife, the company founders, Marshall Pepoon and John Nazro, may have been in financial trouble – or perhaps just been disinclined to help their former employee.[21] "Papoon [sic] and Nazro promised Christensen to pay Emmy

Newtown: Christensen's House," in *Ferdinand Sophus Winslow Letters, September 1861–February 1862* (University of Iowa, Special Collections Department, 1861). Winsløw, "October 24 1861 Newtown: Christensen's House."

[20] Balling, *Erindringer Fra Et Langt Liv [Memories from a Long Life]*, 67.

[21] General C. T. Christensen, "Nogle Blade Af Mit Levnet [Some Sheets of My Life]" (Sayre family archive, Seattle, WA). See also Residents of New York City, "Cleaning the City Streets; Memorial of the Tax-Payers in Behalf of Mr. Smith and His Machines," *New York Times*, March 3, 1860.

$100 a month during his absence, but cheats and rascals as they are they have never paid the first copper yet."[22] Christensen therefore probably enlisted as much for practical reasons as idealism, and the same could be said of his brother-in-law. Though Ferdinand Winslöw also belonged to the group of early volunteers, he made it clear in a letter dated September 22, 1861, that he served as quartermaster of the 9th Iowa Infantry Regiment to avoid being drafted later and having to "go with very bad grace," thereby alluding to the importance of honor more than patriotic zeal.[23]

As it turned out, the schism between idealism and pragmatism was a recurring theme as Scandinavians in other parts of the United States pondered whether to mobilize for the Civil War. Ivar Alexander Hviid (Weid), who had received Old World military training, organized a recruitment meeting in Chicago on July 29, 1861. Weid's call in *Emigranten* was decorated by an eagle holding an "E Pluribus Unum" ribbon, under which the Danish-born immigrant wrote:

Countrymen Scandinavians!
Our adoptive fatherland is threatened by rebels who seek to overthrow the union that now for so many years has brought fortune and blessings to the country. It is every man's duty to defend the country he resides and makes a living in, and as a result we Scandinavians also have an opportunity to show the new world that we have not yet forgotten the heroism that since olden times has personified the Norseman.[24]

Weid thereby publicly appealed to a common Scandinavian ethnicity and greater American values such as the economic prosperity that Scandinavians associated with the Union and the United States' ability to create unity out of diversity. Yet, at the individual level, it was clear that Weid did not necessarily fully embrace the creed of "E Pluribus Unum." When Weid learned that his company would be incorporated into the German-led 82nd Illinois Infantry Regiment, the Danish-born captain felt such urgency to have the decision overturned that he wired the adjutant

[22] Winsløw, "October 24 1861 Newtown: Christensen's House."
[23] "Camp Union. 22 September 1861," in *Ferdinand Sophus Winslow letters, September 1861–February 1862* (University of Iowa, Special Collections Department, 1861).
[24] Ivar Alexander Weid, "Ivar Alexander Hviid," *Middelfart Avis*, September 10, 1862. Also Ivan Alexander Weid, "Landsmænd! Skandinaver! [Countrymen! Scandinavians!]," *Emigranten*, July 28, 1862. Weid's name was spelled Ivan in *Emigranten*, but his name, as evident from other records, was Ivar. See for example Otto Weid, "Los Angeles, Calif., August 7, 1930," in *Weid, Otto + Ivar, 1930–1934. Undated* (Huntington Library, 1930–1934).

general of Illinois, Allen C. Fuller, on September 13, 1862, and argued
that military and political strife originating from the Old World had been
transplanted to the United States: "I think it wrong to order my Company
into Hecker. Germans & Scandinavians never agree[.] They are national
enemies," Weid wrote.[25]

Indicating Scandinavian-born immigrants' limited political leverage,
Weid's complaint changed nothing: the Scandinavian company remained
part of the 82nd Illinois Regiment.[26] Due to their larger share of the
population, however, German immigrants had more opportunities to
enlist in ethnically uniform units and at times even refused to "offer
their Service into a Mixt Regement [sic]," as evidenced by an August 27
letter to Wisconsin's governor Alexander Randall a few months before the
German-led 9th Wisconsin Regiment was mustered into service.[27] Some
German soldiers, as Walter Kamphoefner and Wolfgang Helbich have
suggested, were therefore never part of a multiethnic Civil War crucible as
"general fraternization across ethnic lines simply did not happen."[28]
Scandinavian soldiers, on the other hand, had little choice. The majority
of Scandinavian soldiers in the Civil War served in ethnically mixed units,
and – as the example of Ivar Weid demonstrates – even units at the
company or regimental levels were part of brigades and corps that forced
Norwegians, Swedes, and Danes to interact with their fellow soldiers and
to an extent depend on them for survival.[29]

[25] Ivar A. Weid, "Springfield 13, 1862," in *Civil War Records. 82nd Infantry Regiment. Misc. Letters and Telegrams* (Illinois State Archives, 1862). Also William Burton, *Melting Pot Soldiers: The Union's Ethnic Regiments*, 2nd ed. (New York: Fordham University Press, 1998), 206. In another example of Danish-German rivalry, Danish-born Anders Madsen Smith in his memoirs wrote about sailing across the Atlantic with a German crew: "The hatred that reigned among them and my countrymen caused my stay on the ship to be far from festive. Kicks, blows and terms of abuse were the order of the day." See Anders Madsen Smith, *En Omvandrende Danskers Tildragelser Paa Jagt Efter Lykken* [*A Wandering Dane's Pursuit of Happiness*] (Minneapolis, MN, 1891), 27.

[26] Eric Benjaminson, "A Regiment of Immigrants: The 82nd Illinois Volunteer Infantry and the Letters of Captain Rudolph Mueller," *Journal of the Illinois State Historical Society* 94, no. Summer (2001): 139–143; Ivar A. Weid, "The Deceased Corporal Peter F. Lund," in *Civil War Records. 82nd Infantry Regiment. Orders & Reports* (Illinois State Archive, 1862).

[27] Charles Pauli, "Racine August 27th 1861," in *Archives Division. Wisconsin. Executive Department. Military Correspondence. Series 49. Box 10.* (Wisconsin Historical Society, 1861). See also E. B. Quiner, *Military History of Wisconsin* (Chicago, IL, 1866), 540–547.

[28] Walter D. Kamphoefner and Wolfgang Helbich, eds., *Germans in the Civil War: The Letters They Wrote Home* (Chapel Hill: University of North Carolina Press, 2006), 31–32.

[29] Burton, *Melting Pot Soldiers: The Union's Ethnic Regiments*, 232–233. Also "Oberst Hans C. Heg [Colonel Hans C. Heg]," *Fædrelandet*, August 25, 1864.

Yet in Wisconsin a concerted effort was made to raise a large-scale Nordic Civil War unit. As the summer of 1861 turned to fall and winter, community leaders constructed a pan-Scandinavian ethnic identity based on a common martial Viking past while also acknowledging the practical realities of a political spoils system tied to military service and an idealistic belief in – and duty toward defending – American values and the opportunities associated with American citizenship.[30]

On September 2, 1861, *Emigranten*'s editor Carl Fredrik Solberg reminded his readers that the Scandinavians "owe the country as much as our native-born fellow citizens do" and that since they "in every respect enjoy the same rights" they were obligated to defend the country.[31] Additionally, *Emigranten* printed a text by the Norwegian-born community leader and politician John A. Johnson, who had recruited several Scandinavian volunteers around Wisconsin to "help suppress the slaveholders' insurrection and uphold the country's constitution and laws."[32] In the following weeks, several more letters arguing for Scandinavian volunteerism and idealism appeared in *Emigranten* and simultaneously revealed the connection between recruitment and politics.

In between the practical appeals to ethnicity and the more high-minded appeals to civic nationalism, Scandinavian leaders recognized the political need to field visible Scandinavian military units in order to have political influence in the future. Solberg later remembered an important exchange to that effect with Hans Heg, likely in the late summer of 1861:

One night after I had gone to bed and fallen asleep Mr. Heg came into my room and got in bed with me and woke me up. He said he had decided to enter the military service and had come to Madison for that purpose. We stayed awake the rest of the night talking over his plans of raising a Scandinavian regiment, concerning which he was very enthusiastic. I remember he said, "The men who

---

[30] James M. McPherson, "'Two Irreconcilable Peoples'? Ethnic Nationalism in the Confederacy," in *The Civil War as Global Conflict: Transnational Meanings of the American Civil War*, edited by David T. Gleeson and Simon Lewis (Columbia: University of South Carolina Press, 2014),86–89.

[31] Carl Fredrik Solberg, "Et Skandinavisk Kompagni Af Frivillige Foreslaaet Oprettet," *Emigranten*, September 2, 1861. Also Johnson, *Det Skandinaviske Regiments Historie* [*The Scandinavian Regiment's History*], 14–16.

[32] J. A. Johnson, "Skandinavisk Kompagni," *Emigranten*, September 2, 1861.

conduct this war are going to be the men who will conduct affairs after it is over and if we are going to have any influence then we must get into the war now." He was shrewd enough to see the trend of things.[33]

Initially, Scandinavian leaders aimed even higher than a regiment. On the evening of September 15, prominent Norwegian-Americans gathered at the Capitol House hotel in the center of Madison with the goal of raising a Scandinavian brigade. Capitol House was by 1861 considered Wisconsin's finest hotel, with 120 fashionable rooms inspired by East Coast architecture, and the meeting's setting therefore indicated the Scandinavian elite's level of ambition.[34] Hans Heg was appointed the unit's commanding officer, and in the subsequent weeks the recruitment efforts were stepped up in earnest.[35] By September 25, leading Norwegians in Madison were so confident in their ability to enlist fellow Scandinavians in purely ethnic units that they wrote to the governor of Wisconsin, Alexander Randall, and informed him that "Scandinavians from different parts of this State" had resolved "to raise a Scandinavian Brigade for the war now pending in this our adopted Country."[36]

Underscoring the pragmatic aspects of Civil War enlistments, Johnson received a letter from a countryman, Bernhard J. Madson, suggesting a relatively common quid pro quo for helping to raise the desired ethnic units. On September 27, 1861, Madson assured Johnson that he had enlisted two Norwegian men and soon after wrote that he was "hard to work for the Company" and devoting his "entire time" to recruitment."[37] Madson had read in *Emigranten* that John Johnson's brother, Ole, was "commissioned as recruiting Officer," and he followed his enlistment update with a specific request: "I wish to know, if I am working for the Company for a position or not, since your brother will without doubt be elected Capt."[38] In other words, would Johnson and his brother use their

[33] Albert O. Barton, "Reminiscences of a Pioneer Editor," *NAHA Studies and Records* 1 (1926).
[34] David V. Mollenhoff, *Madison: A History of the Formative Years* (Madison: University of Wisconsin Press, 2003), 47–49.
[35] Johnson, *Det Skandinaviske Regiments Historie* [*The Scandinavian Regiment's History*], 15–17.
[36] J. A. Johnson et al., "Madison Wis Septbr 25th 1861," in *Archives Division. Wisconsin. Executive Department. Military Correspondence. Series 49. Box 11* (Wisconsin Historical Society, 1861).
[37] B. I [Bernt J.] Madson, "Cambridge 27 Sept '61," in *Johnson, John A., 1861–1866, Wis Mss 237s* (Wisconsin Historical Society, 1861). Also B. I. [Bernt J.] Madson, "Cambridge Oct. 6th '61," in ibid.
[38] "Cambridge Oct. 6th '61."

"combined influence" on Madson's behalf "for a Lieut. post?"[39] Johnson's answer, if he ever wrote one, has not been preserved among his personal papers, but Madson, despite his best efforts, never managed to rise above the rank of "sergeant" with the 15th Wisconsin.[40] Madson's lobbying did, however, underline the juxtaposition between the idealism of "upholding the country's constitution" and the practicalities of securing financially attractive leadership positions privately.[41] In another example, Hans Heg, on Monday, September 30, 1861, issued a call for Civil War service through *Emigranten* that revealed both the rhetorical idealism of citizenship duties and the political reality underlying ethnic Civil War units: "The authorities that be in this our new homeland have, as we all know, called the citizens of the country to arms to support the government in its attempt to preserve the Union and its constitution," Heg wrote.[42]

Scandinavians! Let us recognize our present position, our duties and our responsibility as we should understand them. We have still far from carried the part of the war's burdens in respect to delivering personnel as the Scandinavian population's great number here in the country oblige for us ... While the adopted citizens of other nationalities such as the Germans and Irish have put whole regiments in the field, the Scandinavians of the West have not yet sent a single complete Company of infantry to the grand Army. Must the future ask: Where were the Scandinavians, when we saved the mother country?[43]

The appeal was signed by ten prominent Scandinavian businessmen, editors, and opinion-leaders (in all, nine Norwegians and one Dane) and yielded clues to how the ethnic elite wanted Scandinavian identity to be understood in the public sphere.[44] On the one hand, Scandinavians were an exclusive group with a common language and culture competing with Germans and Irish immigrants in displays of loyalty (and by extension

---

[39] Ibid.

[40] Johnson, *Det Skandinaviske Regiments Historie [The Scandinavian Regiment's History]*, 7; Waldemar Ager, *Oberst Heg Og Hans Gutter [Colonel Heg and His Boys]* (Eau Claire, WI: Fremad Publishing Company, 1916), 274.

[41] Carl Fredrik Solberg, "Norske Militærkompagnier," *Emigranten*, September 16, 1861.

[42] Hans C. Heg et al., "Opraab [Call]," ibid., September 30. The following pages in this chapter are partly based on Rasmussen, "'Drawn Together in a Blood Brotherhood': Civic Nationalism amongst Scandinavian Immigrants in the American Civil War Crucible," *American Studies in Scandinavia* 48, no. 2 (2016): 9–26.

[43] Heg et al., "Opraab [Call]."

[44] Johnson et al., "Madison Wis Septbr 25th 1861." See also Olof Nickolaus Nelson, *History of the Scandinavians and Successful Scandinavians in the United States*, vol. I (Minneapolis, MN: O. N. Nelson, 1900), 204–214. Hans Heg, for example, was the first Scandinavian elected to statewide office.

political power); on the other hand, they were part of a greater national project with values that had by now drawn them to become citizens in an adopted homeland.[45]

As proof that these ethnic Scandinavian military units were exclusive in terms of language, *Emigranten*'s editor on October 8, 1861, published a letter by Hans Heg, who emphasized that the "Regiment's officers would be men who speak the Scandinavian languages. Thereby also giving the Scandinavian, who does not yet speak the English language, opportunity to enter into service."[46] This reference to a common Scandinavian origin and identity was a practical construction to maximize recruitment – and perhaps also a necessary one, since Yankee-Americans often were not able to tell Danes, Swedes, and Norwegians apart.[47] Consequently, the exclusive ethnic identity promoted by the Scandinavian regiment's organizers afforded non-English-speaking immigrants the opportunity to fight in the war, to ensure a monthly income, and to contribute to their adopted country maintaining a certain territorial size and certain political ideals.

Secondly, the call for volunteers introduced a political ethnicity, in which Scandinavian unity, and subtle expectations of future political power, was defined in opposition to the "other nationalities such as the Germans and Irish" that had "put whole regiments in the field."[48] Based on the writings of Heg, Solberg, and other ethnic leaders, these exclusive and political perceptions of ethnicity – exclusive ethnicity serving as a foundation for political power – outweighed the more idealistic and universal values also introduced in Heg's petition.[49]

Still, the rhetoric of universal ideals, calling attention to citizenship's duties and adherence to foundational American values of equality and liberty, echoed frequently through the pages of *Emigranten* and the

[45] Heg et al., "Opraab [Call]"; Rasmussen, "'Drawn Together in a Blood Brotherhood': Civic Nationalism amongst Scandinavian Immigrants in the American Civil War Crucible," 12–26; Milton J. Yinger, "Ethnicity," *Annual Review of Sociology* 11 (1985): 159.

[46] Heg, "Opraab [Call]." In the Scandinavian company formed in New York, "drill was conducted and commands were given in Danish," according to the unit's captain, Ole Balling. See Balling, *Erindringer Fra Et Langt Liv* [*Memories from a Long Life*], 67.

[47] Jørn Brøndal and Dag Blanck, "The Concept of Being Scandinavian-American," *American Studies in Scandinavia* 34, no. 2 (2002): 3–5.

[48] Heg et al., "Opraab [Call]."

[49] McPherson, "'Two Irreconcilable Peoples'? Ethnic Nationalism in the Confederacy," 86–89. McPherson defines American civic nationalism as a concept identified with "ideas of liberty, republicanism, manhood suffrage, equality of opportunity, and the absence of rigid class lines."

Swedish-American *Hemlandet* during the Civil War, while less idealistic
motivations appeared in private correspondence.[50]

Emigranten's editor enthusiastically backed the idea of an exclusively
Scandinavian military unit and frequently opened up his newspaper to
contributions aiding the recruitment effort while personally lauding Hans
Heg as "young, forceful and bold, proud, and unwaveringly
trustworthy."[51] Hundreds of Norwegians, a few Swedes, and approximately fifty Danes eventually accepted the call to enlist in the
Scandinavian regiment, but the pace of recruitment also made it clear
that a Scandinavian Brigade was far from realistic.[52] Despite initiating the
recruitment process in September, the regiment did not fill its ranks until
January 1862.[53] The 15th Wisconsin was eventually made up of ten
alphabetized companies with nicknames such as "St. Olaf's Rifles,"
named after the Norwegian king Olav den Hellige (Olaf the Holy), and
"Odin's Rifles," which tied Scandinavian-American recruits to a common
Viking ancestry.[54]

Similar calls for Scandinavian troops, touting a common ethnicity and
defending universal values, with the implicit acknowledgement that there
was political gain to be had from ethnic units, were published across the
Midwest in the fall of 1861 though on a smaller scale. In Illinois and
Minnesota, ethnic leaders who were not affiliated with the recruitment

[50] This complementary identity, meaning the ability to retain an "exclusive" Scandinavian
ethnic identity while still maintaining loyalty to the founding principles of the United
States, was part of the Midwest's appeal to immigrants, as it, according to Jon Gjerde,
"powerfully promoted an allegiance to American institutions" and thus stood in stark
contrast to nativist politicians' call for Anglo-American conformity based on Protestant
American culture. See Jon Gjerde, *The Minds of the West: Ethnocultural Evolution in the
Rural Middle West 1830–1917* (Chapel Hill: University of North Carolina Press, 1997), 8,
12, 59–65. On expression of dual loyalty among Irish immigrants as well, see Susannah
Ural Bruce, *The Harp and the Eagle: Irish-American Volunteers and the Union Army,
1861–1865* (New York: New York University Press, 2006), 47.
[51] Carl Fredrik Solberg, "Oberst Heg," *Emigranten*, October 7, 1861.
[52] Yet, by October 8, 1861, the idea of a "Scandinavian Brigade" was still used as a headline
in *Emigranten*, with the story noting that Captain Andrew Torkildsen was forming
a company for the brigade. See "Den Skandinaviske Brigade [the Scandinavian
Brigade]," *Emigranten*, October 7, 1861.
[53] Johnson, *Det Skandinaviske Regiments Historie [The Scandinavian Regiment's History]*,
16.
[54] Ibid. A third company was named "Wergeland's Guard," for the Norwegian writer
Henrik Wergeland, and a fourth, after Claus Clausen accepted Hans Heg's request to
become regimental chaplain, called themselves "Clausen's Guards," while others were
named "Heg's Rifles," "Norway Bear Hunters," "Scandinavian Mountaineers," and
"Rock River Rangers." See Theodore C. Blegen, "Colonel Hans Christian Heg,"
Wisconsin Magazine of History 4, no. 2 (1920): 155.

effort in Madison, Wisconsin, simultaneously attempted to organize smaller ethnic companies.

Ivar Weid raised his Scandinavian company from a recruiting station in Chicago; a little further west, around Bishop Hill, Illinois, a Swedish company was organized by Captain Emil Forss, who had been an officer in the Old World, and the unit was named the "Swedish Union Guard."[55] On October 2, 1861, Forss announced the company's existence in *Hemlandet* and encouraged his countrymen to "join us" in knowing the duty that they owed to "our adopted country" and thereby "renew honor to the noble Scandinavian name."[56] Swedish-born Hans Mattson organized yet another ethnic unit around the same themes and also likely with a view to turn Civil War service into a political career.[57]

Mattson succeeded in organizing a Scandinavian company for the 3rd Minnesota Infantry Regiment, but in the end the most ambitious and influential Scandinavian ethnic turned out to be the 15th Wisconsin Regiment commanded by Colonel Hans Heg. In the fall of 1861, Heg asked Claus Clausen, his childhood pastor, to be the regiment's chaplain. According to *Emigranten*, Clausen, now forty-one years old, replied that "he regarded it as a calling that it would be his duty to accept, if it could be arranged with his congregations" around St. Ansgar in Iowa.[58]

The Danish-born chaplain's idealism and sense of duty, in some respects, however, clashed with the more practical and immediate daily concerns of the regiment's soldiers. Claus Clausen, who was commissioned on December 11, quickly realized that he faced a tall task regarding the "regiment's moral condition," where drinking and gambling were regular occurrences.[59] Underscoring the ethnic tension between

[55] Captain E. Forss, "Lista På Det Swenska Kompaniet Från Bishop Hill [Muster Roll of the Swedish Company From Bishop Hill]," *Hemlandet*, October 16, 1861. See also Ernst W. Olson, *The Swedish Element in Illinois: Survey of the Past Seven Decades* (Chicago, IL: Swedish-American Bibliographical Association, 1917), 56. According to Olson, "when the Civil War broke out a company of men at Bishop Hill had been drilling for some time under the command of Eric Forsse, formerly of the Swedish Army. The Bishop Hill Company ultimately became part of Company D, of the Fifty-seventh Regiment, Illinois Volunteer Infantry, which was mustered in Dec. 26, 1861."

[56] Forss, "Lista På Det Swenska Kompaniet Från Bishop Hill [Muster Roll of the Swedish Company From Bishop Hill]."

[57] H. Mattson, "Til Skandinaverna i Minnesota [To the Scandinavians in Minnesota]," ibid., September 11.

[58] "Det Skandinaviske Regiments Oprettelse [The Scandinavian Regiment's Creation]," *Emigranten*, November 18, 1861.

[59] Ole A. Buslett, *Det Femtende Regiment Wisconsin Frivillige [The Fifteenth Regiment Wisconsin Volunteers]* (Decorah, IA, 1894), 196.

Scandinavians and Irish immigrants, an alcohol-induced fight broke out on December 24, 1861, between the 15th and 17th Wisconsin Regiments that left several of the participants with "sore noses and black eyes."[60]

The challenge Clausen initially faced in connecting with Scandinavian-born soldiers was in some ways surprising given the theological struggle centered on slavery that raged outside Madison's Camp Randall among Scandinavian clergymen and congregations.[61] In this conflict, Clausen, who for years had worked outside the official church structure, sided more with the worldly concerns of Scandinavian congregations than with trans-planted Norwegian state-church-affiliated clergy and sparked the largest controversy in the Norwegian Synod's history.[62]

When the Civil War broke out in April of 1861, the Norwegian Synod shut down its educational activities at the German-led Concordia College in Missouri.[63] Professor Peter Lauritz (Laur.) Larsen, who was respon-sible for the Norwegian students at the educational institution in St. Louis, issued an "announcement" in *Emigranten* on May 6, 1861, explaining the decision. "[On] account of the political circumstances the faculty at Concordia College, in addition to the supervising committee, have been compelled to suspend instruction and send the students away," Professor

---

[60] Ager, *Oberst Heg Og Hans Gutter [Colonel Heg and His Boys]*, 228.

[61] Karl Jakob Skarstein, *Til Våpen for Det Nye Land: Norske Innvandrere i Den Amerikanske Borgerkrig [To Arms for the New Country: Norwegian Immigrants in the American Civil War]* (Spydeberg: J. W. Cappelens Forlag, 2001), 75–77.

[62] Brynjar Haraldsø, *Slaveridebatten i Den Norske Synode: En Undersøkelse Av Slaveridebatten i Den Norske Synode i USA i 1860-Årene Med Særlig Vekt På Debattens Kirkelig-Teologiske Aspekter [The Slavery Debate in the Norwegian Synod: A Study of the Slavery Debate in the Norwegian Synod in the United States During the 1860 Emphasizing the Debate's Church-Theological Aspects]* (Oslo: Solum Forlag, 1988), 80, 410. See also Claus L. Clausen, "Et Par Ord Til Læserne [A Few Words to the Readers]," *Emigranten*, January 30, 1852.

[63] As early as October 24, 1858, Norwegian-born Caja Munch, who was married to Pastor Peter Storm Munch, had raised some concerns about the partnership with the Missouri Synod but believed that the collaboration would only be temporary "until the Norwegians get strong enough to establish their own university." In the letter to her parents, Munch, however, articulated some uncertainty about project's potential for success: "Several Norwegian boys have already been sent down there to be educated as ministers. God alone knows how this will go. There is some fear that these ministers raised in German will not be suitable for the Norwegian people." See Caja Munch, *The Strange American Way: Letters of Caja Munch from Wiota, Wisconsin, 1855–1859. With an American Adventure Excerpts from "Vita Mea" an Autobiography Written in 1903 for His Children by Johan Storm Munch – Translated by Helene Munch and Peter A. Munch with an Essay Social Class and Acculturation by Peter A. Munch* (Carbondale: Southern Illinois University Press, 1970), 149.

Larsen wrote and asked that his mail now be sent to Madison.[64] Larsen's announcement led *Emigranten*'s editor to ask a simple, but loaded, question regarding the Norwegian pastors' position on slavery given the fact that it is "impossible for anyone at all to remain passive" at the current moment.[65]

The question was important, Solberg argued, because rumors were circulating that the Norwegian pastors exhibited pro-Southern sympathies. Solberg expressed hope that the men "to whom our future pastors' upbringing and instruction is entrusted, is sincerely and unwaveringly devoted to the Union and its government."[66] Solberg extended his political arguments with a religious one by stating that "all authority was of God" and that rebellion against the authorities therefore had to be seen as "ungodly."[67] Norwegian Synod leaders such as Pastor A. C. Preus immediately sensed the question's explosive implications and in a private letter dated May 10 warned Professor Larsen, "For God's sake," against answering publicly.[68]

Less than a month later, however, John A. Johnson revived the issue of loyalty among the Norwegian pastors when he published another piece on the topic in *Emigranten* and increased the pressure on Synod leaders. As Johnson revealed in a letter to his brother Ole on June 1, 1861, the newspaper piece and its content was no coincidence:

My leisure time has been occupied for two or three days in writing an article for the Emigranten concerning the union of our church with the Concordia College, St. Louis. I have been urged to do this and I must say also that it was strictly in accordance with my own inclinations. Perhaps you do not know that the faculty of that college are secessionists, Prof. Larson included, I think it is a great shame that the Norwegians should send their youth to such an institution to be educated. I wish to sever our connection with them, and intended to give som[e] pretty sharp

[64] Laur. Larsen, "Bekjendtgjørelse [Announcement]," *Emigranten*, May 6, 1861. See also Haraldsø, *Slaveridebatten i Den Norske Synode: En Undersøkelse Av Slaveridebatten i Den Norske Synode i USA i 1860-Årene Med Særlig Vekt På Debattens Kirkelig-Teologiske Aspekter [The Slavery Debate in the Norwegian Synod: A Study of the Slavery Debate in the Norwegian Synod in the United States During the 1860 Emphasizing the Debate's Church-Theological Aspects]*, 72.

[65] Carl Fredrik Solberg, "Concordia College," *Emigranten*, May 6, 1861.   [66] Ibid.

[67] Ibid. See Haraldsø, *Slaveridebatten i Den Norske Synode: En Undersøkelse Av Slaveridebatten i Den Norske Synode i USA i 1860-Årene Med Særlig Vekt På Debattens Kirkelig-Teologiske Aspekter [The Slavery Debate in the Norwegian Synod: A Study of the Slavery Debate in the Norwegian Synod in the United States During the 1860s Emphasizing the Debate's Church-Theological Aspects]*, 72–73.

[68] Quoted in Haraldsø, *Slaveridebatten i Den Norske Synode: En Undersøkelse Av Slaveridebatten i Den Norske Synode i USA i 1860-Årene Med Særlig Vekt På Debattens Kirkelig-Teologiske Aspekter [The Slavery Debate in the Norwegian Synod: A Study of the Slavery Debate in the Norwegian Synod in the United States During the 1860s Emphasizing the Debate's Church-Theological Aspects]*, 75, 409.

blows. How well I have succeeded others must judge. It is pretty hard work for me to write, especially in Norwegian, and I know not how the article will appear in print. The editor seems to be well satisfied with it, though he says is it most too severe in some places. I will send you a copy of the paper as soon as it is printed. I do not wish to be known as the author of the article until I am obliged to, so if anyone asks you, keep dark.[69]

Based on Johnson's letter, his response was likely solicited by *Emigranten*'s editor, and it thus provides a peek behind the scenes of the newspaper's editorial processes as well as its editor's conscious attempts to shape Scandinavian public opinion in favor of the Republican Party. J. A. Johnson's letter, signed "X" (but due to a typo published as "H."), appeared in *Emigranten* on June 3, 1861, and added fuel to a smoldering conflict.[70] The rumor that "the faculty at Concordia College was made up of Secessionists or at least men who sympathized with the Secessionists" could only be rebutted by "a denial from one of the Concordia educators themselves," the correspondent argued.[71] "Professor Larsen has been asked by *Emigranten* to explain the issue as a whole and his silence can only be interpreted as a complete confirmation of the rumor's veracity."[72]

To defend secession, Johnson continued, the rebels presented two main arguments: "1) that Slavery is not a sin; 2) that resisting the execution of the United States' legislation in the slave states is not a sin"; the Scandinavian clergy's position on those two assertions was important for the congregations and the ethnic community to know about, Johnson wrote.[73]

Regarding the first argument, Johnson asserted that for centuries slavery had been considered sinful throughout the civilized world: "England, Denmark, and Holland have through great sacrifice and effort set free the slaves in their possessions," and in the North not "one in a hundred" would deny that slavery is a "boundless abomination."[74]

Johnson invoked the founding fathers' idea that "all men are created equal"; regarding the second argument, the Norwegian-born immigrant noted that all government officials took the oath to uphold the Constitution and that the same was true for immigrants wishing to

---

[69] John A. Johnson, "Madison June 1st 1861," in *John A. Johnson Papers. P691. Box 1* (Norwegian-American Historical Association, 1861).

[70] H., "Concordia College Og Oprøret [Concordia College and the Rebellion]," *Emigranten*, June 3, 1861. See also the reply to Johnson the following week where the *Emigranten*'s editor clarified the typo. Jacob Nielsen, ibid., June 10,.

[71] H., "Concordia College Og Oprøret [Concordia College and the Rebellion]."   [72] Ibid.

[73] Ibid.   [74] Ibid.

become American citizens.[75] Consequently, Johnson argued, the Constitution and the officials elected to uphold it should supersede any authority claimed by local or state governments. Yet defenders of the Constitution in the South "were punished with the most outrageous and painful death."[76]

The idea that dissenters in the South were in grave danger found expression on several other occasions during the war's early months and often with a certain narrative hyperbole.[77] If individual states within the Union were able to undermine the national government's authority, contrary to the way societies had been organized in the Western world for ages, the consequences could be severe, Johnson warned. "What would the result be, in case a state had the right to secede at its pleasure? If South Carolina has this right then all other states has it and we could soon have 34 governments instead of 1," Johnson wrote in language indicating threshold principle worries.[78]

It was therefore apparent that the Scandinavian community's position on such matters, not least the influential clergy's, had to be clarified. "We have, in good faith, sent our youth down there to be trained as pastors without knowing that we exposed them to influence of the secessionists' poisonous opinions," Johnson charged and encouraged the Norwegian Synod leaders to sever their ties to the Missouri Synod and create their own institution of learning.[79]

---

[75] Ibid.   [76] Ibid.

[77] As early as January 7, 1861, *Emigranten* published a letter that connected the nation's founding ideals, such as freedom of speech, to threats of violence in the South. "Mr Editor," the letter writer began, "No matter how much I would like to read 'Emigranten' you will realize the reason for my cancellation. I have chosen Texas as my home and am well pleased with this. Concerning the important political question [slavery] I believe that 'Emigranten' has the moral law on its side, but you know how that resonates in a slave state and it often occurs that the Americans, through [different] individuals, learn of the newspaper's political content and thereby one is subject to harassment that might otherwise have been avoided. I am, by the way, against the expansion of slavery and have always thought of it as a moral evil for all of society." See "'Emigranten' i Texas," ibid., January 7. Also a Danish newspaper on July 4, 1861, published an account in which the correspondent alleged he had spoken to "a man, A Dane," from Alabama, who said "that hangings and killings, were the order of the day; if one uttered at single word that indicated sympathy for the North, death was certain." H. L. P., "Amerika [America]," *Lolland-Falsters Stiftstidende*, July 4, 1861.

[78] H., "Concordia College Og Oprøret [Concordia College and the Rebellion]."

[79] Ibid. Also Haraldsø, *Slaveridebatten i Den Norske Synode: En Undersøkelse Av Slaveridebatten i Den Norske Synode i USA i 1860-Årene Med Særlig Vekt På Debattens Kirkelig-Teologiske Aspekter [The Slavery Debate in the Norwegian Synod: A Study of the Slavery Debate in the Norwegian Synod in the United*

The week after Johnson's piece was published in *Emigranten* a self-proclaimed Scandinavian Democratic voter, Jacob Nielsen of Janesville, Wisconsin, indicating the issue's importance to the Scandinavian immigrant community, took issue with "H"'s lack of precision regarding the concept of biblical "sin" and thereby foreshadowed a spiritual and political debate that would bedevil the Scandinavian religious community for the rest of the decade.[80]

Johnson's piece and Nielsen's reply incited Professor Larsen to make a formal statement in *Emigranten* on June 17.[81] Larsen started out by criticizing "a political paper" calling public attention to his political views on the rebellion instead of approaching him privately if it was believed that his position was detrimental to the students he was responsible for educating.[82] Larsen then proceeded to lay out his position on the two main issues on which everything else depended: "1) Slavery and 2) Rebellion or the relation to the authorities altogether."[83]

Countering Johnson's reading of the Bible passage "Do to others as you would have them do to you," Larsen argued that it was unreasonable for a beggar to expect the prosperous to share wealth in excess of alms and unreasonable for the slave to expect freedom from a master in excess of his "duty and conscience"[84] – in short, words far from ideals of equality and liberty to Scandinavian readers. Since slavery "existed among the Jews" and therefore was "allowed by God," Professor Larsen was unwilling to declare slavery sinful. "Of the numerous biblical passages proving that slavery is not a sin, I can just in all haste grasp a few out of many."[85] That slavery was not considered a sin by arguably the most prominent Scandinavian clergyman in America turned out to be a key point.[86]

States During the 1860 Emphasizing the Debate's Church-Theological Aspects] 79–80.

[80] Nielsen, "Concordia College Og Oprøret [Concordia College and the Rebellion]."

[81] Ibid., June 17.

[82] Lauritz Larsen, "Den Christne Og Politiken [The Christian and Politics]," ibid.

[83] Ibid.   [84] Ibid.   [85] Ibid.

[86] Ibid. Slavery, according to Larsen, was far more brutal among the heathen Romans and Greeks than was the case with "ancient Jewish" or "the current American" system of enslavement. Yet, even according to the New Testament it was clear to Larsen that the enslaved should "obey and honor" their masters while "slaveowners" were never compelled to "emancipate" the enslaved, only to "treat them mildly," which American slaveholders implicitly did. In relation to the current rebellions, Larsen's position was that "any rebellion is sinful," but he did not deem himself capable of judging whether secession should be deemed "rebellious." Additionally, underlining the importance of obeying one's authorities, the professor declared himself willing to go to war against the South if so ordered by the governor of Wisconsin.

To *Emigranten*'s anti-slavery editor, Larsen came dangerously close to supporting pro-slavery paternalistic arguments for the institution's benignity in relations between master and slave, thereby ignoring the injustice and by extension the violence, or threat thereof, underlying the whole system of enslavement.[87] *Emigranten*'s opinion, likely voiced by Solberg, disagreed with Professor Larsen on several points and let this be known in the same issue. Describing slavery as the greatest "civic evil" in America, "an absolute enemy of our republican institutions," the newspaper argued for "inherent human sympathy and the conviction" that slavery was "detrimental both to the slaves and the country," which left little room to interpret Larsen's statement as anything other than an expression of Southern sympathy.[88] It came down to a sense of duty coupled with a sense of common human sympathy for people held in bondage, Solberg argued.

We are driven by an instinctive, spirited patriotism, which awakens in all nations in the moment of danger, the same intense patriotism that manifested itself in Norway during the war of 1814 and in Denmark during the Schleswig-Holstein rebellion of 1848 which was far more than just following from the jurists' agreement that Norway and Denmark were right.[89]

Here Solberg introduced a key difference between his text and Larsen's: the emotional and intangibly instinctive aspect of slavery's relationship to ideals of equality and its key role in the current military mobilization occurring both in both the South and the North to such an extent that the Norwegian Synod could no longer maintain its educational mission in Missouri. Where Larsen attempted to separate the issue of slavery from the recently written ordinances of secession – and to an extent succeeded

---

[87] "Concordia College Og Oprøret [Concordia College and the Rebellion]." On paternalism, see Walter Johnson, *Soul by Soul: Life inside the Antebellum Slave Market*, 4th printing ed. (Cambridge, MA: Harvard University Press, 2000), 20–30. Also Eugene D. Genovese, *Roll, Jordan, Roll: The World the Slaves Made* (New York: Vintage Books, 1974), 3–7. According to Genovese, "Southern paternalism, like every other paternalism, had little to do with Ole Massa's ostensible benevolence, kindness, and good cheer. It grew out of the necessity to discipline and morally justify a system of exploitation. It did encourage kindness and affection, but it simultaneously encouraged cruelty and hatred. The racial distinction between master and slave heightened the tension inherent in an unjust social order."

[88] "Despite the most sincere wish to infuse this declaration with its genuine meaning, we could not extrapolate anything other than the Concordia faculty being strongly inclined towards the rebellion and not at all in possession of the patriotism which should warrant them the name Union men," the *Emigranten* piece read. See "Concordia College Og Oprøret [Concordia College and the Rebellion]."

[89] Ibid.

intellectually in making the case for slavery being biblically sanctioned – the professor failed in this particular public debate unfolding in Wisconsin at a time when Scandinavian leaders were recruiting hundreds of Norwegians, Swedes, and Danes to fight against the slaveholding states, run by landholding planters, in rebellion against American authorities.[90]

In the Norwegian township of Perry, Wisconsin, the local pastor's position on the issue of slavery seemingly caused considerable tension. According to a later local account, Pastor Peter Marius Brodahl moved with his wife Johanne "into the Blue Valley parsonage in 1857," but he "endured the hostility of parishioners who disagreed with his stance that holding of slaves was not a sin" during the Civil War.[91] The account further suggested that Brodahl's elite Old World education and resulting "self-conscious" behavior set him apart from his parishioners.[92]

The class-based differences between the Norwegian Synod's leadership and pastors and parishioners not educated in the Old World was also on display after the Norwegian Synod's annual meeting on June 26, 1861. After the meeting, held in Rock Prairie, Wisconsin, where Claus Clausen preached in the 1850s, the ministers issued a joint statement trying to clarify Larsen's theological position by stating that it was "in and of itself not sinful to hold slaves."[93]

The Norwegian Synod's clergymen, many of whom had been educated at Scandinavian universities and were affiliated with the Norwegian state

[90] As Brynjar Haraldsø has noted, "Johnson introduced the question of slavery into the debate and Laur. Larsen provided a theologically substantiated refutation of Johnson's view, but this question became immaterial in this first exchange." See Haraldsø, *Slaveridebatten i Den Norske Synode: En Undersøkelse Av Slaveridebatten i Den Norske Synode i USA i 1860-Årene Med Særlig Vekt På Debattens Kirkelig-Teologiske Aspekter* [*The Slavery Debate in the Norwegian Synod: A Study of the Slavery Debate in the Norwegian Synod in the United States During the 1860s Emphasizing the Debate's Church-Theological Aspects*], 79.

[91] Mary Yeater Rathbun, ed., *The Historic Perry Norwegian Settlement* (Daleyville, WI: Perry Historical Center, 1994), 191–192. I am grateful to Ordelle G. Hill, whose ancestors lived in Dane County, for bringing this account to my attention.

[92] Ibid.

[93] See Larsen, "Den Christne Og Politiken [The Christian and Politics]." See also Rasmus Andersen, *Pastor Claus Laurits Clausen – Banebryder for Den Norske Og Danske Kirke i Amerika. Første Skandinavisk Feltpræst* [*Pastor Claus Laurits Clausen: Trailblazer for the Norwegian and Danish Church in America. First Scandinavian Chaplain*] (Blair, NE: Danish Lutheran Publishing House, 1921), 136. On the Norwegian Synod's annual meeting, see H. A. Preus, "Bekjendtgjørelse [Announcement]," *Emigranten*, May 27, 1861. "According to God's word" it was "in and of itself not sinful to hold slaves" even if it was "an evil and a punishment from God," the Norwegian Synod pastors agreed.

church, generally rejected the Grundtvigian ideas that inspired Claus Clausen, and in late June 1861 they supported a conservative interpretation of slavery's sinfulness.[94] Clausen initially agreed with the joint statement's wording, as it was required in order to be reinstated in the Synod, and he also signed a document admitting to have sinned by resigning from the Synod in the first place. Yet, when Clausen, in his own recollection, had a little more time to consider the statement, he arrived at the conclusion that "slavery in its essence and nature runs counter to the spirit of Christianity generally and the love of God and humanity [*kærlighedsbudet*] specifically and therefore had to be a sin."[95]

In this statement there were echoes of Grundtvig's Old World position on slavery. If Clausen had read Grundtvig's parliamentary debate comments made on December 14, 1848, which he conceivably could have, he would have known of Grundtvig's Old World abolitionism and his position of refuting the right "for one man to possess his fellow men with full right of property; against this I protest in my name, and in the name, I should think, of all friends of humanity."[96]

Thus, after Clausen accepted the position of military chaplain in late 1861, he became even more closely tied to the regiment organizers' public anti-slavery position, which may have contributed to him writing a piece for *Emigranten* called "Tilbagekaldelse" (retraction) on the biblical aspects of the slavery issue, which was published on December 2, 1861.[97]

In words that, to an extent, echoed Grundtvig's first 1839 statement on Danish slavery, Clausen declared "that one human being holds and uses another human being as his property forcefully under the law and that these human beings' position called slavery, is declared to be an evil in itself."[98] Moreover, Clausen, using a general argument that built on Grundtvig's 1843 Easter thoughts about a common Christian humanity

---

[94] See Larsen, "Den Christne Og Politiken [The Christian and Politics]." See also Andersen, *Pastor Claus Laurits Clausen – Banebryder for Den Norske Og Danske Kirke i Amerika. Første Skandinavisk Feltpræst [Pastor Claus Laurits Clausen: Trailblazer for the Norwegian and Danish Church in America. First Scandinavian Chaplain]*, 136.

[95] Claus Laurits Clausen, "Tilbagekaldelse [Retraction]," *Emigranten*, December 2, 1861; Claus L. Clausen, *Gjenmæle Mod Kirkeraadet for Den Norske Synode [Response to the Church Council for the Norwegian Synod]* (Chicago, IL, 1869), 20.

[96] Quoted in K. E. Bugge, "Grundtvig and the Abolition of Slavery," *Grundtvig-Studier* 56, no. 1 (2005): 183.

[97] On Clausen's offer to join the Scandinavian regiment, see "Det Skandinaviske Regiments Oprettelse [The Scandinavian Regiment's Creation]." Also Clausen, "Tilbagekaldelse [Retraction]."

[98] Ibid.

between Black and white, added that slavery "violates the order of nature and all true Christianity."[99] As a result, Clausen was once again thrown out of the Norwegian Synod when he insisted that "slavery was irrefutably sinful."[100]

Thus, by December 1861, when he published his retraction and joined the Scandinavian Regiment as chaplain, Claus Clausen was offering a religious, and somewhat revivalist, anti-slavery vision more in tune with the Scandinavian congregations where many parishioners had acquaintances, friends, or family members serving in the military to suppress the rebellion.[101]

In time this disagreement over slavery's sinfulness, instigated by anti-slavery Norwegian-born leaders, contributed to a split within the Scandinavian-American church and revealed important fault lines between the Scandinavian-American clergy tied to the Old World state churches and pastors, like Claus Clausen, who were critical of state church positions. Additionally, there was a class component tied to the debate as well. To the university-educated synod leaders, the discussion about slavery's sinfulness was primarily intellectual and secondarily political.[102]

To community leaders such as Clausen, Solberg, and Heg, who had lived in small pioneer settlements among the Norwegian Synod's laity (and seen rural hardship up close), it was clear that the issue of slavery's sinfulness was political first and intellectual second. The issue of slavery and the

---

[99] Ibid.

[100] As biographer Rasmus Andersen has noted, "A bitter feud ensued, and some pastors lost their congregations as a result of the different opinions on slavery. For the Norwegian Synod the problem was that it aligned itself with the strongly conservative German Missouri Synod, and their official view was that slavery was not sinful." See Andersen, *Pastor Claus Laurits Clausen – Banebryder for Den Norske Og Danske Kirke i Amerika. Første Skandinavisk Feltpræst* [*Pastor Claus Laurits Clausen: Trailblazer for the Norwegian and Danish Church in America. First Scandinavian Chaplain*], 132–136.

[101] This interpretation is supported by Jon Gjerde, who argues that the Concordia-trained Norwegian clergy "often accepted the conservative political stands that were consistent with those of their Missouri Synod counterparts and at odds with their parishioners." According to Gjerde, parishioners during the Civil war "allied with a minority of the clergy to oppose the Norwegian Synod's official neutrality on the slavery issue." See Jon Gjerde, "Conflict and Community: A Case Study of the Immigrant Church in the United States," *Journal of Social History* 19, no. 4 (1986): 689.

[102] Take, for example, A. C. Preus' argument in *Emigranten* on December 16 on behalf of the Norwegian Synod where he used the word "deduced" in arguing for the lack of connection between "God's word" and slavery's sinfulness. See A. C. Preus, "De Norsk-Lutherske Præsters Erklæring i Slaveri-Spørgsmaalet Nærmere Forklaret," *Emigranten*, December 16, 1861.

Republican Party's deepening fight for emancipation also raised important questions about race relations within American borders as 1861 turned to 1862, and the connection became increasingly clear to the Scandinavian-born men as they went into the field with their respective military units.

Yet, despite the synod conflict's rhetorical and practical ferocity and Clausen's anti-slavery position, it was evident as the war progressed that many of the 15th Wisconsin's leadership were more concerned with liberty and equality as it pertained to opportunities for upward social mobility among Scandinavians than they were with ensuring freedpeople an equal place in an American free labor economy.

***

On a cold, rainy Sunday evening, March 1, 1862, the Scandinavian Ladies of Chicago presented Colonel Hans Heg of the 15th Wisconsin Regiment with a beautiful blue and gold silk banner (see Figure 5.4). "For Gud og Vort Land!" read the flag's inscription (For God and Our Country), an adaptation of the well-known Old World Scandinavian rallying cry "For Gud, Konge og Fædreland" – "For God, King, and Fatherland."[103] The inscription said much about the Scandinavian ethnic elite's public perceptions of Civil War service, as the importance of religion and adherence to "Our Country," a nation where citizenship – theoretically – was based on universal ideas about equality, were recognized by the flag-makers.[104] Additionally, even as it drew inspiration from Scandinavia, the flag also demarcated the Old and the New Worlds, monarchies and republican government, by erasing the word "King" from the Scandinavian-American battle flag.[105]

Yet the Scandinavian regiment was, in part, created because of Scandinavian immigrant leaders' fear that Norwegians, Swedes, and Danes, despite the privilege afforded them due to their white skin and Protestant religion, were somewhat marginalized in relation to the American political and economic establishment, because of language barriers, lack of capital, and lack of access to a political spoils system. For example, the problem of getting Scandinavian-American officers appointed by Wisconsin's governor was described by Colonel Heg in a letter to J. A. Johnson in August 1862: "I have no particular pride of

[103] "Udlandet [Abroad]," *Aarhus Stiftstidende*, April 15, 1862.
[104] McPherson, "'Two Irreconcilable Peoples'? Ethnic Nationalism in the Confederacy," 86.
[105] The flag also alluded to a "complementary identity" as the Danish king Christian VIII, who passed away in January of 1848, had made "Gud og Fædrelandet" (God and Country) his official royal motto and a guiding light for his reign between 1839 and 1848.

FIGURE 5.4 The Scandinavian Regiment's battle flag with the inscription "For Gud og Vort Land" (For God and Our Country). Courtesy Vesterheim Norwegian-American Museum Archives.

nationality in the matter, but I know we have men amongst the Norwegians, capable of being developed – and of becoming good military officers – when modesty prevents them from gaining any position."[106]

Yet modesty did not prevent Bernt J. Madson from receiving his coveted lieutenant position; rather, it was likely the inability of the Scandinavian ethnic elite to expand the pool of available officer slots outside the 15th Wisconsin, which by 1861 was the only regiment where a Scandinavian immigrant with no military experience could realistically hope to be appointed.

As we have seen, Madson wrote J. A. Johnson in early October 1861 petitioning him to throw his and his brother Ole C. Johnson's weight behind a lieutenant appointment; even by late 1862 he was still lobbying

[106] Hans C. Heg, "Private Camp Erickson Aug 12th 1862," in *John A. Johnson Papers. P691. Box 16* (Norwegian-American Historical Association, 1862).

for a better position.[107] Writing from camp near Nashville, Tenneseee, Madson implored J. A. Johnsn to do him a favor by "seeing Gov. Solomon for me" to ask "if he could give me a Lt post in one of the new Reg'ts, Hoping you will do all you can in [sic] behalf."[108] No officer position outside, or even inside, the Scandinavian regiment materialized for Madson, however, and the same was true for the vast majority of Norwegian immigrants, by far the most important voter demographic within the Scandinavian community in Wisconsin.[109] As Olof N. Nelson admitted in his otherwise hagiographic account of the Scandinavian imprint of America, "there were, undoubtedly, Scandinavians in all the fifty-three Wisconsin regiments. But while the Norwegians supplied a large number of common soldiers, they do not appear to have distinguished themselves as officers."[110]

The Scandinavian immigrants who did receive an officer's appointment generally did so because they had been part of Scandinavian ethnic units originally or because they had Old World military experience, which was badly needed in the United States in 1861 and early 1862.

The civic nationalism publicly expressed by Scandinavian leaders in their initial calls for ethnic Civil War units was, however, mirrored and reinforced in the songs the soldiers wrote when they did take the field in 1861 and 1862.[111] Swedish-born Nels Knutson, for example, on a cold and dreary night on picket guard in Missouri, conjured up a song about brotherhood, common humanity, courage, freedom, and religion. "Now brothers and comrades," the song began, the time has come to fight for what is right and the cause of humanity in "God's honor."[112] To achieve

[107] Madson, "Cambridge Oct. 6th '61."
[108] B. I. Madson, "Camp near Nashville Tenn, Dec. 20th 1862," in *John A. Johnson Papers. P691. Box 3* (Norwegian-American Historical Association, 1862).
[109] J. A. Johnson, "Navnefortegnelse," in *Det Skandinaviske Regiments Historie* [*The Scandinavian Regiment's History*], ed. J. A. Johnson (La Crosse: Fædrelandet og Emigrantens Trykkeri, 1869), 7.
[110] Olof Nickolaus Nelson, *History of the Scandinavians and Successful Scandinavians in the United States*, vol. II (Minneapolis, MN: O. N. Nelson & Company, 1900), 121.
[111] The first song, titled "The Volunteer Soldier of the 15th Wisconsin," emphasized the duty to protect the people held dear – "all girls of the North," in fact, as they relied on the Scandinavian soldier. Yet the song also revealed the hesitation in the local community about the war service, articulated in the second verse: "Our folks at home, they thought – / The dear old folks at home – / That all their chaps, not ought to leave." See Rosholt, *Ole Goes to War: Men from Norway Who Fought in America's Civil War*, 43.
[112] Nels Knutson, "Upp Bröder Och Kamrater [Up Brothers and Comrades]," in *Copies of Letters written by Nels Knutson, Moline, IL, during the Civil War. SSIRC. SAC P:315.* (Augustana College, 1862).

this end, Knutson, admitted, hard battles would need to be fought – he invoked help from "the God of War" – but in the "land of the brave and the home of the free," that was the price to pay "for honor, duty, and country."[113]

By 1862, Scandinavian immigrants' understanding of "God and Our Country" had important implications in relation to who they perceived as being worthy of inclusion.[114] As such, the regimental flag, the public recruitment appeals, and the popular culture emanating from Scandinavian Civil War service all reinforced a sense of nationalism based on freedom expressed through commitment to a civic nationalism and often also Protestant religion. The motivations privately expressed, however, revolved around economic and political gain. Old World Scandinavian religion, Protestant and Lutheran as opposed to Irish or German Catholic, played a part in everyday demarcations of "us and them," and, despite anti-slavery rhetoric in the public sphere, everyday practices revealed less than full support for racial equality.

While Grundtvig preached the importance of viewing "all of mankind" as "children of one blood" and army chaplain Claus Clausen called the Norwegian Synod's statement on religiously sanctioned slavery "a web of sophistery," it was clear that Old World ideas of racial

---

[113] Ibid.

[114] From a Scandinavian immigrant perspective, Catholics, Jews, Mormons, and to an extent such Protestants as Baptists and Seventh-Day Adventists were viewed with suspicion even while those same immigrants simultaneously lauded the freedom of religion found in America. Until 1851, the Norwegian Constitution of May 17, 1814, excluded Jewish people from settling in the kingdom, and Scandinavian immigrants thus arrived in the United States with such legislation as part of their cultural baggage. See, for example, Olof Nickolaus Nelson, *History of the Scandinavians and Successful Scandinavians in the United States*, vol. I (Minneapolis, MN: O. N. Nelson & Company, 1900), 129–130. Article II of the Norwegian Constitution read, in part, "Jews shall be kept excluded from the kingdom." Also Julie Allen, *Danish, but Not Lutheran: The Impact of Mormonism on Danish Cultural Identity, 1850–1920* (Salt Lake City: University of Utah Press, 2017), 184–185. Anders Madsen Smith, *En Omvandrende Danskers Tildragelser Paa Jagt Efter Lykken [A Wandering Dane's Pursuit of Happiness]* (Minneapolis, 1891), 67. As nativist political appeal demonstrated, such exclusive views based on religion were not singular to Scandinavian immigrants. Both North and South stereotypes regarding Jewish immigrants and citizens existed and often persisted. The later famed general William T. Sherman wrote in 1862: "We have been annoyed by a crowd of Speculators and Jews who would sell our lives for 10 [percent] profit on a barrel of salt." See W. T. Sherman, "Memphis Aug 4th 1862," in *Samuel Ryan Curtis Papers, 1859–1863. Folder 4* (Manuscript Collections. Abraham Lincoln Presidential Library, 1862). See also Jennifer A. Stollman, *Daughters of Israel, Daughters of the South: Southern Jewish Women and Identity in the Antebellum and Civil War South* (Boston, MA: Academic Studies Press, 2013), 20–23.

superiority, coupled with the allure of land acquisition at the expense of Native people, often influenced Scandinavian-born people's worldview both at the political and the grassroots community levels.[115]

---

[115] Holm and Glenthøj, *Grundtvig: Prædikener i Vartov, 1842–43* [*Grundtvig: Sermons in Vartov, 1842–43*], vol. 5 (Copenhagen: Forlaget Vartov, 2007), 170–178. Also Clausen, "Tilbagekaldelse [Retraction]."

6

Colonization and Colonialism

The second session of the 37th United States Congress convened on Monday, December 2, 1861, the same day that Scandinavian readers out west opened *Emigranten* to Claus Clausen's retraction and an editorial focused on the state of the Union. On December 3, Lincoln's private secretary John George Nicolay "communicated" the president's first annual message to Congress and distributed the content widely.[1]

The president's message, as we have seen, underscored the threshold principle's importance in terms of population growth ("eight times as great" since the 1790 census) and acquisition of territory to "furnish homes for white men" by colonization of "colored men."[2] Lincoln's words immediately spurred a flurry of activity in Danish and American diplomatic circles and demonstrated the racial ideology of white superiority that connected colonization abroad and colonialism at home, rhetorically as well as chronologically and practically. Immediately after Lincoln's message, the Danish charge d'affaires in Washington, DC, Waldemar Raaslöff, alerted the government in Copenhagen (see Figure 6.1). In a December 6 report to the Ministry of Foreign Affairs, Raaslöff directed the ministry's attention to Lincoln's "latest message" and "the planned Colonization of Negroes" who were, or would be, "emancipated due to the progress of the military operations."[3] In Lincoln's message, Raaslöff saw opportunities to revive

---

[1] "The Proceedings of Congress," *New York Times*, December 4, 1861.

[2] Abraham Lincoln, "First Annual Message."

[3] Waldemar Raaslöff, "Kongl. Dansk Gesandtskab. Washington Den 15de December 1861 [Royal Danish Legation. Washington, December 15, 1861]," in *Collection 1175. Koloniernes centralbestyrelse kolonialkontoret. 1855–1918 Immigration af arbejdere. Immigration af arbejdere fra Italien 1884 mm. Box 910* (Copenhagen: Rigsarkivet,

FIGURE 6.1 Waldemar Raaslöff represented the Danish government in Washington, DC, in the Civil War era and helped redirect American colonization policy. But overall his tenure was met with mixed success.

previous discussions over colonization between the United States and Denmark.

Concerns over labor shortages on St. Croix, St. Thomas, and St. John had been a recurring theme since emancipation in 1848. As freedmen and women exercised their newfound, albeit limited, autonomy to seek employment opportunities away from agricultural labor, their former masters and Danish colonial administrators grew increasingly worried. In one estimate, the number of agricultural workers "decreased by one quarter" within the first five years of emancipation, and the lack of laborers in turn created economic challenges that played a role in a brief Danish parliamentary discussion of selling the West Indian "possessions" in 1852.[4] Partly due to worries related to

1861). Also Douma and Rasmussen, "The Danish St Croix Project: Revisiting the Lincoln Colonization Program with Foreign-Language Sources," *American Nineteenth Century History* 15, no. 3 (2014): 10–15. Parts of the colonization research in this chapter has been done in collaboration with Dr. Michael Douma. I am grateful for his, and *American Nineteenth Century History*'s, permission to rewrite and republish those sections here.

[4] Bent Knie Andersen, *Sukker Og Guld [Sugar and Gold]* (Copenhagen: National Museum of Denmark, 2015), 133; *Betænkning Afgiven Af Den i Henhold Til Lov Nr. 294 Af 30. September 1916 Nedsatte Rigsdagskommission Angaaende De Dansk Vestindiske Øer [Report Submitted by the Parliamentary Commission Appointed under Act of*

the threshold principle, Danish politicians voted against selling St. Thomas, St. Croix, and St. John and instead worked consciously to bolster the economic interests of the islands' elites by exploring opportunities for importing foreign labor.[5] The story was not singular to the Danish West Indies. Ever since the downfall of slavery in the Caribbean, European colonial powers had been seeking new sources of labor to remedy shortages across the area.[6] By the 1840s, Caribbean colonies, not least the British West Indies, were receiving "coolies," Asian laborers who worked for such low rates that many observers felt these laborers, themselves only partially free, were also undercutting the costs of slave labor.[7] From 1856 and forward, the St. Croix Burgher Council, a citizens body consisting of elected representatives from the island's international elite, spearheaded an effort to bring in laborers from areas as geographically diverse as "Madeira, Africa, China, and the East Indies."[8] But because the distance to the United States was much shorter and the cost of importing African

September 30, 1916 Regarding the Danish West Indian Islands] (Copenhagen: J. H. Schultz A/S, 1916).

[5] Selling the Danish West Indian islands, "a very historic part of the Danish Kingdom," according to Minster of Finance William C. E. Sponneck, would diminish the nation's territory and population ("a multitude of interests here in the mother country are connected with the colonies," argued conservative politician C. N. David), and partly based on this concern, coupled with the need for post-emancipation stability, the motion did not advance from the Danish parliament by a vote of 53–27. On the topic of Danish "subjects," Sponneck maintained: "The Danish West Indian possessions are a part and a very historic part of the Danish Kingdom . . . and even if the Danish nationality and the Danish language should not be the predominant, I think, that His Majesty's subjects out there are subjects of the Danish state just as well and just as legitimate, as we are." See "Om Fremme Af Jespersens Og Wilkens Indbragte Forslag [On Furthering Jespersen's and Wilkens' Motion]," in *Rigsdagstidende* (1852), 4057–4067.

[6] Moon-Ho Jung, *Coolies and Cane: Race, Labor, and Sugar in the Age of Emancipation* (Baltimore, MD: Johns Hopkins University Press, 2006), 17–20. See also Lomarsh Roopnarine, "The First and Only Crossing: Indian Indentured Servitude on Danish St. Croix, 1863–1868," *South Asian Diaspora* 1, no. 2 (2009). See also Sebastian N. Page, *Black Resettlement and the American Civil War* (Cambridge: Cambridge University Press, 2021), 189–192.

[7] Jung, *Coolies and Cane: Race, Labor, and Sugar in the Age of Emancipation*, 19. See also Roopnarine, "The First and Only Crossing: Indian Indentured Servitude on Danish St. Croix, 1863–1868."

[8] Peter Hoxcer Jensen, *From Serfdom to Fireburn and Strike: The History of Black Labor in the Danish West Indies, 1848–1916* (Christiansted, St. Croix: Antilles Press, 1998), 78–79. See also H[einrich] M[athias] Keutsch, "Chamberlain L. Rothe," in *Collection 1175. Koloniernes centralbestyrelse kolonialkontoret. 1855–1918 Immigration af arbejdere. Immigration af arbejdere fra Italien 1884 mm. Box 910* (Copenhagen: Rigsarkivet, 1860). See also Sharla M. Fett, *Recaptured Africans: Surviving Slave Ships, Detention,*

American laborers therefore much cheaper, the Danish government and the St. Croix Burgher Council started viewing Black laborers in the American South as a more advantageous and economically favorable way to alleviate labor shortages.[9]

Concerned with profit and with an eye toward international exchange markets, St. Croix planters and government officials by 1860 followed American news with particular interest and turned their gaze toward the large slaveholding nation to the north when the United States navy increased its anti-slaving patrols. In the spring of 1860, American naval efforts "near the Cuban coast" resulted in the seizure of three vessels, "the *Wildfire* (26 April), the *William* (9 May), and the *Bogota* (23 May)," with nearly 2,000 enslaved Africans aboard.[10] The "US Home Squadron" transported the ships to Key West in Florida, and the news of this potential labor source spread

and Dislocation in the Final Years of the Slave Trade (Chapel Hill: University of North Carolina Press, 2017), 17.

[9] The St. Croix Burgher Council, consisting of a mix of British citizens, islanders of Dutch and German descent, and Danes, embodied an international outlook and influence. Legally, the Burgher Council had little authority, but as a mouthpiece for the local planter class it played an advisory role in shaping colonization policy. In the early 1860s, Burgher Council meetings on St. Croix were often held at the governor's residence, and, according to an account from a contemporary resident, the governor worked hard alongside the Burgher Council to bring immigrants to the island and thereby further these mutual economic interests. See Ph. Rosenstand, "Fra Guvernør Birchs Dage [from Governor Birch's Days]," in *Tilskueren*, edited by M. Galschiøt (Copenhagen: Det Nordiske Forlag, 1900), 373–375; Douma and Rasmussen, "The Danish St Croix Project: Revisiting the Lincoln Colonization Program with Foreign-Language Sources," 7–11. Also Fridlev Skrubbeltrang, "Dansk Vestindien 1848–1880: Politiske Brydninger Og Social Uro [Danish West Indies 1848–1880: Political Conflict and Social Unrest]," in *Vore Gamle Tropekolonier*, edited by Johannes Brøndsted (Copenhagen: Fremad, 1967), 7–29; P. Andræ, *De Dansk-Vestindiske Øer Nærmest Med Hensyn Til Deres Nuværende Politiske Og Finantsielle Forhold* [*The Danish West Indian Islands Regarding Their Present Political and Financial Conditions*] (Copenhagen: C. A. Reitzel, 1875), 57–59. See also Ove Hornby, *Kolonierne i Vestindien* [*The West Indian Colonies*], edited by Svend Ellehøj and Kristoff Glamann (Copenhagen: Politikens Forlag, 1980), 262–273.

[10] Mrss Culbert & Finlay, "Extract of a Letter from Mrss Culbert & Finlay, Dated New York 8 June 1860 to Finlay & Co St. Croix," in *Collection 1175. Koloniernes centralbestyrelse kolonialkontoret. 1855–1918 Immigration af arbejdere. Immigration af arbejdere fra Italien 1884 mm. Box 910* (Copenhagen: Rigsarkivet, 1860). Also Douma and Rasmussen, "The Danish St Croix Project: Revisiting the Lincoln Colonization Program with Foreign-Language Sources," 8–9.

among the St. Croix planter class in June.[11] By the end of the month, St. Croix governor Vilhelm Birch encouraged the American consul on the island, Robert Finlay, to inquire if the American government, instead of sending "savages" to West Africa, could send 500 to 1,000 of the so-called recaptives to St. Croix, where they would be set to labor for five-year terms.[12]

Finlay responded positively to Birch's question and forwarded the correspondence to the American secretary of state, Lewis Cass.[13] Underscoring the situation's importance, Denmark's King Frederik VII in July personally signed a document dispatching chamberlain Louis Rothe to conduct negotiations with the American government as it debated the recaptives' fate.[14] Rothe soon proposed transferring up to 2,000 Africans to the Danish West Indies as it, in his estimation, would save the Americans the expense of a return journey, help planters on St. Croix acquire cheap labor, and provide "the African race" civilizational uplift through "the advantages" the island of St. Croix offered.[15]

[11] Culbert & Finlay, "Extract of a Letter from Mrss Culbert & Finlay, Dated New York 8 June 1860 to Finlay & Co St. Croix." Also Douma and Rasmussen, "The Danish St Croix Project: Revisiting the Lincoln Colonization Program with Foreign-Language Sources," 8–9.

[12] Culbert & Finlay, "Extract of a Letter from Mrss Culbert & Finlay, Dated New York 8 June 1860 to Finlay & Co St. Croix"; Fett, *Recaptured Africans: Surviving Slave Ships, Detention, and Dislocation in the Final Years of the Slave Trade*, 39.

[13] Vilhelm Birch, "Government House. Saint Croix, June 27th 1860," in *Collection 1175. Koloniernes centralbestyrelse kolonialkontoret. 1855–1918 Immigration af arbejdere. Immigration af arbejdere fra Italien 1884 mm. Box 910* (Copenhagen: Rigsarkivet, 1860). See also Hunter Miller, ed., *Treaties and Other International Acts of the United States of America*, vol. 8, Documents 201–240: 1858–1863 (Washington, DC: Government Printing Office, 1948); R. A. Finlay, "Consulate of the U.S. of America. St. Croix, June 29th 1860," in *RG 59. Records of the Department of State. Despatches from U.S. Consuls in St. Croix, Virgin Islands. 1791–1876.* T233-5 (National Archives at College Park, 1860).

[14] L. [Louis] Rothe, "Washington D.C. 15de Septbr 1860. Til Gouvernøren for De Dansk Vestindiske Besiddelser," in *Collection 1175. Koloniernes centralbestyrelse kolonialkontoret. 1855–1918 Immigration af arbejdere. Immigration af arbejdere fra Italien 1884 mm. Box 910* (Copenhagen: Rigsarkivet, 1860).

[15] "The Africans of the Slave Bark, Wildfire," *Harper's Weekly*, June 2, 1860. See also Ted Maris-Wolf, "'Of Blood and Treasure': Recaptive Africans and the Politics of Slave Trade Suppression," *Journal of the Civil War Era* 4, no. 1 (2014): 60. On September 14, 1860, Rothe wrote to Secretary Cass: "[I seek] an arrangement, by which Africans captured in slavers by the United States vessels of war may be transferred to the Danish Island of St. Croix." See Louis Rothe, "Washington D.C. Septbr. 14th 1860," ibid. (Rigsarkivet). Sending recaptives back across the Atlantic also seemed costly and inconvenient to American politicians like Mississippi Senator Jefferson Davis: "I have no right

In the end, however, President James Buchanan's administration chose to send the recaptives to Liberia and effectively brushed off Danish diplomatic advances with the explanation that "the laws of the United States provide a positive mode of disposal for the slave cargo of all vessels captured in the procuration of the African slave trade."[16] Absent from Buchanan's argument were considerations of the human cost. By late summer, the American government had sent 1,432 recaptives from Key West, but only 823 made it to Liberia, as many other perished from disease.[17] Danish officials' correspondence also demonstrated that economic interests and perceived racial hierarchies, more than concerns over civilizational uplift, determined their policy proposals. As Rothe wrote on September 14, 1860, the "imperfectly civilized population" of Liberia was unfit to continue receiving boatloads of "captured Africans" in need of being "reclaimed from barbarism" on its shores.[18]

Before returning home, Rothe offered his American counterparts an open invitation to reconsider the colonization offer in the future and left instructions to his successor.[19] Thus, Waldemar Raaslöff in December 1861 took it upon himself to again present Caribbean colonization plans when Abraham Lincoln brought up the issue to Congress.

In a meeting with Secretary Seward on December 14, Raaslöff posed the question of "transferring Negroes found on seized slavers" and attempted to gauge the American government's willingness to support larger colonization plans.[20] "Since the number of Negroes" who were or would be emancipated already added up "to several thousand" and was "steadily rising," Raaslöff

---

to tax our people in order that we may support and educate the barbarians of Africa," argued Davis in 1860. Quoted in Maris-Wolf, "'Of Blood and Treasure': Recaptive Africans and the Politics of Slave Trade Suppression," 67.

[16] Quoted in Douma and Rasmussen, "The Danish St Croix Project: Revisiting the Lincoln Colonization Program with Foreign-Language Sources," 9.

[17] Corey Malcolm, "Transporting African Refugees from Key West to Liberia," *Florida Keys Sea Heritage Journal* 19, no. 2 (Winter 2008/2009).

[18] Rothe,."Washington D.C. Septbr. 14th 1860."

[19] To entice Democratic support, President Buchanan at this time considered the annexation of Cuba as a slave state, but in his decision regarding recaptives the president showed little interest in potential future colonization schemes in the Caribbean. See Maris-Wolf, "'Of Blood and Treasure': Recaptive Africans and the Politics of Slave Trade Suppression," 56–66.

[20] Raaslöff, "Kongl. Dansk Gesandtskab. Washington Den 15de December 1861 [Royal Danish Legation. Washington, December 15, 1861]."

argued, it would "be impossible for the United States to provide work for them all."[21] In short, they would soon "be a big burden."[22]

Raaslöff had visited Fort Monroe in the summer of 1861 and was therefore likely familiar with runaways being considered contraband.[23] Moreover, the Union navy's capture of South Carolina's Port Royal and the surrounding Sea Islands in November 1861 made white residents leave while approximately 10,000 formerly enslaved stayed behind.[24] Raaslöff stressed that these so-called contrabands were an important part of an ideal colonization agreement:[25]

The negroes emancipated because of the war, particularly in South Carolina, are among the best and most civilized in the United States and thereby are much above the negroes found on slaveships, as these are completely raw and uncivilized, [and] do not know the language, the work and the entire way of living here and in our colonies.[26]

Seward, in Raaslöff's words, viewed the Caribbean colonization idea favorably and explicitly encouraged the Danish authorities to appoint agents, equip ships, and solicit the labor of "negroes emancipated because of war" along the eastern seaboard.[27] Seward also offered the American government's assistance, a proposal that aligned poorly with the later recollection of his opposition to colonization (always in support of "bringing men and States into the Union" and never "taking any out"),

---

[21] Ibid. See also Douma and Rasmussen, "The Danish St Croix Project: Revisiting the Lincoln Colonization Program with Foreign-Language Sources," 10–15.

[22] Raaslöff, "Kongl. Dansk Gesandtskab. Washington Den 15de December 1861 [Royal Danish Legation. Washington, December 15, 1861]." Also Douma and Rasmussen, "The Danish St Croix Project: Revisiting the Lincoln Colonization Program with Foreign-Language Sources," 10–15.

[23] "From Hon. Charles Sumner to General Butler. Washington, June 24th, 1861," in *Private and Official Correspondence of Gen. Benjamin F. Butler During the Period of the Civil War* (Norwood, MA: Plimpton Press, 1917), 159.

[24] According to James McPherson, these South Carolina contrabands "soon became part of an abolitionist experiment in freedmen's education and cotton planting with free labor." See James M. McPherson, *Battle Cry of Freedom: The Civil War Era* (New York: Oxford University Press, 1988), 371. Also Douma and Rasmussen, "The Danish St Croix Project: Revisiting the Lincoln Colonization Program with Foreign-Language Sources," 10.

[25] Raaslöff, "Kongl. Dansk Gesandtskab. Washington Den 15de December 1861 [Royal Danish Legation. Washington, December 15, 1861]."

[26] Ibid.

[27] Ibid. Raaslöff reported, "Mr. Seward [suggested] ... a suitable agent for the Danish government or the Danish West Indian authorities to sail a ship down the coast and collect emigrants to St. Croix." See also Richard H. Immerman, *Empire for Liberty: A History of American Imperialism from Benjamin Franklin to Paul Wolfowitz* (Princeton, NJ: Princeton University Press, 2012), 112.

but it aligned well with the Lincoln administration's commitment to a white man's republic in the early years of the Civil War.[28]

Colonization would remove Black people to make room for white people, and, if Danish authorities enticed a few thousand fugitive slaves settle in the West Indies, such an arrangement could potentially open the door to much larger agreements with powerful Caribbean colonial powers such as Britain, France, or Holland.[29] Consequently, Seward supported the idea.[30]

The Secretary of State answered me that this idea was actually completely new to him, as he had not thought of placing the above-mentioned emancipated slaves this way, but that he, without having presented it to the President, pronounced himself for the plan and assured me that its implementation would in the best way be supported by the United States government.[31]

According to Raaslöff's description of the December 14 meeting, Seward reiterated the importance of "completely voluntary" emigration to St. Croix but also believed that many runaway slaves would willingly work in the Caribbean and "noted that any foreign government that would try and induce free negroes to emigrate to their West Indian colonies would find the United States government ready to render all possible assistance."[32]

As a result, Danish officials for months worked hard to realize a plan that would facilitate colonization of the "most civilized" emancipated Black laborers.[33] Encouraged by Raaslöff, the governor of St. Croix Peter Birch and the island's Burgher Council quickly formulated a proposal.[34] Governor Birch shared Raaslöff's perspective on runaway "negro slaves," whom he described as a burden on the United States, and confidently wrote to Copenhagen on January 2, 1862, that the American

---

[28] Quoted in Sebastian N. Page, "'A Knife Sharp Enough to Divide Us': William H. Seward, Abraham Lincoln, and Black Colonization," *Diplomatic History* 41, no. 2 (2017): 3. Also Walter Stahr, *Seward: Lincoln's Indispensable Man* (New York: Simon & Schuster, 2012), 341. Also Foner, *The Fiery Trial: Abraham Lincoln and American Slavery*, 234. In the words of Stahr, "sending free blacks away from the United States was inconsistent with Seward's lifelong desire to encourage immigration in order to build up the American population and economy."

[29] Walter Stahr, *Seward: Lincoln's Indispensable Man*, 341. See also Douma and Rasmussen, "The Danish St Croix Project: Revisiting the Lincoln Colonization Program with Foreign-Language Sources," 4, 19.

[30] Raaslöff, "Kongl. Dansk Gesandtskab. Washington Den 15de December 1861 [Royal Danish Legation. Washington, December 15, 1861]."

[31] Ibid.   [32] Ibid.   [33] Ibid.

[34] Peter Vedel, "Udenrigsministeriet. Kjøbenhavn, Den 9 Januar 1862," ibid. (1862). Also Douma and Rasmussen, "The Danish St Croix Project: Revisiting the Lincoln Colonization Program with Foreign-Language Sources," 10.

government was considering "disposing" of "these, under present conditions, inconvenient individuals by colonizing them in Central America or the West Indies."[35]

Following a meeting on January 6, 1862, the council, according to Birch, "declared themselves willing to receive emancipated negro slaves" to the number of 300 to 500.[36] Additionally, Birch added in his letter to Raaslöff, the St. Croix planters were willing to pay the costs of the transportation, as long as they received agricultural workers who would contract to work for at least three years in sugar cultivation on the island in exchange for free housing, a ration of flour and salted fish, and pay of 95 cents per week with twenty-four work days per month.[37] In a flurry of letters aimed at the top of Lincoln's administration, Raaslöff offered free transport to St. Croix for people of "African Extraction," a work day from sun up to sun down, and, echoing Lincoln's annual message, all in an "extremely agreeable and salubrious" climate.[38]

Yet by the spring of 1862 it seemed increasingly clear that the formerly enslaved had little interest in taking advantage of the Danish proposal. African-American perspectives on colonization could be gleaned from the agent appointed to hire laborers by the St. Croix Citizen's Council on February 4, 1862.[39] The agent, George Walker, quickly ran into problems recruiting "refugees from the Southern States" and discussed the nature of his difficulties along the South Carolina Sea Islands in a letter to the

---

[35] Wilhelm Birch, "Gourvenementet for De Dansk Vestindiske Besiddelser [January 2, 1862]," in *Collection 1175. Koloniernes centralbestyrelse kolonialkontoret. 1855–1918 Immigration af arbejdere. Immigration af arbejdere fra Italien 1884 mm. Box 910* (Copenhagen: Rigsarkivet, 1862).

[36] Wilhelm Birch, "St. Croix Den 9de Januar 1862," in *Collection 1175. Koloniernes centralbestyrelse kolonialkontoret. 1855–1918 Immigration af arbejdere. Immigration af arbejdere fra Italien 1884 mm. Box 910* (Copenhagen: Rigsarkivet, 1862). See also Douma and Rasmussen, "The Danish St Croix Project: Revisiting the Lincoln Colonization Program with Foreign-Language Sources."

[37] Birch, "St. Croix Den 9de Januar 1862." See also Douma and Rasmussen, "The Danish St Croix Project: Revisiting the Lincoln Colonization Program with Foreign-Language Sources."

[38] United States Department of State, *Employment of Laborers of African Extraction in the Island of St. Croix. Correspondence between the State Department of the United States and the Chargé D'affaires of Denmark, in Relation to the Advantages Offered by the Island of St. Croix for the Employment of Laborers of African Extraction* (Washington: Government Printing Office, 1862), 4.

[39] "Extra Meeting 4 Febry 1862," in *Collection 691. St. Croix Borgerråd. 1814–1865 Forhandlings- og referatprotokoller 1861–1863. Box 45.3.14* (Copenhagen: Rigsarkivet, 1862).

St. Croix Governor's Mansion:[40] "It is more than probably that I can get the consent of Mr. Seward to go to Fort Monroe, Hatteras, or Port Royal, and hire all the negroes I can get, who will go willingly to St. Croix, as laborers," Walker wrote to Governor Birch on March 16, 1862, "but when I go to the negroes themselves to induce them to go aboard ship and go over the sea, I am afraid all the satisfaction I shall get will be 'no want to go Massa.'"[41]

Walker added:

The negroes are strongly attached to the soil where they live, and their masters tell them that the "Yankees" are making war for the purpose of catching them and selling them off to Cuba, and I fear that field hands, which are the only class you want, will have a great aversion to going on board ship, and the Government will not probably now use any coercion to induce them to go.[42]

Walker seemingly held out hope that the American government could use some form of "coercion" in the future to induce so-called contrabands to leave the country but realized it was almost impossible to attract former slaves, who would "go willingly," because of the comparatively poor labor conditions on the islands.[43] Former slaves hired by the American government in coastal Carolina made $8.00 a month, according to Walker, which was considerably more than the maximum 15 cents a day on weekdays and 20 cents on Saturdays (even when factoring in the plantation laborers' accommodations and garden plots), proposed by the Danish authorities.[44]

Additionally, given Lincoln, Seward, and several other high-ranking Republican supporters' insistence that colonization had to be voluntary, agents like Walker faced an uphill challenge since the African-American community was far from silent on the issue.[45] Despite some internal division regarding the judiciousness of colonization, Black Americans and abolitionists had resisted colonization attempts for decades.[46] On

---

[40] Ibid.; George Walker, "New York March 16th 1862," in *Collection 1175. Koloniernes centralbestyrelse kolonialkontoret. 1855–1918 Immigration af arbejdere. Immigration af arbejdere fra Italien 1884 mm. Box 910* (Copenhagen: Rigsarkivet, 1862).

[41] "New York March 16th 1862." [42] Ibid. [43] Ibid.

[44] Mitchell, *Report on Colonization and Emigration Made to the Secretary of the Interior by the Agent of Emigration* (Washington, DC: Government Printing Office, 1862), 11–15. See also Page, *Black Resettlement and the American Civil War*, 192. As Page points out, "wages in the colonies were, notoriously, one-fourth to one-half their levels in the United States."

[45] Brooks D. Simpson, Stephen W. Sears, and Aaron Sheehan-Dean, eds., "Abraham Lincoln, Annual Message to Congress, December 3, 1861," in *The Civil War: The First Year Told by Those Who Lived It* (New York: Library of America, 2011), 665–666. See also Page, *Black Resettlement and the American Civil War*, 115–125.

[46] According to Martha S. Jones, colonization was "premised in the consent of free black people," but many "viewed proposals for their removal as undercutting their status as

January 23, 1862, a little more than a month after Lincoln's annual message to Congress, freeborn abolitionist and lawyer John S. Rock pointed out the racial discrimination behind the Republican Party's course on colonization and immigration at the Annual Meeting of the Massachusetts Anti-Slavery Society. In his speech, Rock argued that sending Black Americans out of the country instead of utilizing their abilities at home, for example in armed service, undermined the nation's military strength and highlighted the racial discrimination underlying the Republican Party's homestead advocacy. "Why is it that the people from all other countries are invited to come here, and we are asked to go away?" Rock asked. "Is it to make room for the refuse population of Europe?"[47]

Given the opposition to colonization among the Black population and the sensitivity with which the issue was treated by the Lincoln administration, Raaslöff by late spring suggested an alternative to Seward.[48] In a May 26, 1862, letter, Raaslöff reiterated his preference for former slaves with agricultural experience but was prepared "to negotiate and to conclude a special convention for the transfer to that island of Africans who may hereafter be found on board of slavers captured by cruisers of the United States."[49]

While these "captured Africans," from a Danish diplomat's perspective, were far from equal to white men, he reiterated the government line that the opportunity to live with an "excellent and highly civilized colored population" could however expedite the development of these supposedly primitive workers.[50] In the Danish diplomat's mind, and in actual labor practices on St. Croix, a hierarchy of workers clearly existed. As Raaslöff informed Seward, former slaves on St. Croix were divided into first-, second-, and third-class laborers and paid accordingly based on an assessment of their knowledge, ability, physical strength, and endurance.

The captured African, who generally is almost a savage, entirely unaccustomed to and unacquainted with regular agricultural labor, would therefore quite naturally

citizens" and "organized against the ACS." See Martha S. Jones, *Birthright Citizens: A History of Race and Rights in Antebellum America* (Cambridge: Cambridge University Press, 2018), 37. See also Manisha Sinha, *The Slave's Cause: A History of Abolition* (New Haven, CT: Yale University Press, 2016), 160–166.

[47] John S. Rock, "Speech of John S. Rock, Esq., at the Annual Meeting of the Massachusetts Anti-Slavery Society, Thursday Evening, Jan. 23," *The Liberator*, February 14, 1862. See also Edna Greene Medford, *Lincoln and Emancipation* (Carbondale: Southern Illinois University Press, 2015), 57.

[48] Mitchell, *Report on Colonization and Emigration Made to the Secretary of the Interior by the Agent of Emigration*, 16.

[49] Ibid.   [50] Ibid.

and justly have to pass through the lower classes and not become entitled to form part of the first class, which involves the highest pay.[51]

Former slaves with agricultural experience, presumably elevated in their social standing through interaction with Europeans, were at the top of such a hierarchy, which explained Raaslöff's interest in South Carolina; but, realizing the short-term diplomatic and legal obstacles for such an agreement, and perhaps more importantly Black opposition to voluntary colonization, the Danish diplomat settled for what he considered third-class laborers.

Raaslöff's arguments were repeated almost word for word in newspapers such as the *National Intelligencer* after June 10, 1862, when the Government Printing Office officially disseminated the correspondence between Seward and Raaslöff.[52] On June 13, the *National Intelligencer*, based on the *Newark Daily Advertiser*, described the "New Plan of Negro Colonization," where Raaslöff's portrayal of Africans as almost savages was slightly rephrased and the Danish diplomat's position that the endeavor would be "entirely satisfactory" from a "humane and christian" perspective was relayed.[53] Moreover, in a newspaper clipping enclosed by Raaslöff in his report home on July 15, 1862, the *National Intelligencer* lauded the Danish government for its philanthropy in regard to "recaptured Africans" and hoped the Danish proposition "would receive the sanction of Congress" as it offered the "triple advantage" of "a benefit to the productive industry of a friendly Power, a benefit to the poor negroes themselves, and a saving of great expense and inconvenience to us."[54]

Demonstrating the chronological connection between issues of colonization and colonialism, Raaslöff's May 26 offers to "conclude a special convention" on "captured Africans" coincided with Scandinavian editors out west, in an echo of Republican Senator Benjamin Wade, excitedly announcing that "Land for the Landless" had triumphed over "Negroes

---

[51] Ibid.
[52] Department of State, *Employment of Laborers of African Extraction in the Island of St. Croix. Correspondence between the State Department of the United States and the Chargé D'affaires of Denmark, in Relation to the Advantages Offered by the Island of St. Croix for the Employment of Laborers of African Extraction.*
[53] "New Plan of Negro Colonization," *National Intelligencer*, June 13, 1862; "Danmark Og Vore Frigivne Slaver [Denmark and Our Freed Slaves]," *Emigranten*, July 28, 1862.
[54] W. Raaslöff, "Ligation Danoise. Washington a 15 Juilles 1862," in *Collection 0002. Udenrigsministeriet. 1848–1972 Depecher. Washington 1861–1862 mm. Box 155* (Copenhagen: Rigsarkivet, 1862).

for the Negroless" as the long-awaited Homestead Act was finally signed.[55]

Critical perspectives on homestead legislation were absent from Scandinavian newspapers, but abolitionists connected colonization and colonialism and criticized the political establishment's land distribution in favor of white Europeans, a plan that, in their view, further enabled the enslavement of "Africans in the Americas."[56]

The Danish government's active work to amend American colonization policy and Scandinavian-American immigrants' support for Indian removal indicated an acceptance of Old World racial ideology that, in part, shaped life and policy debates within American borders.[57] Danish diplomats like Birch, Rothe, and Raaslöff characterized Africans as "savages" and "barbarians"; only enslaved people who lived among white planters, such as those in South Carolina or the West Indies, were described as having civilized potential and in the American West, Norwegian, Swedish, and Danish immigrants' descriptions of Native people often echoed those of Old World colonial representatives. Designating American Indians as "wild" and "savages" helped settlers justify their pursuit of land.[58] As such, Scandinavian immigrants, as demonstrated by Karen V. Hansen, aided "the US imperial project of

---

[55] "Hjemstedbillen [The Homestead Act]," *Emigranten*, May 26, 1862; "'Land for De Landlösa' Har Wunnit En Seger Öfwer 'Negrer for De Negerlösa' ['Land for the Landless' Has Won a Victory over 'Negroes for the Negroless']," *Hemlandet*, May 28, 1862. Frustrated with the lack of progress on the Homestead Bill, Benjamin Wade asked, on February 25, 1859, "shall we give niggers to the niggerless, or land to the landless?" See Page, *Black Resettlement and the American Civil War*, 112.

[56] Natalie Joy, "The Indian's Cause: Abolitionists and Native American Rights," *Journal of the Civil War Era* 8, no. 2 (2018), 215–216. According to Joy, the anti-slavery movement drew important inspiration from opposition to dispossession of American Indians. Initially focused on resistance to President Andrew Jackson's 1830 policy of Indian removal in the South, the abolitionist movement's advocacy on behalf of American Indian rights "continued well into the 1860s." See also Steven Hahn, *A Nation without Borders: The United States and Its World in an Age of Civil Wars, 1830–1910* (New York: Viking, 2016), 45; Rock, "Speech of John S. Rock, Esq., at the Annual Meeting of the Massachusetts Anti-Slavery Society, Thursday Evening, Jan. 23."

[57] By not distancing themselves from the Danish government's pursuit of colonization policies, Scandinavian-American editors, such as *Emigranten*'s Carl Fredrik Solberg, implicitly supported them. See, for example, "Danmark Og Vore Frigivne Slaver [Denmark and Our Freed Slaves]."

[58] Hansen, *Encounter on the Great Plains: Scandinavian Settlers and Dispossession of Dakota Indians, 1890–1930* (Oxford: Oxford University Press, 2013), 5; Christiansen, *En Pioneers Historie (Erindringer Fra Krigen Mellem Nord- Og Sydstaterne) [A Pioneer's Story: Memoirs from the War between North and South]* (Aalborg: Eget forlag, 1909), 73–74.

seizing and transforming North America," even if they did not arrive as "conscious participants in a colonial scheme."[59] Yet a key policy plank in this "colonial scheme" was the Homestead Act, which for years had found explicit support among the Scandinavian elite and rural communities. The Homestead Act was an important part of their support for the Republican Party, as well as being an important part of their divergence with the abolitionist movement.[60]

To *Emigranten* the Homestead Act also had important transnational implications, as it was clear that it would "benefit the settlers by promoting the nation's development."[61] In part due to the Lincoln administration's conscious efforts, the Homestead Act attracted widespread attention in Europe, not least in Scandinavia, and thereby advanced Republican politicians' combined attempts to grow both territory and population in accordance with the threshold principle.

When Abraham Lincoln spoke in December 1861 of "furnishing homes for white men" through acquisition of territory and colonization of "colored men," he was simultaneously laying the ideological and practical groundwork for further expansion into the west.[62] The Homestead Act's passage in May 1862 (along with the Morrill Land-Grant College Act and the Pacific Railroad Act in early July) further cemented the Lincoln administration's commitment to white settlement on land previously occupied by Native people.[63]

[59] Hansen, *Encounter on the Great Plains: Scandinavian Settlers and Dispossession of Dakota Indians, 1890–1930*, 2–3.
[60] For examples of Homestead Act advocacy before, during, and after the Civil War, see "Hjemstedsloven [The Homestead Act]," *Emigranten*, March 31, 1854. Also C. Fr. Solberg, "Emigranten under Præsidentvalgkampen [The Emigrant During the Presidential Election]," ibid., July 2, 1860. Also "Hjemstedbillen [The Homestead Act]." See as well "Atter Om Homesteadloven [Once Again on the Homestead Act]," *Fædrelandet*, March 5, 1868. And "Wigtigt För 'Homesteadsettlare' i Minnesota [Important for Homestead Settlers in Minnesota]," *Hemlandet*, May 19, 1868.
[61] "Hjemstedbillen [The Homestead Act]." See also Thomas C. Mackey, ed. *A Documentary History of the Civil War Era: Legislative Achievements*, vol. 1 (Knoxville: University of Tennessee Press, 2012), 63–66.
[62] Lincoln, "First Annual Message."
[63] Stephen Kantrowitz, "'Not Quite Constitutionalized': The Meaning of 'Civilization' and the Limits of Native American Citizenship," in *The World the Civil War Made*, edited by Gregory P. Downs and Kate Masur (Chapel Hill: University of North Carolina Press, 2015), 80; Alyssa Mt. Pleasant and Stephen Kantrowitz, "Campuses, Colonialism, and Land Grabs before Morrill," *Native American and Indigenous Studies* 8, no. 1 (2021). See also Keri Leigh Merritt, *Masterless Men: Poor Whites and Slavery in the Antebellum South* (Cambridge: Cambridge University Press,

To *Emigranten* the Homestead Act's "benefit to settlers without means" was "too evident to warrant any explanation," and its importance underlined by the fact that it was translated word for word (just as an earlier homestead proposal had been as far back as 1854).[64] Similarly, *Hemlandet* praised it a victory for free labor as the landless could now become free men.[65] The Homestead Act, which allowed citizens to claim seemingly free land if they were willing to inhabit the area and improve the land for five years, thereby fulfilled a long-standing Scandinavian immigrant dream as well as a long-standing Republican goal.[66]

Scandinavian-American immigrants quickly seized on the opportunities provided by the Lincoln administration, but tellingly there was no mention of the Dakota people living in Minnesota – or indigenous people living elsewhere – when the Homestead Act's potential was espoused in Midwestern immigrant enclaves. On August 6, 1862, *Hemlandet* published a letter from Andrew Jackson, a Swedish-American pastor living in Minnesota, which drew Scandinavian immigrants' attention to homestead opportunities:

It is known that the Swedes and Norwegians have taken up a section of approximately 15 square miles that is very sparsely settled. I had hoped that our countrymen would come and settle among us to fill the empty space, especially as the Homestead Act makes it so easy to acquire land here.[67]

Time was of the essence, however. According to Jackson, who first arrived at Green Lake in 1859, Americans were eyeing the land, and so the

2017), 267–269; Foner, *Free Soil, Free Labor, Free Men: The Ideology of the Republican Party before the Civil War*, 27–29.

[64] "Hjemstedbillen [The Homestead Act]"; "'Land for De Landlösa' Har Wunnit En Seger Öfwer 'Negrer for De Negerlösa' ['Land for the Landless' Has Won a Victory over 'Negroes for the Negroless']." See also "Hjemstedsloven [The Homestead Act]." See also Foner, *Free Soil, Free Labor, Free Men: The Ideology of the Republican Party before the Civil War*, 27–29. Homestead legislation, as demonstrated by Foner, had since the mid-1850s been one of the Republican Party's preferred precepts for alleviating urban poverty and attracting white foreign-born voters. See also Mackey, *A Documentary History of the Civil War Era: Legislative Achievements*, 63–66.

[65] "'Land for De Landlösa' Har Wunnit En Seger Öfwer 'Negrer for De Negerlösa' ['Land for the Landless' Has Won a Victory over 'Negroes for the Negroless']."

[66] Mackey, *A Documentary History of the Civil War Era: Legislative Achievements*, 63–66. For a person to formally stake out a homestead claim, he or she had to be the "head of a family," at least twenty-one years of age, and "a citizen of the United States" or an immigrant who had "filed his declaration intention to become such" that had never "borne arms against the United States government or given aid and comfort to its enemies."

[67] Andrew Jackson, "Från Green Lake [from Green Lake]," *Hemlandet*, August 6, 1862.

Swedish pastor's countrymen needed to be both faster and bolder if they were to get a slice of "empty" Minnesota farmland before the Americans did.[68] Otherwise Scandinavian newcomers would have to settle even further west where there would be no pastors, no schools, and no fellow Scandinavians: in short, immigrant sheep without a herder. Hurry to Minnesota, Jackson pleaded.[69]

Pastor Jackson's 1862 letter fit a broader pattern among Nordic settlers. As we have seen, since the first Scandinavian newspaper broadside was published in the Midwest in 1847, editors and correspondents in immigrant enclaves had regularly expressed support for territorial expansion as well as general disregard for Native people's interests and rights.[70] In a letter dated November 16, 1857, Norwegian-born pastor Johan Storm Munch wrote to his brother in Norway about Minnesota extending westward "to the possessions of the Indians" and noted that the Norwegians had "occupied the best land" while only briefly alluding to American Indians' presence in travel descriptions.[71] "Here and there (although now seldom) a forlorn Indian, wrapped in his blanket, curiously stares," Munch wrote in an account of a journey down the Mississippi, which included observations from a trip inland:[72]

The road went over desolate, wild prairies, and from there into thick, dark woods, where only a couple of years ago hordes of Indians had their home. Now, however, hardly one was to be seen.[73]

Pastor Munch's wife, Caja, in a letter home relayed the idea that "here in America all were equal," yet her impressions of Native people in a letter to her parents dated October 24, 1858, made it clear that she did not consider them so.[74] Caja Munch described "Indians" as "howling like wild

---

[68] E. Norelius, "Dr Andrew Jackson," in *Korsbanneret*, ed. J. G. Dahlberg and A. O. Bersell (Rock Island: Lutheran Augustana Book Concern, 1902), 179.

[69] Jackson, "Från Green Lake [from Green Lake]."

[70] Arlow William Andersen, *The Immigrant Takes His Stand: The Norwegian-American Press and Public Affairs, 1847–1872* (Northfield, MN: Norwegian-American Historical Association, 1953) 34–51. See also "Den Enstemmige Erklæring Af De Tretten Forenede Stater Af America [The Unanimous Declaration of the Thirteen United States of America]," *Nordlyset*, July 29, 1847.

[71] Peter A. Munch, *The Strange American Way: Letters of Caja Munch from Wiota, Wisconsin, 1855–1859. With an American Adventure Excerpts from "Vita Mea" an Autobiography Written in 1903 for His Children by Johan Storm Munch – Translated by Helene Munch and Peter A. Munch with an Essay Social Class and Acculturation by Peter A. Munch* (Carbondale: Southern Illinois University Press, 1970), 114–115.

[72] Ibid.   [73] Ibid.   [74] Ibid., 11.

animals," travelling in big bands, instilling fear in Scandinavian women, and, in an anecdote about alcohol, lacking self-control.[75]

While Scandinavian-born men and women on several occasions also expressed some empathy for Native people, it was often with the assumption of inevitable Indian dispossession.[76] Thus, even Scandinavian immigrants who "wrote of shameful treatment of Indians" did not, as Betty Bergland points out, challenge "the justice of federal policies ceding land."[77] This justification of land-taking was rooted in a notion of white superiority: civilized Europeans as opposed to "half-wild children of nature."[78] In this sense, the Scandinavian immigrants' whiteness (and their Protestant religion) set them apart in their own eyes from American Indians and people of African heritage. In Jon Gjerde's words:

As they began to label themselves in relation to others, European immigrants transposed the despotism of Europe to the unfreedom of the nonwhite as a vehicle to juxtapose their freedom in the United States. As historians have illustrated time and time again, this transformation from the unfree European to the free American tragically was connected to the denial of freedom to others.[79]

Often Scandinavian immigrants did not reflect on the fact that they were settling on land formerly inhabited by American Indian tribes, though

---

[75] Ibid., 148–149. See also Betty Bergland, "Norwegian Immigrants and 'Indianerne' in the Landtaking, 1838–1862," *Norwegian-American Studies* 35 (2000): 333–334. Duus, along with women like Elise Wærenskjold and Elisabeth Koren, according to Betty Bergland conveyed "empathy in the few references to Indians found in their letters," even if the latter two only initially had few if any interactions with native bands, as American Indians had been removed from the lands they were now inhabiting. Thus, Elise Wærenskjold, who settled in Texas, wrote home in 1851 that "as yet I have not seen a single Indian," and Elisabeth Koren, married to Pastor Ulrich Vilhelm Koren, wrote home that the Indians lived in "the very westernmost part of Iowa and we in the easternmost; here it is peaceful enough."

[76] "Norwegian Immigrants and 'Indianerne' in the Landtaking, 1838–1862," 341. As Bergland has noted, Norwegian-born H. A. Preus, for example, acknowledged the tragic outcome of both Indian removal and slavery. "Among the various heathen tribes there are hardly any who have been in closer contact with Christians than Indians, but with the exception of the unhappy Negro slaves, neither is there anyone who has suffered more from the cruel treatment of Christians than Indians. They are therefore entitled to a special sympathy of Christians, a sympathy that can only be increased by a closer familiarity with this, in many respects, distinctive and excellent peoples."

[77] Ibid., 340–342.   [78] Ibid.

[79] Jon Gjerde, "'Here in America There Is Neither King nor Tyrant': European Encounters with Race, 'Freedom,' and Their European Pasts," *Journal of the Early Republic* 19, no. 4 (1999): 690.

they were clearly aware of the fact. Norwegian-born Ole Andersen, for example, hoped to attract fellow immigrants to the newly organized Dakota territory in 1861 by detailing how settlers were benefiting from native people's agricultural practices. "In the James Valley and along the Missouri wheat yields are 26 bushels an acre. Corn, grown on old Indian plantings, yields 78 bushel an acre," Andersen wrote.[80]

Also C. C. Nelson, who settled in Minnesota and recounted his experiences later in life, noted the presence of indigenous people. "We arrived on the 10th day of July, 1858, and found the country a complete wilderness, with the exception of Indians who were there only human beings around here," Nelson wrote, before adding, "We didn't find them very pleasant or agreeable."[81]

Moreover, Pastor Jackson's letter from August 6, 1862, described the area around Green Lake, Minnesota, as "empty space," despite the fact that it was located on recently ceded Native lands and located only about 30 miles east of the Yellow Medicine Agency where Dakota people retained an ever-decreasing slice of land west of the Minnesota River.[82]

Though the Homestead Act gave the impression that the "unappropriated public lands" offered were indeed uninhabited land, the situation in Minnesota proved more complex.[83] Despite negotiations throughout the 1850s with the Dakotas, which led to Indian bands ceding "millions of acres," including ancestral grounds, the American government's failure to survey reservation borders until 1858 strained the relationship between Native Americans and Northern European settlers.[84]

Tension between Dakota bands and immigrants had been on the rise at least since late 1854 when German-born settlers moved into "abandoned

---

[80] Ole Andersen, "Det Norske Settlement i Dakota [The Norwegian Settlement in Dakota]," *Emigranten*, May 20, 1861.

[81] C. C. Nelson, "Lafayette, Minnesota, April 13th, 1926," in *Dakota Conflict of 1862 Manuscripts Collection* (Saint Paul: Minnesota Historical Society, 1926). As a potential indication of the Dakota War's divisiveness for decades to come, the *Lafayette Ledger* omitted Nelson's description of American Indians as "human beings" when it published his account in 1926. See "The Lafayette Ledger. Lafayette, Minnesota. C. C. Nelson Writes Interesting History of Indian Massacre in New Sweden and Bernadotte," in *Bent Vanberg Manuscript. Mss P1104* (Northfield, MN: Norwegian-American Historical Association, 1926).

[82] Jackson, "Från Green Lake [from Green Lake]."

[83] Mackey, *A Documentary History of the Civil War Era: Legislative Achievements*, 64.

[84] Gary Anderson, *Kinsmen of Another Kind: Dakota-White Relations in the Upper Mississippi Valley, 1650–1862* (Lincoln: University of Nebraska Press, 1984), 226–237. See also Hahn, *A Nation without Borders: The United States and Its World in an Age of Civil Wars, 1830–1910*, 245–246.

summer lodges" built by Sisseton bands.[85] As described by Gary Anderson, European immigrants thereby effectively reduced the land available for hunting, and, when Dakota bands returned in the spring of 1855, newly arrived settlers were confronted by Indian women angrily pounding their fists into the ground, signifying possession of the land.[86] As more German and Scandinavian settlers moved into the river valleys, lack of cultural understanding caused ever-simmering conflict.

Most of these settlers were foreigners who knew nothing about the Indians and did not understand the importance of reciprocity in Sioux society. If they aided a passing hunting party, it was usually out of fear rather than from a willingness to share. Consequently many Dakota men came to hate their German and Scandinavian neighbors.[87]

Additionally, the Dakota community, split between farmers and hunters, disagreed on how to deal with settlers. Spurred by government agents, who handed out "annuity money and food only to Indians who showed some inclination to become farmers," a faction of Dakota tried to adopt white people's practices and appearances, but the hunter bands continued to view white people as trespassers.[88] The settlers, however, remained in place and – bolstered by a series of treaties signed between 1837 and 1858 – over time only augmented their presence.[89]

According to the 1850 census, 6,038 white people (and thirty-nine "free colored") lived in the Minnesota territory, whereas 8,000 "Sioux" were counted.[90] By 1860, however, Native people made up just 1.4 percent of Minnesota's population (2,369 out of 172,023), while foreign-born residents accounted for 34.1 percent (58,728) with 6.84 percent of the recently admitted state's population registered as Scandinavians (mainly Norwegians and Swedes).[91]

---

[85] Gary Anderson, *Kinsmen of Another Kind: Dakota–White Relations in the Upper Mississippi Valley, 1650–1862* (Lincoln: University of Nebraska Press, 1984), 240.

[86] Ibid.   [87] Ibid., 242.

[88] Gary Clayton Anderson and Alan R. Woolworth, eds., *Through Dakota Eyes: Narrative Accounts of the Minnesota Indian War of 1862* (Saint Paul: Minnesota Historical Society Press, 1988), 12.

[89] Ibid., 8–9.

[90] *The Seventh Census of the United States: 1850* (Washington, DC: Robert Amrstrong, Public Printer, 1853), ix, xciv.

[91] Joseph C. G. Kennedy, ed., *Population of the United States in 1860* (Washington, DC: Government Printing Office, 1864), xxix, 252–254. For comparative purposes, German immigrants accounted for 10.7 percent of the state's population (18,400 in all). See Jeppesen, *Danske i USA 1850–2000. En Demografisk, Social Og Kulturgeografisk Undersøgelse Af De Danske Immigranter Og Deres Efterkommere* [*Danes in the*

Thus, in the spring of 1861, when a conflict over stolen pigs from a nearby farm was on the verge of escalating to violence, the Dakota made clear that both land and animals belonged to them and that Scandinavian immigrants, in turn, belonged east of Fort Snelling. Still, settlers kept coming.[92]

By the summer of 1862, the US government's failure to deliver promised food supplies and money, along with the immigrants' encroachment, had stretched Dakota hunters' trust to the breaking point.[93] Out of desperation, a band of Dakota raided a warehouse in early August, which allegedly prompted one "Indian agent" to exclaim, "If they are hungry, let them eat grass."[94] On August 17, four Dakota hunters, in a tragic attempt to demonstrate bravery, attacked and killed five settlers in Acton, Minnesota, and in the early morning of August 18 asked the support of Little Crow, the most influential leader of the Mdewakanton band.[95] As Gary Anderson and Alan Woolworth have explained, several of the Dakota hunters who sought out Little Crow were part of an influential hunting lodge that had "increasingly become an instrument for resisting government acculturation and a forum for voicing discontent with the reservation system."[96] The hunting lodge denied admittance to Indians who, in accordance with the American government's wishes, had taken up farming, and the hunters' position was strengthened by the delay of provisions and annuities. Thus, "faced with the full force of about

United States 1850–2000. A Demographic, Social and Cultural Geographic Study of The Danish Immigrants and Their Descendants] (Odense: University Press of Southern Denmark, 2005), 131.

[92] Victor E. Lawson, Martin E. Tew, and J. Emil Nelson, *The Illustrated History of Kandiyohi County, Minnesota* (Saint Paul, MN: The Pioneer Press Manufacturing Departments, 1905), 16. Also Anderson, *Kinsmen of Another Kind: Dakota–White Relations in the Upper Mississippi Valley, 1650–1862*, 233–237. See also Hansen, *Encounter on the Great Plains: Scandinavian Settlers and Dispossession of Dakota Indians, 1890–1930*, 2–13. See also Anderson and Woolworth, *Through Dakota Eyes: Narrative Accounts of the Minnesota Indian War of 1862*, 8. I am grateful to Gunlög Fur for alerting me to this Scandinavian-Dakota encounter.

[93] Anderson, *Kinsmen of Another Kind: Dakota-White Relations in the Upper Mississippi Valley, 1650–1862*, 226–27. Also Hansen, *Encounter on the Great Plains: Scandinavian Settlers and Dispossession of Dakota Indians, 1890–1930*, 36–37. As well as Jennifer Graber, "Mighty Upheaval on the Minnesota Frontier: Violence, War, and Death in Dakota and Missionary Christianity," *Church History* 80, no. 1 (2011): 81–88.

[94] Gary Clayton Anderson, "Myrick's Insult: A Fresh Look at Myth and Reality," *Minnesota History*, no. Spring (1983): 199–201. Also Hahn, *A Nation without Borders: The United States and Its World in an Age of Civil Wars, 1830–1910*, 245.

[95] Anderson and Woolworth, *Through Dakota Eyes: Narrative Accounts of the Minnesota Indian War of 1862*, 13, 34–36.

[96] See, for example, Big Eagle's narrative of the Dakota War. Ibid.

a hundred members of the soldiers' lodge, Little Crow reluctantly agreed to join the war."[97]

Shortly thereafter, at 7 a.m., the attack, supported by the majority of Dakota men, began in response to broken treaties, hunger, and foreign-born advances onto what they considered their lands.[98] Scandinavian immigrants in the area where Pastor Jackson had advocated future settlements were among the first attacked. Soon letters recounting the trauma of violence started appearing in Scandinavian-American newspapers and reinforced widespread disdain for the Dakota Indians' humanity and their claims to land.

On August 27, 1862, two lengthy articles appeared in *Hemlandet* under a large typeset heading "Fiendtligt anfall af Indianerne i Minnesota" (Hostile attack by Indians in Minnesota) followed by the subheader that in translation read "Horrible bloodbath among the settlers on the borders." A correspondent, who was only identified as "A Minnesotan," described a community that within a month had gone from blissful ignorance of the Civil War to feeling the conflict's consequences in a shockingly concrete manner:

We did not think we were in any danger or that we should have any need for our soldiers here at home, but we were deceived. The Indians, both the Sioux and the Chippewa, have just now attacked our settlements on the border and are raging forward like wild animals, burning, stealing, and murdering anything in their path.[99]

The Dakota initially targeted settlements along the southern part of the state: New Ulm, Mankato, Fort Ridgeley, and, a little further to the north, Norway Lake. In Wisconsin, *Emigranten* in a September 1 article under the headline "Indian Unrest in Minnesota – a Norwegian-Swedish Settlement Attacked" brought the war's horrors into Scandinavian log cabins:[100]

The Norway Lake settlement is chiefly made up of Norwegian and Swedes. They were gathered in church Wednesday afternoon on August 20 and on the way back from service they were attacked by a roaming mob of Indians. Some rode ponies,

[97] Ibid.
[98] Graber, "Mighty Upheaval on the Minnesota Frontier: Violence, War, and Death in Dakota and Missionary Christianity," 88. See also Hahn, *A Nation without Borders: The United States and Its World in an Age of Civil Wars, 1830–1910*, 245.
[99] Minnesotabo, "Minnesota D. 21. Aug 1862."
[100] Graber, "Mighty Upheaval on the Minnesota Frontier: Violence, War, and Death in Dakota and Missionary Christianity," 81–89. See also Hahn, *A Nation without Borders: The United States and Its World in an Age of Civil Wars, 1830–1910*, 244–248.

other[s] were on foot and approximately fourteen people were killed and horribly mutilated ... There is now no communication between Green Lake and Norway Lake.[101]

The reports published in *Hemlandet* were equally grim. "A number of countrymen killed," read a headline on September 3, 1862, where a letter from Red Wing, Minnesota, named some of the war's casualties: "Lars Lindberg, Anders Lindberg, August Lindberg, A. B. Brobäck and their child Daniel Brobäck" among several others.[102] Andrew Jackson, who had advocated land claims in Minnesota three weeks earlier, doubted his survival when he penned a letter on August 25. "[The Indians] are on horseback and seem to be well trained in their hellish doings," Jackson wrote. "God help us."[103]

The assaults on civilians and ensuing military engagements were harrowing for all involved. Pastor Jackson, perhaps too traumatized to describe the violence, wrote to fellow pastor Erik Norelius on August 20, 1862, in the middle of the attacks, but did not devote a single word to his experience or those of congregations by Eagle Lake, Nest Lake, Wilson Prairie, or Norway Lake. Similarly, Swedish-born Erik Jönsson could apparently never bring himself to send a letter, written on March 3, 1863, to his Old World family detailing the trauma.[104]

You may have heard that the Indians have ravaged in Minnesota. They came over here on August 23, six savages on horseback, just as we were ready to drive to St. Peter ... Unfortunately, in our fear when we hid in the grass we became separated. I had son Nils and son Olof, three years old, and my wife had a little ten-month-old son [August] with her as well as the girl [Inga] and Pehr ... When the savages came back they found my wife right away and the three children lying in the grass beside their mother. When they heard the savages talking, Inga said (afterwards) that mother prayed, Lord Jesus, receive my soul into your bosom. They shot her in the chest. Then they

---

[101] "Indianerurolighederne i Minnesota – Et Norsk-Svensk Setlement Angrebet. [Indian Unrest in Minnesota – A Norwegian-Swedish Settlement Attacked]," *Emigranten*, September 1, 1862.

[102] E. Norelius, "Red Wing Minn. Den 27. Aug. 1862," *Hemlandet*, September 3, 1862.

[103] Andrew Jackson, "Från Pastor A. Jackson," ibid., September 3, 1862.

[104] Erik Jönsson, "Skandiangrof Den 3die Mars 1863 [Scandian Grove, March 3, 1863]," in *Jønsson (Johnson) Erik and Erickson, Ingar papers 1863; n.d. SSIRC SAC P:81* (Augustana College, 1863). Jönsson's letter, written to his Swedish relatives, is preserved in the archives of Augustana College in Rock Island, Illinois, but according to a note written by a Jönsson descendant, the letter was never sent.

took Inga and dragged her around in the grass until her skin as torn and lacerated from the hips to the feet, but the Lord gave her strength. She was as still as if she were dead. They felt of her pulse and opened her eyes, but when they saw no sigh of life they let her lie. Then they took Pehr a little distance away and shot him.[105]

The Dakota Indians, according to Jönsson, then burned the family home as well as that of five neighbors. Jönsson acknowledged receiving a letter from his family in Sweden in September 1862, but "because of my great sorrow and misery I neglected to write." In his postscript, Jönsson added a few words about his youngest son, who had initially survived the Dakota attack: "August, who was born October 21, 1861, became ill with measles on January 22 and died on February 2, 1863."[106]

With accounts in the vein of Jönsson's flowing east, the Scandinavian-language newspapers were soon brimming with reports of "hostile" Indian attacks – "wild animals," burning, stealing, and plundering.[107] The two main Scandinavian newspapers *Emigranten* and *Hemlandet* at times shared content and *Emigranten* on September 15, 1862, published an account from *Hemlandet* under the heading "More on the Indian Unrest in Minnesota," in which the writer described his encounter with "the savage enemy" and corroborated the main details of the letter that Erik Jönsson never sent.[108] Perhaps understandably, little attention was paid to the conflict's causes in these particular accounts.[109] When a Scandinavian correspondent, Lars Lee in South Bend just outside Mankato, finally did venture an explanation in *Emigranten*, he acknowledged that "the Sioux Indians have not received their government pensions yet," but he then added, "We now hope they will get them in lead and steel."[110]

[105] Ibid.
[106] Andrew Jackson, "Columbia, Monongalia Co Minn D. 20de Aug '62," in *Eric Norelius papers, 1851–1916. Letters 1851–1864. SSIRC MSS P:1* (Augustana College, 1862). See also Norelius, "Dr Andrew Jackson," 185. See as well Jönsson, "Skandiangrof Den 3die Mars 1863 [Scandian Grove, March 3, 1863]."
[107] Minnesotabo, "Minnesota D. 21. Aug 1862." See also Jackson, "Från Pastor A. Jackson."
[108] "Mere Om Indianer-Urolighederne i Minnesota [More on the Indian Unrest in Minnesota]," *Emigranten*, September 15, 1862.
[109] Anderson and Woolworth, *Through Dakota Eyes: Narrative Accounts of the Minnesota Indian War of 1862*, 8–13.
[110] Lars Lee, "South Bend, Blue Earth Co., Minnesota, August 22de, 1862, [South Bend, Blue Earth Co., Minnesota, August 22nd, 1862]" *Emigranten*, September 1, 1862.

To quell the Dakota uprising, President Lincoln in early September appointed Major General John Pope, fresh from defeat at the battle of Second Manassas in the war's eastern theatre. Pope's army, the Department of the Northwest, included the 3rd Minnesota Infantry Regiment with a sizeable contingent of Scandinavian soldiers (Company D), and the new commander did not hide his contempt for the enemy he was about to face. "They are to be treated as maniacs or wild beasts, and by no means as people with whom treaties or compromises can be made," Pope instructed.[111]

Within six weeks, the government forces and Minnesota militia gained the strategic upper hand. Chief Little Crow's defeat at the hands of Colonel Henry H. Sibley's troops at the battle of Wood Lake on September 23, 1862, effectively ended the conflict.[112] Close to 500 settlers, soldiers, and militia men had lost their lives along with an "unknown but substantial number" of Dakota Indians.[113] With an additional 303 Native people condemned by a military commission, it was obvious from the Minnesota settlers' perspective that many American Indians would have to pay a physical price in order for the Lincoln administration to escape paying a political price.

While subsequent interviews with Dakota Indians, mediated through, and recorded by, white missionaries, demonstrated that not everyone had taken active part in the bloodshed, Scandinavian immigrants and the American government's response did not differentiate between Dakota bands – and initially not between individual Dakota men either.[114]

[111] Major General John Pope, quoted in Hahn, *A Nation without Borders: The United States and Its World in an Age of Civil Wars, 1830–1910*, 246–247.
[112] Pelle, "Korrespondens Fra Col. Sibleys Expedition Mod Indianerna [Correspondence from Col. Sibley's Expedition against the Indians]," *Hemlandet*, October 22, 1862. See also Graber, "Mighty Upheaval on the Minnesota Frontier: Violence, War, and Death in Dakota and Missionary Christianity," 90.
[113] Anderson and Woolworth, *Through Dakota Eyes: Narrative Accounts of the Minnesota Indian War of 1862*, 1. See also Carol Chomsky, "The United States-Dakota War Trials: A Study in Military Injustice," *Stanford Law Review* 43, no. 13 (1990): 21–22. Based on varying estimates of the war's casualties, Chomsky arrives at twenty-nine Dakota warriors killed, while Isaac V. D. Heard in his 1865 account writes that the "admitted losses of the enemy in 1862" totaled forty-two. See Isaac V. D. Heard, *History of the Sioux War and Massacres of 1862 and 1863* (New York: Harper & Brothers, Publishers, 1865), 248.
[114] A. W. Williamson, "Information Got from Indian Prisoners in Camp Mcclellan in Reference to the Outbreak," in *Williamson family papers 1854–1950. Mss 122. Box 1* (Augustana College, 1863). Robert H. Caske (or Chaska), who had helped save missionary Thomas Williamson's life before seemingly reluctantly joining the Dakota war effort, was initially sentenced to death but found himself among the 260 Dakota warriors

Pope's view of American Indians as "maniacs or wild beasts" was echoed in letters from Scandinavians who survived the conflict.[115] The inhabitants of Minnesota, a loyal Republican state, for months remained so anxious that trepidation even crossed state lines to Wisconsin. Within Minnesota, fear of the "savage Indians" also crossed ethnic and political lines. The pro-Republican Scandinavian newspapers were far from the only outlets concerned with the US–Dakota War. In Brown County, the Democratic *Green Bay Advocate* expressed the same ideology of white superiority as was found in *Emigranten*, but its editor also implicitly criticized the government for lack of vigor in dealing with "the Sioux" and their "savage outbreak."[116]

In the end Lincoln, after his assistants' careful review, assented to the execution of thirty-eight Indians who were hanged on December 26, 1862, in the "largest official mass execution" in American history.[117] On December 31, 1862, Wisconsin's adjutant general, August Gaylord, submitted his annual report to the governor and tied the Dakota War directly to the need for a state militia in order to continue population growth in the region.[118]

[The Indian raid in Minnesota] also gave rise to uneasiness on our northern frontier, and for a time threatened serious consequences, the result of panic rather than of actual danger. The settlers along the frontier rushed terror stricken from their homes ... some have left entirely; preferring to sacrifice their homesteads, than to

---

pardoned by President Lincoln. Caske was removed from Mankato in Minnesota to Camp McClellan in Davenport, Iowa, after the December execution and told Thomas Williamson's son, Andrew, about his experiences when interviewed in January 1863. According to Andrew W. Williamson, Caske initially remained home (having taken up farming in the vicinity of Williamson's mission along the Yellow Medicine River) but was eventually pressured into joining the war on the Dakota side around the area of New Ulm. See also Curt Brown, "Minnesota History: Caught in the Middle of the Dakota War," *Star Tribune*, April 2, 2015.

[115] As an example, see Alan Swanson, "The Civil War Letters of Olof Liljegren," *Swedish Pioneeer Historical Quarterly* 31, no. 2 (1980): 101–104. While Liljegren, according to Swanson, was prone "to speak in extreme terms," his letters revealed the emotional frenzy brought on by the war. Liljegren supported vigilante action against the arrested Dakota Indians and did not distance himself from "secret clubs organized" in Minnesota to kill any Indian pardoned by the president.

[116] "Matters in Minnesota."

[117] Anderson, *Kinsmen of Another Kind: Dakota–White Relations in the Upper Mississippi Valley, 1650–1862*, 260. See also Hahn, *A Nation without Borders: The United States and Its World in an Age of Civil Wars, 1830–1910*, 247. See also Anderson and Woolworth, *Through Dakota Eyes: Narrative Accounts of the Minnesota Indian War of 1862*, 15.

[118] August Gaylord, *Annual Report of the Adjutant General of the State of Wisconsin for the Year 1862* (Madison: Atwood & Rublee, State Printers, 1863), 55.

remain subjects to continued fear. A State military organization would do much to reassure the timid, and give confidence to those in the more exposed localities, and thereby prevent what might otherwise prove a serious hindrance to immigration.[119]

The 1862 US–Dakota War, in time, became part of the argument for continued settlement on former or current indigenous land, a practice of elimination that Patrick Wolfe has termed "settler colonialism" (see Figure 6.2).[120] The war also continued to play a role at the national

FIGURE 6.2 The dispossession of American Indians in Minnesota forced many native bands further west into the Dakota territory where they soon again encountered Northern European immigrants in pursuit of landownership. This May 28, 1928, photo shows the Redfox family – Solomon (standing left), June, Mary, Louise, Esther, George Two Bear, and Archie – with Reverend Mathias B. Ordahl (standing right), who baptized the infant, and his grandchild sitting in front. Courtesy of Louis Garcia.

[119] Ibid.
[120] Patrick Wolfe, "Settler Colonialism and the Elimination of the Native," *Journal of Genocide Research* 8, no. 4 (2006): 388; Stephen Kantrowitz, "White Supremacy, Settler Colonialism, and the Two Citizenships of the Fourteenth Amendment," *Journal of the Civil War Era* 10, no. 1 (2020): 29–53; Gunlög Fur, "Indians and Immigrants – Entangled Histories," *Journal of American Ethnic History* 22, no. 3 (2014): 65.

level. To prevent further political consequences, the Republican-led Congress, "with Lincoln's assent," exacted an even higher toll on the Dakota community than the mass execution. As Steven Hahn has noted, by early 1863, Congress effectively stripped the Dakota of "their reservation along the Minnesota River, abrogating all claims they might have, terminating the payment of annuities and forcing them out of the state and onto the open plains, along Crow Creek, in southeastern Dakota Territory."[121] Thereby, the US–Dakota War, and the memory of that war, helped Scandinavian immigrants more clearly articulate a settler colonial mindset that was mostly implicit before the struggle over landownership turned violent – but a mindset that persisted subsequently.[122]

As the Homestead Act's colonial consequences were beginning to show in Minnesota, concrete colonization steps were simultaneously taken in Washington. Consequently, Waldemar Raaslöff made his way up the stairs of the United States Capitol, on a warm Wednesday in the middle of July 1862.[123] The Danish chargé d'affaires sensed he was on the cusp of

---

[121] Hahn, *A Nation without Borders: The United States and Its World in an Age of Civil Wars, 1830–1910*, 246–247. Robert H. Caske was among the Dakota removed to Crow Creek after his imprisonment.

[122] Wolfe, "Settler Colonialism and the Elimination of the Native." See also Hansen, *Encounter on the Great Plains: Scandinavian Settlers and Dispossession of Dakota Indians, 1890–1930*, 30–39; Karl Jakob Skarstein, *The War with the Sioux*, (Digital Press Book, 2015), https://co mmons.und.edu/cgi/viewcontent.cgi?article=1004&context=press-books, xxii. In the following decades, and even well into the twentieth century, US–Dakota War experiences reflecting a sense of white superiority were handed down and recounted within the Scandinavian communities; it was eventually named "the Sioux massacre." See Louis Pio, "The Sioux War in 1862," *Scandinavia*, March, 1884, 142. See also O. J. Wagnild, "History of the Norwegian Settlements in Jackson, County, Minnesota," in *P1523 Local History: Minnesota – Jackson County* (Norwegian-American Historical Society, 1944). See also Ole D. Sando, "Til Fædrelandets Redaktion," *Fædrelandet*, April 30, 1868. See as well Wilhelm Moberg's immensely popular historical fiction account of Swedish immigrants in Minnesota where the main character Karl Oskar Nilsson becomes visibly upset when accused of settling on land "stolen from Indians." Wilhelm Moberg, *Sista Brevet Till Sverige [Last Letter Home]* (Stockholm: Alb. Bonniers boktryckeri, 1968), 61. I am grateful for Professor Dag Blanck's recommendation of Moberg's book.

[123] Waldemar Raaslöff, "Kongelig Dansk Gesandtskab. P.t. New York Den 30te Juli 1862 [Royal Danish Legation, Presently New York, July 30, 1862]," in *Collection 1175. Koloniernes centralbestyrelse kolonialkontoret. 1855–1918 Immigration af arbejdere. Immigration af arbejdere fra Italien 1884 mm. Box 910* (Copenhagen: Rigsarkivet, 1862). See also Robert Krick, *Civil War Weather in Virginia* (Tuscaloosa: University of Alabama Press, 2007), 65. See also "Local," *Alexandria Gazette*, July 16, 1862. Officially Raaslöff was designated "Envoy Extraordinary and Minister Plenipotentiary" when presenting his credentials to the Lincoln administration. See Waldemar Raaslöff, "Address Delivered on the 15th January 1864," in

a binding agreement that would fundamentally alter American colonization policy. Despite acknowledging to the Danish Ministry of Foreign Affairs that anything "touching on the great Negro question [is] treated by the [United States] government with the utmost caution," Raasløff was optimistic about eventually bringing African-American laborers to St. Croix.[124]

To ensure smooth passage, Senate Judiciary Committee chairman Lyman Trumbull and Secretary Seward had personally helped Raasløff edit the proposed document by striking words such as "treaty," "convention," and "apprenticeship," as these terms would draw political opponents' attention and result in undesirable debates or votes on the Senate floor.[125]

Amended to the liking of Trumbull and Seward, and bearing the official name "An act to amend an act entitled 'an act in addition to the acts prohibiting the slave trade,'" the bill passed the Senate, by a vote of 30–7, late in the evening of Tuesday, July 15, thanks to Trumbull's efforts.[126] The following day, Raasløff "had the pleasure of seeing the bill pass the House of Representatives unamended," and on July 17 President Lincoln approved the act followed by a go-ahead for further negotiations.[127]

Raasløff therefore met with Secretary of the Interior Caleb Blood Smith on July 19 and, in the presence of two witnesses, signed an agreement regarding "recaptured Africans," which was understood by the parties involved, as well as Confederate Secretary of State Judah P. Benjamin when he later learned of it, as a first step to pursuing concrete colonization

Washington D.C., diplomatisk repræsentation. 1854–1909 Korrespondancesager (aflev. 1918). Politisk Korrespondance 1864–1868 (Copenhagen: Rigsarkivet, 1864).

[124] Raasløff, "Kongelig Dansk Gesandtskab. P.t. New York Den 30te Juli 1862 [Royal Danish Legation, Presently New York, July 30, 1862]," 65. See also John C. Rivers, ed., *The Congressional Globe: Containing the Debates and Proceedings of the Second Session of the Thirty-Seventh Congress* (Washington, DC: Congressional Globe Office, 1862), 3997.

[125] Raasløff, "Kongelig Dansk Gesandtskab. P.t. New York Den 30te Juli 1862 [Royal Danish Legation, Presently New York, July 30, 1862]." Instead of "apprenticeship," Seward and Trumbull, with Raasløff's blessing, settled on the phrase "to employ them at wages"; this, according to the Danish diplomat, was consistent with the labor regulations existing in the Danish West Indies since the authorities' reluctant abolition of slavery in 1848.

[126] Rivers, *The Congressional Globe: Containing the Debates and Proceedings of the Second Session of the Thirty-Seventh Congress*, 3358–3359.

[127] Raasløff, "Kongelig Dansk Gesandtskab. P.t. New York Den 30te Juli 1862 [Royal Danish Legation, Presently New York, July 30, 1862]."

plans for current so-called contrabands or even future freedpeople in the Caribbean.[128]

The agreement between the United States and Denmark stipulated that for the next five years, "all negroes, mulattos or persons of color seized by the US armed vessels onboard vessels, employed in the prosecution of the Slave Trade," would be transported to St. Croix and employed as third-class agricultural laborers earning 5 cents a - day.[129] It was an "unconditionally advantageous" agreement, asserted Raaslöff proudly in his letter home to the Danish Ministry.[130] The congressional bill did not explicitly mention colonization of refugees, contraband slaves, or freedpeople within American borders, but it expanded the president's options for negotiating with "foreign Governments having possessions in the West Indies or other tropical regions" regarding so-called recaptured Africans; and politicians, both North and South, with the help of the Second Confiscation Act, understood it as opening the door to what was called voluntary emigration to a colony "beyond the limits of the United States."[131] In other words, the agreement was read with great concern in the Confederacy.

Confederate Secretary of State Judah P. Benjamin, who incidentally had been born on St. Croix in 1811, clearly interpreted the Danish-American agreement as a legislative step to undermine Southern slavery. After reading about the colonization agreement, Benjamin wrote to his European commissioner Ambrose Dudley Mann on August 14, 1862 and instructed him to ensure that Danish leaders "reject any possible complicity, however remote, in the system of confiscation, robbing, and murder which the United States have recently adopted to subjugate a free people." According to Benjamin, Confederate president Jefferson Davis

---

[128] Judah P. Benjamin, "Department of State. Richmond, 14 August. 1862," in *Ambrose Dudley Mann letters, 1850–1889* (LSU Libraries, Baton Rouge, 1862). See also Douma and Rasmussen, "The Danish St Croix Project: Revisiting the Lincoln Colonization Program with Foreign-Language Sources," 16–18.

[129] Secretary, "Monday 18 Augt 1862. Meeting at Governmenthouse According to Invitation of His Excellency." See also Miller, *Treaties and Other International Acts of the United States of America.*

[130] Raaslöff, "Kongelig Dansk Gesandtskab. P.t. New York Den 30te Juli 1862 [Royal Danish Legation, Presently New York, July 30, 1862]."

[131] Rivers, *The Congressional Globe: Containing the Debates and Proceedings of the Second Session of the Thirty-Seventh Congress.* See also James Oakes, *Freedom National: The Destruction of Slavery in the United States, 1861–1865* (New York: W. W. Norton & Company, 2013), 235–239.

specifically feared that the Lincoln administration was corrupting a "neutral and friendly power by palming off our own [Confederate] slaves seized for confiscation by the enemy as Africans rescued at sea from slave-traders."[132]

Though Benjamin admitted to not knowing "the precise terms" of the Danish-American agreement, his and Davis' fears were not wholly unfounded. Raaslöff had, as we have seen, on more than a few occasions expressed desire to use former Confederate slaves for labor in the Danish West Indies.[133] This link between "recaptured" Africans and emancipated "negroes" remained clear to Danish, American, and Confederate officials. The silver lining, from a Confederate perspective, was the fact that the Danish-American agreement "only" included "Africans captured at sea from slave-trading vessels," and, in addition, it seemed near inconceivable to Benjamin that the Lincoln administration could garner widespread support for emancipation among a xenophobic white electorate.[134] "The prejudice against the negro race is in the Northern States so intense and deep-rooted that the migration of our slaves into those States would meet with violent opposition both from their people and local authorities," assessed Benjamin in his letter to Mann.[135] "Already riots are becoming rife in Northern cities, arising out of conflicts and rivalries between their white laboring population and the slaves who have been carried from Virginia by the army of the United States," Benjamin added.[136]

In some ways Benjamin's letter was both obvious and prophetic. In the late summer of 1862, "prejudice against the negro race" *was* intense in the North, and riots *were* becoming rife in Northern cities. Senator Lyman Trumbull, a supporter of colonization who had helped Raaslöff edit the document that led to a change in American policy in July 1862, also expressed ambivalence about the role of future freedpeople in American society. As Eric Foner has noted, Trumbull, "who included a colonization provision in the original

[132] Benjamin, "Department of State. Richmond, 14 August. 1862."
[133] Raaslöff, "Kongl. Dansk Gesandtskab. Washington Den 15de December 1861 [Royal Danish Legation. Washington the 15th of December, 1861]."
[134] Benjamin, "Department of State. Richmond, 14 August. 1862."
[135] Ibid. Also Oakes, *Freedom National: The Destruction of Slavery in the United States, 1861–1865*, 225.
[136] Ibid.

version of the Second Confiscation Act, explained candidly, 'There is a very great aversion in the West ... against having free negroes come among us. Our people want nothing to do with the negro.'"[137]

Inadvertently underscoring Benjamin's point, President Lincoln on August 14, 1862 – the very same day that the Confederate Secretary of State wrote to Ambassador Mann – held a meeting with five leading delegates from Washington's Black community.[138] At this meeting Lincoln advocated colonization more directly than ever before.

Black people, Lincoln said, were cut off from "many of the advantages" that "the white race" enjoyed.[139] Even when slavery would eventually end, there was little prospect of racial equality. "On this broad continent, not a single man of your race is made the equal of a single man of ours. Go where you are treated the best ... I do not propose to discuss this, but to present it as a fact with which we have to deal," Lincoln plainly stated.[140] While the president acknowledged that free Blacks could be unwilling to leave the country where they were born, he called such a position "selfish" on their part and reiterated that voluntary emigration from the United States was his preferred solution. "It is better for us both, therefore, to be separated ... There is an unwillingness on the part of our people, harsh as it may be, for you free colored people to remain with us."[141]

Such comments fit well with Raaslöff's impression of the American president. In the wake of the April 16, 1862, compensated emancipation act in Washington, DC, the Danish diplomat reported home that he had "heard people say" they regretted the president's approval of the bill and that, if Lincoln had not signed the emancipation bill, it would have been in accordance with the views he had always maintained.[142] These statements indicated a lack of belief in Black people's capacity for citizenship in the

---

[137] Quoted in Foner, *The Fiery Trial: Abraham Lincoln and American Slavery*, 222.

[138] Medford, *Lincoln and Emancipation*, 57. According to Medford, the "five men selected were all prominent members of the African American community – Edward Thomas, leader of the group and active in various fraternal orders and in fund-raising for the National Freedmen's Relief Assocation; John F. Cook Jr., like his father, an educator; Benjamin McCoy, founder of the Asbury Methodist Church; Cornelius Clark, a member of the Social Civil and Statistical Association (an organization whose membership consisted of some of the most elite Black men in the city); and John Costin, whose family had been a prominent fixture in the African American community for decades."

[139] Roy P. Basler, ed., *Collected Works of Abraham Lincoln*, vol. 5 (New Brunswick: Rutgers University Press, 1953), 370–375.

[140] Ibid.   [141] Ibid.

[142] W. Raaslöff, "Ligation Danoise, Washington a 28 April 1862," in *Collection 0002. Udenrigsministeriet. 1848–1972. Depecher. Washington 1861–62 mm. Box 155* (Copenhagen: Rigsarkivet, 1862).

Lincoln administration, a perspective supported by the DC emancipation bill's appropriation of $100,000 for "voluntary colonization of African Americans living in the capital," which, as Kate Masur has noted, was "a nod to those, including Lincoln, who doubted that black and white people could peacefully coexist in the United States once slavery was over."[143]

Thus, it was likely that Raaslöff's hearsay regarding the public's surprise over Lincoln signing the bill, if credible, could be traced to the fact that the bill in some respects went further than Lincoln then had hoped.[144] After hesitating for a few days, Lincoln, who had drafted a bill to abolish slavery in the nation's capital in 1849 but privately advocated gradual, compensated emancipation, supported by a popular vote, did sign the bill, as he felt "a veto would do more harm than good."[145] Moreover, by August 1862, Lincoln had, according to Secretary of the Navy Gideon Welles, already started thinking of widespread and potentially also uncompensated emancipation. In his July 13, 1862, diary entry, Welles wrote of a carriage ride to a funeral that he shared with President Lincoln:

It was on this occasion and on this ride, that he first mentioned to Mr Seward and myself the subject of emancipating the slaves by Proclamation in case the rebels did not cease to persist in their war on the government and the Union, of which he saw no evidence. He dwelt earnestly on the gravity, importance and delicacy of the movement – said he had given it much thought and said he had about come to the conclusion that we must free the slaves or be ourselves subdued.[146]

Welles added that this discussion on July 13, 1862, marked an important break with the president's previous thinking on the emancipation as Lincoln had previously "been prompt and emphatic in denouncing any interference by the general government with the subject."[147]

---

[143] Kate Masur, *An Example for All the Land: Emancipation and the Struggle over Equality in Washington* (Chapel Hill: University of North Carolina Press, 2010), 25.

[144] In Foner's words, the "measure did provide for compensation to loyal owners, up to a maximum of $300 per slave (well below their market value, critics charged). But emancipation was immediate, not gradual, and the law made no provision for a popular vote on the subject." See Foner, *The Fiery Trial: Abraham Lincoln and American Slavery*, 57–58, 199–201.

[145] Ibid., 57–58, 199–200.

[146] Howard K. Beale, ed. *Diary of Gideon Welles, Secretary of the Navy under Lincoln and Johnson*, 3 vols., vol. 1 (New York: W. W. Norton & Company, 1960), 70–71.

[147] Ibid.

While Lincoln, prodded by abolitionists, was clearly considering the idea of emancipation, his August 14 meeting and his administration's subsequent pursuit of large-scale voluntary colonization suggests that the president was at this point following a dual strategy with continued belief in colonization as a viable partial solution for dealing with race relations within American borders.[148]

Opposition to colonization among Black Americans, however, remained widespread. Abraham Lincoln's August 14 demand for voluntary emigration received a cordial but clear rebuttal from the African American community.[149] Frederick Douglass described the president as "silly and ridiculous" in his inconsistent advocacy of colonization, but Lincoln's preliminary Emancipation Proclamation on September 22, 1862, nevertheless included a provision for the freed people to "be colonized, with their consent."[150] Additionally, Welles noted in his diary on Friday, September 26, 1862:

> On Tuesday last the President brought forward the subject and desired the members of the Cabinet to each take it into serious consideration. He thought a treaty could be made to advantage, and territory secured to which the negroes could be sent. Thought it essential to provide an asylum for a race which we had emancipated, but which could never be recognized or admitted to be our equals. Several governments had signified their willingness to receive them. M. Seward said some were willing to take them without expense to us. Mr. Blair made a long argumentative statement in favor of deportation. It would be necessary to rid the country of its black population, and some place must be found for them. He is strongly for deportation, has given the subject much thought, but yet seems to have no matured system which he can recommend. Mr. Bates was for compulsory deportation. The negro would not, he said, go voluntarily, had great local attachments but no enterprise or persistency. The President objected unequivocally to compulsion. Their emigration must be voluntary and without expense to themselves. Great Britain, Denmark, and perhaps other powers would take them.[151]

After Lincoln's August 14 meeting with Black leaders, Raaslöff, who himself had called Africans "almost savages," seemed to believe that colonization continued to be a key part of Lincoln's racial policy, and when the preliminary emancipation proclamation was issued it therefore took Raaslöff by surprise.[152]

---

[148] Medford, *Lincoln and Emancipation*, 56–57.   [149] Ibid., 57–59.   [150] Ibid., 62.

[151] Beale, *Diary of Gideon Welles, Secretary of the Navy under Lincoln and Johnson*, 152.

[152] W. Raaslöff, "Ligation Danoise. Washington a 23 Septbr. 1862," in *Collection 0002. Udenrigsministeriet. 1848–1972 Depecher. Washington 1861–1862 mm. Box 155* (Copenhagen: Rigsarkivet, 1862). See also Foner, *The Fiery Trial: Abraham Lincoln and American Slavery*, 231–234.

Still, on September 30, 1862, eight days after President Lincoln's preliminary Emancipation Proclamation, American diplomats in European countries with "colonial possessions" such as Great Britain, France, Holland, and Denmark, were instructed to invite the respective prime ministers to a convention regarding emigration of "free persons of African derivation."[153] Secretary of State Seward authorized his ambassador in Copenhagen, Bradford R. Wood, to "inquire whether the Danish govt" had "a desire to enter into such a negociation [sic]," and suggested a treaty running for ten years regarding the free Blacks and former slaves, many of whom Seward claimed, despite significant evidence to the contrary, had "made known to the President their desire to emigrate to foreign countries." Moreover, Seward wrote, "it is believed that the number of this class of persons so disposed to emigrate is augmenting and will continue to increase."[154]

In part pressured by Confederate emissaries, the Danish government declined to pursue further negotiations with the American government despite the September 30 overtures.[155] The decision was influenced by the Danish Kingdom's declining international stature following the Napoleonic Wars, and dependence on Europe's great powers to resolve the Schleswig War of 1848, coupled with continued tension in relation to the German confederation and the Danish Kingdom's German-speaking residents.[156] In the belief that the July 19 agreement would send thousands of recaptives to St. Croix and the knowledge that it would be close to impossible to attract freedpeople from the United States, the Danish

[153] William H. Seward, "Department of State, Washington, 30th September 1862, Bradford R. Wood, Esquire," in *Collection 1175. Koloniernes centralbestyrelse kolonialkontoret. 1855–1918 Immigration af arbejdere. Immigration af arbejdere fra Italien 1884 mm. Box 910* (Rigsarkivet, 1862). See also *Mitchell, Report on Colonization and Emigration Made to the Secretary of the Interior by the Agent of Emigration*, 28. Diplomats in Britain, France, Holland, and Denmark were all instructed to broach the subject of "emigration" with leading politicians.

[154] Seward, "Department of State, Washington, 30th September 1862, Bradford R. Wood, Esquire."

[155] A. Dudley Mann, "Copenhagen, October 24, 1862," in *Records of the Confederate States of America* (Library of Congress, 1862); Peter Vedel, "Udenrigsministeriet, Departementet for De Politiske Sager. Kjøbenhavn Den 21de November 1862," in *Collection 1175. Koloniernes centralbestyrelse kolonialkontoret. 1855–1918 Immigration af arbejdere. Immigration af arbejdere fra Italien 1884 mm. Box 910* (Copenhagen: Rigsarkivet, 1862).

[156] Rasmus Glenthøj, "Pan-Scandinavism and the Threshold Principle?," in *A History of the European Restorations: Governments, States and Monarchy*, edited by Michael Broers and Ambrogio Caiani (London: Bloomsbury Academic, 2019), 9–11.

diplomats tacitly accepted their lack of *Grossstaat* status and agreed to heed Confederate warnings.[157]

As the Danish Ministry of Foreign Affairs phrased it in a missive from November 21, 1862, it would be wise not to negotiate about importation of labor with the Lincoln administration currently, "as it was doubtful if the North American Union would emerge victorious from the war with the separatist movement."[158] With that, official Danish colonization interest petered out, and the same seems to have been the case within American borders. Seward's circular in many respects was the pinnacle of official optimism regarding colonization initiatives from the Lincoln administration, though there is evidence that the idea continued to hold sway over the president privately.[159]

The main Scandinavian-born actor driving the colonization negotiations in the United States, Waldemar Raaslöff, was sent on a mission to China, and his successor, Swedish count Edward Piper (see Figure 6.3), less actively pursued implementation of the July 19 agreement. As it turned out, no recaptives were ever transported to St. Croix by the United States navy, and instead the Danish government's simultaneous negotiations with Great Britain proved somewhat more fruitful. On June 15, 1863, 321 laborers from India, so-called coolies, arrived at St. Croix and were provided housing that a British official who later visited found "totally inadequate." As Kalyan Kumar Sircan has pointed out, men and women were "lodged indiscriminately together in one room," and provided such poor diet that within "18 months of their arrival twenty-two [Indians] had died."[160]

Importantly, also in this case of labor importation, Denmark had to rely on a more powerful international player. In comparison to Great Britain or

---

[157] Benjamin, "Department of State. Richmond, 14 August. 1862." See also Walker, "New York March 16th 1862."

[158] Peter Vedel, "Udenrigsministeriet, Departementet for De Politiske Sager. Kjøbenhavn Den 21de November 1862," ibid.

[159] Philip W. Magness and Sebastian N. Page, *Colonization after Emancipation: Lincoln and the Movement for Black Resettlement* (Columbia: University of Missouri Press, 2011); Guelzo, "Review: Phillip W. Magness and Sebastian N. Page. Colonization after Emancipation: Lincoln and the Movement for Black Resettlement. Columbia: University of Missouri Press, 2011. Pp. 164"; Philip W. Magness and Sebastian N. Page, "Lincoln, Colonization, and Evidentiary Standards: A Response to Allen C. Guelzo's Criticisms of Colonization after Emancipation: Lincoln and the Movement for Black Resettlement in the Journal of the Abraham Lincoln Association, Winter 2013" (2013).

[160] Kalyan Kumar Sircar, "Emigration of Indian Indentured Labour to the Danish West Indian Island of St. Croix 1863–1868," *Scandinavian Economic History Review* 7, no. 19 (1971): 139–141.

FIGURE 6.3 Count Edward Piper, sitting on the far left, is pictured here with fellow diplomats (e.g. France's Henry Mercier, third from the right) and William Seward at Trenton Falls, New York, in 1863. Piper proved less active in high-level colonial negotiations than his predecessor, Waldemar Raaslöff. Courtesy of the Library of Congress.

the United States, Denmark's international influence had for years been waning and the nation was no longer able to affect change internationally without outside help. Yet, this realization did not directly dawn on key Danish politicians until an even further descent into *Kleinstaaterei* starting in 1864 and culminating in 1870 with diplomatic fiascos in both the Old and the New Worlds, the latter at the hands of the United States.

By 1862, however, Danish and American diplomatic relations were relatively strong, though one particular piece of legislation would prove to be the source of much diplomatic energy exerted over the coming years. The transnational connection between the issue of conscription and immigration in relation to the 1862 Homestead Act was immediately recognized by European, Confederate, and American diplomats. In Europe, Confederate diplomat A. Dudley Mann – who saw immigration to the United States as a direct threat to the Confederate war effort and "was convinced that in every part of Europe [there] were scores of Union agents who existed for the sole purpose of recruiting soldiers" – warned the Confederate government about the bill and its consequences.[161]

---

[161] Robert L. Peterson and John A. Hudson, "Foreign Recruitment for Union Forces," *Civil War History* 7, no. 2 (1961): 178–179.

On at least "twelve occasions," Mann sent reports home about European immigrants serving the cause of the Union armies. Without Irish and German troops, Mann claimed, "the war against the South could not have been carried on," and the Midwest especially was becoming "a receptacle for foreign emigrants, who are chiefly controlled by out-and-out abolition propagandists, driven from Germany on account of their red-republican, socialistic demonstrations."[162]

Thus, as colonization faded from the forefront of international diplomacy and domestic policy, the interrelated issues of citizenship and American empire persisted.

The Homestead Act laid the foundation for further territorial expansion based on white settlement and, in time, provided an almost irresistible incentive for landless and smallholding European immigrants to add to the American population. As Don Doyle has noted, the Homestead Act's transnational appeal was "a remarkable campaign to replenish the Union army and score a clever public diplomacy coup in the bargain."[163]

Consequently, on August 8, 1862, Secretary Seward issued Circular No. 19 to his American envoys in Europe, aiming to spread knowledge about the agricultural, manufacturing, and mining opportunities the Homestead Act provided. "You are authorized and directed to make these truths known in any quarter and in any way which may lead to the migration of such people to this country," Seward wrote.[164] Soon thereafter, on August 12, 1862, the American consul in Bergen, Norway, O. E. Dreutzer, reported back that he had translated the Homestead Act and was working to get it published locally.[165]

Other American envoys followed suit. The Homestead Act was prepared for publications in both Sweden and Norway, while the same approach was followed by American diplomats in other European countries such as Germany and France.[166] When the Homestead Act was

[162] Ibid, 178–179.

[163] Don H. Doyle, *Cause of All Nations: An International History of the American Civil War* (New York: Basic Books, 2013), 168–169, 77–81. I am grateful to Dr. Michael J. Douma for guiding me to these sections of Doyle's book. See also Foner, *Free Soil, Free Labor, Free Men: The Ideology of the Republican Party before the Civil War*, 236–237.

[164] Ella Lonn, *Foreigners in the Union Army and Navy* (Baton Rouge: Louisiana State University Press, 1951), 418–420.

[165] Halvdan Koht, "When America Called for Immigrants," *Norwegian-American Studies and Records* 14, no. 8 (1944). See also Theodore C. Blegen, *Norwegian Migration to America: The American Transition* (New York: Haskell House Publishers, 1940), 408–413.

[166] Ibid. See also Lonn, *Foreigners in the Union Army and Navy*, 419.

distributed and advocated in Scandinavia by local consuls directed by the State Department in August 1862, it renewed interest in questions of emigration and citizenship on both sides of the Atlantic.[167]

On the one hand, American authorities were trying to detail the wondrous opportunity within American borders and were helped by the fact that living conditions for many smallholders in Scandinavia was equated with poverty.[168] On the other hand, the Civil War, and thus fear of forced military service, diminished Old World emigration enthusiasm some. Scandinavian-language migration pamphlets were increasingly critical of the United States after the federal draft in the fall of 1862, and foreign-born consuls within the United States complained regularly over immigrants being forced into military service.

American attempts to promote the Homestead Act led to heightened diplomatic activity, as European governments charged the Lincoln administration with what can be termed an indirect draft due to the Homestead Act's attraction for impoverished Europeans. Additionally, the Homestead Act raised two interrelated issues of importance to European immigrants: on the one hand, citizenship's relation to military service; and on the other, as we have seen, the notion of the American West as empty land.[169]

The Homestead Act stipulated that American citizenship, or intended citizenship, was required to claim land. Yet, in their quest for landownership, Scandinavian immigrants often did not contemplate the potential consequences of this prerequisite for a homestead claim, but after the Militia Act and Enrollment Act passed in 1862 and 1863 respectively it was clear that the right to a homestead claim equalled eligibility for military service. As Ella Lonn pointed out:

President Lincoln, in order to avoid misapprehension concerning the obligations of foreigners under the law of 1863, issued a proclamation on May 8, 1863, declaring no alien exempt who had declared his intention of becoming a citizen of the United States or a state or had exercised other political franchise. Such an alien was allowed sixty-five days to leave the country if he so desired.[170]

---

[167] "Lidt Om Udvandringen Fra Norge Og De Formentlige Aarsager Til Samme [About the Emigration from Norway and Its Presumed Causes]," *Emigranten*, August 18, 1862.

[168] Ibid.

[169] Smith, *Virgin Land: The American West as Symbol and Myth*, 190–200. According to Smith, the Republican Party with its support of a Homestead Bill succeeded in establishing the myth of an agrarian utopia in the West, which, "among recent German immigrants as well as among the descendants of pioneer settlers," was a crucial issue.

[170] Lonn, *Foreigners in the Union Army and Navy*, 440–41. See also James M. Geary, *We Need Men: The Union Draft in the Civil War* (DeKalb: Northern Illinois University Press, 1991), 28.

Thus, a noticeable shift in migration patterns from Scandinavia occurred in the wake of the 1862 US–Dakota War and Militia Act.[171] The Danish emigration writer Rasmus Sörensen spent the early summer of 1862 in Wisconsin and specifically recommended New Denmark and several other places in the Midwest subsequently. Yet, when Sörensen published an updated pamphlet with emigration advice in 1863, he explicitly made the Lincoln administration's draft policies part of the reason why he now recommended Canada. Scandinavian immigrants were encouraged by Sörensen to settle north of the United States because of the "insecurity" brought on by the "incessant recruiting and equipping of their people and money for warfare."[172]

Sörensen did, however, try to dismiss rumors that circulated in Scandinavian newspapers about immigrants being kidnapped for military service, potentially due to some highly publicized British cases, but he acknowledged that countrymen could try to coax newly arrived immigrants into the army so they would not have serve themselves.[173]

Perhaps just as importantly, Sörensen directly tied the opportunities under the Homestead Act to potential military service, as he recognized the Homestead Act's provision that, since only citizens

---

[171] Blegen, *Norwegian Migration to America: The American Transition*, 408–409.

[172] Rasmus Sørensen, *Er Det for Tiden Nu Bedre for Danske Udvandrere at Søge Arbeidsfortjeneste Og Jordkjøb i Canada, End i Wisconsin Eller i Nogen Anden Af De Vestlige Fristater i Nord-Amerika? [Is It Now Better for Danish Emigrants to Seek Profit and Land in Canada Than Wisconsin or Any Other of the Western Freestates in North America?]* (Copenhagan: Græbes Bogtrykkeri, 1863), 1.

[173] Ibid., 3. The following year M. A. Sommer also advocated emigrating to Canada, since the "war in America over the past three years had damaged the country in many respects." Sommer did not mention the draft specifically, but he made it clear that Canada offered "peace, security, calmness, and good order," which the United States by implication did not. See M. A. Sommer, *Nogle Bemærkninger Til Det Skandinaviske Folk Angaaende Udvandring Til Amerika Især Til Den Store Engelske Provinds Canada Samt Oplysning Om Befordring Til Australien, Ny Seland Og Nord Amerika [Some Remarks to the Scandinavian People Regarding Emigration to America Especially the Large English Province Canada as Well as Information About Transportation to Australia, New Zeeland and North America]* (Copenhagen: J. Cohens Bogtrykkeri, 1864). For cases of British subjects alleging kidnapping, see Michael J. Douma, Anders Bo Rasmussen, and Robert O. Faith, "The Impressment of Foreign-Born Soldiers in the Union Army," *Journal of American Ethnic History* 38, no. 3 (2019): 93–95.

or intended citizens could take out land under the 1862 Act, doing so equalled military obligations to the American government:

It is true that every settler can attain unsold free land, namely 160 acres ... by pledging to become a citizen and thereby assume duty of military service and committing to settle and cultivate as much of this free land as he can for 5 years before he thereupon gets the deed.[174]

The draft's impact on issues of citizenship, as well as the American government's aim of growing the population through European emigration, was also noticeable in immigrant naturalization petitions. Whether newly arrived immigrants were sought out as targets for countrymen trying to evade either the draft, Yankee Americans trying to collect their draft bounty, or felt cultural pressure to volunteer in small close-knit communities, this indirect draft was perceived as a significant problem among prospective Scandinavian emigrants.

The diplomatic tension based on the issue of forced military service was less pressing for the Scandinavian governments than was the case for the British or German legations, but thinly veiled recruitment by American consuls in Norway and Sweden did cause smaller diplomatic incidents. When Seward directed his European envoys to spread information about the Homestead Act's opportunities, he also indirectly raised the ire of Sweden's King Karl (Charles) XV.[175] According to Seward's representative in Stockholm, Jacob S. Haldeman, the Swedish government had since 1861 been fierce opponents of American attempts to recruit laborers whether in agricultural or industrial sectors:

It is well known that the King and his brother Prince Oscar are violently and bitterly hostile to all who recommend or encourage immigration, and I find if I wish to stand well with the King and his Ministers the less said for the present on this subject the better.[176]

The Swedish authorities, likely linking the solicitation of laborers to the solicitation of military men, expressed such opposition to recruitment that Foreign Minister Count Manderström advised "the American Embassy in

---

[174] Sørensen, *Er Det for Tiden Nu Bedre for Danske Udvandrere at Søge Arbeidsfortjeneste Og Jordkjøb i Canada, End i Wisconsin Eller i Nogen Anden Af De Vestlige Fristater i Nord-Amerika? [Is It Now Better for Danish Emigrants to Seek Profit and Land in Canada Than Wisconsin or Any Other of the Western Freestates in North America?]*, 8–16.

[175] Quoted in Lonn, *Foreigners in the Union Army and Navy*, 418–420.

[176] Quoted in ibid., 427.

Stockholm that his government could not condone the solicitation of soldiers by United States consuls in Sweden."[177]

Yet, both in the Old World and the New World, fear of forced military service was the main story.[178] While the concrete influence of emigration writers warning against forced military service in the United States is difficult to measure, the hesitancy to travel to the United States during wartime – partly due to fear of an indirect military impressment – is supported quantitatively. In a demographic study based on millions of census pages, Danish historian Torben Grøngaard Jeppesen found that Norwegian, Swedish, and Danish immigration, along with that from Germany and Holland, fell "fairly significantly" during the Civil War.[179] In other words, the fear of forced military service for some time contributed to undermining the Lincoln administration's goal of growing the population through the Homestead Act.

[177] Quoted in ibid., 416–427.

[178] As early as November 1861, Danish newspapers had published stories about opportunity in the United States after the Civil War's outbreak now being correlated with potential loss of life. Anyone not willing to be killed, it was suggested in a letter from "a country-man," was strongly advised "to say home until conditions improve, the prospects of which presently unfortunately only seem poor." See En Landsmand, "Af Et Brev Til Redact. Af 'Aarhuus Stiftstidende'. New-York Den 14de Octbr. 1861 [From a Letter to the Editorial Office of 'Aarhus Stiftstidende.' New York, October 14, 1861]," *Aarhuus Stifts-Tidende*, November 9, 1861.

[179] While the official emigration numbers from Denmark recorded in the United States fluctuated during the 1850s from a low of three in 1852 to peak of 1,035 in 1857, there was a perceptible fall of Scandinavian immigrants after 1862 despite information circulating about the Homestead Act. See Torben Grøngaard Jeppesen, *Danske i USA 1850–2000. En Demografisk, Social Og Kulturgeografisk Undersøgelse Af De Danske Immigranter Og Deres Efterkommere* [Danes in the United States 1850–2000. A Demographic, Social and Cultural Geographic Study of the Danish Immigrants and Their Descendants], 124–125.

7

Duties of Citizenship

Few Civil War issues were as complex, confusing, and fear-inducing in immigrant communities as the federal draft implemented in the wake of the 1862 Militia Act. The Militia Act, which passed on the same day that President Lincoln authorized the St. Croix negotiations, enabled the president to call state militia into the service of the United States for up to nine months and implement a draft if individual states could not fill their quotas with volunteers. The act also requested the states' enrollment of all male citizens between eighteen and forty-five years of age, if need be, and enabled the military to employ African-American laborers.[1]

The Militia Act thus vastly expanded the pool of potential recruits for the United States military and, in Steven Hahn's words, "marked an enormous shift in policy."[2] At a time when "martial manhood and citizenship went hand in glove," the Lincoln administration's policy reignited long-standing discussions over who was eligible to enjoy the rights of

---

[1] Thomas C. Mackey, ed., *A Documentary History of the Civil War Era: Legislative Achievements*, vol. 1 (Knoxville: University of Tennessee Press, 2012), 93–97. See also Roy P. Basler, *Collected Works of Abraham Lincoln*, vol. 3 (New Brunswick, NJ: Rutgers University Press, 1953), 296–297. See as well James M. McPherson, *Battle Cry of Freedom: The Civil War Era* (New York: Oxford University Press, 1988), 491–494. James W. Geary, *We Need Men: The Union Draft in the Civil War* (DeKalb: Northern Illinois University Press, 1991), 28.

[2] Hahn, *A Nation without Borders: The United States and Its World in an Age of Civil Wars, 1830–1910* (New York: Viking, 2016), 253–254. Importantly, by removing the word "white" from the "free able-bodied white male citizens" written in the 1792 Militia Act, the 1862 Militia Act laid the foundation for expanding military service to "persons of African descent."

American citizenship and who, in turn, should carry out the duties associated with such citizenship.[3]

Consequently, high-level policy discussions over colonization, military service, and homesteading in Washington, DC, aimed at expanding the white population, pool of military recruits, and the nation's territory (the basis for American Empire), had important implications for Scandinavian immigrants' perceptions of citizenship. By the summer of 1862, two questions took on increased significance within the Scandinavian-American community: Who belonged within the borders of the United States? And what rights and duties were associated with belonging?

On August 4, the War Department ordered 300,000 militia men to "be immediately called into service," and assigned state quotas based on population count.[4] As letters from anxious Danish-born immigrants started to flow to his office, it became clear to Waldemar Raaslöff (who had temporarily moved his legation base to Long Branch, New Jersey, to enjoy the soothing "sea, air, and bath") that there was no escaping the Militia Act's consequences.[5]

"The introduction of forced conscription will have an effect on filling the army ranks," Raaslöff wrote home on August 12; "[the spending] will be increased considerably by the employment of thousands of negroes, fugitive slaves who are de facto emancipated." And, added Raaslöff, there was now real concern that the ranks would be filled by his countrymen.[6]

In a "private and confidential" letter, Raaslöff wrote to Frederick William Seward, the son and assistant of the secretary of state, on August 14 to ask if the US government was planning on issuing general instruction for the exemption of foreigners drafted into military service for the Union forces. "I have had a great many applications from Danish Consuls and Danish subjects," Raaslöff wrote, "and although no drafting has yet taken place, the apprehensions of my countrymen do not appear altogether groundless."[7]

[3] Ibid.

[4] The United States War Department, *The War of the Rebellion: A Compilation of the Official Records of the Union and Confederate Armies. Series 3*, vol. 2 (Washington, DC: Government Printing Office, 1899), 291–292, 333–335.

[5] Waldemar Raaslöff, "Private and Confidential. Mansion near Long Branch N. J. August 14th. 1862," in *William Henry Seward Papers. Microform Edition* (University of Rochester, Department of Rare Books, Special Collections and Preservation, 1862).

[6] W. Raaslöff, "Ligation Danois, New York a 12 Aout 1862," in *Collection 0002. Udenrigsministeriet. 1848–1972. Depecher. Washington 1861–62 mm. Box 155* (Copenhagen: Rigsarkivet, 1862).

[7] Raaslöff, "Private and Confidential. Mansion near Long Branch N. J. August 14th. 1862."

Even though Frederick Seward assured the Danish diplomat, in a letter dated August 17, that the War Department's regulations for a potential draft emphasized "drafting only of citizens of the U.S. not of aliens," Raaslöff's suspicion was not unfounded.[8] Categories such as "citizens of the U.S." and "aliens" were complex. The underlying problem was the fact that American citizenship by 1862 was only loosely defined. In Christian Samito's words, "the rights and privileges one enjoyed depended on a complicated network of factors, including whether one was a naturalized or native-born citizen, where one lived, and one's race, slave status, gender, political office, job, position within a family, and membership in different associations."[9] Even Attorney General Edward Bates, writing in November 1862, had to admit that he could not find the "exact meaning" or the "constituent elements" of citizenship anywhere.[10]

Moreover, the War Department's call for 300,000 militia men now made it necessary for the government to reconcile notions of citizenship duties at the state, federal, and international levels to avoid widespread resistance to, and diplomatic fall-out from, a possible draft in the fall of 1862. The issue of defining citizenship duties was critical to ensure a fair draft for both native- and foreign-born men living within the Union; since diplomatic issues fell within William Seward's purview, the State Department, building on the War Department's directives, played a critical role in establishing parameters for citizenship in relation to foreign governments both publicly and behind the scenes in the fall of 1862.[11]

In its work to define American citizenship, the Lincoln administration could draw on a few general guidelines such as the ones established by the Naturalization Act of 1790, which in Linda Kerber's words was "generous in requiring only two years of residency, proof of 'good character,' and an oath to 'support the constitution of the United States'" but included only "free white persons."[12] Still, the 1790 Act served as inspiration for subsequent

---

[8] F. W. Seward, "Monday Aug 17 1862," ibid.

[9] Christian G. Samito, *Becoming American under Fire: Irish Americans, African Americans, and the Politics of Citizenship During the Civil War Era* (Ithaca, NY: Cornell University Press, 2009), 1.

[10] See also Edward Bates, *Opinion of Attorney General Bates on Citizenship* (Government Printing Office, 1862), 3–4.

[11] Stephen Kantrowitz, *More Than Freedom: Fighting for Black Citizenship in a White Republic, 1829–1889* (New York: Penguin Press, 2012), 35–36.

[12] Linda K. Kerber, "The Meanings of Citizenship," *Journal of American History* 84, no. 3 (1997): 841. See also William J. Novak, "The Legal Transformation of Citizenship in Nineteenth-Century America," in *The Democratic Experiment: New Directions in*

naturalization acts and state constitutions on the question of citizenship (even if individual states tweaked the wording slightly).

Hence, diplomatic tension revolving around the definition of citizenship ran high in the fall of 1862. In the span of a few months, the US Department of State was forced to investigate close to 1,000 cases, from mainly British and German subjects, of alleged wrongful enlistment. At the local level, ethnic groups, not least Scandinavian immigrants, developed draft resistance strategies to avoid military service.[13] For two reasons, foreign-born residents' concern with the 1862 draft was concentrated in Wisconsin. First, according to the 1860 census, 36 percent of Wisconsin residents were born outside American borders (and the number even higher for draft-eligible men), which was a significantly greater proportion than in other states struggling to field enough volunteers.[14] More Norwegian, Swedish, and Danish immigrants lived in Wisconsin (23,265) than in any other state in the Union, and Scandinavian Wisconsin residents therefore far outweighed countrymen in other states such as Ohio, Indiana, Maryland, and Pennsylvania that had to resort to drafting in the fall of 1862.[15]

Second, in Wisconsin, there was significant confusion and tension regarding draft regulations, quotas, and enrollment of foreign-born residents that was exacerbated by the difficulty of procuring volunteers during harvest season. Thus, Wisconsin quickly became the Scandinavian epicenter around which questions of American citizenship, as it related to the duty of federally mandated military service, revolved. All five Scandinavian cases challenging

---

American Political History, edited by Meg Jacobs, William J. Novak, and Julian E. Zelizer (Princeton, NJ: Princeton University Press, 2003), 89–91.

[13] Together with two American researchers, Michael J. Douma and Robert O. Faith, I have gone over all 1,040 cases of alleged wrongful conscription (often due to claims of "alienage"). See Michael J. Douma, Anders Bo Rasmussen, and Robert O. Faith, "The Impressment of Foreign-Born Soldiers in the Union Army," *Journal of American Ethnic History* 38, no. 3 (2019). The process and the results of these investigations can be brought together through an examination of the State Department's "Case Files on Drafted Aliens," which concretely reveals the American government's position on citizenship in the fall of 1862 and the geographic distribution of draft complaints.

[14] Some Wisconsin counties, such as Ozaukee in the eastern part of the state (54 percent of its 15,682 residents were foreign-born, according to the 1860 census), had an even higher share of foreign-born residents. For comparative purposes, other states that struggled to fill their military quotas in 1862 include Pennsylvania with 15 percent foreign-born, Ohio with 14 percent, and Maryland with 13 percent. Kennedy, *Population of the United States in 1860*, 215, 398, 439, 544.

[15] Ibid. Combined only 1,663 Scandinavian immigrants lived in Ohio, Indiana, Maryland, and Pennsylvania combined, according to the 1860 census.

conscription that made it to William Seward's desk in the fall of 1862 originated from Wisconsin.

Even though these five cases from Scandinavian-born individuals constitute only 1.1 percent of the State Department's "Case Files on Drafted Aliens" from Wisconsin during the Civil War, the relatively small number masks the consequences of the draft at the community level. A close reading of selected medical exemption records, census data, diary entries, letters, and newspaper articles reveals widespread draft anxiety and myriad strategies in the Scandinavian immigrant communities aimed at avoiding military service. Moreover, this examination also shows that draft resistance in Wisconsin cut across otherwise deep political and ethnic divisions and further demonstrates that immigrants actively used the vagueness of citizenship definitions to obtain draft exemptions.[16]

While it is certainly true that the Republican-leaning secular Scandinavian newspapers *Emigranten* and *Hemlandet* supported the Lincoln administration's expansion of citizenship duties, many, if not most, of the Scandinavian immigrants who had not volunteered for military service in 1861 resisted the militia draft even if they were active supporters of the Republican Party. Flight from enrollment officers (at times across state borders), dubious attempts at securing medical exemptions, and mutual aid societies organized to hire non-Scandinavian substitutes were just some of the attempts made by Scandinavian-born residents in Wisconsin to escape the draft.[17]

After Abraham Lincoln's July 1 call for 300,000 volunteer troops for three-year service, there was some confusion in Wisconsin about the state's exact quota. Since Wisconsin had raised more troops than required in

---

[16] See, for example, McPherson, *Battle Cry of Freedom: The Civil War Era*, 493; Tyler Anbinder, "Which Poor Man's Fight? Immigrants and the Federal Conscription of 1863," Civil War History 52, no. 4 (2006): 352. Peter Sørensen Vig, *Danske i Krig i Og for Amerika* [*Danes Fighting in and for America*] (Omaha, NE: Axel E. Andersen, 1979), 185–197. The story of draft resistance has been almost completely absent in Scandinavian ethnic Civil War historiography, though Vig does briefly acknowledge that several settler families had their "sons flee either to Denmark or Canada until the war was over," and Johannes Wist notes in passing that "it is evident from a quite lively newspaper discussion that many of our countrymen do everything possible to avoid military service." See Johannes B. Wist, ed. *Norsk-Amerikanernes Festskrift* (Decorah: The Symra Company, 1914), 33). See also Waldemar Ager, *Oberst Heg Og Hans Gutter* [*Colonel Heg and His Boys*], 223–261.

[17] Close to 80 percent of foreign-born residents' cases claiming military exemption on the grounds of "alienage" occurred between October 1862 and January 1863 at the height of controversy over the fall draft. See, for example, Peter Kotvis, "State of Wisconsin. County of Milwaukee," in *RG 59. General Records of the Department of State. Civil War Papers, 1861–1865. Case Files on Drafted Aliens. 1862–64. Entry 970. Box 3* (National Archives at College Park, 1862).

previous calls, state Adjutant General Augustus Gaylord operated from the
assumption that Wisconsin should raise six regiments, roughly the equivalent
of 6,000 men.[18] Yet, when the War Department called for an additional
300,000 troops on August 4 (and assigned Wisconsin a quota of an additional 11,904 men), Wisconsin's German-born governor Edward Salomon
quickly realized that trouble was looming. Throughout the month of August,
Salomon communicated almost frantically with Secretary of War Stanton to
buy time for additional volunteering and gain clarity regarding draft proced-
ures. At the same time, Wisconsin residents, especially foreign-born men,
organized community meetings, filled ethnic newspapers with draft-related
articles, and when possible got in touch with local consulates.[19]

On August 9, the War Department issued regulations for "the enrollment of and draft of 300,000 militia" to specify how actual draft proceedings were to be conducted and thereby made fears of forced military
service even more concrete across the Union. State governors were now
directed to appoint officials who could enroll all able-bodied men between
eighteen and forty-five by recording their "name, age, and occupation," as
well as any information that might exempt them from duty.[20]

Consequently, on August 10, Gaylord sent out instructions to local
sheriffs and tasked them with collecting enrollment information statewide
to ensure that everyone eligible for military service was registered for the
potential upcoming draft. Adding up all previous calls for troops, on
August 11 Gaylord calculated that Wisconsin still needed to raise
18,150 troops through volunteering and – if need be – a statewide draft.[21]

Knowing that resistance to a draft would be substantial, Governor
Salomon wrote Secretary of War Stanton on August 11, 1862, pleading

---

[18] August Gaylord, *Annual Report of the Adjutant General of the State of Wisconsin for the
    Year 1862* (Madison: Atwood & Rublee, State Printers, 1863), 76. See also McPherson,
    Battle Cry of Freedom: The Civil War Era, 492.
[19] United States War Department, *The War of the Rebellion: A Compilation of the Official
    Records of the Union and Confederate Armies. Series 3*, vol. 2 (Washington, DC:
    Government Printing Office, 1899), 333–335.
[20] Ibid. When the Enrollment Act of 1863 passed, the country, according to Ella Lonn, was
    divided "into enrollment districts, corresponding roughly to the Congressional districts;
    each of these was headed by a provost marshal, and in turn were under a provost-marshal-
    general at the head of a separate bureau in the War Department. All male citizens, and all
    male aliens who had declared on oath their intention of becoming citizens, who were
    physically fit and between the ages of twenty and forty-five must be enrolled and were
    liable to be drafted for the service of three years." See Ella Lonn, *Foreigners in the Union
    Army and Navy* (Baton Rouge: Louisiana State University Press, 1951), 440–441.
[21] United States War Department, *The War of the Rebellion: A Compilation of the Official
    Records of the Union and Confederate Armies. Series 3*, vol. 2, 291.

to have the deadline for volunteering extended past August 15, so as to not "check the spirit among the loyal people of this State."[22] Additionally, Salomon assured the secretary of war that Wisconsinites were determined "to fill all by volunteering, if they can be allowed to do so by giving them time enough … To cut off volunteering in this State when it takes ten days to reach the most distant portions is unfair and unjust, and our people so feel it."[23]

The following day, August 12, 1862, Salomon wrote again expressing concern that "one-half of the able-bodied men between eighteen and forty-five years in this State are foreign-born."[24] Salomon's letter claimed that the foreign-born had all "declared their intention to become citizens of the United States" and were eligible to vote. Perhaps out of necessity, this led the governor to reveal a more expansive understanding of citizenship when he concluded that "great injustice will be done to our State if they are exempt. Cannot those who are not willing to subject themselves to draft be ordered to leave the country?"[25]

Stanton's prompt answer made clear that "foreigners who have voted at our elections are regarded as having exercised a franchise that subjects them to military duty," but added that a declaration of intention to become a naturalized citizen was "not of itself sufficient to prevent their taking advantage of their alienage."[26]

Stanton's indirect clarification of what constituted American citizenship – voting but not a declaration of intent to become a citizen – was so important that Salomon immediately ordered it "published for the information of the people of the state."[27]

Meanwhile, Secretary of State Seward initially took a less encompassing approach to draft eligibility. As previously noted, Seward's State Department answered Raaslöff on August 17 that the draft only included "citizens of the U.S. not of aliens," and the Secretary of State personally reiterated this position in a response to the British legation on August 20, which was later published, when he wrote that "none but citizens are liable to military duty in the country"; he added, "This Department has never regarded an alien who may have merely declared his intention to become a citizen, as entitled to a passport."[28]

---

[22] Ibid., 357.   [23] Ibid.   [24] Ibid., 369.   [25] Ibid.   [26] Ibid.
[27] Gaylord, *Annual Report of the Adjutant General of the State of Wisconsin for the Year 1862*, 78–79.
[28] Seward, "Monday Aug 17 1862." See also "Aliens and the Draft," *New York Times*, August 25, 1862.

Perhaps not surprisingly, many immigrants at the community level were confused by the ambiguity between Seward's statement that "none but citizens" were liable to military service and the War Department's position that "foreigners who have voted at our elections are regarded as having exercised a franchise that subjects them to military duty."[29]

On September 1, 1862, *Emigranten* printed Secretary of State William Seward's letter from August 20, 1862, in an attempt to assure Scandinavian readers that only immigrants who had become citizens were subject to the draft. Yet, Seward's letter translated into Norwegian was prefaced by an editorial comment, likely from *Emigranten*'s editor, Carl Fredrik Solberg, that it would be "reprehensible" for anyone eligible to vote to shun military service. "When we have a citizen's rights we should also recognize a citizen's duties," the editor lectured.[30]

As such, *Emigranten*'s position supported Stanton's view that anybody who had voted was liable for the draft, and the newspaper writer actually expanded on Stanton's definition with his editorial call to have anyone enjoying the *right* to vote should recognize their *duty* to serve in the American military. According to *Emigranten*, such a position seemed both "fair and right," and the resolution of the confusion surrounding draft eligibility now depended on "whether the Secretary of State or the Secretary of War shall be obeyed."[31]

The secretary of state indirectly answered *Emigranten*'s question on September 5, 1862, in a response to an inquiry from Indiana Governor Oliver P. Morton. Seward's response demonstrated he had reconciled his position with that of Stanton's August 12 directive to Salomon. Though Seward initially proclaimed that "there is no principle more distinctly and clearly settled in the law of nations, than the rule that resident aliens not naturalized are not liable to perform military service," the secretary of state ended his letter by underscoring the connection between voting and draft eligibility (which would conveniently also expand the pool of potential militia recruits):

It is proper to state, however, that in every case where an alien has exercised suffrage in the United States he is regarded as having forfeited allegiance to his native sovereign, and he is, in consequence of that act, like any citizen, liable to

---

[29] Gaylord, *Annual Report of the Adjutant General of the State of Wisconsin for the Year 1862*, 78–79.

[30] "Udskrivningen [the Conscription]," *Emigranten* September 1, 1862. See also editorial comments in *Emigranten* August 11, 1862; August 18, 1862.

[31] Ibid.

perform military service. It is understood, moreover, that foreign governments acquiesce in this construction of the law. It is hoped that under this construction your militia force will not be sensibly reduced.[32]

Thus by September, when a handful of states were preparing for a draft, the State Department's position was that any foreign-born resident within the United States who had voted was eligible for military service. The state most severely affected by this expansion of draft eligibility was Wisconsin. While Stanton, in response to Salomon's pleas, agreed to extend the deadline for accepting volunteers (September 1 for old regiments being replenished with new volunteers, and August 22 for entirely new regiments), the chronological cut-off points left Wisconsin with too little time to fill the state quota due to logistical and practical problems.[33]

Because of the difficulty of attaining accurate draft rolls in a timely fashion, a frustrated Governor Salomon wrote to Stanton on August 26 with first a question and, as he frequently did, then a demand for a quick reply: "What course shall I take where in a township no man will serve as enrolling officer and the people refuse to give their names and abandon their houses when an officer comes to enroll them? Answer." The somewhat exasperated reply came back from Stanton the next day: "In the case supposed in your telegram of yesterday afternoon I do not know anything better than to 'let them slide.'"[34]

The sheriffs and their deputies tasked with collecting accurate enrollment regularly had to travel on bad roads to remote locations and at times encountered resistance in ethnic communities to such a degree that Adjutant General Gaylord in his annual report had to admit that the initial draft rolls were "too incomplete to be relied upon as furnishing accurate and trustworthy data, and they were, with few exceptions, returned to the sheriffs for correction."[35]

---

[32] John Bassett Moore, *A Digest of International Law*, vol. 4 (Washington, DC: Government Printing Office, 1906), 52–54.

[33] United States War Department, *The War of the Rebellion: A Compilation of the Official Records of the Union and Confederate Armies. Series 3*, vol. 2, 380–381.

[34] Ibid., 471–477.

[35] Charles E. Estabrook, ed., *Annual Reports of the Adjutant General of the State of Wisconsin for the Years 1860, 1861, 1862, 1863, 1864* (Madison, WI: Democrat Printing Co., State Printers, 1912), 98, 162–163. Governor Salomon reiterated to Secretary of War Stanton that he needed more time "as it takes several days to spread the news through the state." See United States War Department, *The War of the Rebellion: A Compilation of the Official Records of the Union and Confederate Armies. Series 3*, vol. 2, 387.

Additionally, evidence of medical examinations that raised questions in terms of both quality and ethics started to trickle into Gaylord's office.[36] Though the theme of duty to "our adopted country" was frequently found in *Emigranten*, actual practice in the medical examiners' offices revealed that the Scandinavian martial enthusiasm was not what it appeared in the newspaper pages.

In Dane County, where the state capital Madison was located, *Emigranten* on August 18 proudly reported that the "Norwegian" town of Vermont had procured thirteen volunteers out of the settlement contingent of eighteen allegedly "almost all Norwegian," and the nearby "Norwegian town Pleasant Springs" held a meeting on August 14 where it was decided to spur volunteer enlistment by providing a bounty of $50.[37] In the same issue, *Emigranten* relayed reporting from the *Toronto Globe* that Toronto was being overrun by people (the editor did not offer specifics on ethnicity) fleeing conscription while foreigners specifically were reported leaving Baltimore to avoid the draft. Additionally, the Scandinavian editor singled out Irish "secessionists" in Missouri and chastised them for claiming to be subjects of Great Britain in order to avoid military service.[38]

Yet the Scandinavian recruitment success reported by *Emigranten* masked draft resistance even within Dane County where the newspaper was published (see Figure 7.1). As the American state apparatus suddenly reached tangibly into the Scandinavian communities and demanded that the rights associated with citizenship also be accompanied by acknowledgement of duties, otherwise seemingly able-bodied Scandinavians started showing up at their local draft and medical examiners' offices seeking exemptions by late August.

In Dane County, more than 75 percent of the 1,014 exemptions granted were issued as medical exemptions between August 24 and September 11, 1862, by examining surgeon John Favill. As it turned out, Dane County's rate of 1,014 exemptions out of 7,466 draft enrollees, which translated to

---

[36] By December 10, the Wisconsin adjutant general sent out a general order citing "gross injustice" done "by the manner in which the surgical examination of the militia from Manitowoc county" had been conducted. But even more importantly, many Wisconsin men were able to purge themselves from the draft rolls by gaining medical exemptions even before the draft was eventually held on November 10. See Estabrook, *Annual Reports of the Adjutant General of the State of Wisconsin for the Years 1860, 1861, 1862, 1863, 1864*, 98, 162–163.

[37] "Indkaldelsen Af De 600,000 Mand [The Call for the 600,000 Men]," *Emigranten*, August 18, 1862.

[38] Ibid.

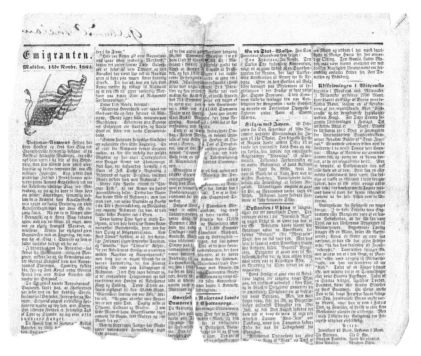

FIGURE 7.1 "Udskrivningen i Wisconsin" (The Conscription in Wisconsin) reads the far-right column headline of *Emigranten* on November 14, 1863, testifying to the draft's enduring importance for the newspaper's readership. Courtesy of Vesterheim Norwegian-American Museum Archives.

a 14 percent exemption rate, was actually below the state average, while Brown County (29 percent), Manitowoc County (35 percent), and Ozaukee County (50 percent), among others, pulled up the statewide average.[39]

However, even in a county like Dane with relatively few draft exemptions, Scandinavians in towns like Perry and Springdale seem to have been disproportionally successful in gaining medical exemptions. According to the 1860 census, 169 men in the town of Springdale were between the ages of eighteen and forty-five in 1862, with 37 percent being Norwegian. Yet a conservative estimate based on common Scandinavian names (even

[39] See, for example, John Favill, "Certificate of Disability," in *County Clerk. Civil War Draft Records, 1862. Dane Series 42. Box 1* (Wisconsin Historical Society, 1862). See also Estabrook, *Annual Reports of the Adjutant General of the State of Wisconsin for the Years 1860, 1861, 1862, 1863, 1864*, 220–230. Out of 127,894 men enrolled by the sheriffs, 28,012 – or 22 percent – were exempted from the draft in 1862. The War Department's August 9 instructions had stipulated that certain professions (e.g. telegraph operators, locomotive engineers, and mailmen) were exempted from the draft.

when recorded with spelling errors) such as Arne Anderson, Thore Oleson, and Peter Arnison, as well as the names matching specific census information regarding nationality, suggests that at least ten Norwegians (out of twenty medical exemptions preserved at the Wisconsin Historical Society) escaped the initial draft for conditions such as "want of constitutional vigor," "a bad hand," "injury of the knee," and so on after being examined by Favill.[40] In Perry, 80 percent of the 137 draft-eligible men were Norwegian-born, but at least fourteen out of the sixteen medical exemptions granted (88 percent) seem to have been given to Norwegians. In other words, Norwegians likely made up a larger share than their numbers warranted of medical exemptions granted to draft-eligible men from towns like Springdale and Perry. And the Scandinavian pattern of seeking draft exemption in Wisconsin was not limited to Dane County.

On September 15, 1862, *Emigranten* – after first decrying the disgrace of people "prostituting" themselves by dressing up as women to slip over the border to Canada – published an anonymous letter from a reader in the southern part of Wisconsin who claimed to have seen first-hand the Scandinavian reluctance regarding military service. "I fear that a great deal of the draft-eligible Norwegians, at least the ones around Janesville and Beloit," would try to escape the draft, the correspondent noted. Norwegians usually considered "strong and energetic" were now trying to dodge the draft by actively seeking medical exemptions. "I thought of sending you a list over such patriots, but the meetings [medical examinations] are not yet over, and I am also afraid that the list would have been quite long."[41]

The correspondent's use of "Norwegians" instead of "Americans" highlights the ambiguity surrounding citizenship and national allegiance. Following *Emigranten*'s editorial position, which perhaps was not entirely coincidental, the anonymous letter here argued for Norwegians serving in the military even if they were not fully naturalized citizens.[42]

---

[40] Kennedy, *Population of the United States in 1860*, 534. See also Favill, "Certificate of Disability."

[41] "Udskrivningen [The Conscription]," *Emigranten*, September 15, 1862.

[42] John A. Johnson, "Madison June 1st 1861," in *John A. Johnson Papers. P691. Box 1* (Norwegian-American Historical Association, 1861). As Johnson's 1861 letter on working behind the scenes at *Emigranten* suggests, some anonymous letters in the ethnic press may have been solicited – at least, that seems to have been the case later. In a study of the later Scandinavian-American press's role in policy discussions after 1890, Jørn Brøndal found that the "large proportion of anonymous letters might suggest" fabrication on the editors' part. See Jørn Brøndal, *Ethnic Leadership and Midwestern Politics: Scandinavian Americans and the Progressive Movement in Wisconsin, 1890–1914* (Chicago, IL:

In Brown County, where 49 percent of the population according to the 1860 census was foreign-born, Scandinavians in New Denmark established a mutual aid society demarcated along ethnic lines to allow drafted countrymen to hire substitutes.[43] On August 30, 1862, the Scandinavian inhabitants met to "support and comfort the families of persons who may be conscripted" for the United States army. The solution, after lengthy discussions, was a monthly fee of $2 from everyone who attended the meeting and wanted to be a member. What was left unsaid in the meeting minutes, but what the meeting's secretary Fritz Rasmussen made clear in his diary (and later through his and his community members' actions), was that many residents were prepared to hire substitutes, feign invalidity, or invoke ambiguous citizenship status to avoid conscription.[44] "Draft fear," Rasmussen noted, was the principal topic of conversation.[45]

The New Denmark residents' worst fears were realized when Wisconsin proved unable to fill the federally mandated military quota. On October 27, 1862, *Emigranten* reported that, out of twenty-eight Wisconsin counties, the northeastern part of the state would be comparatively hard hit. Brown County, for example, was to provide 155 men (out of 1,324 subject to the draft), Ozaukee County 529 men (out of 1,229 subject to the draft), and Washington County 807 men (out of 2,282 subject to the draft).[46] All told, the state of Wisconsin was going to draft 4,131 men, with the qualification

University of Illinois Press, 2004), 212–215. On the topic of draft resistance, *Emigranten* in March 1863 also published an article with the heading "Norwegian Deserters" and named names based on an announcement from General Pope with both a carrot and a stick toward the end of the article. "As announced last week, the President will exempt all the deserters who voluntarily report by their Regiment or nearest military post before April 1 for all punishment other than loss of pay for the time they have been away, whereas anyone who has not reported will be punished as deserters. See "Norske Deserterede [Norwegian Deserters]," *Emigranten*, March 23, 1863.

[43] Kennedy, *Population of the United States in 1860*, 526–43. Brown County in 1860 was home to 2,244 men between the ages of fifteen and forty and 5,817 foreign-born men and women out of a total county population of 11,795 (49 percent).

[44] Fritz W. Rasmussen, "Forhandlinger [Negotiations, August 30, 1862]," in *Fritz Rasmussen Papers. Additions, Genealogy notes. Green Bay Mss 4. Box 9, Folder 7* (Wisconsin Historical Society, 1862). See also Vig, *Danske i Krig i Og for Amerika [Danes Fighting in and for America]*, 275.

[45] Rasmussen, "The 12. Friday [September]." See also "The 20. Saturday [September]," in *Fritz William Rasmussen Papers. Diaries, 1857–1876* (Wisconsin Historical Society, 1862).

[46] "Drafting in Wisconsin," *Emigranten*, October 27, 1862. See also Kennedy, *Population of the United States in 1860*, 527–534. See as well Estabrook, *Annual Reports of the Adjutant General of the State of Wisconsin for the Years 1860, 1861, 1862, 1863, 1864*, 190, 230.

that "returns from Milwaukee" were yet incomplete and the adjutant general had not received all information from Dunn, Kewaunee, Rock, and Shananaw County (the quotas for these counties were to "be announced when complete").[47] Despite the laborious attempts to get draft rolls right and ensure transparency in the process, the statewide draft when it was implemented on November 10, 1862, was, in Gaylord's words, met with such "stubborn" and in some cases "armed resistance" in eastern Wisconsin that Governor Salomon had to intervene.[48]

The Draft Commissioner [in Ozaukee County] was violently assaulted, escaping with his life only by flight, and the records were destroyed. But the authors of this had kindled a flame, which soon outran their control, and an infuriated mob ran riot through the town; old personal differences were made the occasion of attack; houses, with their contents, were demolished, and the wrecks of once happy homes, now stand through the village of Port Washington, as a sad memento of lawless violence.[49]

Following the November 10 riots, Governor Salomon wrote to the state's appointed provost marshal, Walter D. McIndoe, and authorized him to "proceed immediately to Port Washington with a sufficient military force to enforce the draft, and arrest the leaders and aiders and abetters in the riotous proceedings."[50] Ozaukee County's many German and Luxembourg residents were primarily involved in agriculture, and the area had a "low enlistment rate" along with strong support for the Democratic Party – a connection that *Emigranten*, in its November 17 issue, did not fail to point out. *Emigranten* laid the blame for the insurrection squarely at the feet of a seemingly unholy trinity of Catholicism, German-born immigrants, and the Democratic Party, which in combination produced what was reported as "gross violence."[51]

[47] Gaylord, *Annual Report of the Adjutant General of the State of Wisconsin for the Year 1862*, 96–97. In the end, the draft in Milwaukee and Kewaunee County was postponed to November 19 and "the earliest practicable moment" for the two counties respectively. Eventually Milwaukee County was assigned a quota of 728 men.

[48] Deborah Beaumont Martin, *History of Brown County, Wisconsin: Past and Present* (Chicago, IL: S. J. Clarke Publishing Company, 1913), 204–205. See also "Udskrivningen Af Værnepligtige i Wisconsin – Optøier i Milwaukee, Ozaukee Og Washington Countier [The Conscription of Draftees in Wisconsin – Riots in Milwaukee, Ozaukee and Washington Counties]," *Emigranten*, November 17, 1862.

[49] Estabrook, *Annual Reports of the Adjutant General of the State of Wisconsin for the Years 1860, 1861, 1862, 1863, 1864*, 163.

[50] Edward Salomon, "Nov. 11, 62," in *Letters Madison 1862. Volume 5. Series 33 of Governors Correspondence General, 1838–1926* (Wisconsin Historical Society, 1862). See also Lawrence Larsen, "Draft Riot in Wisconsin, 1862," *Civil War History* 7, no. 4 (1961): 421–423.

[51] "Udskrivningen Af Værnepligtige i Wisconsin – Optøier i Milwaukee, Ozaukee Og Washington Countier [The Conscription of Draftees in Wisconsin – Riots in

The German-speaking immigrants' actions in Ozaukee County were described as conducted by "a furious mob" that, in addition to assaulting the draft commissioner and much else, had broken into a Masonic lodge. "The Free Masons is a society that the German-Catholic clergy most definitely is opposed to," noted *Emigranten* with a thinly veiled reference to the nativist movement of the 1850s.[52]

Moreover, detailing a revolt in Milwaukee's 9th Ward and once again using religion to partially explain disorderly deeds, *Emigranten* noted that a large crowd of Germans "strongly influenced by the pro-slavery catholic paper Milwaukee 'Seebote'" were largely responsible for the unrest.[53]

Events unfolded less violently in Brown County as the larger towns of Green Bay, De Pere, and Fort Howard, according to a later historical account, had filled their quotas ahead of November 10.[54] The draft burden therefore fell on the smaller communities with fewer resources to organize widespread resistance, but violence – or threats thereof – simmered just below the surface. Foreign-born men "who had come to the United States to escape the military conscription laws enforced in Germany, France and other countries and were not yet long enough in America to understand or sympathize with the Union" voiced their discontent loudly, and Belgian immigrants in Green Bay and Scott "refused to comply with the governor's order."[55]

Milwaukee, Ozaukee and Washington Counties]." See also "Udskrivningen i Wisconsin [the Conscription in Wisconsin]," *Emigranten*, September 24, 1862. Later historical accounts agreed with *Emigranten*'s assessment of ethnicity. See for example Mischa Honeck, "Men of Principle: Gender and the German American War for the Union," *Journal of the Civil War Era* 5, no. 1 (2015): 56–57.

[52] "Udskrivningen Af Værnepligtige i Wisconsin – Optøier i Milwaukee, Ozaukee Og Washington Countier [The Conscription of Draftees in Wisconsin – Riots in Milwaukee, Ozaukee and Washington Counties]." See also "Udskrivningen i Wisconsin [The Conscription in Wisconsin]." *Emigranten*'s reference to the Freemasony harkened back to the role the society played in the anti-immigrant and anti-Catholic Know-Nothing movement in the middle of the 1850s. See for example McPherson, *Battle Cry of Freedom: The Civil War Era*, 130–144.

[53] "Udskrivningen Af Værnepligtige i Wisconsin – Optøier i Milwaukee, Ozaukee Og Washington Countier [the Conscription of Draftees in Wisconsin – Riots in Milwaukee, Ozaukee and Washington Counties]."

[54] Martin, *History of Brown County, Wisconsin: Past and Present*, 204.

[55] Martin, *History of Brown County, Wisconsin: Past and Present*, 204–05. Also Fritz W. Rasmussen, "Den 10de Mandag [November]," in *Fritz William Rasmussen Papers. Diaries, 1856–1876. Green Bay Mss 4. Box 8* (Wisconsin Historical Society, 1862).

The resistance was slightly more muted in the Scandinavian immigrant communities, but the amount of time and space devoted to draft issues in *Emigranten* testified to the importance of the forced military service in the minds of the paper's subscribers. To Norwegian, Swedish, and Danish immigrants, it was not only the concrete fear of being drafted that took its toll mentally, and for some physically; it was also the amount of time spent planning for the draft, which had economic consequences. In New Denmark, the frequent meetings held in the "Scandinavian War Aid Association" drained the time and energy from the association's secretary's farm work, to such an extent that he skipped an important meeting on November 14 just the day after rumors of the draft results had started circulating in town.[56]

On Thursday November 13, Rasmussen had learned from a community member that "they had finally begun drawing for the draft" and that five members "were chosen – unfortunately – from the Scandinavian Association," while another four were drafted without being members of the association. All told, nine men were drafted from New Denmark on top of the sixteen volunteers the community had already furnished "out of 69 able-bodied men," or, as Rasmussen noted, "between every second and every third."[57]

Rasmussen's numbers were off by one compared to the adjutant general's office (twenty-four out of sixty-eight able-bodied men in the official tabulation), but with a quota of nine draftees out of sixty-eight men (13 percent), New Denmark in November was harder hit by the draft than the county in general (where 155 out of 1,814 men, or 9 percent, of the able-bodied men were drafted).[58]

The reality of military service in the short term, however, proved less severe for county's communities. Out of 155 men drafted from Brown

[56] Fritz W. Rasmussen, "Den 22. Løverdag [November]," in *Fritz William Rasmussen Papers. Diaries, 1856–1876. Green Bay Mss 4. Box 8* (Wisconsin Historical Society, 1862).

[57] "Den 13. Torsdag [November]," in *Fritz William Rasmussen Papers. Diaries, 1856–1876. Green Bay Mss 4. Box 8* (Wisconsin Historical Society, 1862). See also Adjutant General, "County Draft Book No. 1. 1862–1863," in *Adjutant General. Draftee Substitutes (ca. 1861–1865), Camp Washburn. Series 1137. Box 7* (Wisconsin Historical Society, 1862).

[58] Daniel M. Whitney, "List of Persons Liable to Military Duty in the Town of New Denmark," in *Wisconsin. Adjutant General. Draft Records, 1862–1865. Series 1137. Reel 1* (Wisconsin Historical Society, 1862). When factoring in earlier volunteers, New Denmark and the greater Brown County eventually, however, ended up with the same share on paper – more than one third of the draft eligible population – called up for military service after November 10.

County, forty-four did not report and another forty-four were discharged, leaving just sixty-seven men mustered in by the time the adjutant general gave his annual report in 1863. Gaylord, in the case of Washington County, explained the fact that "few drafted men" had reported by noting the lack of transportation to Camp Washburn in Milwaukee where they, along with draftees from Brown and other nearby counties, eventually were to report.[59] While poor infrastructure and lack of transportation definitely played a role in towns like New Denmark, the underwhelming number of recruits at Camp Washburn was also explained by the continued unwillingness to accept the draft.

In addition, foreign-born residents within American borders from the fall of 1862 and forward recognized the importance of their citizenship status. In Brown County, the district to which New Denmark belonged, only eight "declarations of intention" to become a citizen were taken out in 1863. In comparison, 177 Brown County declarations of intention survive from 1860, sixty-nine from 1861, and twenty-five from 1862.[60] According to the 1860 census, Brown County numbered 6,148 men, 2,302 of them between the approximate military age of twenty and fifty years; and of the eight declarations taken out in 1863, five (two Danes, one Dutchman, one German, and one Irishman) were born between 1814 and 1818, thereby making them older than forty-five years and consequently ineligible for the 1862 draft.

At the local level, only one draftee from New Denmark ended up in the army as a consequence of the 1862 draft, while the remaining eight employed different strategies for initially avoiding military service. Out of the nine foreign-born men drafted from New Denmark, four were Danes, two Norwegians, two Irish and one from France. Five of the nine could use funds from their membership in the "Scandinavian War Aid Association" to defray the costs of hiring a substitute, but the non-Scandinavian members of the town had to look for other measures. In desperation, thirty-year-old Dennis Devan's Irish-born wife threatened the local sheriff with violence when he came around to deliver the draft results:

[The sheriff] was most excited and dreadfully flustered as he well knew what it meant to come around to people with such messages, as he said, "not very pleasant

---

[59] August Gaylord, "Document N: Annual Report of Adjutant General Gaylord for 1863," in *Message of the Governor of Wisconsin, Together with the Annual Reports of the Officers of the State, for the Year A.D. 1863* (Madison: William J. Park, State Printer, Harding's Block, 1864), 1074. Also Estabrook, *Annual Reports of the Adjutant General of the State of Wisconsin for the Years 1860, 1861, 1862, 1863, 1864*, 163, 211.

[60] Kennedy, *Population of the United States in 1860*, 526–27. Also *Wisconsin, County Naturalization Records, 1807–1992, Images*.

news." Dennis Devan's wife had met him in the door with a pitchfork and a "don't come in here."[61]

Devan eventually got exempted, though it is difficult to ascertain the exact reason why in the surviving records, but it is likely that he received a medical exemption, through either real or feigned injury, or was able to fight the authorities' enrollment information in other ways. Medical exemption, as we have seen, or the ability to convince the enrollment officers that the draft rolls contained wrongful information were strategies regularly employed by drafted men in the community. Underlining the ethnic differences that guided life in New Denmark, Fritz Rasmussen in a April 11, 1863, diary entry noted about Devan's wife that she was "the only Irish wife I have thus far met who can converse just somewhat decently," and reiterated his perception of Irish men as being (too)heavy drinkers, which he thought impacted their ability to be productive farm laborers.[62]

In rural communities, age likely had an effect on medical exemptions, due to cumulative bodily wear and tear, but age could also be a factor in and of itself as the draft-eligible age was set between eighteen and forty-five. Mads Rasmussen, for example, who was listed as being forty-four years old on the draft rolls made up in August 1862, seemingly found a different (and cheaper) solution to avoiding military service than hiring a substitute when he, according to a later document, "got out of [the draft] by getting old in a Hurry."[63] What that likely meant was that Rasmussen, who was a member of the Scandinavian War Aid Association, went to Green Bay, which was an initial county rendezvous point, and acted even older than his age (he was born in 1820) at the medical examination, which eventually earned him an exemption.[64]

At least two other New Denmark draftees succeeded in having a substitute accepted by the military authorities, and one of them was Fritz Rasmussen's brother-in-law, Celius Christiansen. Christiansen, who

[61] Fritz W. Rasmussen, "Den 20. Torsdag [November]," in *Fritz William Rasmussen Papers. Diaries, 1856–1876. Green Bay Mss 4. Box 8* (Wisconsin Historical Society, 1862).

[62] Fritz W. Rasmussen, "Den 11 Löverdag [April]," in *Fritz William Rasmussen Papers. Diaries, 1856–1876. Green Bay Mss 4. Box 8* (Wisconsin Historical Society, 1863).

[63] R. C. Johnsen, "New Denmark 3/8 Ad 1882 [March 8th]," in *Civil War Mother's Pension. Application 258778* (National Archives, 1882). See also Rasmussen, "Record! Of Skandinavians, Who Have Been Settled and Lived in the Town of New Denmark."

[64] On Mads Rasmussen getting exempted in Green Bay (the reason for exemption is not stated though), see "Consolidated Lists of Civil War Draft Registrations, 1863–1865," in *Records of the Provost Marshal General's Bureau (Civil War), Record Group 110. NM-65, entry 172* (Washington, DC: National Archives, 1863), 314.

married Fritz Rasmussen's sister Inger in 1857, was also a member of the Scandinavian War Aid Society and therefore had approximately $70 in mutual aid that he could parlay into finding a substitute instead of risking his life in the military.[65] Thus, as soon as it was rumored that Christiansen had been drafted, he anxiously started searching for a substitute and was able to convince the recently married twenty-three-year-old August Hauer to enlist in his place in exchange for $170.[66]

Yet, in these discussions over substitutes as well as in the creation of the Scandinavian War Aid Association, Old World notions of ethnicity seemingly complicated New World notions of citizenship duties. When August Hauer, who was born in Schleswig (one of the duchies that had rebelled against Danish rule in 1848), told his father, Hans, that he had enlisted as a substitute for Celius Christiansen, the family patriarch – who according to Fritz Rasmussen was "a mortal enemy of anything Danish" – angrily attempted to change his son's mind and make him go back on the promise to be a substitute.[67] Interestingly, Hans Hauer had lived among Danish people most of his life: four of his children were born in Denmark prior to the 1848 revolution, but the next four were born in the United States between 1852 and 1862. Importantly, however, Hans Hauer's actions may well also have been shaped by the fact that his son Johan (a little brother of August) had died from disease in the service of the Union Army on February 15, 1862.[68]

Christiansen had previously served in the Danish military, which likely made claims for medical exemption less plausible, and he had voted in an

---

[65] Celius Christiansen, *En Pioneers Historie (Erindringer Fra Krigen Mellem Nord- Og Sydstaterne) [A Pioneer's Story: Memoirs from the War between North and South]* (Aalborg: Eget forlag, 1909), 41.

[66] Ibid. In his memoirs, Christiansen wrote: "My name was among the ones drawn and this caused sorrow and worry to an extent that only the ones who have tried it actually understand. I had wife and kids and a relatively good farm that I was now forced to leave." See also Rasmussen, "Record! Of Skandinavians, Who Have Been Settled and Lived in the Town of New Denmark."

[67] "Den 17. Mandag [November]." See also Vig, *Danske i Krig i Og for Amerika [Danes Fighting in and for America]*, 275.

[68] Rasmussen, "Record! Of Skandinavians, Who Have Been Settled and Lived in the Town of New Denmark," 36–60. Hauer in all likelihood was among the 40 percent of residents within Danish borders that identified as German after Norway was incorporated into the Swedish kingdom in 1814. See Rasmus Glenthøj, "Pan-Scandinavism and the Threshold Principle?," in *A History of the European Restorations: Governments, States and Monarchy*, edited by Michael Broers and Ambrogio Caiani, pp. 245–255 (London: Bloomsbury Academic, 2019). For information about Johan Hauer, see Peter Sørensen Vig, *Danske i Amerika [Danes in America]*, vol. 1, (Minneapolis, MN: C. Rasmussen Company, 1907), 356.

American election as early as 1854, which made exemption due to "alien-age" unlikely.[69] Despite this initial setback, Christiansen continued the negotiations with August Hauer and eventually secured him as a substitute. Yet, even if an accord was mutually agreed to, there was no guarantee that the substitute would be accepted by the American author-ities; and thus, on top of the expense of paying the substitute, draftees incurred the added expenses (not least in terms of laboring hours lost) associated with travelling to Green Bay or Milwaukee to report for military duty.[70] As Fritz Rasmussen complained in his diary, "that is of course the universal rule: that the poor man can not thrive, who must bear the expenses, but that the rich man grows fat on the crumbs stolen from the poor one."[71]

The only New Denmark resident that served as a result of the first draft was Hans Gundersen from Norway, who had declared his intent to become a naturalized citizen on March 30, 1861, less than two weeks before the Civil War's outbreak. Gundersen's forced war service led to fierce debates in the Association in late November, as Gundersen had not signed on to the original pact.

Being single with neither wife nor children, Gundersen in August volunteered to support the Scandinavian War Aid Association with a pledge of a dollar every month. Yet, one dollar was only half of the monthly fee, which made him "neither a half nor full member," according to Fritz Rasmussen.[72] Yet when Gundersen's name was drawn up, he requested support from the Association, which the members reluctantly agreed to provide, perhaps underscoring a sense of ethnic obligation.[73]

---

[69] Christiansen, *En Pioneers Historie (Erindringer Fra Krigen Mellem Nord- Og Sydstaterne) [A Pioneer's Story: Memoirs from the War between North and South]*, 15.

[70] Though writing about Massachusetts before the Civil War, Christopher Clark's point that "the aspiration for household 'independence' relied on the necessity of exchanging goods and labor with neighbors and kin" applied to Scandinavians in New Denmark as well during the Civil War. Christopher Clark, *The Roots of Rural Capitalism: Western Massachusetts, 1780–1860* (Ithaca, NY: Cornell University Press, 1990), 38. See a lso Fritz W. Rasmussen, "The 8th Monday [December]," in *Fritz William Rasmussen Papers. Diaries, 1856–1876. Green Bay Mss 4. Box 8* (Wisconsin Historical Society, 1862).

[71] "The 8th Monday [December]." In order to make it to Green Bay in time, Hauer had to borrow Rasmussen's sleigh while another New Denmark resident drove all through the night to make it in time. In his diary Rasmussen added, "The Order for transportation to the camp of rendezvous, had namely come so precipitately, that sufficient time was hardly given them to send for their substitutes; a considerable expense for the poor Conscripts, to be forced to bring their Substitutes to Milwaukee instead: that they might as well have been excted [accepted] at Green Bay."

[72] Rasmussen, "Den 22. Løverdag [November]."   [73] Ibid.

The meetings in the Scandinavian War Aid Association continued well after the draft, and in late November it was resolved that the secretary, Fritz Rasmussen, should publish information about the Association's proceedings in the local *Green Bay Advocate*. "Dear Sir," Rasmussen wrote on November 24, 1862, in a letter that underscored his reluctance to serve in the United States military despite his support for the Republican Party:

I take this opportunity to ask the favor individually of you, as well as in [sic] behalf of quite a large proportion of the settlers of the town, to give these lines a publication in your paper – if for nothing else – to show the neighbors that we have not all left the country to avoid the trouble and travail of the land, but are here yet, able to give a hand at reefing the canvass if the storm should be still stronger should we be commanded to do so, for all our – I was going to say patriotic (?) men have gone long before this. We had lately, grown somewhat callous to the subject of drafting, which at first, was only imagined as *possible*. Although, among the weaker part of our members, it created considerable sensation: but they being descendants of ... war-faring people ... mustered courage enough to manage looking the monster straight in the eyes, and adopt measures to alleviate the curse somewhat.[74]

With the help of the War Aid Association, questionable medical exemptions, and related efforts, most Scandinavians in New Denmark avoided military service in the first draft. For several others, however, the draft was a potential tragedy. French-born Peter Kiefer had to leave "a young wife and six small kids all under the age of seven," and Fritz Rasmussen's neighbor, Knud, asked him to write a will stipulating that he wanted to leave all his earthly possessions to his wife.[75] When the draft finally got underway in Keewaunee County, Rasmussen noted that twenty-six people had been drafted in the town of Franklin, and that several, who were "in very dire straits," had "small children."[76] That these were not singular incidents was supported by Gaylord's annual report, in which he noted that "peculiar hardship" had occurred in cases where "large families, from whom one or more had previously volun-teered, were deprived of their only remaining support of the family."[77]

[74] F. W. Rasmussen, "Aid to Families of Drafted Men," *Green Bay Advocate*, November 27, 1862.

[75] Fritz W. Rasmussen, "Den 24. Mandag [November]," in *Fritz William Rasmussen Papers. Diaries, 1856–1876. Green Bay Mss 4. Box 8* (Wisconsin Historical Society, 1862).

[76] "Den 29. Løverdag [November]," in *Fritz William Rasmussen Papers. Diaries, 1856–1876. Green Bay Mss 4. Box 8* (1862).

[77] Gaylord, *Annual Report of the Adjutant General of the State of Wisconsin for the Year 1862*, 55.

Although draft resistance was most pronounced in the eastern part of Wisconsin, a handful of Scandinavians in Racine, Kenosha, and Dane County, along with hundreds of German and Irish immigrants, tested the nature of American citizenship by taking their claims of alienage all the way to the State Department.

One of the young Norwegians who tried, and failed, to get an exemption from military service due to his foreign-born status, not medical disability, was Ole Hanson in Dane County. Hanson appeared before draft commissioner Levi Vilas on Monday, September 1, but he was denied exemption, along with his countryman Helge Hanson, for having already taken out naturalization papers and voted.[78] As it turned out, Hanson was drafted in November and, not willing to accept the local draft commissioner's ruling, on December 12, 1862, with the help of his father, took his case to a local attorney who forwarded it to the State Department.[79]

On February 27, 1863, Hanson was notified that his exemption request had to be submitted through more official channels (either a local consul or the state executive), but on March 18 the Norwegian-born Wisconsin resident was finally given an exemption "unless evidence controverting" his statements of having "never declared his intention to become a citizen" nor "exercised the privilege of the elective franchise" was unearthed.[80]

The wording of the State Department's answer to Ole Hanson was revealing. Not only was voting deemed a factor in draft eligibility, but it was also clearly stated that having declared one's "intention to become a citizen" was as well.[81] In other words, between August 17, 1862, when Frederick Seward assured Raaslöff that the American government's draft only included citizens, and March 18, 1863, when Hanson was finally released from military service, the State Department had expanded draft eligibility to include both voting and intent, in essence broadening the

---

[78] Levi B. Vilas, "Wednesday Augt. 27th 1862," in *County Clerk. Civil War Draft Records, 1862. Dane Series 42. Box 1* (Wisconsin Historical Society, 1862). See also "Monday Sept. 1st 1862," in *County Clerk. Civil War Draft Records, 1862. Dane Series 42. Box 1* (Wisconsin Historical Society, 1862).

[79] Ole Hanson, "Madison, Wisconsin, December 12th, 1862," in *RG 59. General Records of the Department of State. Civil War Papers, 1861–1865. Case Files on Drafted Aliens. 1862–64. Entry 970. Box 3* (National Archives at College Park, 1862).

[80] F. W. Seward, "Department of State, Washington, March 18, 1863," in *RG 59. General Records of the Department of State. Civil War Papers, 1861–65. Letters sent Regarding Drafted Aliens. 1862–64. Entry 972* (National Archives at College Park, 1863).

[81] Ibid.

federal government's definition of American citizenship and thereby increasing the pool of recruits.[82]

Since Ohio, Indiana, Maryland, and Pennsylvania drafted before Wisconsin, the State Department received alienage claims as early as August and September 1862, which soon kept the secretary of state so busy that Ella Lonn later marveled that "Seward had time to attend to any of the other duties incident to the secretaryship of state."[83]

By the time the draft rolled around in Wisconsin on November 10, Seward was working hard to clarify the draft procedure and that same day attempted the following explanation in a letter to France's envoy, Henry Mercier:[84]

This is a complex government, consisting of State governments, within their sphere independent of the federal government; the federal government, its sphere, independent of the State governments. Collisions between them cannot be prevented by executive action. They must, however, be reconciled when they have occurred. The government calls on the States to furnish troops by draft of the militia. The States determine for themselves who constitute the militia, and they make the draft. They respectively provide for ascertaining who are liable to the draft and who are exempt from it, and they have State commissioners to hear, try, and determine such cases. Those commissioners render accounts of their doings to the governors of the States, and act with entire independence of the federal government, and are in no way responsible to them. If the governor of a State errs, and subjects to military duty a person who is entitled to exemption of the ground of alienage, a question is thus raised between the United States and the nation which is entitled to protect the complainant. This department then receives and promptly and effectually decides the case. It would indeed be very agreeable to communicate in advance to representatives of the foreign powers the principles upon which the department would proceed in such cases. But, on the other hand, it must be allowed there are few subjects more productive of conflicting legislation and adjudication than that of alienage. It seems, therefore, to be prudent to refrain from anticipating merely what speculative questions involve, and to confine the action of the government to those cases which, being practically brought before it, must necessarily receive its solution.[85]

---

[82] For a broader discussion of citizenship and the status of foreign-born residents within the Union in relation to the draft, see Douma, Rasmussen, and Faith, "The Impressment of Foreign-Born Soldiers in the Union Army."

[83] Lonn, *Foreigners in the Union Army and Navy*, 469–471.

[84] George W. Childs, ed. *The National Almanac and Annual Record for the Year 1863* (Philadelphia: George W. Childs, 1863), 82.

[85] *Papers Relating to Foreign Affairs Accompanying the Annual Message of the President to the First Session of the Thirty-Eight Congress*, Part II (Washington, DC: Government Printing Office, 1864), 744–745. See also Douma, Rasmussen, and Faith. "The Impressment of Foreign-Born Soldiers in the Union Army," 83–84.

Underscoring the confusion that reigned in immigrant communities (and the measures some were willing to take to avoid military service), Milwaukee's Prussian-born consul Adolph Rosenthal wrote to William Seward on November 24 with a long list of residents born within the German states who claimed to be exempt from service. The arguments forwarded by Rosenthal can in many ways be seen as a microcosm of the citizenship issues that the State Department based their decisions on in order to avoid diplomatic incidents of transnational consequence. Additionally, while patterns in the State Department's decision-making did emerge, it is also evident from Seward's letter to Mercier that the United States government attempted to retain some leeway in its handling of cases. Ultimately the burden of proof therefore fell on the immigrant claiming alienage, and if the paperwork was not sufficient then a military discharge was no guarantee.

At the one end of the spectrum, Rosenthal presented cases that were "such that the right to claim exemption is unquestionable" and pointed to thirteen foreign-born residents, "being subjects of foreign powers" as well as "having taken no steps to become citizens of the United States nor exercised any rights as such," as clear-cut examples.[86]

In the next paragraph followed the description of eleven subjects who "ceased to be subjects of their former sovereign, but have likewise not declared their intention to become citizens of the United States," and – one step further removed from being a subject of foreign power – six applications from individuals who "who it seems have ceased to be subject of their former sovereign and have declared their intention, to become citizens of the United States, but have not become such."[87] Rosenthal also submitted three cases of German immigrants who seemed to have moved closer to American citizenship. Despite having made affidavits that they were "still subjects of their homegovernments [sic]," these three immigrants had "declared their intention to become citizens of America" and had voted.[88] Finally, the German consul submitted two applications on behalf of Andreas Sollar and Franz Wolfgram, who had "ceased to be subjects of their former sovereigns" and had "declared their intention and voted" but had "not become citizens of the United States."[89]

---

[86] Adolph Rosenthal, "To His Excellency William H. Seward," in *RG 59. General Records of the Department of State. Civil War Papers, 1861–1865. Case Files on Drafted Aliens. 1862–64. Entry 970. Box 6* (National Archives at College Park, 1862).
[87] Ibid.   [88] Ibid.
[89] Ibid. The same reasoning, being a native of a foreign country and not having completed the naturalization process, appears throughout the "Case Files on Drafted Aliens." See, for example, Hanson, "Madison, Wisconsin, December 12th, 1862."

This, in other words, was the continuum on which issues of forced military service and citizenship existed, in the eyes of a foreign consul; from having made no declaration of intent to naturalize and exercised no rights of American citizenship to having declared intent and voted but not finalized the process of naturalization. Highlighting the case-by-case decision-making outlined by Seward in his letter to Mercier, ten out of the initial thirteen cases in which Rosenthal deemed "the right to claim exemption" unquestionable resulted in discharge from the military.[90] At the other end of what one might call the "citizenship continuum," both Sollar and Wolfgram, who had declared their intention and voted, were denied discharge.[91]

Apart from the Dane County case of Ole Hanson, a small handful of successful Danish exemption cases from Kenosha and Racine County, all arguing for exemption based on alienage and supported by claims of not having voted or taken out papers intending to become American citizens, survive in the State Department records. Those cases, decided in late 1862 and early 1863, all resulted in discharge.[92]

Given the fact that Norwegians were much more numerous than Swedes and Danes in Wisconsin, it is perhaps surprising that only Ole Hanson's case made it all the way to the State Department in 1862, but a few explanations can be offered. Ella Lonn points out that the Swedish foreign minister saw little reason for granting Swedish and Norwegian nationals protection that they had voluntarily renounced by emigrating.[93]

Thus, the low number of high-level Swedish and Norwegian cases (only two out of the 436 Wisconsin cases that survive in the State Department archives) for an immigrant group that constituted more than 8 percent of all foreign-born Wisconsin residents in 1860 can partly be explained by lack of Old World political will to defend their former subjects against the American government's draft policies.[94] The Danish representative

[90] Rosenthal, "To His Excellency William H. Seward."   [91] Ibid.

[92] See, for example, Geo P. Hansen. "Vice Consulate for Denmark. Chicago Dec 12 1862," in *RG 59*. *General Records of the Department of State. Civil War Papers, 1861–1865. Case Files on Drafted Aliens. 1862–64. Entry 970. Box 5* (National Archives at College Park, 1862). See as well Hendrik Schmidt. "State of Wisconsin. Racine Co," in *RG 59*. *General Records of the Department of State. Civil War Papers, 1861–1865. Case Files on Drafted Aliens. 1862–64. Entry 970. Box 5* (National Archives at College Park, 1862). Additionally, Paul Quigley has found that the United States government, early in the war, usually granted "foreign subjects" exemptions to maintain good relations with European powers. See Paul Quigley, "Civil War Conscription and the International Boundaries of Citizenship," *Journal of the Civil War Era* 4, no. 3 (2014): 378.

[93] Lonn, *Foreigners in the Union Army and Navy*, 469–477.

[94] See Hanson, "Madison, Wisconsin, December 12th, 1862."

Raaslöff, who had developed close personal relationships to top American politicians early in the war and actively sought to have draft regulations clarified in August of 1862, helps explain why the four Danish cases taken to the State Department in 1862 resulted in exemption.[95]

Additionally, Scandinavian settlements patterns in rural areas, shaped by Norwegian, Swedish, and Danish immigrants mostly finding agricultural work, likely contributed to the relatively few Scandinavian "alienage" cases in comparison to the prevalence of cases from the area around Milwaukee, which was heavily populated by German immigrants and well represented by German consuls.[96] Living in rural Wisconsin, it was practically and economically difficult for Scandinavian immigrants to travel to Chicago, where the closest Scandinavian consuls at this time were located.[97]

In sum, the draft had much larger ramifications at the community level than what can be gleaned from the diplomatic correspondence and official draft rolls that are often used to gauge the level of draft resistance.[98] While 1,042 cases of alleged wrongfully forced military service survive in the State Department's records, including at least two Norwegians and five Danes, it is on the ground level, in the medical exemption offices, in the community meetings, and in the homes visited by enrollment officers that the real ramifications of the federally mandated draft must be sought. As

[95] W. Raaslöff, "Danish Legation. P.t. New York November 5th 1861," in *M-52. Notes from the Danish Legation in the U.S. to the Dept. of State, 1801–1906. Roll T3* (National Archives at College Park, 1861). See also Lonn, *Foreigners in the Union Army and Navy*, 458. For examples of Raaslöff's correspondence with high-level American politicians, see Michael J. Douma and Anders Bo Rasmussen, "The Danish St Croix Project: Revisiting the Lincoln Colonization Program with Foreign-Language Sources." *American Nineteenth Century History* 15, no. 3 (2014): 311–342.

[96] Torben Grøngaard Jeppesen, *Danske i USA 1850–2000*, 131–135. See also Alison Clark Efford, *German Immigrants, Race, and Citizenship in the Civil War Era* (Washington, DC: Cambridge University Press, 2013), 10.

[97] Geo P. Hansen, "Vice Consulate for Denmark. Chicago Dec 12 1862," in *RG 59. General Records of the Department of State. Civil War Papers, 1861–1865. Case Files on Drafted Aliens. 1862–64. Entry 970. Box 5* (National Archives at College Park, 1862). On December 12, 1862, the Danish vice-consul in Chicago, George P. Hansen, wrote to the legation in Washington, DC, about two cases of wrongful enlistment but alluded to several other; he also praised a local Wisconsin colonel for allowing the Danish subjects furlough "in all cases . . . to visit this city to consult me." For the geographical location of Danish consuls and vice-consuls, see Childs, *The National Almanac and Annual Record for the Year 1863*, 84–85.

[98] See for example, Quigley, "Civil War Conscription and the International Boundaries of Citizenship"; Anbinder, "Which Poor Man's Fight? Immigrants and the Federal Conscription of 1863."

demonstrated here, the draft impacted and complicated the labor relations that had previously characterized a small town like New Denmark by sending more than one out of three draft-eligible males to war between 1862 and 1865, and it challenged these foreign-born men who had come to the United States to enjoy the fruits of American citizen rights to grapple with the consequences of American citizenship duties. The Scandinavian immigrants' eagerness to participate in American democracy (and through the process of voting to further their own economic interests) left them unable to claim "alienage," and they thus had to resort to other ways of getting exempted from the draft rolls. Norwegian-born immigrants in some localities were quite successful in acquiring medical exemptions, while the Scandinavians in New Denmark initially were able to defer military service through mutual aid that allowed for the hiring of substitutes and likely also medical exemptions.

Yet, the draft, as James McPherson has pointed out, presented the potential for "an enormous expansion of federal power at the expense of the states," and by denying claims of "alienage" throughout the fall of 1862 to foreign-born residents who had either voted or declared their intent to become naturalized citizens, the State Department did expand the meaning of American citizenship before the legislative process caught up on March 3, 1863 with the Federal Conscription Act that by law expanded draft eligibility to "persons of foreign birth who shall have declared on oath their intention to become citizens."[99]

Thus, with a congressional legislative stroke, immigrants who had declared their intention to become citizens unambiguously became legally subject to military duty. As it turned out, the Federal Conscription Act and the related acts that followed would within the next two years have tremendous impact on communities like New Denmark and further reduce Scandinavian immigrants' incentive to naturalize or even emigrate in the first place.

To Scandinavian-born community members, these draft laws challenged American ideas of liberty and equality, since the state now coerced prospective citizens into the military and undermined opportunities for economic equality by putting a greater burden on less affluent immigrants than was the case for rich people.

---

[99] Mackey, *A Documentary History of the Civil War Era: Legislative Achievements*, 129–138.

8

A Rich Man's War

Along with the draft, economic hardship, exacerbated by the Civil War, filled the pages of Fritz Rasmussen's diary throughout the fall of 1862.[1] Faithfully, Rasmussen described the local economic prospects but often also the "quite variable" weather (one day surprisingly hot, the next chilly and cloudy). As October drew closer, however, the entries gradually shifted from meteorology to military tidings. With mounting Union casualties, dark clouds were gathering on the horizon.[2] On September 20, 1862, Rasmussen sarcastically noted that he might as well serve in the army, with all the difficulties and dangers that would bring, rather than endure the daily grind in New Denmark.[3] "It is most enough, to derange minor minds, those circumstances that both country and commerce are involved in," Rasmussen wrote:

> [For years,] I have been borrowing and going in debt, constantly increasing my property and very well [felt], that if things would continue, I would easily be able to clear up and splendidly, but now everything is down as a bog; and too, the fear of a possible "draft" compelling to go into the war. ... I have had but little of worldly comfort, when exepting [sic] the greatest of all comforts; a incomparable <u>good health</u>; as I have had to work

---

[1] F. W. Rasmussen, "Aid to Families of Drafted Men," *Green Bay Advocate*, November 27, 1862.

[2] See, for example, Fritz W. Rasmussen, "The 12. Friday [September]," in *Fritz William Rasmussen Papers. Diaries, 1857–1876* (Green Bay: Wisconsin Historical Society, 1862). On the military situation in 1862 and mounting Union casualties, see James M. McPherson, *Crossroads of Freedom: Antietam* (New York: Oxford University Press, 2002), 84–108.

[3] Fritz W. Rasmussen, "The 20. Saturday [September]," in *Fritz William Rasmussen Papers. Diaries, 1857–1876* (Green Bay: Wisconsin Historical Society, 1862).

most hard and in every way tried, to make both ends meet, which I as yet, have not been able to. But the present greatest aggravation and most contemptable [sic] of all: is to hear those in pecuniary regard, well off, to complain and expressing their patriotism, in the most pitiable manner. So much for human Senserity [sic].[4]

The war had made it increasingly difficult to procure cash, and trade opportunities were suppressed.[5]

In addition, Fritz Rasmussen also recorded his wife Sidsel's dissatisfaction "with things and circumstances" over the summer.[6] According to Fritz Rasmussen, Sidsel had compared their condition with that of others and was "gritty and grumbling," as she was "quite adverse to farming" and considered "a farmer nothing more or less than a hireling or working-animal, for society in general."[7] Rasmussen, however, expressed the hope that her feelings would change "when the dice" would "turn up a little richer" in his favor.[8]

In late May, Rasmussen had written of "work work, steady and allways [sic], so that it blackens up before the eyes; and no time [for] any relax in work," and yet he was not able to procure even the "most necessary wants in the household."[9] Moreover, on May 5, 1862, Rasmussen, "celebrated" his twenty-ninth birthday with a diary tirade rejecting the notion that "life is sweet."[10] To the Danish immigrant, life's sweetness only came true for one in a thousand, while he himself had a difficult time even writing: due to another hard day's work, "the hand will not lay steady," Rasmussen scribbled.[11] At the root of the problem were people, often "those well off," who constructed or maintained hierarchies, Rasmussen argued.[12] One such person was

---

[4] Ibid.

[5] For an example of cash scarcity in New Denmark, see Fritz W. Rasmussen, "The 25 Monday," in *Fritz Wiliam Rasmussen Papers. Diaries, 1856–1876 Green Bay Mss 4. Box 8* (Green Bay: Wisconsin Historical Society, 1863).

[6] "The 8. Sondag [June]," in *Fritz William Rasmussen Papers. Diaries, 1856–1876. Green Bay Mss 4. Box 8* (Green Bay: Wisconsin Historical Society, 1862).

[7] Ibid.   [8] Ibid.

[9] Fritz W. Rasmussen, "The 27. Tuesday [May]," in *Fritz William Rasmussen Papers. Diaries, 1856–1876. Green Bay Mss 4. Box 8* (Green Bay: Wisconsin Historical Society, 1862).

[10] Fritz W. Rasmussen, "The 5th Monday [May]," in *Fritz William Rasmussen Papers. Diaries, 1856–1876. Green Bay Mss 4. Box 8* (Green Bay: Wisconsin Historical Society, 1862).

[11] Ibid.

[12] Rasmussen, "The 20. Saturday [September]"; "Den 31. Søndag. Paaske [The 31st Sunday. Easter]," in *Fritz William Rasmussen Papers. Diaries, 1856–1876. Green Bay Mss 4. Box 8* (Green Bay: Wisconsin Historical Society, 1862).

Frederik Hjort, who was described on March 31, 1861, as having Old World class sensibilities.[13]

Since he is a schoolmaster's son from Denmark [he] naturally possesses – to a pretty great extent – the inherent European power-seeking spirit that the poor smallholder or farm hand and the lower classes in Denmark as well as all of Europe sighs under and must tip their hat to. This is not found here and the constitution can therefore not be reconciled with such views, since regardless of how wealthy he is, he must nonetheless settle for being on an equal societal rung with the common man.[14]

If the affluent had been in a different position in life, Rasmussen posited, they would yearn for "Liberty, Equality and the Rights of man," even if the "present government" was admittedly imperfect (though the American "form of government" was not).[15] The opportunity to use one's free will in the United States, with nobody judging or punishing one's actions (and implicitly thereby allowing for upward social mobility), was the freedom attainable only in the New World, according to Rasmussen.[16]

As we have seen, the class-based discussion between Rasmussen and Hjort that centered on equality also tied into conflicts over slavery between mainly rural congregations and well-educated clergymen in the Scandinavian communities in the North and a year later shaped opinions of the draft as well.[17]

Yet it was not solely in the northern villages that debates raged over who were the producers of economic growth and who were the beneficiaries of that labor. The deepening sense that the rich and powerful were exploiting the poor, a perception familiar to Old World immigrants, was apparent in the South as well.[18]

---

[13] Peter Sørensen Vig, *Danske i Amerika [Danes in America]*, 2 vols., vol. 1 (Minneapolis, MN: C. Rasmussen Company, 1907), 261–262. See also "Indbetalt På Emigr. [Paid to Emigranten]."

[14] Rasmussen, "Den 31. Søndag. Paaske [The 31st Sunday. Easter]."   [15] Ibid.

[16] Ibid. An intellectual who did not understand the meaning of freedom in the Old and New World, in Rasmussen's view, was destined – "here as well as there" – to remain with his "plow or axe" and accept that, in the United States, a man would not be able to "earn his bread with his mouth" like the preacher and the dog. See also John Gotlieb Matteson, *Matteson Liv Og Adventbevægelsens Begyndelse Blandt Skadinaverne – En Selvbiografi [Matteson's Life and the Adventist Movement's Origin among the Scandinavians – an Autobiography]* (College View, NE: International Publishing Association, 1908), 63–64.

[17] Mary Yeater Rathbun, ed., *The Historic Perry Norwegian Settlement* (Daleyville, WI: Perry Historical Center, 1994), 191.

[18] Discussions over the relationship between slaveholders and non-slaveholders and slavery's central role in the South as well as in a Northern (rural) capitalist system were apparent across the country. On rural capitalism, see Christopher Clark, *The Roots of*

Accounts of the Norwegian, Swedish, and Danish immigrants' experiences with life in the slaveholding South appeared periodically in newspapers and private letters. These depictions demonstrated that Scandinavians in the South benefited economically from slavery even if they did not directly support slaveownership or the Confederate state-building experiment.[19]

Still, while there is evidence that several Scandinavians were reluctant participants in the slaveholding economy, class, in combination with significant social pressure, often trumped race in the struggle to achieve upward social mobility. In other words, few Scandinavian immigrants in the South challenged the institution of slavery since many indirectly benefited economically from it. Yet, tacit acceptance of the surrounding slavery-based society did not mean widespread embrace of secession. On the contrary, opposition to the planter class grew stronger as the Civil War progressed even as dissidents found themselves in a perilous position.

In *Emigranten* on May 20, 1861, a Norwegian-born correspondent warned that anarchy reigned in New Orleans: people were being

Rural Capitalism: Western Massachusetts, 1780–1860 (Ithaca, NY: Cornell University Press, 1990), 226–229, 72–80. For the connection between slavery and capitalism, see Sven Beckert, *Empire of Cotton: A Global History* (New York Alfred A. Knopf, 2014), 146–147. On discussions within the Scandinavian community, see "Negerslaveriet Og Fremtiden [Negro Slavery and the Future]." In this piece, published in the Democratic newspaper *Den Norske Amerikaner*, the writer argued: "Slavery probably impoverishes the South, as they say, but from there it does not necessarily follow, that it necessarily impoverishes the individual slaveholders themselves. Slavery impoverishes Virginia, but it enriches a John Taylor, a John Mason, a Wm. Smith, who rule Virginia. . . . In reality, slave labor is a highly profitable and advantageous monopoly and its great advantages are only restrained by competition amongst itself. Slavery is no different in its harmful repercussions than other monopolies."
[19] Some Scandinavian immigrants, for example, inherited enslaved people upon marrying or rented slaves when they needed work done. See Marco Giardino and Russell Guerin, *Mississippi's No-Man's Land: An Echo of the Koch Family Letters* (Denver, CO: Outskirts Press, 2006), 4–11. Also *The Swedes in Texas* asserts that Swante Magnus Swenson, who owned more than 100,000 acres in Travis County, Texas, had become a slaveowner through marriage but sold the family's slaves when the Civil War broke out. See Ernest Severin et al., *Svenskarne i Texas i Ord Och Bild, 1838–1918* [*The Swedes in Texas in Text and Images, 1838–1918*], vol. I (Austin, TX: E. L. Steck, 1919), 160–167. See also Carl T. Widen, "Texas Swedish Pioneers and the Confederacy," *Swedish Pioneer Historical Society* 12, no. 3 (1961): 101. See also "Mississippi Dec. 28, 1860," *Hemlandet*, January 16, 1861.

forced into military service and intimidation was ever-present.[20] A Dane living in Alabama in 1861 also alleged that "hangings and killings ... were the order of the day," for people who displayed sympathy for the North.[21]

Moreover, the threat of violence forced a Scandinavian company into Confederate service around New Orleans. Along with all other residents in New Orleans, Norwegians, Swedes, and Danes had been directed to report for drill training. As Union forces approached the city in the spring of 1862, the "the Scandinavian Guard" was presented with documents to sign up for six months of military service.[22] Few, if any, of the company's soldiers, however, wanted to join the Confederate cause, and the unit's leaders, according to an anonymous correspondent, explicitly framed the conflict as a rich man's war.

Almost all of us balked at signing and said that we had nothing to fight for until the enemy came within 3 miles of the city. Moreover, we found it more suitable if they would enlist one of the regiments consisting of rich Americans, many of whom had property and negroes worth more than 2 million dollars; these people had started the war and had something to fight for. We were foreigners who had to support ourselves through work. But all arguments were in vain.[23]

The powerlessness articulated by the Danish-born immigrant was far from isolated to Scandinavian residents in New Orleans. As Keri Leigh Merritt has demonstrated in her study of non-slaveholding whites, attaining political influence in the South was "an unrealistic dream" for most, as voting

---

[20] "Skandinaverne i New Orleans [The Scandinavians in New Orleans]," *Emigranten*, May 20, 1861. According to the writer, a sizable group of Scandinavian immigrants who continued to participate in the slave-based economy existed. "A Norwegian, who has just returned from New Orleans, recounts that the Scandinavian residents there are mainly rebels," the correspondent noted, adding that a Swedish immigrant had even attempted to form a Scandinavian company to fight for Jefferson Davis. This observation is backed up by a study of Norwegian soldiers in the Confederacy where the authors maintain that it is "probably correct to say, as one source puts it, 'The Texas Norse were divided over the Civil War. Though most were Union men ... the records show that [many] served in the Confederate Armies.'" See C. A. Clausen and Derwood Johnson, "Norwegian Soldiers in the Confederate Forces," *Norwegian-American Studies* 25 (1972).

[21] "Skandinaverne i New Orleans [The Scandinavians in New Orleans]"; H. L. P., "Amerika [America]," *Lolland-Falsters Stiftstidende*, July 4, 1861.

[22] "Skandinaverne i Syden [The Scandinavians in the South]," *Emigranten*, December 1, 1862.

[23] Ibid.

restrictions in a state like Louisiana barred the majority of "white men from the polls."[24]

Along with poor whites, slaveholders in the South worried about immigrant influence to such a degree that they incarcerated newcomers, especially men and women from Ireland, at a higher rate than their proportion of the population would otherwise warrant.[25] Despite such hardship, and their initial reluctance to support secession, many Irish immigrants still chose to join the Confederate ranks when war broke out. As an ethnic group, the Irish earned a reputation for bravery, but also, in the words of David Gleeson, "had a propensity to desert" and thereby challenged the notion of a "united Confederate nation."[26]

The relatively few Scandinavian immigrants' wartime actions further undermined the alleged Civil War era Solid South. When "the Scandinavian Guard" was forced into Louisiana's Chalmette Regiment, they, in their own words, did everything they could to resist and delay their service while consciously trying to set themselves apart by embracing Old World Scandinavian symbols as opposed to identifying with the newly formed Confederacy. The company named the throughway between their tents "Scandinavian Street" and the first tent on the street "Dannevirke," inspired by the historic and mythical Danish fortification in Schleswig that dated back to the pre-Viking age.[27]

When the threat of a Union invasion became real, the entire Chalmette Regiment refused to ship out toward Fort St. Philip but were forced at the point of guns and bayonets to do so.[28] In an act of defiance, the correspondent noted that the Scandinavian soldiers, by then, "had taken down the rebel flag but the Danish one still flew."[29]

The Scandinavians were positioned as sharpshooters at Fort Jackson in the middle of Louisiana's swamp region, surrounded by "snakes and

---

[24] Keri Leigh Merritt, *Masterless Men: Poor Whites and Slavery in the Antebellum South* (Cambridge: Cambridge University Press, 2017), 165–166. According to Merritt, "Louisiana's poor whites were so removed from the voting process" that some considered "the state an oligarchy."

[25] Ibid., 73–75, 191.

[26] There was, for example, widespread support for the national Democratic candidate Stephen Douglas in New Orleans during election of 1860. See David T. Gleeson, *The Green and the Gray: The Irish in the Confederate States of America* (Chapel Hill: University of North Carolina Press, 2013), 7–8, 33–42.

[27] "Skandinaverne i Syden [The Scandinavians in the South]."   [28] Ibid.   [29] Ibid.

insects as well as crocodiles," but when the attack came on April 24 at 3 a.m. the Chalmette Regiment, with its contingent of Scandinavian troops, surrendered "without firing a shot."[30] As Michael Pierson has shown, the surrender at Fort Jackson indicated "just how little resistance" nonvolunteers around New Orleans were willing to offer, and the lack of Confederate zeal was underlined a few days later in a mutiny at Fort Jackson involving many German and Irish immigrants.[31]

THE
BATTLE OF NEW ORLEANS
Philadelphia LEE & WALKER

FIGURE 8.1 The Union Navy's attack on Fort Jackson and Fort St. Philip on the way to New Orleans on April 24, 1862, is here depicted as more dramatic than the parts of the battle where Old World immigrants were involved. Photo by MPI/ Stringer/Archive Photos/Getty Images.

[30] Michael D. Pierson, *Mutiny at Fort Jackson: The Untold Story of the Fall of New Orleans* (Chapel Hill: University of North Carolina Press, 2008), 112. See also "Skandinaverne i Syden [The Scandinavians in the South]."

[31] Pierson, Mutiny at Fort Jackson: The Untold Story of the Fall of New Orleans, 68–112; Keating, *Shades of Green: Irish Regiments, American Soldiers, and Local Communities in the Civil War Era* (New York: Fordham University Press, 2017), 100–102.

With the fall of New Orleans, the only Scandinavian ethnic unit in the Confederate military ceased to exist, but the class-based tension under-lying its military service persisted. In an example of subtle criticism of the Confederate ruling class, Danish-born A. J. Miller wrote a satirical letter to a friend on June 26, 1862, about the absence of patriotism he and his sons felt. Both of Miller's sons, Jon and Charles, had been conscripted "into the great Confederate States' army to fight for freedom and against – I don't know what," Miller wrote and continued with a comment on the hardship the Civil War had already visited on the community as evidenced by the condition of his poultry.[32] "The fowl had consumption – as it was said – from lack of something to consume."[33]

Christian Koch, a Danish-born sailor who had married into an American family and settled in Bogue Homa north of New Orleans, quickly experienced the fear and privations of Civil War as well. Koch operated a schooner which was seized by Union forces early in the war and therefore had to navigate the borderlands between Union-held territory around New Orleans and his family home in Confederate-held Hancock County, Mississippi. Writing from New Orleans on September 10, 1862, Koch urged his wife Annette to help their sons avoid military service by hiding from Confederate authorities. "If they have not yet taken Elers, send him, for Gods sake, of[f] at once, let him stay in the swamp," Koch wrote, "I think Emil had also better keep out of theyr vay [sic], as I hear the[y] take boys from 16 years."[34]

Additionally, in a testament to challenges both North and South, Swedish-born Frans O. Danielson in his November 20, 1862, letter home from Helena, Arkansas, explained to his family that southern politicians had passed a law "that no man" owning "twenty Negroes" could be drafted.[35] "That will make some of the lower classes open their eyes," Danielson added.[36]

---

[32] Vig, *Danske i Amerika* [*Danes in America*], 1, 241.

[33] Ibid. Miller's one son, John, came home after twelve months of service, but when the letter was sent his "poor Charles" was "still in the grip of these great champions of freedom."

[34] Christian Ditlev Koch, "No. Sept 10 1862," in *Christian D. Koch and Family Papers, Mss. 202, Louisiana and Lower Mississippi Valley Collections. Box 1* (LSU Libraries, Baton Rouge, Louisiana, 1862). See also Giardino and Guerin, *Mississippi's No-Man's Land: An Echo of the Koch Family Letters*, 5–13.

[35] F. O. Danielson, "Helena, Arkansas November 5, 1862," in *Mathilda Cassel Peterson Danielson (1834–). SSIRC Mss P: 55* (Augustana College, 1862). See also Check and Johnson (translator), "Civil War Letters to New Sweden, Iowa," *Swedish-American Historical Quarterly* 36, no. 1 (1985): 3–25

[36] F. O. Danielson, "Helena, Arkansas November 5, 1862," in *Mathilda Cassel Peterson Danielson (1834–). SSIRC Mss P: 55* (Augustana College, 1862).

In time, poor whites and immigrants in the South did open their eyes, at least if measured by their opposition to military service. According to Merritt, "the Confederacy suffered incredibly high rates of desertion" among "poor whites" fighting against their will, and David Gleeson observes that "Irish soldiers deserted more often than their native-born colleagues," while a predominantly German company in the Army of Northern Virginia had the worst desertion rate of all.[37]

Though the number of surviving records is small, a similar development seems to have taken place among Scandinavian immigrants in the South. In a letter home, Elers Koch, who by 1863 was conscripted into the 9th Mississippi Cavalry, expressed support for his Uncle George who had seemingly deserted, and Christian Koch, in an April 13, 1863 letter, cursed "the 'rascals' who caused the war."[38] Moreover, forty-eight-year-old Charles Stevens, another Danish-born sailor, only reluctantly joined a cavalry unit in Georgia in 1864 and was later claimed to have opposed secession.[39] In short, the class tension underlying military service revealed itself repeatedly whether it was around New Orleans or New Denmark.

Fritz Rasmussen's brother-in-law, Celius Christiansen, hired a fellow immigrant to serve in his place when he was drafted in 1862, but two years later, when Christiansen was forced into the military again, he no longer had any "pretense about hiring a substitute": by then "it was only

[37] Merritt, *Masterless Men: Poor Whites and Slavery in the Antebellum South*, 36; David T. Gleeson, *The Irish in the South, 1815–1877* (Chapel Hill: University of North Carolina Press, 2001), 150. See also Gleeson, *The Green and the Gray: The Irish in the Confederate States of America*, 221.

[38] Elers Koch, "Monticello, April 3, 1863," in *Christian D. Koch and Family Papers, Mss. 202, Louisiana and Lower Mississippi Valley Collections. Box 1* (LSU Libraries, Baton Rouge, Lousiana, 1863). Earlier correspondence also supports Christian Koch's reservations toward the slaveholding elite's power even if at times he benefited from using enslaved people as laborers. On July 15, 1856, Koch wrote Annette from his hometown in Denmark and expressed frustration over the family lumber business in Mississippi. In Christian Koch's view, "indeed there" was "a heap more liberty here than in the Southern states." See Christian Ditlev Koch, "Kirkeby, July 15, 1854," in *Christian D. Koch and Family Papers, Mss. 202, Louisiana and Lower Mississippi Valley Collections. Box 1* (LSU Libraries, Baton Rouge, Louisiana, 1854). The quote from Christian Koch appears in Giardino and Guerin, *Mississippi's No-Man's Land: An Echo of the Koch Family Letters*, 15–18.

[39] Charles E. Pearson, "Captain Charles Stevens and the Antebellum Georgia Coasting Trade," *Georgia Historical Quarterly* 75, no. 3 (1991): 505. I am grateful to David J. Gerleman for bringing this story to my attention.

the rich man who enjoyed that right."[40] Christiansen's rural draft experience mirrored that of numerous immigrants in American cities. As Tyler Anbinder has found, "immigrants were far less likely than natives to buy their way out of the draft."[41] However, different strategies for draft resistance strategies ensured that urban immigrants, often German and Irish, overall were underrepresented in the United States military while the onus of the draft fell "disproportionately" on "native-born laborers, especially those residing in rural areas."[42]

While there were several exemption categories, it was clear that immigrant enclaves, urban and rural, would now even more concretely have to decide what citizenship meant to them. To Scandinavian immigrants, exercising the right to vote was a key part of citizenship, and the war's ebbs and flows led some to a reassessment of political allegiances.

While Fritz Rasmussen generally supported the Republican Party's economic ideals, he at times also considered its policy implementations flawed. For the Danish-born New Denmark resident, the disillusionment with the war and the country's overall economic circumstances likely led him to stray from the Republican Party. In his diary on November 4, 1862, Rasmussen noted that he went down to the local schoolhouse in the morning to "observe 'the general election'" and afterward brought home salt for a neighbor who had to split a barrel with a countryman due to the rising prices.[43] In the early afternoon, Rasmussen and his Uncle Knud both voted for the Democratic county clerk candidate Myron P. Lindsley, who had written to Rasmussen personally to ask for his vote.[44]

At the state level, the 1862 midterm election also proved difficult for Republican candidates. The Democratic Party picked up three of Wisconsin's six seats in the House of Representatives in Washington,

---

[40] Celius Christiansen, *En Pioneers Historie (Erindringer Fra Krigen Mellem Nord- Og Sydstaterne) [A Pioneer's Story: Memoirs from the War between North and South]* (Aalborg: Eget forlag, 1909), 48–49. "It was now the third time I had to leave home to go to war, once in Denmark and twice in America," Christiansen recounted.

[41] Tyler Anbinder, "Which Poor Man's Fight? Immigrants and the Federal Conscription of 1863," *Civil War History* 52, no. 4 (2006): 351.

[42] Ibid., 347–351.

[43] Fritz W. Rasmussen, "November 4, 1862," in *Fritz William Rasmussen Papers. Diaries, 1856–1876. Box 8. Green Bay Mss 4* (Green Bay: Wisconsin Historical Society, 1862).

[44] Ibid.

DC, and thereby split the number of representatives equally with their Republican opponents.[45]

At the national level, however, Fritz Rasmussen gave the impression of being a solid, though not uncritical, supporter of the Republican Party as evidenced by his December 1862 exchange with the local Bohemian doctor, Mr. Patrzizny, "as fanatical a democrat as any."[46] On their political differences, Rasmussen noted, "Laying that aside we are very sincere freinds [sic], he not having the remotest idea; of my adheranse [sic] to a different creed."[47]

A few weeks earlier, partly demonstrating his frustration with the draft, Rasmussen recorded a derisive description of Brown County's Irish-born draft commissioner, Henry S. Baird, who, in Rasmussen's view, had "branded" himself as "thorough Democrat" and normalized "aristocracy" in handling his responsibilities.[48] Still, most community members in New Denmark managed to avoid the draft in 1862, and Fritz Rasmussen's somewhat intermittent surviving diary entries in the early part of 1863 dealt more with local than national news. Partly because of the Danish-born immigrant tiring of the daily writing and partly because of a diary having gone missing, little is known of Fritz Rasmussen's end to 1862, but on Friday, March 20, he picked up the pen for the first time in 1863.[49] "Finally I thought to have become true to my oft taken decision of ending my scribbling or diary-writing and observations," Rasmussen began before citing his reasons to

[45] "The Next Congress," *Wisconsin State Journal*, November 8, 1862. *Emigranten* on November 10 attempted to explain the results as something to be "expected" but also made the losses seem smaller than they actually were by, perhaps inadvertently, reporting a Republican 4–2 advantage. See "Valgene," *Emigranten*, November 10, 1862.

[46] Fritz W. Rasmussen, "Sunday December 14, 1862," in *Fritz William Rasmussen Papers. Diaries, 1856–1876. Green Bay Mss 4. Box 8* (Green Bay: Wisconsin Historical Society, 1862).

[47] Ibid. Rasmussen voted for Lincoln in 1860, cast a Union vote in November of 1863 and voted to elect Ulysses S. Grant in 1868. See "November 1860. Den 7de. [November 1860. The 7th]." Also "Tuesday November 3, 1863." Also "The 3rd Tuesday [November]," in *Fritz William Rasmussen Papers. Diaries, 1856–1876. Green Bay Mss 4. Box 8* (Green Bay: Wisconsin Historical Society, 1868).

[48] Fritz W. Rasmussen, "Den 27. Torsdag [November]," in *Fritz William Rasmussen Papers. Diaries, 1856–1876. Green Bay Mss 4. Box 8* (Green Bay: Wisconsin History Society, 1862).

[49] Fritz W. Rasmussen, "Den 20de Fredag [Marts]," in *Fritz William Rasmussen Papers. Diaries, 1857–1876; Account Books, 1856–1909; "Record of Skandinavians Who Have Been Settled and Lived in the Town of New Denmark, Brown County, Wisconsin." Box no. 8* (Green Bay: Wisconsin Historical Society, 1863).

contemplating quitting; difficulties getting paper, poor lighting, and weariness after a day's work were all reasons, yet in the end he had to admit that keeping his journal had become a habit and a few years later also admitted that writing had a therapeutic quality to it, as it helped dispel his "troubled thoughts."[50]

The following months provided ample opportunity for "troubled thoughts" concerning both local draft politics and national party politics. In addition, local tragedies provided immediate grounds for reflection in the early summer.

In his diary entry from June 5, 1863, Fritz Rasmussen noted that he had passed the early part of the day "with talk and political discourses and differing opinions about the same (politics)" with his work crew before going up to Einar Quisling to attend the funeral of the Norwegian farmer's youngest who "died the other day."[51] A number of neighbors congregated at Quisling's home after the funeral to pay their respects, and just as people finished greeting each other, "yet another little girl (the second oldest), who laid 'saddled with with death,' died":[52]

It was decided to lay the second child to rest that Sunday and that morning Rasmussen helped prepare the grave for Quisling's little one and attended the funeral with his father and father-in-law. At one point later in the day, Sidsel, seven months pregnant with her and Fritz's third child, feared that their daughter Rasmine also had fallen ill with the same symptoms as the two children who had just passed way. The Rasmussen family, however, breathed a sigh of relief when it turned out that Rasmine's condition improved quickly.[53]

In short order, illness had taken two of the youngest New Denmark community members, and the Civil War was threatening to take several older ones. As previously noted, Johan Hauer died from disease on February 15, 1862, his older brother August had since volunteered as a substitute, and Niels Peter Pedersen had been gravely wounded on June 2, 1863, during the siege of Vicksburg.[54] Now, as the draft rolls

[50] "The 26th Friday [July]," in *Fritz William Rasmussen Papers. Diaries, 1856–1876. Green Bay Mss 4. Box 8* (Green Bay: Wisconsin Historical Society, 1867).
[51] "Den 5te Fredag [June]," in *Fritz William Rasmussen Papers. Diaries, 1856–1876. Green Bay Mss 4. Box 8* (Green Bay: Wisconsin Historical Society, 1863).
[52] Ibid.   [53] Fritz W. Rasmusssen, "Den 7de Søndag [June]," ibid.
[54] Vig, *Danske i Amerika [Danes in America]*, 1, 356.

were once again being made up in Wisconsin during July and August 1863, Fritz Rasmussen, along with his twenty-nine-year-old neighbor Theodore Hansen and several others, found their names on the official "draft registration" list.[55]

Hansen, who was born in the same Old World village as Fritz Rasmussen's wife and regularly swapped labor with Fritz Rasmussen in America, owned a plot of land close to the Rasmussen family.[56] In March 1861, Fritz Rasmussen recorded in his diary that Theodore Hansen, who had been part of the New Denmark community since 1855, was looking to buy yet another plot of land in New Denmark and thereby indicated that the relatively young immigrant was on his way to realizing upward social mobility through landownership in America.[57]

Military service could be an avenue to upward social mobility with enlistment bonuses and, theoretically, a steady monthly income, but Theodore Hansen's dreams were tied to farming not fighting. Hansen's stepfather, Mads Rasmussen, who had avoided military service likely due to his age and marital status, harbored little affection for his stepson and might have exerted pressure, directly or indirectly, to make the younger family member enlist in his place.[58] A later account, at least, maintained that Theodore Hansen enlisted to avoid Mads Rasmussen's having to serve.[59]

After enlisting in the 22nd Wisconsin Infantry on November 13, 1863 (and initially expressing satisfaction with the lighter workload in the army compared to life on the farm), Hansen's subsequent letters demonstrate that his motives for enlisting were not tied to economic aspirations or patriotic sentiment.[60] Hansen's reluctance to serve mirrored dynamics

[55] Ibid.

[56] Fritz W. Rasmussen, "20. Løverdag [Juni]," in *Fritz William Rasmussen Papers. Diaries, 1856–1876* (Geren Bay: Wisconsin Historical Society, 1863).

[57] "Den 20. Onsdag [Og Indlæg Fra Marts Også]," in *Fritz William Rasmussen Papers. Diaries, 1857–1876; Acount Books, 1856–1909; "Record of Skandinavians Who Have Been Settled and Lived in the Town of New Denmark, Brown County, Wisconsin."* Box No. 8. Green Bay Mss 4 (Green Bay: Wisconsin Historical Society, 1861).

[58] For Fritz Rasmussen's assessment of Mads Rasmussen and Theodore Hansen's relationship, see Fritz W. Rasmussen, "Den 13de Tirsdag [September]," in *Fritz William Rasmussen Papers. Diaries, 1857–1876; Account Books, 1856–1909; "Record of Skandinavians Who Have Been Settled and Lived in the Town of New Denmark, Brown county, Wisconsin."* Box no. 8 (Green Bay: Wisconsin Historical Society, 1864).

[59] Johnsen, "New Denmark 3/8 Ad 1882 [March 8th]."

[60] Theodore Hansen, "Murfreesboro Feb 13[,] 64," in *Civil War Mother's Pension. Application 258778* (Washington, DC: National Archives, 1864).

within the German immigrant community, where Mischa Honneck has found that the "compulsory features" of the 1863 Enrollment Act even "invited comparisons to slavery and tyranny."[61]

Still, despite the draft resistance apparent on the ground in immigrant communities, important political differences remained between the Scandinavians and larger ethnic groups.[62]

Hans Borchsenius, the recently converted Democrat (and, on account of illness, recently discharged army adjutant), specifically warned against backing his former party. "I know that the Democrats are working hard to assume government power and are attempting to persuade people in every possible way," Borchsenius wrote in a piece published by *Emigranten* on October 27, 1862.[63] Democratic critique of high taxes and hard times, however, rang hollow when considering their unrealistic political platform, Borchsenius maintained. "Everyone ought to have their attention directed at the congressional elections, as the nation's fate might depend on a fortunate outcome," Borchsenius argued, and the soldiers of the 15th Wisconsin Regiment responded with strong Republican support.[64]

With the exception of three men, the 15th Wisconsin voted unanimously for a Republican candidate in the 1862 midterm election and counted 239–0 votes for the Republican candidate in Wisconsin's chief justice election in April 1863, along with 41–0 in Wisconsin's gubernatorial election on November 3, 1863 (in comparison, 82 percent of the

---

[61] Mischa Honeck, "Men of Principle: Gender and the German American War for the Union," *Journal of the Civil War Era* 5, no. 1 (2015): 56.

[62] On the political differences, an unnamed immigrant wrote home to the Old World Danish newspaper *Flyveposten* on July 30, 1863, that the political situation in the North was "disintegrating in every respect." The two main parties, "the Democrats and the Republicans (the black negro Republicans)," hated each other, and, added the letter writer, who seemingly identified with neither party, "now conscription has arrived, but the Democrats won't join." Everyone were so tired of war that they wanted peace at any price, the writer claimed, before noting, "The wisest thing for me to do might not even be to stay here until next year, as I risk conscription for the army with the next draft." See "Af Et Brev Fra En Dansk i America [Of a Letter from a Dane in America]," *Flyveposten*, September 24, 1863.

[63] Borchsenius, "Et Par Ord Om Valgene [A Few Words on the Elections]."

[64] Ibid. "Let us support the Union and the Constitution and we shall yet experience a fortuitous and honorable end to the war while having the fond knowledge that we, through out votes, have contributed to bring about the implementation of old Jackson's saying 'The Union must and shall be preserved.'"

predominantly German 9th Wisconsin and 25 percent of the mainly Irish 17th Wisconsin supported the Republican candidate, James D. Lewis).[65] Fritz Rasmussen also threw his support behind the party in power during the gubernatorial election of 1863:[66]

In the afternoon gone down to Schoolhouse No. 1, to vote, at the general Election; of course "Union vote" and, what a clamour [sic] the "Catholics" made; who are all without national distinction – "Democrats."[67]

To Rasmussen it seemed as if American society, no matter how great the expression of "adherence to republican sentiments and institutions," was becoming increasingly hierarchical and undermining opportunities for individual expression.[68] "'Dog over Dog,' that is human nature," he noted, but much of his frustration was also tied to renewed worries over the draft.[69] *Emigranten* recorded the 1863 election results on November 9 and described the outcome as the largest Republican victory in Wisconsin since Lincoln's election in 1860, but the paper quickly turned its attention to draft-related issues as well.[70]

Given the draft's magnitude in the Scandinavian-American community it therefore seemed only fitting that Fritz Rasmussen ended 1863 on a conscription-related note. In his December 31 entry, Rasmussen described his farm-related chores (chopping stove wood) and community-related work (helping residents with official and personal

[65] A. C. Johnson et al., "Statement of Votes Polled for State Senators by the Electors of Company B of the Fifteenth Wisconsin Regiment of Infantry at an Election Held at Bowling Green Ky. On Tuesday, the Fourth Day of November, A.D. 1862," in *Wisconsin. Governor Military Votes, 1862–1865. Series 60. Box 2* (Madison: Wisconsin Historical Society, 1862); "Wisconsin Military Vote-1863 and 1864," *Prescott Journal*, December 10, 1864.

[66] The "Wisconsin Seventh" and the "Third Wisconsin" also voted overwhelmingly for the Republican candidate. Frank Klement, "The Soldier Vote in Wisconsin During the Civil War," *Wisconsin Magazine of History* 28, no. 1 (1944): 45. Regarding Irish and German support for the Democratic Party, see Keating, *Shades of Green: Irish Regiments, American Soldiers, and Local Communities in the Civil War Era*, 74, 141; Walter D. Kamphoefner and Wolfgang Helbich, eds., *Germans in the Civil War: The Letters They Wrote Home* (Chapel Hill: University of North Carolina Press, 2006), 12.

[67] Fritz W. Rasmussen, "Tuesday November 3, 1863," in *Fritz William Rasmussen Papers. Diaries, 1856–1876* (Green Bay: Wisconsin Historical Society, 1863).

[68] Ibid.   [69] Ibid.

[70] "Novembervalgene – Unionsmændene Seire i Wisconsin [The November Election – Union Men Triumph in Wisconsin]," *Emigranten*, November 9, 1863.

correspondence). On the final day of the year, Rasmussen paid out money from the "public (Volunteer) fund" to the wife of a local Civil War soldier, and later he helped a countryman, Lars Andersen, write a couple of letters, "one to his son in the Army and one to the Office of the 'Emigranten' with a part of his contingent." On his last line for the year 1863, Rasmussen neatly and gloomily noted, "So ended this year too and has entered the space of nothingness, as many of its predescessors [sic] before it; gone! gone!! And, we are going too."[71]

[71] Rasmussen, "Thursday December 31."

9

Echoes of Emancipation

While Fritz Rasmussen closed out 1863 thinking about the draft, that same year had begun with discussions about issues of race. In its first editorial of 1863, *Hemlandet* celebrated "a new epoch" in "this country's history" as slavery had been abolished, the rebellion's backbone broken, and freedom reestablished.[1] Still, *Hemlandet*'s articles demonstrated continued widespread feelings of vengeance toward Dakota bands, and the lead-up to emancipation revealed a lack of support for racial equality within the Scandinavian-American community.[2]

Throughout 1862, expressions of racial superiority occurred regularly even among professed anti-slavery officers. On January 15, 1862, Ferdinand Winslöw, chief quartermaster for the Army of the Southwest, described his "elegant free darkie" servant, Homer Grimes, as a "nigger" ready "for any command," and a few months later Colonel Hans Heg noted his young Black servant working hard while acting as "a good Nigger."[3] Additionally, in an

---

[1] "Nytårshelsning [New Year's Greeting]," *Hemlandet*, January 7, 1863.

[2] On expressions and feelings of vengeance toward the Dakota, see N., "Til Red. Af Hemlandet [To the Editor of Hemlandet]," ibid.; Andrew Jackson, "Scandia, Carver Co., Minn. D. 13 Dec. 1862," ibid.

[3] Ferdinand Sophus Winsløw, "Pacific, Mo. 15 January 1862," in *Ferdinand Sophus Winslow letters, September 1861-February 1862* (University of Iowa, Special Collections Department, 1862). In describing his breakfast ritual, Winslöw, who paid Grimes $20 a month, wrote: "In the morning he makes fire, brushes all my clothes and blackens my boots, stands over me while I dress; he has charge of all my trunks and clothes, sees to the washing, and altogether I have first rate comfort by his attendance. When I am dressed, he spreads the table, comes back with a waiter with my coffee, milk, sugar, steak and other eatables, and there I sit in my lordly solitude,

undated letter to his Danish-born father, seemingly composed in 1862, seventeen-year-old Charles Adolphus Lund wrote from Racine, Wisconsin: "I do not believe in letting the Negro free, not by a good deal."[4]

Yet military developments prompted renewed assessment of race relations, not least within the Lincoln administration, and the Scandinavian-American press followed events closely. As the main Union Army frantically chased Robert E. Lee's Army of Northern Virginia into Maryland during the first half of September 1862, the Scandinavian-American press, drawing on east coast newspapers, published weekly situation reports.[5] In a by-now well-known turn of events, a Union corporal's discovery of Lee's Special Order 191, detailing the Confederate Army's movements, gave the government troops an unprecedented advantage, and the subsequent costly battle around Antietam Creek on September 17 forced the invaders back.[6] The victory gave President Lincoln a successful military pretext for issuing the Preliminary Emancipation Proclamation on September 22, which *Emigranten* (notably commenting on the proclamation's military instead of moral impact) described as a "mighty step forward in suppressing the rebellion."[7] Lincoln's proclamation proposed to compensate states in the Union that set "immediate or gradual" abolition in motion but, as we have seen, also kept the option of colonization, with freedpeople's consent, open.[8] Thus, the Preliminary Emancipation Proclamation implicitly reinforced a view of white citizenship that was also demonstrated in Secretary Seward's Homestead Act promotion in Europe and further underlined by his September 30

---

the nigger standing in front, ready for any command." Also Theodore C. Blegen, *The Civil War Letters of Colonel Hans Christian Heg* (Northfield, MN: Norwegian-American Historical Association, 1936), 57. Heg added that his Black servant strutted around "as big as a monkey" when the colonel got him a pair of pants.

[4] Lund, "Dear Father."

[5] "Madison. 27de Septbr. 1862," *Emigranten*, September 29, 1862; "Reballarna i Maryland [The Rebels in Maryland]," *Hemlandet*, September 17, 1862; "Krigen i Virginia [The War in Virginia]," *Emigranten*, September 8, 1862.

[6] Charles B. Dew, "How Samuel E. Pittman Validated Lee's 'Lost Orders' Prior to Antietam: A Historical Note," *Journal of Southern History* 70, no. 4 (2004): 865–869.

[7] "Madison. 27de Septbr. 1862."

[8] "Madison. 27de Septbr. 1862," *Emigranten*, September 29, 1862; Edna Green Medford, *Lincoln and Emancipation* (Carbondale: Southern Illinois University Press, 2015), 61–62. See also James Oakes, *Freedom National: The Destruction of Slavery in the United States, 1861–1865* (New York: W. W. Norton, 2013), 301–302, 14–17.

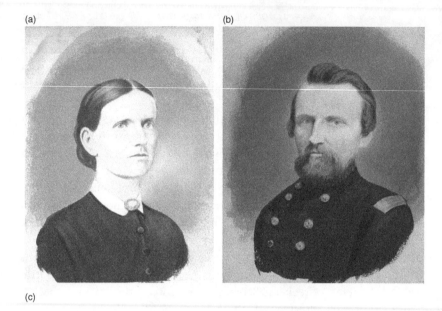

(a)   (b)

(c)

FIGURE 9.1 Ferdinand Winslöw (bottom right) wrote more than 100 letters to his wife, Wilhemina, during the Civil War, as did Hans Heg to his wife, Gunild, and both at times expressed a sense of white racial superiority. Courtesy Winslow Family Private Collection and Vesterheim Norwegian-American Museum Archives.

attempt to open colonization negotiations with Great Britain, France, Holland, and Denmark.[9]

Yet, even with its underlying premise of a continued white man's republic, the Preliminary Emancipation Proclamation was controversial. From 1862 and forward, Democrats, according to Eric Foner, raised fears that "Emancipation would produce 'scenes of lust and rapine' in the South and unleash 'a swarthy inundation of negro laborers and paupers' on the North."[10] With a message amplified through sympathetic editors, the Democratic Party hammered at the lack of military success, the ineffective leadership, the poor economy, and the Preliminary Emancipation Proclamation's impotence ahead of the 1862 midterms. As *Green Bay Advocate* editor Charles D. Robinson opined on October 2, 1862, you had to "catch your rabbit" before you could cook it, and the proclamation had no effect until "the States in rebellion" were once again brought "under the jurisdiction of the constitution."[11]

During this time of economic and military anxiety, Democratic viewpoints, as we have seen, appealed to some Scandinavian-born immigrants in New Denmark, and even among otherwise solid Republican supporters in the Scandinavian community, the Preliminary Emancipation Proclamation received a lukewarm reception. Swedish-born Frans O. Danielson, serving in the 29th Iowa, wrote to his siblings that he was glad to hear that the Republican Party had a lot of support back in New Sweden before commenting on the soldiers' reaction to Lincoln's proclamation: "There are some bitterly opposed to it but they will have to grin

---

[9] As Ella Lonn reminds us, Seward did everything he could to encourage immigration with the related aim of adding potential white military personnel. See Ella Lonn, *Foreigners in the Union Army and Navy* (Baton Rouge: Louisiana State University Press, 1951), 418–420. See also James Mitchell, *Report on Colonization and Emigration Made to the Secretary of the Interior by the Agent of Emigration* (Washington, DC: Government Printing Office, 1862), 28. See also Phillip W. Magness and Sebastian N. Page, *Colonization after Emancipation: Lincoln and the Movement for Black Resettlement* (Columbia: University of Missouri Press, 2011), 73. See also Seward, "Department of State, Washington, 30th September 1862, Bradford R. Wood, Esquire."

[10] Eric Foner, *The Fiery Trial: Abraham Lincoln and American Slavery* (New York: W. W. Norton, 2010), 234–235.

[11] "The President's Proclamation," *Green Bay Advocate*, October 2, 1862. A few weeks later, Robinson also charged Republicans with undermining the Constitution and depicted New York's Democratic governor Horatio Seymour as one "of the men who have stood upright amid the storm of fanaticism." See "Gov. Seymour and the War," October 23, 1862.

and bear it," Danielson wrote.[12] Perhaps more revealing, Danielson, who had observed runaway slaves up close as part of the Army of the Southwest in Helena, Arkansas, added: "Let me know if you have got Niggers up in Iowa yet, and what you think of freeing them and sending them North. We have got thousands of the buggers down here. For my part I don't think much of them."[13]

In expressing views of Black people's inferior status, however, Scandinavian immigrants were far from alone.[14] Responding to an equipment request from the Army of the Southwest, Major-General Henry W. Halleck suggested that the army's commander, Samuel R. Curtis, and his "antislavery politics" were part of a larger problem, as Congress was "so busy discussing the eternal nigger question" that they failed to make the necessary appropriations.[15] Moreover, as Curtis' army advanced toward Helena in the spring and summer of 1862, enslaved people by the thousands "abandoned their masters" and joined the march, which foreshadowed the challenges and criticism of emancipation along the banks of the Mississippi River.[16] Curtis, who was closely aligned with German-born anti-slavery radicals in his ranks and personally close with Ferdinand Winslöw, liberally issued free papers and allowed former slaves to sell cotton from nearby plantations, which opened him up to censure from more conservative officers.[17]

When Curtis was transferred for a higher command in August 1862, his division commander Frederick Steele, an opponent of emancipation, took

---

[12] F. O. Danielson, "Helena, Arkansas November 5, 1862," in *Mathilda Cassel Peterson Danielson (1834–). SSIRC Mss P: 55* (Augustana College, 1862); Earl D. Check and Emeroy Johnson (translator), "Civil War Letters to New Sweden, Iowa," *Swedish-American Historical Quarterly* 36, no. 1 (1985):3–25.

[13] Danielson, "Helena, Arkansas November 5, 1962."

[14] As commander of the Army of the Southwest, Samuel R. Curtis' anti-slavery views, for example, proved problematic when he prepared to bring "war by emancipation" into Arkansas in early 1862. See Anders Bo Rasmussen, "The Spoils of the Victors: Captain Ferdinand Winslow and the 1863 Curtis Court of Inquiry," *Annals of Iowa* 76, no. 2 (2017): 162.

[15] Quoted in Andrew Zimmermann, "From the Rhine to the Mississippi," *Journal of the Civil War Era* 5, no. 1 (2015): 25–26.

[16] Carl H. Moneyhon, "From Slave to Free Labor: The Federal Plantation Experiment in Arkansas," in *Civil War Arkansas: Beyond Battles and Leaders*, ed. Anne J. Bailey and Daniel E. Sutherland (Fayetteville: University of Arkansas Press, 2000), 178; Oakes, *Freedom National: The Destruction of Slavery in the United States, 1861–1865*, 249. See also Rasmussen, "The Spoils of the Victors: Captain Ferdinand Winslow and the 1863 Curtis Court of Inquiry."

[17] "The Cotton Court of Inquiry; Testimony of Maj.-Gen F. Steele Important Developments Gen. Curtis Implicated," *New York Times*, May 24, 1863.

FIGURE 9.2 Major-General Samuel Curtis and Staff photographed in St. Louis in late 1861 or early 1862. Winslöw is seated to the far left. Courtesy Sadovnikoff Family Private Collection.

command at Helena and detailed his view of the Army of the Southwest's condition in a letter to President Lincoln dated February 15, 1863:

> [In August 1862] our camps and the town of Helena were overrun with fugitive slaves of both sexes, from infancy up to old age. Vice, immorality and distress, the usual accompaniments of vagrancy and destitution followed. The women were prostituted to a fearful extent, I believe by officers as well as by men, the feeble died in the streets in great numbers, from neglect and want. Disease and the elements of disorganization were introduced into my command by these miserable creatures.[18]

Thus, Steele placed blame for the army's poor condition on fugitives, but – in shaping conditions on the ground – the Union Army's white officers bore the primary responsibility. At Helena, some Union officers even took advantage of the situation to advance their personal economic interests by confiscating cotton from nearby plantations. One such officer, among several, was Ferdinand Winslöw. While attempting to control chaotic conditions around Helena, the Danish-born quartermaster sold horses, demanded a stake in a local business, and in all likelihood profited

---

[18] Frederick Steele, "Head Quarters 1st Division 13th Army Corps. In Camp near Vicksburg Miss. Feby. 15th 1863. To His Excellency the President," in *General Frederick Steele Papers, Mo191* (Stanford University Libraries, Department of Special Collections, 1863).

privately from cotton sales that were meant by Curtis to help support the numerous refugees living under desperate conditions.[19] In other words, Winslöw, by taking advantage of his position as chief quartermaster, in several instances chose pecuniary gain at the expense of his professed abolitionist values of "equality and freedom."[20]

The soldiers on the ground understood the situation clearly. Danish-born Anders M. Koppel wrote about the soldiers' "disgust" with the "cotton expeditions" in the summer of 1862.[21] Additionally, Calvin P. Alling, who like Koppel served in the 11th Wisconsin, pointed out Colonel Charles Hovey of the 33rd Illinois Infantry Regiment as one of the central actors engaged in illegal speculation around Helena and wrote that "some of the regiments engaged in stealing and smuggling cotton, in the name of the Government," but shipped it north to St. Louis and sold it "as their own."[22]

The cotton speculation going on around Helena in 1862 – and the private gain that followed – led to a "Court of Inquiry" in 1863 that implicated several high-ranking Union officers such as General Curtis (and his quartermaster Winslöw) in an attempt to ascertain, among other things, whether "officers in the service have been engaged, or directly or indirectly participated in traffic in Cotton or other produce on the Mississippi River."[23] The court case was mostly presented to the public as a problem of officers overstepping their responsibilities as public servants in relation to the government, but that same government was by 1862 also responsible for providing for thousands of runaways.[24] The

[19] The Steele quote and parts of this paragraph is also appears in Rasmussen, "The Spoils of the Victors: Captain Ferdinand Winslow and the 1863 Curtis Court of Inquiry."

[20] Winslow, "Brooklyn. 11th Septbr. 1856. Religion Og Politik [Brooklyn. September 11th, 1856. Religion and Politics]," 168; Rasmussen, "The Spoils of the Victors: Captain Ferdinand Winslow and the 1863 Curtis Court of Inquiry."

[21] A. M. K., "Korrespondance Fra Det 11te Wisconsin-Regiment [Correspondance from the 11th Wisconsin Regiment]," *Emigranten*, October 13, 1862.

[22] Calvin P. Alling, "Four Years in the Western Army: In the Civil War of the United States, 1861 to 1865," in *Manuscript Collection. Reminiscences. Wis Mss 102S* (Madison: Wisconsin Historical Society, undated).

[23] Captain Robert A. Howard (recorder), "Proceedings and Report of a Court of Inquiry on the Sale of Cotton and Produce at St. Louis, Missouri, 1863. Volume 1," in *Record Group 159: Records of the Office of the Inspector General* (National Archives, Washington, DC, 1863). See also Rasmussen, "The Spoils of the Victors: Captain Ferdinand Winslow and the 1863 Curtis Court of Inquiry."

[24] Earl J. Hess, "Confiscation and the Northern War Effort: The Army of the Southwest at Helena," *Arkansas Historical Quarterly* 44, no. 1 (1985): 62–71. See also Rasmussen, "The Spoils of the Victors: Captain Ferdinand Winslow and the 1863 Curtis Court of Inquiry."

human cost of Union officers' private profit, however, was only cursorily considered by the court and the press, though the lack of resources in and around Helena, in part due to the cotton traffic, was underscored in a letter – loaded with assumptions about Black people's capacity for citizenship – written by Acting Assistant Quartermaster B. O. Carr and sent to Winslöw on July 24, 1862:[25]

Capt., There is a perfect "cloud" of negroes being thrown upon me for Sustenance and Support, out of some 50 for whom I draw rations this morning but twelve were working stock, all the rest being women and children. What am I to do with them? If this taking them in and feeding them is to be the order of the day, would it not be well to have some competent man employed to look after them and keep their time; draw their rations; look after their Sanitary Condition. Etc. Etc? As it is, although it is hard to believe that such things can be, Soldiers & Teamsters (white) are according to common reports indulging in intimacy with them which can only be accounted for by the doctrine of Total Depravity.[26]

Steele and Carr's description of Black fugitives revealed the unequal power relationships between white soldiers and future freedpeople, as well as an ideology of white superiority that was also mirrored by civilians in the Midwest. In Leslie A. Schwalm's words:

Among many midwesterners, emancipating and aiding former slaves who intended to stay in the South were viewed as a humanitarian issue. But when former slaves – by their own volition or with the help of others – made their way north, emancipation became an increasingly critical and vigorously debated matter of public policy. Revealing a deep-seated belief in the benefits and necessity of a racially stratified society, many whites assumed that any black gains in the region would diminish their own status and citizenship. For those midwesterners whose understanding of white supremacy had been premised on their right and ability to exclude first Native Americans and then African Americans from the region, the physical mobility of former slaves suggested an undesirable change in racial boundaries and practices in a postslavery nation.[27]

---

[25] Howard (recorder), "Proceedings and Report of a Court of Inquiry on the Sale of Cotton and Produce at St. Louis, Missouri, 1863. Volume 1"; "The Cotton Court of Inquiry; Testimony of Maj.-Gen F. Steele Important Developments Gen. Curtis Implicated," *New York Times*, May 24, 1863; Ferdinand (Fred) Sophus Winsløw, "Novbr 18 1863 My Dear General" (Missouri History Museum Digital Content, 1863).

[26] B. O. Carr, "Helena, Ark. July 24th 1862," in *Samuel R. Curtis Papers. Testimonies in investigation of Curtis for alleged cotton speculation. 1862–1863. Box 2* (State Historical Society of Iowa, 1862). See also Jim Downs, *Sick from Freedom: African-American Illness and Suffering during the Civil War and Reconstruction* (New York: Oxford University Press, 2012), 22–25.

[27] Leslie A. Schwalm, *Emancipation's Diaspora: Race and Reconstruction in the Upper Midwest* (Chapel Hill: University of North Carolina Press, 2009), 83–84.

Concerns of freedpeople's mobility were also voiced in *Hemlandet* on October 22, 1862. The paper warned that "a certain party" was trying to stir up the Irish as well as the working class by inciting fear of wage-based competition if "masses" of freedpeople should migrate to the North.[28] *Hemlandet*, however, reassured its readership that, while "black migration lowers the wages for white labor," there was no reason to despair:[29] "The South is the black race's natural home, the negro thrives the most in the tropical regions."[30]

News of the Preliminary Emancipation Proclamation had likely reached civilian Scandinavian-born immigrants a month earlier, when *Hemlandet* on September 24 announced it as "a fatal blow to the rebellion" and *Emigranten* a few days later noted that the president would declare "all slaves free" in the states where the rebellion was maintained by the end of the year.[31] Still, the Scandinavian-American press spent little subsequent editorial energy on emancipation and instead devoted itself mostly to weekly description of military affairs, coverage of the US–Dakota War in Minnesota, and updates on the draft.[32]

A sense of Scandinavian immigrants' position on emancipation could, however, be gleaned from later published letters and editorials. Henrik (Henry) Syvertsen, a Norwegian immigrant with a degree from the Royal Frederick University in present-day Oslo, was curiously silent on the Preliminary Emancipation Proclamation when he penned a letter, focused on military matters, to *Emigranten* on October 18, 1862, from Kentucky; but later in the war he published a letter in the Norwegian-language *Fædrelandet* (the Fatherland) about the teachings of phrenology and his belief that "a negro [is] unfit for higher education."[33]

In his letter, dated May 30, 1864, Syvertsen reinforced his view of racial superiority, as he sought to allay his Scandinavian-American readers' fear over amalgamation by stating: "I doubt, that a time should come when an

---

[28] "Skola De Swarte Komme Til Norden? [Should the Blacks Come to the North?]," *Hemlandet*, October 22, 1862.

[29] Ibid.   [30] Ibid.

[31] "Presidenten Utfärdar En Emancipations-Proklamation [The President Issues an Emancipation Proclamation]," *Hemlandet*, September 24, 1862. See also "Madison. 27de Septbr. 1862."

[32] See, for example, "Drafting i Wisconsin [Drafting in Wisconsin]," *Emigranten*, October 27, 1862; "Soldaterna Från Illinois [The Soldiers from Illinois]," *Hemlandet*, October 31, 1862.

[33] H. S., "Korrespondance Fra Det Skandinaviske Regiment [Correspondence from the Scandinavian Regiment]," *Emigranten*, November 3, 1862. Also Henry Syvertsen, "Lexington, Ky., Mai 30te 1864," *Fædrelandet*, June 9, 1864.

educated, moral woman would marry a Negro. The loathsome stench alone that comes off a Negro in the summertime would be an insurmountable obstacle."[34] Leading up to the 1864 presidential election, Syvertsen also penned a long letter for *Fædrelandet* with a sense of sensation and ironic distance about local residents' reaction to the newly deployed Black provost guards: "Just imagine, that Negroes, whom these aristocratic Lexingtonians always have treated and considered animals, that these now should guard them, that was over the top."[35]

Fædrelandet, published out of La Crosse, Wisconsin, launched its first edition on January 14, 1864 and claimed to be an unabashedly Union paper, but not because of President Abraham Lincoln, nor because of "Negro emancipation"; rather, it was a Union paper because the pure American republic, created "on liberty and equality," was a truly "glorious institution in accordance with human and divine law."[36]

Though the Union war effort by 1864 was intimately tied to liberty through abolition, the connection was less pronounced in *Fædrelandet*'s coverage.[37] The paper's distinction between "Negro emancipation" on the one hand and American foundational values of "Liberty and Equality" on the other indicated that, despite freedpeople's crucial contributions to the United States military, support for their future economic and political rights in American society could not be taken for granted among opinion leaders in the Scandinavian-American community.[38]

---

[34] Ibid. See also Rasmussen, "'Drawn Together in a Blood Brotherhood': Civic Nationalism Amongst Scandinavian Immigrants in the American Civil War Crucible," *American Studies in Scandinavia* 48, no. 2 (2016): 14. Syvertsen's countryman, B. A. Frøiseth, an avowed Democrat and part of the Scandinavian community leadership, continued the theme of amalgamation when he before the important presidential election of 1864 warned that electing Lincoln would lead to the "sacrifice of the citizens' blood for the Negro's liberation and equality with the rest of the citizen, by which an abolitioned mongrel race will be the consequence." See B. A. Frøiseth, "St. Paul, 1864, Sept. 30," *Fædrelandet*, October 13, 1864.

[35] Henry Syvertson, "Lexington, Ky., Sept. 29, 1864," *Fædrelandet*, October 13, 1864.

[36] "Til Fædrelandets Læsere [To Our Fatherland's Readers]," ibid., January 14; Anders Bo Rasmussen, "'On Liberty and Equality': Race and Reconstruction among Scandinavian Immigrants, 1864–1868," in *Nordic Whiteness and Migration to the USA: A Historical Exploration of Identity*, ed. Jana Sverdljuk et al. (New York: Routledge, 2020).

[37] James M. McPherson, "A. Lincoln, Commander in Chief," in *Our Lincoln*, ed. Eric Foner (New York: W. W. Norton, 2008), 28.

[38] "Til Fædrelandets Læsere [To Our Fatherland's Readers]." See also the English-language article that accompanied the first Norwegian-language editorial "To the American People," *Fædrelandet*, January 14, 1864. Also Arlow William Andersen, *The Immigrant Takes His Stand: The Norwegian-American Press and Public Affairs, 1847–1872* (Northfield, MN: Norwegian-American Historical Association, 1953), 80–82.

In an April 7, 1865, editorial with distinct echoes of the racial stereo-types put forth by *Hemlandet* in 1862, *Emigranten*'s editor Carl Fredrik Solberg penned an editorial asking "what will be done with these freedmen."[39] Solberg painted a scenario where freedpeople could "come up here and flood our Northern states" and change the cities' appearances with "black or yellow skin, their wooly head, and white teeth." Even more ominously, the editor asked: "Would they not, with government authority, come and acquire space and become our neigh-bors and (oof!) our in-laws?"[40] *Emigranten* continued: "Would not these poor, helpless, poor, wretched, perplexed colored people," lacking legal rights, come North and cause difficulties as a "new and priviledged class of beggars and paupers?"[41] The answer, *Emigraten* assured its readership, was comforting:

The negro does not thrive outside the South. We even have an intelligent Negro's own word that many blacks from the North will venture South as soon as any colored there can have his full freedom and his weightiest argument was that "the black people is not regarded at all" here in the North.[42]

The racial ideology expressed in the Scandinavian-American public and private spheres regarding emancipation would continue to inform percep-tions for years. The conclusion drawn, almost universally, was that slav-ery was a stain on American democracy and the institution's demise consequently a blessing, but freedom did not equal a broad embrace of liberty and equality for nonwhites. Moreover, emancipation debates often played a marginal role on the homefront in midwestern communities even as draft legislation sent an ever-increasing proportion of Scandinavian-born men South. Probably hundreds, if not thousands, of Norwegians, Swedes, and Danes witnessed Black soldiers' war service up close as part of the armed forces where they were confronted directly with the question of freedpeople's rights. Those left behind, however, mainly discussed the duties of citizenship.

As we have seen, liberty in the eyes of Scandinavian immigrants often meant a liberal government, freedom of religion, and equality in societal matters. The Lincoln administration's conscription policy was therefore regularly perceived as undermining the ideal of a limited government protecting individual rights. Yet the paradox between love of liberty and

---

[39] David W. Blight, *Frederick Douglass: Profet of Freedom* (New York: Simon & Schuster, 2018), 370–372. Also "Madison, 7de April 1865," *Emigranten*, April 10, 1865.
[40] Ibid.   [41] Ibid.   [42] Ibid.

reluctance to defend it was almost completely absent in discussions in the Scandinavian-American public and private spheres by 1864.

A week before *Fædrelandet*'s first edition, on January 7, 1864, Fritz Rasmussen described correspondence with the local provost marshal about conscription. Rasmussen's inquiry was prompted by conversations with several inhabitants of New Denmark about avoiding the draft – specifically Rasmussen's ability to cheaply make out papers vouching for residents who had not declared their intent to naturalize.[43] Little more than a month later, on February 15, 1864, Rasmussen detailed a special meeting by New Denmark's residents at the local schoolhouse with the sole purpose "of voting a tax upon the town, to procure Volunteers, so as to avoid the Draft, so much the dread of the community."[44] Usually local meetings ran long due to disagreement, but this was different. "I must say that I have, as yet, not attended any kind of meeting, for whatever purpose, which have proved so unanimous to the subject matter for consideration as this one," Rasmussen wrote:[45]

Very little Descention [dissent] or opposition brought forward, as those, wishing as to do, plainly felt that internal rebuke, of the thought to do so by learning and seeing the mind of the gathering. It was finally resolved, to have the town authorities procure Volunteers at what price they could get them, though not exceeding $150.00 each; and the whole sum to be emploied [sic], not to exceed $1500.00.[46]

On February 24, 1864, Rasmussen again dealt with draft-related issues, as his father-in-law came over and wanted his help with paperwork related to draft exemption.[47] Additionally, in March the Brown County–based vice-consul for Sweden and Norway, Otto Tank, published several "Consular Announcements" in the Scandinavian-American newspapers dealing concretely with the issue of citizenship.[48] Swedish or Norwegian subjects could obtain a consular certificate to ensure exemption from military service, if they paid $2; had sworn testimony certifying their "place of birth," "age," "arrival in the United States," and "places lived"; and confirmed "not having voted nor declared their intent to

[43] Fritz W. Rasmussen, "Den 7de Torsdag [January]," in *Fritz William Rasmussen Papers. Green Bay Mss 4. Box no. 8* (Green Bay: Wisconsin Historical Society, 1864).

[44] Fritz W. Rasmussen, "15. Monday [February]," in *Fritz William Rasmussen Papers. Green Bay Mss 4. Box no. 8* (Green Bay: Wisconsin Historical Society, 1864).

[45] Ibid.   [46] Ibid.

[47] Fritz W. Rasmussen, "The 24th Wednesday [February]," in *Fritz William Rasmussen Papers. Green Bay Mss 4. Box no. 8* (Green Bay: Wisconsin Historical Society, 1864).

[48] See for example, Otto Tank, "Consulat-Bekjendtgjørelse [Consular Announcement]," *Fædrelandet*, March 3, 1864.

become citizen of the United States."[49] The related issues of citizenship, duty, and conscription only took on increased importance given the mounting Union losses in eastern and western theaters during the spring and early summer of 1864 and revealed a continued chasm between ethnic elite rhetoric and the sentiment in Scandinavian communities – though also a realization on the part of Scandinavian editors that the draft issue was a prime concern among their readers.[50]

On November 16, 1863, *Emigranten* had warned its readership that "the conditions for exemption" were "very strict," but it nevertheless provided a very detailed description of what conditions *could* lead to draft exemption.[51] *Emigranten's* message had been clear: it was more the exception than the rule to get out of military service because of one's physical condition.[52] A week later, however, a reader emphasized that there was also an important legal component to military exemption. On November 23, 1863, a pointed critique aimed at the Norwegian consul in Wisconsin appeared in the pages of *Emigranten*:

> There are a number of Norwegians, among the most recent conscripted or drafted men, whose claim to exemption from the draft rests on "no citizenship," or in other words, who never have voted in municipal or national elections and never having declared intention to become citizen of the United States.

These Norwegians surely fell under the protection of the Norwegian consul, the correspondent B. W. Suckow, argued, and he chastised the allegedly inexperienced representative for consulting American authorities before issuing "protection-documents." As an example of the consul's incompetence, Suckow recounted the story of a twenty-four-year-old Norwegian immigrant

[49] Ibid.

[50] "Nyheder [News]," ibid., January 14; "Forandringer Og Tillæg Til Udskrivningsloven [Changes and Amendments to the Conscription Act]," *Fædrelandet*, March 3, 1864. For a description of Union offensives and the resulting casualties – approximately 90,000 Union soldiers killed and wounded in May and June alone – in 1864, see James M. McPherson, *Battle Cry of Freedom: The Civil War Era* (New York: Oxford University Press, 1988), 718–750. In an account published in 1865, Danish-born Baptist minister Lars Jörgensen claimed to have cared for thousands of "sick and wounded" in hospitals and camps in the preceding years; see L. Jörgensen, *Amerika Og De Danskes Liv Herovre [America and the Danes' Existence over Here]* (Copenhagen: Louis Kleins Bogtrykkeri, 1865), 4–5.

[51] "Udskrivningen i Wisconsin [The Draft in Wisconsin]," *Emigranten*, November 16, 1863. Though neither "toothlessness" nor "the loss of a finger" would excuse one from military service, the loss of a thumb or the "index finger on the right hand" would. Also, the loss of a "big toe" along with being "deaf, mute, more or less blind" or having a "strong stutter" could ensure exemption, according to *Emigranten*.

[52] Ibid.

who sought "protection papers against the draft."[53] The consul, however, had stated that the immigrant's father, who had declared his intention to become a citizen before the son reached legal age, made the son eligible for military service as well. The consul's interpretation of draft legislation was claimed by the writer to be fallible, as only the father's full-fledged citizenship could have led to the son being draft-eligible. In the wake of the March 3, 1863, Enrollment Act, which specifically tied draft eligibility to "intention," the claim seemed tenuous, however.[54]

Absent from the discussion in *Emigranten* was the question of whether a seemingly healthy, twenty-four-year-old Norwegian-born man, who had lived in the United States for a number of years, was actually duty-bound to serve in the military. The American government's perspective was by 1863 clear: "All able-bodied male citizens" between twenty and forty-five years of age "ought willingly to contribute" to ensure the "maintenance of the Constitution and Union, and the consequent preservation of free government," but Suckow's letter indicated a slight shift in the Scandinavian public sphere.[55]

By publishing Suckow's letter, *Emigranten* now included voices that ran counter to the discourse of duty – so prevalent in the Scandinavian ethnic elite's push for volunteer recruitment in 1861 and 1862 – and thereby demonstrated an openness to discussing military exemption in an era marked by conscription.[56] By late 1863 it had seemingly become more acceptable within their own communities for Scandinavian immigrants to seek exemption from military service, and Old World officials were increasingly expected to help obtain it.

Yet elite rhetoric surrounding the duties of citizenship persisted. As an example, John A. Johnson, who was one of the principal organizers behind the 15th Wisconsin regiment in 1861, addressed the question of duty and sacrifice in a Fourth of July address aimed at an English-speaking audience in 1864.

[53] B. W. Suckow, "Den Norske Vicekonsul i Wisconsin," ibid., November 23.
[54] Ibid. See also Thomas C. Mackey, ed., *A Documentary History of the Civil War Era: Legislative Achievements*, vol. 1 (Knoxville: University of Tennessee Press, 2012), 129–138. The Enrollment Act, in its clarification of the 1862 Militia Act, specifically incorporated the phrase "persons of foreign birth who shall have declared on oath their intention to become citizens" as "liable to perform military duty."
[55] Mackey, ed., *A Documentary History of the Civil War Era: Legislative Achievements*, 129–138.
[56] Hans C. Heg et al., "Opraab [Call]," *Emigranten*, September 30, 1861. See also Ivar Alexander Weid, "Ivar Alexander Hviid," *Middelfart Avis*, September 10, 1862. See also H. Mattson, "Til Skandinaverna i Minnesota [To the Scandinavians in Minnesota]," *Hemlandet*, September 11, 1861.

The speech initially echoed Lincoln's at Gettysburg in November 1863 and then turned to the importance of territorial growth, with an implicit nod to the threshold principle, before ending with a discussion of duty. "Eighty-eight years ago today," Johnson noted, "the immortal Continental Congress" made clear to the world that "all men were created free and equal."[57] Like several Scandinavian-born orators and editors before him, Johnson lauded the nation's founders for their seemingly infallible commitment to freedom and equality and criticized the slave-holding states for undermining these values:

It has been said by some, "why not let the South go?" Have we not without their territory enough resources to make the greatest nation on earth. We have one foot upon the Atlantic the other upon the Pacific with territory between of almost exhaustless fertility, enough to farm 50 great States capable of supporting more than 100 millions of people . . . but if the South may secede why may not any other section, or even single states. And where would it end if a section or state as soon as it felt a little aggrieved should practice the doctrine of secession? Would we not soon be divided into immensurable petty states, without the power to protect our industry or commerce or to enforce respect from foreign nations?[58]

On the importance of maintaining national unity for the sake of continued territorial and population growth, Johnson added: "No one doubts this. Then our only salvation is to put forth every effort to make every necessary sacrifice of blood and treasure to reunite the shattered Republic."[59] Yet the rhetoric of "every necessary sacrifice," by ethnic leaders such as Johnson, was often not shared on the ground in the Scandinavian immigrant enclaves, and increasingly the resistance was reflected in the press.

A little more than a month later, *Fædrelandet* focused less on the nation's founding ideals than on the pressing reality of the draft. On August 25, 1864, acknowledging its readership's hopes and wishes, *Fædrelandet* noted a sense "that Wisconsin will not have to furnish much more than 12,000 men."[60] In Illinois, focus was even more clearly directed at draft avoidance. On September 7, 1864, *Hemlandet* reported to its mainly Swedish-born readership, that the "draft is on everybody's mind" and added that "every town does whatever possible to dodge it."[61] *Hemlandet* informed its readers that anyone who was not yet a citizen, had not voted, and had not taken out papers with intent to naturalize

[57] J. A. Johnson, "88 Years Ago to Day the Immortal Continental Congress," in *John A. Johnson Papers. P691. Box 12* (Northfield, MN: Norwegian-American Historical Association., 1864).
[58] Ibid.   [59] Ibid.   [60] "Draften i Wisconsin," *Fædrelandet*, August 25, 1864.
[61] "Draften," *Hemlandet*, September 7, 1864.

could contact "W. H. Church, Clerk of Circuit Court," in Chicago's 1st Ward, and get proof of exemption from the draft.[62]

By 1864, the framing of duty by the Scandinavian press was less specifically tied to military service in defense of the nation's values than to an acceptance of Old World countrymen also contesting the definition and duty of citizenship in order to avoid military service. Residents in New Denmark seemingly explored every exemption option. An increasingly desperate Fritz Rasmussen penned the following complaint in his diary on October 2, 1864, after his neighbor Knud had stopped by to borrow a recent issue of *Fædrelandet*:

So goes Sunday, even with Monday, worrying and drudging; more so now, under the dreadfull [sic] anxiety of the "War" i.e. the fear of being drafted, to "serve my Country" (?) Yes, to serve a few overrich, vainglorious and diabolical creatures, in the shape of human beings. ... Honest, Hold [old], Hoary "Abe" is certainly to[o] honest and old, for the position he holds, blessed be the generous heart to the contrary![63]

Resigned, Fritz Rasmussen by October 3, 1864, had started to make arrangements for travelling to Green Bay for a medical examination with his brother-in-law James.[64] On October 6, James stopped by to notify Fritz Rasmussen that they had both been drafted along with New Denmark community members Marcus Pedersen, Rasmus "Sejler" (sailor), Anton Christiansen, Johan Hartman, Niels Mogland, Ferdinand Larke (Lærke), and several others. According to Fritz Rasmussen, James "staid [stayed] talking a little while, about which best to do: 'run away or stand.'"[65]

On October 11, Rasmussen went down to James to see if "he had come back from Green Bay and 'the Provost Marshals Office' and what might be the news."[66] James was not home yet, however, and Rasmussen made plans with his countryman Ferdinand Larke to go the following day. When Rasmussen got back to his own place, an Irish community member, in Rasmussen's diary referred to as Brady's wife, came to talk and put "forth all Kinds of arguments to induce me to 'not report' or 'run away.'"[67]

---

[62] Ibid.   [63] Rasmussen, "Oct Sunday 2nd."
[64] "The 3rd. Monday [October]," in *Fritz William Rasmussen Papers. Green Bay Mss 4. Box no. 8* (Green Bay: Wisconsin Historical Society, 1864).
[65] "The 6. Thursday [October]," in *Fritz William Rasmussen Papers. Green Bay Mss 4. Box no. 8* (Green Bay: Wisconsin Historical Society, 1864).
[66] "The 11. Tuesday [October]," in *Fritz William Rasmussen Papers. Green Bay Mss 4. Box no. 8* (Green Bay: Wisconsin Historical Society, 1864).
[67] Ibid.

Yet, in the end, Rasmussen and several other community members could not bring themselves to run away. On a beautiful and mild fall day, October 12, Rasmussen and his travel companions went to Green Bay to report for military service.[68] In the "forenoon" of October 13, Rasmussen went in for his medical examination, hoping to get exempted, and got the impression that a bribe, which was not an uncommon occurrence, could have secured such an outcome.

As J. Matthew Gallman has shown, bribery was so prevalent that numerous humorists with a wide audience portrayed "those weak kneed, cowardly, despicable types who came up with ridiculous schemes to avoid the draft."[69] Some showed draft dodgers running off to Canada, "creating an expatriate community of cowards in Windsor"; others men dressing up as women; and the cartoonist Austin A. Turner depicted an early draft evader complaining of weakness in his back but in fact carrying a "stack of bills strapped to his back, as a generous bribe to the doctor" (see Figure 9.3).[70]

The word around Green Bay was that it was possible, with the right stack of bills, to find a similar exemption solution in the local examiner's office, but at the moment of truth Fritz Rasmussen failed to take advantage of the situation:

If I had only been bold and present-minded enough, I might, I think, very probably have been exemted [sic] for, I had or to all appearances, was given, all the chance, that the Doctor possibly could give a person, to offer a bribe, if really he would have taken any, as the general belief is that he does.[71]

While Fritz Rasmussen could not bring himself to pay for a fraudulent medical exemption, Ferdinand Larke was willing to pursue other options. The Danish-born blacksmith, who was examined just a few minutes after Rasmussen, "pretended a stiff knee," "made himself a miserable cribble [sic]," and complained loudly though he, in Rasmussen's estimation, was as "sound in the leg as if he never had any ailment in it."[72] In an unexpected turn of events, Larke also told the examining surgeon, who "worked at" him considerably, that Fritz Rasmussen could vouch for his injury.[73] Put on the spot, Rasmussen

[68] "The 26th Wednesday [October]," in *Fritz William Rasmussen Papers. Green Bay Mss 4. Box no. 8* (Green Bay: Wisconsin Historical Society, 1864).

[69] J. Matthew Gallman, *Defining Duty in the Civil War: Personal Choice, Popular Culture, and the Union Home Front* (Chapel Hill: University of North Carolina Press, 2015), 143–49.

[70] Ibid., 149–153.   [71] Rasmussen, "The 26th Wednesday [October]."   [72] Ibid.

[73] Ibid.

FIGURE 9.3 Underlining the prevalence of draft resistance, and its echoes in broader American culture, the draftee in this cartoon says, "Doctor I'm weak in the back," to which the examining surgeon replies, "Yes, I see it – can't go – too delicate." Courtesy Library Company of Philadelphia.

explained that he had known Larke for "the last 11 or 12 years" and also bended the truth when adding:

[I] had often heard him tell of suffering extremely, in that knee once; [and] had allways [sic] thought that he drew that leg a little awkward, when walking; yes: that he was considered an upright character, through our neighborhood; that I didn't think it nescessary [sic] to make use of cloroform [sic].

Describing the incident in his diary, Rasmussen was somewhat shocked that Larke "dared to try" without even having consulted or hinted at his intention before turning to his fellow New Denmark resident for support:

During the scuffling, Ferdinand once cried out most pitiable and said "Oh 'Doctor' I didn't come here to get hurt. I came to be examined." To which the Surgeon answered: "No, but we are not here to be fooled." But most assuredly as I have heard Ferd. to have said since – they were most damnably fooled. By nine oclock P.M. on the 13th we again made home, most dreadfully tired; and, I, by no means very contended [sic].[74]

Approaches to the draft and medical examination processes underscored the desperate measures foreign-born residents would take to avoid the draft. For some, the strategies for avoiding military service succeeded. Larke, for example, was declared exempt because of "lameness in the right Knee," while Rasmussen – along with several community members, Norwegian-born Einar Quisling among them – was "held" for the army instead.[75] The news shook Fritz Rasmussen, who could not bring himself to record anything in his diary for two weeks after going to Green Bay. "I have been rather puzzled in my mind; hardly knowing what to lay hands to, on account of the being 'drafted' to serve 'Oncle Samuel' [sic]," Rasmussen finally wrote on October 26.[76]

The thirty-one-year-old immigrant now had to leave his wife and three daughters in New Denmark. As it turned out, Rasmussen would also serve alongside soldiers of native-born, German-born, and Irish-born heritage while experiencing the effects of slavery up close. Thus, Rasmussen – who, like many of his fellow countrymen in Brown County, would have preferred to stay out of the Civil War – had to contemplate the merits and drawbacks of American citizenship to an even greater degree over the following year. Yet when the Danish-born immigrant, weary from countless hours of hard farm work, sat down on October 26, 1864, to take up his diary, optimism about life in America had temporarily vanished. Rasmussen's entry captured his mood: "Perhaps I may soon come to write with the sword or bayonet, making gory figures. Thou Lord and Ruler of us miserable beings, have mercy upon us and save us from the Evils to come."[77]

---

[74] Ibid.   [75] Ibid.   [76] Ibid.

[77] Ibid. Fritz Rasmussen's mood was moreover affected by false rumors circulating in New Denmark about the deaths of previously drafted community members Anthon Christiansen, T.C. Johansen, Marcus Pedersen and John Hartmann, who allegedly had been killed, either by guerrillas or by a train running into the river.

As Fritz Rasmussen and other New Denmark community members prepared to travel south, the officers and men of the 15th Wisconsin were
getting ready to travel north. The *remaining* officers and men, that is – the
past two years had been trying for the approximately 800 Scandinavians
who had originally enlisted. Battles at Perryville, Stones River,
Chickamauga, Pickett's Mill, and Atlanta had taken such a toll that, by
late 1864, only 320 men remained on active duty.[78]

Yet, throughout the war, soldiers in the Scandinavian Regiment continued to describe warfare as something Scandinavians withstood better
than any other ethnic group. As Henry Syvertsen noted after the regiment's first major battle in Kentucky on October 8, 1862, "the
Norwegians must be a quite peculiar, composed race"; despite "cannonshot after cannonshot and musketvolley after musketvolley thundering"
around them, "the coffee pots were immediately over the fire as soon as
the order to rest was given."[79]

The narrative of calmness under fire, often traced back to a martial
Viking past, was common in descriptions of the Scandinavian Regiment
during and after the Civil War.[80] The underlying idea was a sense of
Scandinavian superiority that, to some degree, was earned on the battlefield
but also reflected in civilian accounts. In his memoirs, for example, former
Union officer, Ole Balling, even contended that Abraham Lincoln in the fall
of 1864, had greeted him "with great affection" and mentioned that the
Norwegians he knew in the Midwest were "the very best settlers."[81]

Among the Norwegians in the Midwest who served in the military, the
15th Wisconsin Regiment was the most visible unit and therefore received
the most attention in both contemporary and subsequent accounts.[82] For its

[78] E. B. Quiner, *Military History of Wisconsin* (Chicago, IL, 1866), 630–631. During the
war, 267 soldiers in the 15th Wisconsin Infantry lost their lives, twenty-two went missing,
and a sprinkling of others deserted, were reassigned, or discharged.
[79] H. S., "Korrespondance Fra Det Skandinaviske Regiment [Correspondence from the
Scandinavian Regiment]," *Emigranten*, November 3, 1862.
[80] John Fitch, *Annals of the Army of the Cumberland: Comprising Biographies, Descriptions
of Departments, Accounts of Expeditions, Skirmishes, and Battles* (Philadelphia:
J. B. Lippincott & Co., 1864), 231. Fitch in 1864 wrote that thousands of Scandinavinas
were "found in every regiment organized in the Northwest" and counted among "the best
and bravest of our soldiers. Descendants of the sturdy Vikings of medieval times."
[81] O. P. Hansen Balling, *Erindringer Fra Et Langt Liv* [*Memories from a Long Life*]
(Kristiania: S. & Jul Sørensens Bogtrykkeri, 1905), 82–83.
[82] For an attempt to get part of the 15th Wisconsin mustered out of war service a few months
early, see K. J. Fleischer, "Petition Fra Det Skandinaviske Selskab i Madison Til Guvernør
Lewis Af Wisconsin [Petition from the Scandinavian Society in Madison to Governor
Lewis of Wisconsin]," *Fædrelandet*, October 13, 1864.

FIGURE 9.4 Portrait of Hans Heg by Herbjørn Gausta. The Norwegian-born colonel fell at the battle of Chickamauga on September 20, 1863. Courtesy Vesterheim Norwegian-American Museum Archives.

part, the 15th Wisconsin was hit hardest during the battle of Chicakamauga on September 19 and 20, 1863. Colonel Hans Heg, shortly after having been promoted to brigade commander, fell victim to a sharpshooter's bullet, while Ole C. Johnson, who succeeded Heg as regimental commander, was captured and sent to Libby Prison in Virginia.[83] In all, the 15th Wisconsin sustained 177 casualties during the battle, and afterward stories of Hans Heg's sacrifice, valor, and coolness under fire, along with that of his soldiers, came to exemplify the Scandinavian war effort.[84]

[83] J. A. Johnson, ed., *Det Skandinaviske Regiments Historie* [*The Scandinavian Regiment's History*] (La Crosse: Fædrelandet og Emigrantens Trykkeri, 1869), 103–111.

[84] Ole C. Johnsen, "De Norske Krigsfanger i Libby Prison [The Norwegian Prisoners-of-War in Libby Prison]," *Emigranten*, November 23, 1863. See also Johnson, *Det Skandinaviske Regiments Historie* [*The Scandinavian Regiment's History*], 109. See also "Oberst Hans C. Heg [Colonel Hans C. Heg]," *Fædrelandet*, August 25, 1864.

Still, the fact that many Scandinavians did not serve in pan-Scandinavian units and instead were scattered in numerous regiments across the midwest was lamented by *Fædrelandet* on August 25, 1864:

Unity makes for strength and respectability. Heg wanted his countrymen to reap the full fruit of what they did for the fatherland. He realized that if Norwegians were shoved into the American regiments under the American regimental names, then the Americans would appropriate all the officers' positions – everything that would yield money and honor – and only leave the Norwegians the cold honor to cover the battlefield with its bodies, without even in death mentioning their actual names.[85]

The necessity of gaining ethnic recognition for political gain through units like the 15th Wisconsin, and the underlying premise of pure Scandinavian units performing better than ethnically mixed units, was underscored in the same article by *Fædrelandet*.[86]

Furthermore, the idea of Scandinavian military superiority was on full display in *Fædrelandet* leading up to the 1864 presidential election. At this moment, agitation against Democrats, not least German and Irish supporters of the Democratic Party, had reached a pinnacle, as demonstrated by the October 13 editorial penned by *Fædrelandet*'s editors:

In the Democratic meetings some big-name Gentlemen are sitting intelligently, a smile on their lip and clever stratagem behind their ears, but the masses are formed by the Irish and Germans, who never knew what the constitution contained and blindly follow their leaders' say ... When we see Norwegian farmers among this crowd, we have to believe that either they seek office at the presidential election or they have degraded themselves to being equals with the Irish and intellectually inferior Germans.[87]

Ramping up the anti-Democratic agitation, the editorial also compared writers of Democratic campaign pamphlets with animals, Irish, and "wild-Germans" (*Vildtydskere*).[88] As a demonstration of the Democratic Party's

---

[85] "Oberst Hans C. Heg [Colonel Hans C. Heg]."

[86] Ibid. "[It is] a shame that the many thousand Scandinavians, who serve in the Union army, did not follow this example and form their own Regiments. Instead they are spread around in nearly all Regiments, and no matter how brave they have proven themselves they have to be content with the praise or shame the Yankees' behaviour gets their Regiment."

[87] "Et Ord, Demokrater! [A Word, Democrats!]," *Fædrelandet*, October 13, 1864.

[88] Ibid. See also Rasmussen, "'Drawn Together in a Blood Brotherhood': Civic Nationalism Amongst Scandinavian Immigrants in the American Civil War Crucible," 18.

lack of appeal among Scandinavians, the 15th Wisconsin, which by late fall of 1864 was finally stationed in the rear to guard a bridge at Whiteside Station, sent a clear message when the soldiers cast their presidential election votes on November 8.[89]

Through votes for presidential electors, state superintendent, members of congress, state senators, members of assembly, and county officers, it became clear that Abraham Lincoln's Union Party continued to enjoy overwhelming support. With Company B detached at Lookout Creek, 177 soldiers in the 15th Wisconsin Regiment had their votes registered in the surviving records, and 176 votes (99 percent) were cast for electors who supported Abraham Lincoln.[90]

Norwegian-born Second Lieutenant George Hovden of Company G marked the election in his diary and noted that everyone in the company "went for Lincoln."[91] A little north, at US hospital no. 8 in Nashville, Tennessee, Gunvold Johnsrud, who served in the 16th Minnesota Infantry on November 4, 1864, wrote about the "great Union Procession for the A. Lincoln & Johnson party," held in the streets ahead of the election, and added: "It was quite a wonder to see so many lights at one time and place." During the election, four days later, the Norwegian-born Johnsrud offered the assessment that "little Mack will have a poor show for president."[92]

In Arkansas, a Swedish-born correspondent to *Hemlandet* reported that the 3rd Minnesota, which included a Scandinavian company, had voted before leaving Pine Bluff. "All the votes 'cast' were for Abraham Lincoln," the correspondent noted, though "one or two intended to vote for Mac but refrained from doing so, out of shame, when they saw how everyone else voted (they were 'conscripts')."[93]

[89] "Det Skandinaviske Regiments Major Georg Wilson [The Scandinavian Regiment's Major Georg Wilson]," *Emigranten*, November 21, 1864.

[90] Chief Clerks of the Senate and Assembly, ed., *The Legislative Manual of the State of Wisconsin* (Madison, WI: Atwood & Rublee, 1865), 172. See also Joseph Mathieson, "Statement of Votes Polled for Electors of President and Vice-President of the United States," in *Wisconsin. Governor Military Votes, 1862–1865. Series 60. Box 11* (Madison: Wisconsin Historical Society, 1864).

[91] O. M. Hovde, ed., *The Civil War Diary of George Johnson Hovden Translated by Norma Johnson Jordahl* (Decorah, IA: Luther College Library, 1971), 63.

[92] Gunvold Johnsrud, "1864 at U.S. Hospital No 8. Novbr 4," in *Civil War Diary. Gunvold Johnsrud, 1841–1923. P468* (Northfield, MN: Norwegian-American Historical Association, 1864).

[93] En af de få Qwarwarande, "Soldat-Korrespondens. Duvalls Bluff, Ark. D. 1:Ste Dec. 1864 [Soldier Correspondence. Duvall's Bluff, Ark. the 1st of December 1864]," *Hemlandet*, January 11, 1865.

Reporting about a mock vote involving his "invalid company" in Lexington, Kentucky, Henry Syvertsen distanced himself from the Democratic candidate George McClellan and reported it as a "happy sign of the times" that 44 out of 50 supported Lincoln.[94] Moreover, Ole Steensland, an imprisoned Norwegian-born soldier from the 15th Wisconsin, later remembered how support for Lincoln remained strong even in the infamous Georgia prison camp Andersonville where thousands died from illness and malnutrition.[95]

The New Yorkers went around with ballots and said "vote for little Mac(Clellan) and let us have peace and get out of here and not lie here to rot for Lincoln and the Negroes." We said: Vote for Lincoln; – a Man, who is loyal to the Unions and will not give up until he has [clamped] down on the Confederacy.[96]

The Scandinavian soldiers thereby helped justify the rationale behind the Lincoln administration's decision to let soldiers vote. Wisconsin Republicans had taken the lead regarding this electoral issue, and several other states modeled their voting practice after Wisconsin's example.[97] Across the country, more than three out of four soldiers, 78 percent, supported Abraham Lincoln in the 1864 election, and the Scandinavian 15th Wisconsin Regiment's 176 out of 177 votes for the incumbent turned out to be the strongest support for the president among any Wisconsin regiment.[98] In the 9th Wisconsin Regiment, made up of a sizeable German contingent, close to 80 percent of the soldiers (396 out of 498) supported Lincoln, while that number was less than 30 percent in the 17th Wisconsin, a predominantly Irish regiment.[99]

---

[94] Syvertson, "Lexington, Ky., Sept. 29, 1864."
[95] William Marvel, *Andersonville: The Last Depot* (Chapel Hill: University of North Carolina Press, 1994), 58–59.
[96] "We were there during the election and the rebels liked to know the spirit among the prisoners and thus wanted us to vote and campaign," private Ole Steensland later remembered. See Waldemar Ager, *Oberst Heg Og Hans Gutter [Colonel Heg and His Boys]* (Eau Claire, 176).
[97] Oscar Osburn Winther, "The Soldier Vote in the Election of 1864," *New York History* 25, no. 4 (1944): 441.
[98] Assembly, *The Legislative Manual of the State of Wisconsin*, 172. See also Joseph, "Statement of Votes Polled for Electors of President and Vice-President of the United States." See also Frank Klement, "The Soldier Vote in Wisconsin During the Civil War," *Wisconsin Magazine of History* 28, no. 1 (1944): 46.
[99] "Wisconsin Military Vote – 1863 and 1864," *Prescott Journal*, December 10, 1864.

Such voting patterns among Scandinavians, Germans, and Irish extended outside of Wisconsin's military units.[100] As Walter Kamphoefner and Wolfgang Helbich have pointed out, the "percentage of support" for Lincoln among Germans "declined slightly" between 1860 and 1864, and Milwaukee, with its strong German influence, "was one of only two big cities where Lincoln lost ground between elections."[101] Even more pronounced was Irish-American opposition to Lincoln. As Susannah Ural has shown, "Irish-Americans turned out in droves" to vote for George McClellan in 1864, which, in one example, led to 90 percent of the vote in a heavily Irish New York ward being cast for Lincoln's opponent.[102]

The Scandinavian immigrant vote in New Denmark was less clear. Despite his frustrations with the Lincoln administration, Fritz Rasmussen probably supported the sitting president, whom he had described as "honest" a month earlier. Yet in the same diary entry Rasmussen, as we have seen, also maintained that Lincoln was too "old, for the position he holds."[103] In his diary, Rasmussen wrote that he had gone "to schoolhouse No. 1 for election," but in contrast to 1860, where he voted "for Abraham Lincoln and H. Hamlin," he did not disclose which candidates received his support in 1864.[104] Fritz Rasmussen did, however, maintain, or at least regain, his admiration for Lincoln, and if he followed the recommendations in the Scandinavian-language newspapers circulating in New Denmark, he would again have voted "for Lincoln."[105]

---

[100] On Scandinavian civilian support for Lincoln, see for example, Sw. Tragordh, "Hvem Bör Blifwa President För Nästa 'Term' [Who Should Be President for the Next 'Term'?]," *Hemlandet*, May 4, 1864.

[101] Walter D. Kamphoefner and Wolfgang Helbich, eds., *Germans in the Civil War: The Letters They Wrote Home* (Chapel Hill: University of North Carolina Press, 2006), 12. Support for the Republican Party also declined slightly, from 81.6 to 79.5, in the 9th Wisconsin between the gubernatorial election in 1863 and the presidential election in 1864. See "Wisconsin Military Vote – 1863 and 1864."

[102] Susannah Ural Bruce, *The Harp and The Eagle: Irish-American Volunteers and the Union Army, 1861–1865* (New York: New York University Press, 2006), 231.

[103] Rasmussen, "Oct Sunday 2nd."

[104] Fritz W. Rasmussen, "Den 8de Tirsdag [November]," in *Fritz William Rasmussen Papers. Green Bay Mss 4. Box no. 8* (Green Bay: Wisconsin Historical Society, 1864). See also "November 1860. Den 7de. [November 1860. The 7th]."

[105] "Den 8de Tirsdag [November]"; "New Denmark. Brown Co. Wis. January 27th 1894," in *Rasmussen, Fritz. Additions, 1860–1918. Green Bay Mss 4. Box 9* (Green Bay: Wisconsin Historical Society, 1894). On the different newspapers read in New Denmark, see "Den 27de Løverdag [April]," in *Fritz William Rasmussen Papers.*

If Fritz Rasmussen did indeed vote for Lincoln, he likely did so along with most Scandinavian immigrants.[106] Even along the Pearl River in the deep South, Christian Koch, who had been navigating life between New Orleans and his home in Hancock County since 1862, was clear about his political preferences.[107] "I am glad Lincoln is elected again, I dont [sic] want to see peace now till the South is whipped, if it last 10 years longer, I begin to feel as if I could help to fight them myself," Koch wrote.[108]

In the end, Lincoln won all the states in the North, with the exception of New Jersey, and also enjoyed electoral success in states such as Maryland, Missouri, and West Virginia. *Emigranten* celebrated the president's reelection on November 14, 1864, while praising the voters' support of the "war policy hitherto followed to suppress the rebellion."[109]

Lincoln's reelection ensured that the conscripted New Denmark farmers would have to help suppress the rebellion and ensure emancipation.

Diaries, 1856–1876. Green Bay Mss 4. Box 8 (Green Bay: Wisconsin Historical Society, 1867). The election of 1864 did, however, reveal one specific example of Scandinavian ethnicity trumping otherwise solid editorial Republican sentiment. Hans Heg's younger brother Ole, who had served briefly as quartermaster in the 15th Wisconsin, ran for the assembly candidate position in Racine County on a Democratic ticket. Despite Ole Heg's political affiliation, *Emigranten*'s editor endorsed his candidacy based on the premise that too few Scandinavian-born immigrants had been nominated by the nation's two major parties and thus deserved Scandinavian support when they were nominated. "Preferably we feel that for such local functions, little attention should be paid to the party, but as much as possible always be on the side of a fellow countryman ... Had it been for a more important political office, such as Congress ... we should have expressed the hope that he would not be elected." See "Kandidat Til Assembly i Racine Co., Wis., – En Normand Nomineret [Candidate to Assembly in Racine Co., Wis., – A Norwegian Nominated]," *Emigranten*, October 17, 1864.

[106] *Fædrelandet* reported the margins of victory across the states on November 24, 1864. See "President Lincoln Og De Forenede Staters Fremtid [President Lincoln and the Future of the United States]," *Fædrelandet*, November 24, 1864. See also McPherson, *Battle Cry of Freedom: The Civil War Era*, 803–805. Helped, in part, by the soldier vote, Lincoln won 212 votes to 21 in the electoral college, though the election was closer in states such as Indiana where absentee ballots were disallowed.

[107] Marco Giardino and Russell Guerin, *Mississippi's No-Man's Land: An Echo of the Koch Family Letters* (Denver: Outskirts Press, 2006), 15–49.

[108] Christian Ditlev Koch, "Nelsons Mill Novb 19 1864," in *Christian D. Koch and Family Papers, Mss. 202, Louisiana and Lower Mississippi Valley Collections. Box 2* (LSU Libraries, Baton Rouge, Louisiana, 1864).

[109] "Madison, 12te Nov. 1864," *Emigranten*, November 14, 1864. With the "exception of a lone scuffle by a polling place in Minnesota," everything had proceeded peacefully, *Emigranten* reported, "the government had taken its precautions against the expected assults from fanatical rebels and draft dodgers and the northern border town were not interfered with." See also Richard H. Abbott, *The Republican Party and the South, 1855–1877* (Chapel Hill: University of North Carolina Press, 1986), 38–39.

Two months later, Fritz Rasmussen therefore started his own journey toward the deep South along with 150 other closely guarded draftees.[110]

Fritz Rasmussen left Madison as part of the 14th Wisconsin Regiment on a clear, cold Tuesday, January 17, 1865, en route to join the Union campaign against Mobile in Alabama.[111] For months the draft had impacted life in Wisconsin, and for months it would continue to do so. Thus, in one of Edward Rasmussen's first letters to his son in the army, dated January 23, 1865, he included information on the draft that demonstrated how closely the community followed the quota system and how much they by 1865 knew about it:

Now the draft is again upon us and this time I am thinking that it will be the last as here will not be many remaining for additional drafting. I saw in the [Green Bay] Advocate that Green Bay must deliver 45 of their able-bodied men and since there are here in this town around 30 and they therefore must have 12 men but will draft 24, then it will soon even out.[112]

Additionally, on February 20, 1865, Rasmussen's in-laws, Ane and N. C. Hansen, referenced the impending draft scheduled for March, which seemed to make it impossible for any of the remaining foreign-born men to avoid military service. Consequently, several Danish immigrants struck out for Green Bay to voluntarily enlist and procure the $300 bonus associated therewith.[113]

Fritz Rasmussen's brother-in-law, Celius Christiansen, who was drafted in 1862 but avoided service by hiring a substitute, likely knew that he was on the short list for the upcoming draft and volunteered in Green Bay along with at least ten other New Denmark residents, which caused "quite a commotion" in the immigrant community.[114] The problem, as Fritz Rasmussen's father described it, was that by volunteering in Green Bay and being paid there, the volunteers would be credited there and not in New Denmark, which likely meant that "the few remaining will have to go as soldiers since there will be no one left to draft from."[115]

---

[110] Fritz W. Rasmussen, "Dagbog: Madison Jan: Den 17/65," in *Fritz William Rasmussen Papers. Correspondence, 1834–1942. Green Bay Mss 4. Box no. 1.* (Green Bay: Wisconsin Historical Society, 1865). See also Ager, *Oberst Heg Og Hans Gutter* [*Colonel Heg and His Boys*], 58.

[111] Rasmussen, "Dagbog: Madison Jan: Den 17/65."

[112] Edward Rasmussen, "New Denmark T. O. Den 23 Januar 1865," in *Fritz William Rasmussen Papers. Correspondence, 1834–1942. Green Bay Mss 4. Box no. 1* (Green Bay: Wisconsin Historical Society, 1865).

[113] Ane Hanson, "New Danmark D. 20 Feb. 1865 Kjere Sviger Søn," ibid.

[114] Edward Rasmussen, "New Denmark 26 Fbr. 1865," ibid.   [115] Ibid.

Rasmussen's wife Sidsel made the same point when she wrote to her husband from New Denmark on March 22, 1865, and revealed in a new letter the following day that the draft's pressure exacerbated ethnic tension in the community: "Dennis Devan was drafted and ran away like every other Irishman. [Johan] Goldsmidt was also Drafted and had to go."[116] Yet also within the Danish immigrant community, the draft revealed both ethnic and class tension. Indicating the continued conflict between German and Irish immigrants and their Scandinavian counterparts, not least perceptions of who was bearing, and who was skirting, the duties of citizenship, Fritz Rasmussen's father notified his son of the draft's results on March 23, 1865:

> The draft has come to an end here 14 days ago and now I believe it will end for good, as there is not one single able-bodied man left fit for service. Here the draft was later. Linhardt, Mads Rasmussen, Anders Petersen, Goldsmidt, Dines Duan [Dennis Devan], Hofman and several Germans and Irish but all three Danes were rejected and they only got a hold of a few Germans. The rest had run away.[117]

Edward Rasmussen also recounted a story of a failed attempt at bribery by Goldsmidt, who as a result was compelled to serve even without a medical examination, before turning his attention to the community volunteers that had enlisted. "That concludes the draft," Rasmussen asserted.[118] Otherwise, most of the Rasmussen family letters sent to Fritz revolved around concern for his safety, local news (a town election on April 4 and a deadly smallpox outbreak in May), and national news from the war (the fall of Richmond and Petersburg).[119]

One topic completely absent from the letters sent south to Fritz Rasmussen was the issue of emancipation and the plight of four million freedpeople after the end of hostilities. This was perhaps not surprising given the relatively small number of free Black people living in the Upper Midwest (in Brown County, Wisconsin, twenty "free colored" out of approximately 12,000 residents were counted in the 1860 census), but while the New Denmark letter-writers may never have met a Black community member, they would have known about policy debates through newspapers circulating in

---

[116] Sidsel Rasmussen, "Onsdag Den 22 Marts," ibid. See also "New Danmark Marts 23," in *Fritz William Rasmussen Papers. Correspondence, 1834–1942. Green Bay Mss 4. Box no. 1* (Green Bay: Wisconsin Historical Society, 1865).
[117] Edward Rasmussen, "Denmark Den 23. Martz 1865," ibid. [118] Ibid.
[119] See, for example, Sidsel Rasmussen, "Juni Den 22," ibid.

town.[120] Moreover, thoughts on abolition, and the fight to achieve it, had clearly taken on increased importance outside of Brown County.

For Fritz Rasmussen, the shared fate of soldiering created an even greater sense of solidarity, also across ethnic lines, for the already class-conscious Wisconsin farmer. As an example, the thirty-one-year-old immigrant's first letters home from the campaign against Mobile in March 1865 detailed spending miserable, rainy days huddled up on a pile of coal with his Irish comrade-in-arms Patrick Terry, and a week later sharing his tobacco with a Prussian-born neighbor from New Denmark named George Böhme.[121] Yet in Alabama's subtropical climate, surrounded by unknown and often unwashed men, the drafted farmer had come down with a painful bout of diarrhea. Weakened by hot flashes and chills, Rasmussen time and again had to leave the ranks and let yellowish pus mixed with bloody stool fertilize the swamps of Alabama. "I am seemingly in no small danger of losing this fragile life, either by enemy bullets or disease in this climate," Fritz Rasmussen warned his wife Sidsel in a letter on March 24.[122] Three days later, the Army of West Mississippi came into contact with Conforederate defenders by Mobile Bay in Alabama, and, judging by the way the Danish draftee recorded the encounter, he thought he was going to lose his life in the confrontation.[123]

The noise, Rasmussen wrote, was intense, almost to the point of deafening. Only when darkness fell over southern Alabama did the shooting wane, but even then the Danish immigrant's life was still in danger due to feverish shivering and, by day, the continued Confederate bombardment.[124] Over the following days, one shell landed in a group of soldiers but only knocked over their coffee pot; another snapped a pine like a twig; a third tore the head off a man; and as the siege around Mobile's Spanish Fort and Fort

---

[120] Joseph C. G. Kennedy, *Population of the United States in 1860* (Washington, DC: Government Printing Office, 1864), 529.

[121] Fritz W. Rasmussen, "Camp on Fish River, Alabama. Marts Den 24de 1865," in *Fritz William Rasmussen Papers. Diaries, 1857–1876. Green Bay Mss 4. Box no. 8* (Wisconsin Historical Society, 1865). See also "April Den 1ste 1865," in *Fritz William Rasmussen Papers. Diaries, 1857–1876* (Green Bay: Wisconsin Historical Society, 1865).

[122] Rasmussen, "Camp on Fish River, Alabama. Marts Den 24de 1865." See also Anders Bo Rasmussen, *I Krig for Lincoln* [*To War for Lincoln*] (Copenhagen: Informations Forlag, 2014), 23–24.

[123] "Den 28de Klok 2 Eftermid. [Marts]," in *Fritz William Rasmussen Papers. Diaries, 1857–1876* (Green Bay: Wisconsin Historical Society, 1865). Also ibid., 257–66.

[124] Ibid.

Blakely continued, Rasmussen reported on several wounds suffered by both Black and white soldiers in his vicinity:[125]

This morning an Indian was carried in, shot in the head, and who was, I think, drawing his last breaths. Just as we had had dinner they started to throw shells in here again so one was not safe anywhere and an old poor English-man (Isaac Brigham) who had gone as a "substitute" and like me came from Green Bay had his right leg torn a quarter off three inches below the knee by a piece of a bomb.[126]

Rasmussen's military experience, shared with thousands of comrades, strengthened his sense of belonging to a national community and in some ways mirrored that of the Irish and Black soldiers.[127] As Christian Samito has pointed out, "military service had explicit links to citizenship and inclusion as part of the American people," and the fact that Rasmussen and others of Scandinavian heritage served alongside American Indians, Germans, Irish, English, and native-born soldiers helped shape a broader view of American citizenship.[128]

Fritz Rasmussen in his writings regularly exhibited concern for, and friendship with, fellow soldiers of many different backgrounds.[129] The reluctant recruit sympathetically described a fellow soldier of Stockbridge Indian heritage who helped an ill Irish-born comrade-in-arms; and on

---

[125] Fritz W. Rasmussen, "Marts Den 31de Klokken 7–8," in *Fritz William Rasmussen Papers. Diaries, 1857–1876* (Green Bay: Wisconsin Historical Society, 1865).

[126] "April Den 3de 1865," in *Fritz William Rasmussen Papers. Diaries, 1857–1876* (Green Bay: Wisconsin Historical Society, 1865).

[127] Fritz W. Rasmussen, "History! Of the Town of New Denmark, Brown Co. Wis," in Fritz William Rasmussen Papers. Correspondence, 1834–1942; Records of the New Denmark Home Guards, 1876–1883, and Evangelical Christian Society, 1871–1897; "History of the Town of New Denmark," 1876, 1881; and Miscellaneous Material. Box no. 1. Green Bay Mss 4. (Green Bay: Wisconsin Historical Society, 1876); Rasmussen, "'Drawn Together in a Blood Brotherhood': Civic Nationalism amongst Scandinavian Immigrants in the American Civil War Crucible," 22–24; William Burton, Melting Pot Soldiers – The Union's Ethnic Regiments, 2nd ed. (New York: Fordham University Press, 1998), 175. Burton argues that "geography, personal friendships, occupation, class, non-ethnic politics, and ambition" weighed heavier than ethnicity for most soldiers.

[128] Christian G. Samito, *Becoming American under Fire: Irish Americans, African Americans, and the Politics of Citizenship During the Civil War Era* (Ithaca, NY: Cornell University Press, 2009), 40.

[129] McPherson, *For Cause and Comrades – Why Men Fought in the Civil War* (New York: Oxford University Press, 1997), 85. Based on his draft experience, Rasmussen's writings add support to James McPherson's argument that a Civil War soldier's primary group was partly made up of "the men from his town or township with whom he enlisted."

March 30, 1865, he mourned another Stockbridge Indian friend from northern Wisconsin, Thomas Anthony, who had died of illness:[130]

This saddened me even more than if it had been someone from a different part of the country[.] This man was, so to speak, from home and we had practically formed a brotherly relationship that, for my part went closer to the heart than perhaps his but which encouraged me more than any others except my comrade Terry.[131]

Interestingly, Rasmussen's statement alludes both to the entanglement of Native Americans and white European settlers and the distance between them.[132] On the one hand, the Danish immigrant felt a real bond between him and Anthony based on their mutual Wisconsin background, but Rasmussen also realized that the warm "brotherly" feelings were not necessarily shared by Anthony, who in his lifetime would have witnessed large-scale European settlement on American Indian land in the Midwest.[133] Though motivations for joining the military were multifarious among Native people, Anthony's volunteer service is noteworthy due to the association between martial manhood and American citizenship.[134] Thomas Anthony's service in a regular military unit such as the 14th Wisconsin could well have been motivated by economic concerns but could also potentially have been a way to establish a claim to citizenship.[135]

---

[130] Celius Christiansen, En Pioneers Historie (Erindringer Fra Krigen Mellem Nord- Og Sydstaterne) [A Pioneer's Story: Memoirs from the War between North and South] (Aalborg: Eget forlag, 1909), 19–21. See also Fritz W. Rasmussen, "Marts Den 30de 1865," in Fritz William Rasmussen Papers, 1834–1942. Green Bay Mss 4. Box no. 1 (Green Bay: Wisconsin Historical Society, 1865).

[131] "Erindringer Fra Mit Feldtliv. Camp near Montg. Ala. Juni Den 26. 1865," in *Fritz William Rasmussen Papers. Correspondence, 1834–1842. Box 1. Folder 1* (Green Bay: Wisconsin Historical Society, 1865).

[132] For other examples, see Gunlög Fur, "Indians and Immigrants – Entangled Histories," *Journal of American Ethnic History* 33, no. 3 (2014): 55–76.

[133] Russell Horton, "Unwanted in a White Man's War: The Civil War Service of the Green Bay Tribes," *Wisconsin Magazine of History* 88, no. 2 (2004): 18–26.

[134] Louis P. Masur, *Lincoln's Last Speech: Wartime Reconstruction and the Crisis of Reunion* (Oxford: Oxford University Press, 2015), 9–10, 146–150.

[135] As Stephen Kantrowitz has shown, Ho-Chunk bands in Wisconsin consciously adopted "Western" expectations of "civilized" behavior, such as buying land and wearing perceived Western cloting, to gain the rights of American citizenship, but such attempts were also met with significant resistance. A few Wisconsin Indians were successful in using the vagueness of American citizenship categories to their advantage by buying small tracts of land and adopting "Western" garb. By doing so, Wisconsin Indians would "demontrate their fitness by embracing a matrix of values and behaviors: the principles of private

Military service did often lead to increased standing in the surrounding society, not least among white Americans with political power. Native people, however, continued to struggle to achieve recognition as citizens in Wisconsin and elsewhere for years after the Civil War.[136] American Indians, for example, were notably absent when Republican congressman George S. Boutwell, on the Fourth of July, 1865, pointed to the service by "whites and negroes born on this continent," as well as "the Irish and the Germans" and "representatives from every European race," as proof that they all deserved voting rights and, by extension, recognition as citizens.[137]

For many, war service was therefore not without importance – but even in this final push to reunite the nation was also not without risk. While digging trenches outside Fort Spanish by Mobile Bay, Fritz Rasmussen on April 6 described one shell wounding twenty-one men, filling the trench with smoke, and the blast wave nearly concussing the entire unit.[138] On April 8, Rasmussen and several veterans was shocked "terribly and horribly" by a rifle bullet cutting the neck artery of a fellow soldier while another hit an "Indian" from Rasmussen's own company in the leg.[139] Mercifully, by 5:30 p.m. on April 8, the end of the campaign was in sight. In a mass bombardment, more than ninety-six artillery pieces opened fire on the forts around Mobile and, according to one witness observing from a safe distance, created a moment of almost surreal beauty: "The fire of so many large guns, and the loud explosion of shells, produced one of those sublime scenes which seldom occur, even in the grandest operations of

---

property and contract; habits of fixed settlement, market orientation, and patriarchal household organization; and particular modes of dress, speech, and worship." See Stephen Kantrowitz, "'Not Quite Constitutionalized': The Meaning of 'Civilization' and the Limits of Native American Citizenship" (New York: Penguin Press, 2012), 75–76. On the complexity of American Indians' motivation for military service, see William McKee Evans, "Native Americans in the Civil War: Three Experiences," in *Civil War Citizens: Race, Ethnicity, and Identity in America's Bloodiest Conflict*, edited by Susannah J. Ural (New York: New York University Press, 2010), 188–189.

[136] Kantrowitz, "'Not Quite Constitutionalized': The Meaning of 'Civilization' and the Limits of Native American Citizenship," 75–77.

[137] Quoted in Samito, *Becoming American under Fire: Irish Americans, African Americans, and the Politics of Citizenship During the Civil War Era*.

[138] Fritz W. Rasmussen, "April Den 6. Klok 2 Eftermid," in *Fritz William Rasmussen Papers. Diaries, 1857–1876. Green Bay Mss 4. Box no. 8* (Green Bay: Wisconsin Historical Society, 1865).

[139] "April 8de, 1865 Formid. Klok. 9," in *Fritz William Rasmussen Papers, 1834–1942. Green Bay Mss 4. Box 1* (Green Bay: Wisconsin Historical Society, 1865).

war," recalled Brigadier General (and later US Minister to Sweden and Norway) Christopher C. Andrews.[140]

The bombardment set a chain reaction in motion. The 8th Iowa initiated the attack and succeeded in planting the American flag on top of the breastworks despite fierce Confederate resistance before the defenders retreated further into the fortress. For a brief moment, Rasmussen thought his regiment would be called upon to finish the attack. Shortly before midnight on April 8 Rasmussen and his fellow soldiers were sent to the frontlines "double quick, forward march!" and from this vantage point witnessed other units move toward the breastworks.[141] "We expected to see and hear a horrendous sight every moment," Rasmussen wrote.[142] But the Confederate defenders were gone. Spanish Fort was in Union hands. The following day, on April 9, Fort Blakely fell, and Ferdinand Winslöw – the 9th Iowa's former quartermaster, who seemed on the cusp of another logistics appointment in Major General Edward Canby's army – wrote to his wife Wilhemina about the elation.[143] Winslöw arrived in Canby's camp just as the battle ended and found his brother-in-law, Christian Christensen, who had helped recruit the war's first Scandinavian company, along with several high-ranking generals.

I had hardly been there half an hour before one Aide-de-Camp after another came with the glorious news of the assault on and taking of Fort Blakely. So there were congratulations, and as the night set in, and the camp fires shone all around in these magnificent pine woods and everything around looked like a fairy-world all the Generals – Steele, A. J. Smith, Carr, Granger, Osterhaus and others sat down in a circle back of Christensen's tent around the quiet, happy Canby, who lit and smoked his cigarre [sic] with an apparent delight and gusto.[144]

The fact that Winslöw had brought along "all kinds of nice" food and a "demi-john with 5 gallons of whiskey" likely did nothing to dampen the mood, and when the Union Army entered Montgomery, the Confederacy's

[140] Christopher Columbus Andrews, *History of the Campaign of Mobile; Including the Coöperative Operations of Gen. Wilson's Cavalry in Alabama (1867)* (New York: D. Van Nostrand, 1867), 149–151.

[141] Fritz W. Rasmussen, "April Den 9de 1865 – Palme Søndag!," in *Fritz William Rasmussen Papers. Diaries, 1857–1876. Green Bay Mss 4. Box no. 8* (Green Bay: Wisconsin Historical Society, 1865).

[142] Ibid.

[143] Edward Canby, "New Orleans La Mar 5th 1865," in *Letters received by the Commission Branch of the Adjutant General's Office, 1863–1870* (Washington, DC: National Archives, 1865); Ferdinand Sophus Winslöw, "Close by Fort Blakely Apr. 10, 1865," in *Ferdinand Sophus Winslow letters, September 1862–April 1865* (University of Iowa, Libraries, Special Collections Department, 1865).

[144] "Close by Fort Blakely Apr. 10, 1865."

FIGURE 9.5 Ferdinand Winslöw (left) surprised his brother-in-law, Christian Christensen, in Alabama in April of 1865, and they likely had this photo taken together in New Orleans shortly thereafter. Courtesy Sadovnikoff Family Private Collection.

first capital city, three days later, it was an important step toward territorial reunification.[145]

Brevet Lieutenant Colonel Stephan Vaugh Shipman, from Madison, Wisconsin, described the occupation of Montgomery in his diary and noted that they "reached the City about 9 o'clock and amid loud cheering the Flag was run up over the State House where the first rebel Congress

[145] Ibid.

met!"[146] The end of combat, however, raised larger questions about the nation's future, not least the role of freedpeople. According to William Warren Rogers Jr., the "sentiments of rejoicing blacks were not in doubt," and that was also the way Fritz Rasmussen described his experience around Montgomery on April 22, 1865.[147] As his regiment prepared to march through Montgomery to a camp a few miles outside of town, Rasmussen touched on the unit's experience with the formerly enslaved. "This morning we again drew rations for two days that should last for three," Rasmussen wrote, giving the reason that "Negroes" were "rushing to our lines" and causing depleted rations for the soldiers due to the larger numbers of mouths to feed.[148] The reaction among the soldiers was mixed, Rasmussen wrote: "Many find it hard but many just laugh and think that they thereby have a good excuse for 'fourage' (stealing)."[149]

Rasmussen himself seems to have been more sympathetic to the plight of freedpeople. But if he specifically recorded his impression of marching through Montgomery on April 23, 1865, those diary pages have now been lost. Rasmussen did, however, describe the experience many years later. When asked to recount his war experience almost a half century afterward, the reluctant veteran's memory allowed for the following:

I helped occupy "the Rebel Capital City" and [I] marched in to the high-pitched tune of "Yankee Doodle" but hardly saw a white person, on the contrary cheered by the black, many of whom could be called white, especially the women.[150]

In his recollection, Rasmussen likely alluded to the sexual violence inflicted on enslaved women by their masters before and during the Civil War, and the attempts to cling to such patterns of domination among white southerners when they returned after the war.[151] Throughout 1865, Rasmussen and other Union soldiers serving in the deep South had a chance to immerse themselves more in their surroundings and consequently also contemplate southern society then and now, not least the impact of emancipation. By

---

[146] Stephan Vaughn Shipman, "Wednesday, April 12th, 1865," in *Stephen Vaughn Shipman, Diary, 1865, Transcription* (Madison: Wisconsin Historical Society, 1865).

[147] William Warren Rogers Jr., *Confederate Home Front: Montgomery During the Civil War* (Tuscaloosa: University of Alabama Press, 1999), 147–148.

[148] Fritz W. Rasmussen, "Near Greenville, Alabama April Den 22de 1865 Eftermid. Kl. 3–4," in *Fritz William Rasmussen Papers. Correspondence, 1834–1942. Box 1* (Green Bay: Wisconsin Historical Society, 1865).

[149] Ibid.   [150] Vig, *Danske i Amerika* [*Danes in America*], 1, 357.

[151] Hannah Rosen, *Terror in the Heart of Freedom: Citizenship, Sexual Violence, and the Meaning of Race in the Postemancipation South* (Chapel Hill: University of North Carolina Press, 2009), 9–11, 70–73.

July 1865, Rasmussen's critique of the Old World nobility and the New World elite mirrored, in important ways, his thoughts on slavery and his antipathy toward slaveowners.

What spendour, yes to put it plainly, Paradise – these people have lived in, not to speak of money or riches, it is therefore no wonder that they became haughty and arrogant. ... It is also no wonder that when war came that they fought for their slavery, since without slavery their circumstances can not possible [sic] be what they were before. But, whether splendor for them or not, I say, splendid, splendid that slavery is abolished.[152]

Thus, Rasmussen interpreted the Civil War as a class conflict; but it was still not clear how much support for abolition also meant support for freed-people's equality and citizenship rights. Such discussions were playing them-selves out at all levels of American society, not least among the Republican leadership in Washington, DC, where plans of freedpeople's future role in the nation were made simultaneously with plans for expanding the nation's territory and population.

---

[152] Fritz W. Rasmussen, "Camp at Montgomery, Ala. Juli Den 23de 1865," in *Fritz William Rasmussen Papers. Correspondence, 1834–1942. Green Bay Mss 4. Box 1* (Green Bay: Wisconsin Historical Society, 1865).

PART III

COLONIALISTS

Lincoln's American Empire

American attempts to expand its territory and population ramped up in early 1865.[1] On January 7, 1865, Waldemar Raaslöff attended a dinner hosted by the French chargé d'affaires, L. De Geoffroy, with several Washington dignitaries present including US Secretary of State William Seward. The presence of both Seward and Raaslöff was no coincidence. Authorized by President Lincoln, who had shown Raaslöff an "exceptional" amount of attention at the White House New Year's reception five days earlier, Seward suggested that he and Raaslöff sit down before dinner in a room adjacent to the dining room to discuss a proposition that Raaslöff almost immediately thereafter relayed to the Danish Ministry of Foreign Affairs in a dispatch labeled "Confidential."[2]

Seward wanted to bring it to "the Danish government's attention" that the United States "desired through purchase to attain possession of our West Indian Islands."[3] The American proposition was motivated by the perceived need for a naval and coaling station in the Caribbean, and St. Thomas was at the top of empire-building Americans' wish list.

---

[1] For stories of American interest stretching back to 1864, see "Dansk-Vestindien," *Fædrelandet*, November 17, 1864; Halvdan Koht, "The Origin of Seward's Plan to Purchase the Danish West Indies," *American Historical Review* 50, no. 4 (1945): 764–766. See also Charles Callan Tansill, *The Purchase of the Danish West Indies*, reprint ed. (New York: Greenwood Press, Publishers, 1968), 7. Writing from Copenhagen in the summer of 1864, the American minister to Denmark, Bradford Wood, considered the partial territorial dismemberment of Denmark an accomplished fact and wondered what nations would get a share in "the plunder."

[2] Waldemar Raaslöff, "Kongelig Dansk Gesandtskab. Washington D. 9de Januar 1865," in *Udenrigsministeriet. 1856–1909 Samlede sager. Vestindien 1865–1909. Box number 771* (Copenhagen: Rigsarkivet, 1865).

[3] Ibid.

In Raaslöff's account, Seward had wanted to "put forward this Overture" for "quite some time" but had until now not been able to find "a suitable moment."[4] The reason was an Old World conflict, now known as the Second Schleswig War, that turned out to be an important first step in Otto von Bismarck's *Grossstaatenbildung* – the unification of the German states – the consequences of which had only recently become clear.[5]

For Danish politicians, military personnel, and civilians alike, the conflict was devastating.[6] The war reduced Denmark's territorial size by one-third and its population by 40 percent and thrust the country further into international *Kleinstaat* status – so much so that people wondered if Denmark could even survive as a nation and whether it offered economic prospects worthy of future generations' pursuit.[7]

At the peace conference in London, Danish delegates had, "in confidence" and ultimately unsuccessfully, suggested ceding the islands of St. Croix, St. Thomas, and St. John to Prussia and Austria in exchange for a redrawn border, but there were still raw emotions – and potential real political ramifications – associated with a sale.[8] The Civil War, however, had shown the need for the United States, as part of its own *Grossstaatenbildung*, to become a "naval power," and, now that the peace agreement between "Denmark and the German great powers had taken effect," Seward trusted that negotiations could be conducted with "the greatest possible delicacy and discretion."[9]

---

[4] Ibid.

[5] Rasmus Glenthøj and Morten Nordhagen Ottosen, *Union Eller Undergang: Kampen for Et Forenet Skandinavien* [*Union or Ruin: The Struggle for a United Scandinavia*] (Copenhagen: Gads Forlag, 2021). See also Tom Buk-Swienty, *1864: The Forgotten War That Shaped Modern Europe* (London: Profile Books LTD, 2015), xviii.

[6] See for example Rasmus Glenthøj, *1864: Sønner Af De Slagne* [*1864: Descendants of the Defeated*] (Copenhagen: Gads Forlag, 2014). Also Lucie Koch, "Riserup Ds: 2de Juli 1865," in *Christian D. Koch and Family Papers, Mss. 202, Louisiana and Lower Mississippi Valley Collections. Box 2* (LSU Libraries, Baton Rouge, Louisiana, 1865).

[7] Rasmus Glenthøj, "Skandinavismen Som En Politisk Nødvendighed [Scandinavism as a Political Necessity]," in *Skandinavismen: Vision Og Virkning [Scandinavism: Vision and Effect]*, ed. Ruth Hemstad, Jes Fabricius Møller, and Dag Thorkildsen (Odense: Syddansk Universitetsforlag, 2018), 246–248; Buk-Swienty, *1864: The Forgotten War That Shaped Modern Europe* (London: Profile Books, 2015), xviii; Koch, "Riserup Ds: 2de Juli 1865."

[8] Quoted in Ove Hornby, *Kolonierne i Vestindien [The West Indian Colonies]*, edited by Svend Ellehøj and Kristoff Glamann (Copenhagen: Politikens Forlag, 1980), 294. See also Raaslöff, "Kongelig Dansk Gesandtskab. Washington D. 9de Januar 1865."

[9] "Kongelig Dansk Gesandtskab. Washington D. 9de Januar 1865."

Still, the Schleswig question complicated American imperial pursuits. As Erik Overgaard Pedersen has shown, Denmark's foreign policy after 1864 was primary determined by attempts to regain at least part of Schleswig and minimize any further loss of territory or population. To affect such an outcome, support from France and Great Britain – who were wary of the United States extending its strategic and military position into the Caribbean – was crucial. On the other hand, a successful sale of the Danish West Indies would bolster the depleted Danish treasury while also resolving a complicated – and by 1865 no longer economically beneficial – colonial relationship in a far-away region.[10]

These intricate international relationships would, along with the American domestic tension over citizenship questions, determine the negotiations for the next five years. In the end, despite a treaty signed by both American and Danish diplomats, the United States, in Seward's words, chose "dollars" over "dominion" as the Senate never ratified the agreement and thereby revealed the limits of small state diplomacy as Danish politicians had little, if any, leverage.[11]

Initially, however, it was Danish fear related to the threshold principle that hampered the negotiations.[12] Raaslöff, for example, described the thought of losing the West Indian Islands as "too painful for me to entertain" and sensed that a sale "would be contrary" to King Christian IX's "feelings."[13] The origins of such "painful" thoughts, and Schleswig's future importance, were found in an attempt to consolidate the Danish Kingdom more clearly along ethnic and linguistic lines.[14] On November 13, 1863, the Danish parliament passed the so-called November Constitution aiming to divide Schleswig from the mainly German-speaking Holstein.[15] This move,

---

[10] Erik Overgaard Pedersen, *The Attempted Sale of the Danish West Indies to the United States of America, 1865–1870* (Frankfurt am Main: Haag + Herchen, 1997), 14–16.

[11] William Seward, quoted in Edward Lillie Pierce, *A Diplomatic Episode: The Rejected Treaty for St. Thomas* (Boston, MA: 1889), 30.

[12] Raaslöff, "Kongelig Dansk Gesandtskab. Washington D. 9de Januar 1865."

[13] Ibid.; Tansill, *The Purchase of the Danish West Indies*, 12.

[14] Glenthøj, "Skandinavismen Som En Politisk Nødvendighed [Scandinavism as a Political Necessity]," 228, 40–41. Concurrently, with the November Constitution there were important discussions taking place related to increased pan-Scandinavian cultural and political cooperation.

[15] Inge Adriansen and Jens Ole Christensen, *Første Slesvigske Krig 1848–1851: Forhistorie, Forløb Og Følger [First Schleswig War 1848–1851: Causes, Course, and Consequences]* (Sønderborg: Sønderborg Slot, 2015), 33.

however, was seized upon by leading politicians within the German Federation, the Prussian minister-president Otto von Bismarck among them, as a breach of the London Treaty following the First Schleswig War. Within months, war between Denmark and Prussia – the former aided by a contingent of Swedes, Norwegians, and Finns, the latter allied with Austria – broke out.

These Old World developments were followed closely in America by politicians, diplomats, and Scandinavian immigrants alike.[16] *Emigranten, Fædrelandet,* and *Hemlandet* ran weekly updates, and in New York Scandinavian leaders and diplomats, led in part by Waldemar Raaslöff, organized a fundraising drive.[17] The war found its decisive military moments at the battles of Dybböl and Als. After a two-month-long siege, numerically superior Prussian troops overran the Danish ramparts at Dybböl on April 18, 1864, and by late June seized all of mainland Jutland. As noted, the war's consequences were deeply felt in Northern Europe.[18] Not only had Denmark lost sizable territory and population to emerging great powers in Europe, the post-war years also saw Denmark, Sweden, and Norway lose population to emigration, in part due to Seward's promotion of the Homestead Act.

While the Second Schleswig War for some months made it more difficult for Scandinavians to emigrate to North America, as passage between Denmark and northern Germany (e.g. Hamburg) for a period was not possible, the end of the war led a number of Scandinavian immigrants

[16] Koht, "The Origin of Seward's Plan to Purchase the Danish West Indies," 764–765.

[17] "The war that is now raging in Denmark has misery and suffering in its wake," read a joint resolution of Scandinavian-born New Yorkers. Scandinavian immigrants in the United States were encouraged to donate 10 cents weekly to help the war's casualties. See H. Dollner, "Bekjendtgørelse [Announcement]," *Fædrelandet,* March 23, 1864. Moreover, on June 5, 1864, Danish immigrants again met in New York and wrote a statement that was later published in *Emigranten:* "With the keenest attention we Danes here in America have followed the events in our dear Fatherland and today, the anniversary of the Danish Kingdom's Constitution, we have gathered to send you our salute and thanks ... To the Danish warriors from countrymen in America ... the ca[n]non's thunder from Dybböl's redoubts reached us and with pride we received the accounts of your heroic defense." See "De Danske i New York [The Danes in New York]," *Emigranten,* August 22, 1864. Also "Sorgliga Underrättelser [Sad News]," *Hemlandet,* May 4, 1864.

[18] See, for example, Lucie Koch, "Riserup Ds: 2de Juli 1865," in *Christian D. Koch and Family Papers, Mss. 202, Louisiana and Lower Mississippi Valley Collections.* Box 2 (LSU Libraries, Baton Rouge, Louisiana, 1865).

FIGURE 10.1 The mill at Dybböl came to symbolize the military defeat in 1864 for generations of Danes as the battlefield and surrounding territory was annexed by the emerging German *Grossstaat*. Photo by Hulton-Deutsch Collection/Corbis via Getty Images.

west. For Swedish, Norwegian, and Danish citizens returning home with military experience in the summer of 1864, the United States became an increasingly attractive place to resume a military career.

On September 16, 1864, American consul William W. Thomas Jr. wrote from the Kingdom of Sweden and Norway that Swedish volunteers from the war of 1864 were arriving "in squads of five, ten, and twenty" and that all heartily wished to "go to America and join the forces of the Union."[19]

---

[19] W. W. Thomas, "United States Consulate. Gothenburg September 16, 1864," in *RG 59 Records of the Department of State. Despatches from U.S. Consuls in Gothenburg, Sweden 1800–1906. T 276* (National Archives at College Park, 1864).

Thomas personally arranged for these soldiers' travel by raising money and working out arrangements with captains in Hamburg. While acknowledging that "as consul I can have nothing to do with enlisting soldiers," Thomas nevertheless wrote with pride that he had "forwarded over thirty [Swedish veterans] this week" whose fare had been paid by "good friend[s] in America, including the Consul himself."[20] Thus, Thomas knowingly leveraged Swedish veterans' post-war economic anxiety to add military manpower in opposition to the interest of Swedish authorities but claimed to provide a valuable opportunity that the veterans' themselves sought.[21]

Thomas' example was far from singular. While recruitment in Germany was officially illegal, more than 1,000 men in Hamburg were enlisted through Boston-based agents in the latter years of the war, and British diplomats raised numerous complaints of "fraudulent enlistment" as well.[22]

Additionally, as described in *Emigranten*, the German Press reported that "several" Danish officers, some of whom may have been living south of the recently redrawn Danish-German border, were about to leave for America from Hamburg and Bremen in December 1864. According to an article in *Hamburg Nachrichten* (Hamburg Intelligencer), eleven war veterans had arrived in the port city and "a large number of comrades were expected to follow."[23]

---

[20] Ibid. Also Nels Hokanson, *Swedish Immigrants in Lincoln's Time* (New York: Arno Press, 1979), 27, 69. The idea of enlisting Swedes in the Union army had been on Thomas' mind throughout 1864. On February 12, 1864, Thomas specifically advocated transferring as many of "these descendants of the Vikings" as possible to bolster the war effort. W. W. Thomas, "United States Consulate. Gothenburg Feb. 12. 1864," in *RG 59 Records of the Department of State. Despatches from U.S. Consuls in Gothenburg, Sweden 1800–1906. T 276* (National Archives at College Park, 1864).

[21] On December 1864, news of "several former Danish officers" in Hamburg about to embark for New York to "enlist in the Union army" was published in the local newspapers with the expectation that they would be "followed by a larger number of comrades." See "Udvandring Af Danske Officerer Til Amerika [Emigration of Danish Officers to America]," *Emigranten*, January 9, 1865.

[22] Andrea Mehrländer, "'. . . Ist Daß Nicht Reiner Sclavenhandel?' Die Illegale Rekrutierung Deutscher Auswanderer Für Die Unionsarmee Im Amerikanischen Bürgerkrieg ['Is That Not Pure Slavetrade?' The Illegal Recruitment of German Emigrants for the Union Army During the American Civil War]," *Amerikastudien/American Studies* 44, no. 1 (1999). I am grateful to Dr. Michael Douma for unearthing the Mehrländer study. See also Michael J. Douma, Anders Bo Rasmussen, and Robert O. Faith, "The Impressment of Foreign-Born Soldiers in the Union Army," *Journal of American Ethnic History* 38, no. 3 (2019): 76–106.

[23] "Udvandring Af Danske Officerer Til Amerika [Emigration of Danish Officers to America]." Yet, toward the end of the Civil War, life in the United States was not always as promising as immigrants had hoped. Danish Consul Harald Döllner revealed in a letter

These Scandinavian war veterans were, in part, looking for opportunities to use their military experience in the American Civil War, but the Homestead Act, which had taken effect in 1863, also became an increasingly powerful pull factor. After 1864, Scandinavian immigrants, with limited opportunity for upward social mobility in the Old World, thereby played into Seward's Homestead vision of European migration adding to the nation's population, pool of recruits, and territory through the Confederacy's defeat and western expansion when Old World conditions became too desperate.[24]

The Scandinavians who did arrive expressed pride in the nation they had now become part. "At the present time America has a great army and perhaps more than all of Europe's armies," wrote Norwegian-born Ole Jakobsen Berg in January 1865, adding that no country could measure up to the United States. Yet how the newly adopted nation would maintain this appeal and simultaneously reconstruct itself, with the South's added population and territory, after four years of Civil War remained an open question. To Seward, part of the answer was continued expansion.

Despite being a small state diplomat, Raaslöff had cultivated a fruitful relationship with William Seward stretching back to at least 1861, when the two agreed to explore colonization of "now emancipated negroes" in the Caribbean.[25] The mutual trust made Seward confident that he could count on Raaslöff's "discretion" when he opened negotiations for the purchase of St. Thomas, St. Croix, and St. John on January 7, 1865, and

---

written on January 10, 1865, and published in the Copenhagen newspaper *Fædrelandet* some questionable recruiting techniques in the New World that warranted a warning to people back home. "Many Danes come to New York without means and without understanding English, among them officers of the Danish army, who expect to be placed in the same position as they had at home. As many educated young men have served in the American Army for several years, it presently does not need more foreign officers. For privates there will undoubtedly be adequate opportunity for some time ... The Danish emigrants must at their arrival here guard themselves against impostors. Usually they [the emigrants] come to the consulate after they have fallen into financial difficulty or have fallen into the hands of impostors who have sold them as soldiers, and at a time when the Consul can't help them." See Fædrelandet, "Kgl. Dansk Consulat i New York [Royal Danish Consulate in New York]," *Fædrelandet*, February 1 1865.

[24] Ole Jakobsen Berg, "Clinton Den 8de Janny 1865," in *America Letters and Articles. 1860–1890. P435. Box 2* (Northfield, MN: Norwegian-American Historical Association, 1865).

[25] Raaslöff, "Kongl. Dansk Gesandtskab. Washington Den 15de December 1861 [Royal Danish Legation. Washington the 15th of December, 1861]."

Raaslöff on the other hand reported that Seward was "entirely serious" and acted on behalf of the president.[26] According to Raslöff's report of the meeting, Seward stated that "the United States naturally would not want to see" the islands fall into the hands of "another power" and promised the "most loyal and most friendly" negotiating position toward Denmark.[27] If Seward's proposal did indeed give "occasion for negotiations," the American secretary of state promised that they would be conducted in the "most 'generous,' 'chivalrous' and 'delicate' manner."[28]

The meeting sparked high-level negotiations between Seward's Department of State and the Danish government often represented by Raasläff. Despite the Danish king's hesitancy, which initially put negotiations on hold, Raasläff was notified by the Danish Ministry of Foreign Affairs on February 24, 1865, that the country's "financial and political position" necessitated a thorough consideration of the American proposal and that "on an occasion such as this, personal feelings should not be the sole factor."[29]

Yet the negotiations were derailed – as were so many other lives and policy decisions – on April 14, 1865, by John Wilkes Booth's fateful shot in Ford's Theater and Lewis Powell's knife-wielding attack on Seward.[30] The following day, Raasläff received a melancholic message from Acting Secretary of State William Hunter, who had the "great misfortune" to inform him that:

The President of the United States was shot with a pistol last night while attending a theatre in this City, and expired this morning from the effects of the wound at about the same time an attempt was made to assassinate the Secretary of State [,] which though it fortunately failed, left him severely, but it is hoped not dangerously wounded, with a Knife or Dagger. Mr. F. W. Seward was also struck on the head with a heavy weapon and is in a critical condition from the effect of the blows. Pursuant to the provision of the Constitution of the United States Andrew Johnson, the Vice President, has formally assumed the functions of President.[31]

---

[26] "Kongelig Dansk Gesandtskab. Washington D. 9de Januar 1865."   [27] Ibid.   [28] Ibid.
[29] Quoted in Tansill, *The Purchase of the Danish West Indies*, 12.
[30] For the assassination plans, see Martha Hodes, *Mourning Lincoln* (New Haven, CT: Yale University Press, 2015), 1–5. Raasläff's assessment of the attacks and their consequences for Danish-American diplomacy can be found in Waldemar Raasläff, "Confidentielt. No. 6. Washington D: 22 April 1865" (Copenhagen: Rigsarkivet, 1865).
[31] William Hunter, "Department of State, Washington 15 April, 1865," in *Washington D.C., diplomatisk repræsentation. 1854–1909 Korrespondancesager (aflev. 1918). Politisk Korrespondance 1864–1868* (Copenhagen: Rigsarkivet, 1865).

Raaslöff, who responded to Hunter's news with "deep and sincere grief," on April 22, 1865, reported home to the Danish government that a planned meeting with the secretary of state would now be postponed indefinitely.[32]

It was soon clear that the assassination of President Lincoln, who had recently laid out a vision of reconstruction with "malice towards none" and a personal preference for Black men's suffrage, had far-reaching consequences inside and outside American borders.[33] Lincoln's successor, Andrew Johnson, shared the late president's homestead advocacy and vision of expansion into the Caribbean through purchase of "the Virgin Islands," but in his opposition to freedpeople's landownership and equality he helped legitimize ideas of Black inferiority and helped exacerbate splits in the Republican Party.[34] Such nationwide debates over expansion and equality also rippled through Scandinavian-American communities.

---

[32] Waldemar Raaslöff, "Washington D: 22 April 1865," in *Udenrigsministeriet. 1856–1909 Samlede sager. Vestindien 1865–1909. Box number 771* (Copenhagen: Rigsarkivet, 1865). In the meantime, Raaslöff requested detailed instructions about how to proceed with the negotiations "in the always conceivable event that Mr. Seward dies." See also William Hunter, "Department of State, Washington 15 April, 1865," in *Washington D. C., diplomatisk repræsentation. 1854–1909 Korrespondancesager (aflev. 1918). Politisk Korrespondance 1864–1868* (Copenhagen: Rigsarkivet, 1865).

[33] Hodes, *Mourning Lincoln*, 38.

[34] Andrew Johnson, "Third Annual Message" (online by Gerhard Peters and John T. Woolley, The American Presidency Project; www.presidency.ucsb.edu/ws/index.php?pid=29508, 1867); Hodes, *Mourning Lincoln*; Paul Frymer, *Building an American Empire: The Era of Territorial and Political Expansion* (Princeton, NJ: Princeton University Press, 2017), 21–22.

I I

The Principle of Equality

Cannons boomed in celebration across the South toward the end of the Civil War. In Little Rock, Arkansas, Nels Knutson described a 100-cannon tribute to General Philip Sheridan's victory in the Shenandoah Valley in October 1864. In Alabama, Christian Christensen noted a 100-gun salute to celebrate the victory over Lee's army in April 1865 and a 200-gun salute when Mobile fell.[1] In New Orleans, Elers Koch, who had been forced to serve in the Confederate cavalry for part of the war, described a "great illumination" and salute "on account of the surrender" and added: "I feel like I want to Hurrah all the time, I feel so elated by the Federal success."[2]

But euphoria soon turned to sorrow. With news of Lincoln's death, troops such as the 54th Massachusetts in Charleston, South Carolina, "lowered flags, fired guns, tolled bells," and a "silent gloom" fell over the Union Army's encampments while military and civilian buildings were draped in black.[3] As far north as New Denmark, Wisconsin, Fritz

---

[1] Nels Knutson, "Little Rock Ark October 4th 1864," in *Copies of Letters written by Nels Knutson, Moline, IL, during the Civil War. SSIRC. SAC P:315* (Augustana College, 1864). See also C. T. Christensen, "Headquarters, Army and Division of West Mississippi, Mobile, Ala., April 16th, 1865. General Field Orders, No. 23.," in *General Frederick Steele Papers, M0191* (Dept. of Special Collections, Stanford University Libraries, Stanford, CA, 1865). See also Christopher Columbus Andrews, *History of the Campaign of Mobile; Including the Cooperative Operations of Gen. Wilson's Cavalry in Alabama (1867)* (New York: D. Van Nostrand, 1867), 230.

[2] Elers Koch, "New Orleans April 17th 1865," in *Christian D. Koch and Family Papers, Mss. 202, Louisiana and Lower Mississippi Valley Collections. Box 2* (LSU Libraries, Baton Rouge, LA, 1865).

[3] Quoted in Martha Hodes, *Mourning Lincoln* (New Haven, CT: Yale University Press, 2015), 57–58.

Rasmussen's father noted the "great general mourning" associated with the "murder," and his son-in-law, Celius Christiansen, years later described a similar experience in Missouri.[4] "Never will I forget the impression, I got, by seeing the great city, St. Louis, in a mourning garb," Christiansen wrote: "Everything was draped with black cloth even down from all the church spires. Thousands of dollars had been spent in this city alone to express the people's deep mourning of the president."[5]

The Confederate capitulations, Lincoln's assassination, and the attempt at Secretary Seward's life, along with all the other "events over the last month," led to a sense at *Emigranten* that April 1865 had surpassed "everything that has thus far taken place in the continent's history."[6] With Lincoln's assassination, thoughts of retribution, for a moment, supplanted thoughts of reconciliation.[7] Writing from Nashville, Tennessee, in late April or early May, Norwegian-born Julius Steenson struggled to find the words to describe his feeling of "horror" and "vengeance" toward "the assassin Booth" in a letter to his cousin Mary.[8] Steenson was glad that the "murderer" had been caught but sorry that Booth was killed in the process, feeling that "to die so quick was not enough punishment for such an act as to kill that man of so great private life and public worth."[9]

Retribution was also on Edward Rasmussen's mind: "You have probably heard that they have caught the traitor Jeff. Davis and I hope that before you receive these lines that he is strung up in a gallow as high as

[4] Edward Rasmussen, "New Denmark, Brown Co. Den 29. Maj 1865 Wis.," in *Fritz William Rasmussen Papers. Correspondence, 1834–1942. Green Bay Mss 4. Box no. 1* (Green Bay: Wisconsin Historical Society, 1865).

[5] Celius Christiansen, *En Pioneers Historie (Erindringer Fra Krigen Mellem Nord-Og Sydstaterne) [A Pioneer's Story: Memoirs from the War between North and South]* (Aalborg: Eget forlag, 1909), 55.

[6] "Emigranten. "Madison, 17de April 1865," *Emigranten*, April 24 1865. See also "Forfærdelige Efterretninger – Præsidenten Og Statsministeren Myrdede [Terrible News: The President and Secretary of State Murdered]," *Emigranten*, April 17, 1865.

[7] Richard White, *The Republic for Which It Stands: The United States During Reconstruction and the Gilded Age, 1865–1896* (Oxford: Oxford University Press, 2017) 12. White notes that there was "little violence against Confederate sympathizers," but feelings of vengeance were clearly expressed; see Julius Steenson, "Cousin Mary I Would Say Some Thing About the Assasination of Our President," in *Kestol Family Papers* (In family possession, 1865).

[8] Steenson, "Cousin Mary I Would Say Some Thing About the Assasination of Our President."

[9] Ibid.

Hans Mattson
1832–1893

FIGURE 11.1 Hans Mattson became one of the best-known Swedish-American Civil War officers and later one of the best-known Scandinavian-born politicians in the United States.

Haman's," Rasmussen noted with an Old Testament reference, in a letter to his son Fritz.[10] In a similar vein, the Swedish-born colonel Hans Mattson, stationed in Jacksonport, Arkansas, wrote to his wife that several "persons were shot dead by soldiers at Little Rock for rejoycing [sic] over Lincoln[']s murder – it served them right."[11]

    Mattson's letter alluded to the simmering tension and the potential for violence between former Confederates and the Union Army tasked, in part, with ensuring public safety, not least that of freedpeople. Guerrilla attacks, robberies, Union soldiers' own looting, and attacks on the formerly enslaved at times found their way into accounts, demonstrating both prejudice and empathy toward freedpeople among Scandinavian soldiers.

    Maintaining law and order proved difficult in numerous instances during this early part of Reconstruction. Norwegian-born Ole Stedje,

[10] Fritz Rasmussen, "New Denmark, Brown Co. Den 29. Maj 1865 Wis."
[11] H. Mattson, "Sunday Morning Apr 23. 1865," in *Hans Mattson and Family Papers. Box 1* (Minnesota Historical Society, 1865). See also Donald J. Simon, "The Third Minnesota Regiment in Arkansas, 1863–1865," *Minnesota History* (1967): 292.

writing from Duvall's Bluff, Arkansas in March 1865, noted the importance of winning over the local population in a larger effort against
paramilitary bands, and Danish-born Wilhelm Wermuth described "violence so common here that there is not much to say about it," after falling
victim to guerrillas in Kansas.[12]

Fritz Rasmussen, who spent the majority of his one-year service in
Alabama, also witnessed instances in which tension between white southerners and freedmen likely turned violent. Describing a boat being loaded
with confiscated rebel weapons, Rasmussen on August 2, 1865, saw one gun
go off and hit "a negro in one side of the abdomen," tearing a "hideous" hole
to the intestines.[13] "Several people thought that the carpenter aboard had
shot him," Rasmussen noted, "as it was known that they had exchanged
words."[14]

While Rasmussen did not specifically note the carpenter's ethnicity, the
fact that he, unlike the victim, was not described as "a negro" possibly
makes it an instance of a white laborer shooting a Black man. If so, it was
part of a larger pattern during the early part of reconstruction. As Carole
Emberton has noted, "the violence recorded by the [Freedmen's] Bureau
attests to both its pervasiveness in postwar society as well as the indeter-
minacy of power relations in everyday life."[15] In Missouri, Rasmussen's
brother-in-law Celius Christiansen contemplated violence and the consequences of slavery when he arrived at "Væverly" (Waverly); in his memoirs he recounted the aftermath of a guerrilla attack in 1865:

They had so little respect for the military that they, in broad daylight a Sunday
afternoon, attacked a plantation close to town. Here they shot three negroes,
whereof one died immediately, and the two others survived by pretending to be
dead. I spoke to one of them who had three bullets in his head and someone had

---

[12] O. O. Stedje, "Fra Arkansas. Duvall's Bluff, Arkansas, 2den Marts, 1865," *Emigranten*,
April 3, 1865. See also Wilhelm Wermuth, "Atchison Kansas D 20 Maj," in
*Håndskriftsafdelingen. Ny Kongelig Samling 2719. II. Folio. Karl Larsen's Collection,
Unused material. Wilhelm Adolf Leopold Wermuth, USA (Soldat, guldgraver, mine-ejer)*
(Copenhagen: Det Kongelige Bibliotek, 1865). The Danish-born veteran had left Chicago
around Christmas of 1864 and hoped to make money further south but lost all. "It pains
me that I can not send you some money but I have had bad luck myself," Wilhelm
Wermuth wrote to his mother from Kansas in May 1865. "These guerrillas took it from
me and I barely escaped with my life."
[13] Fritz W. Rasmussen, "August Den 2de 1865," in *Fritz William Rasmussen Papers.
Correspondence, 1834–1942. Green Bay Mss 4. Box no. 1* (Green Bay: Wisconsin
Historical Society, 1865).
[14] Ibid.
[15] Carole Emberton, *Beyond Redemption: Race, Violence, and the American* (Chicago, IL:
University of Chicago Press, 2013), 80.

knocked his teeth in, so it was horrible to watch. That such an outrageous attack frightened the black population is quite natural and I remember that I felt great compassion with them by hearing their lamentations and seeing their misery and sadness.[16]

Christiansen claimed the attack was committed by the famed outlaw brothers Frank and Jesse James, who had returned to their family farm in nearby Clay County, Missouri, in late 1865, but the chronology does not quite add up, as the 50th Wisconsin left Waverly in the summer.[17] It is, however, possible that Christiansen did witness the aftermath of an attack by bushwackers in the summer of 1865, as Waverly was situated in a "triangle of counties" where the anti-Unionist – and by extension anti-Black – sentiment, according to T. J. Stiles, "was fiercest."[18]

Importantly, Christiansen's memoir also revealed a certain ambivalence about race and ethnicity in the post-war moment, as he expressed sympathy for "the poor black slaves" who suffered in bondage, disdained the many shabby slave huts he encountered, and applauded abolition of "the gruesome slavery" but also, to an extent, admired ex-confederates and supported American Indians' removal.[19] Christiansen became "intimate friends" with an alleged former bushwacker and later praised a victory against Lakota people that opened up "large expanses of the best lands."[20]

Christiansen's story exemplifies the complexities on the ground in the post-war South but indicates Scandinavian immigrants' lack of postbellum reflection regarding Native people and freedpeople's precariousness in the

---

[16] Christiansen, *En Pioneers Historie (Erindringer Fra Krigen Mellem Nord-Og Sydstaterne)* [*A Pioneer's Story: Memoirs from the War between North and South*], 62–63.

[17] T. J. Stiles, *Jesse James: Last Rebel of the Civil War* (New York: Alfred A. Knopf, 2002), 160–167.

[18] Ibid., 164.

[19] Christiansen in his memoirs also described the economic advantages based on exploitation that the planter class enjoyed: "Little wonder that the property-owning class were so reluctant to give up the priviledges they were born with. The had usurped power to such an extent that they just sent people out to survey the richest and best land to then acquire it, but the greatest advantage was the cheap labor as the poor black slaves were not given anything else than paltry food and clothing." See Christiansen, *En Pioneers Historie (Erindringer Fra Krigen Mellem Nord- Og Sydstaterne)* [*A Pioneer's Story: Memoirs from the War between North and South*], 58, 73–74.

[20] Christiansen, *En Pioneers Historie (Erindringer Fra Krigen Mellem Nord-Og Sydstaterne)* [*A Pioneer's Story: Memoirs from the War between North and South*], 58–65, 73–74. Speaking to Scandinavian immigrants' concern with a quick return to post-war life without explicitly engaging issues issues of racial equality, Christiansen recalled that Waverly became a better place when Confederate soldiers returned because of the returned soldiers' hospitality. See also Stiles, *Jesse James: Last Rebel of the Civil War*, 164.

face of violence as well. Yet, even as Scandinavian-born soldiers often abhorred violence against freedpeople, few examples exist of them pro-actively fighting for Black citizenship, voting rights, and equality in the Civil War's immediate aftermath.

War service in the South helped transform some perceptions of race among Scandinavian-born soldiers, as was the case for a correspondent who wrote to *Hemlandet* in October 1863 from Helena, Arkansas, to express his admiration of the service performed by a "Corps d'Afrique."[21] Moreover, in *Emigranten* on April 25, 1864, Ole Stedje from the Army of the Cumberland wrote: "When one, as we do, move about down here for a longer period of time, and can see all of slavery's conditions revealed, the thought forces itself upon one that even if one previously was a stiff Democrat, slavery has been the South's most depraved institution."[22]

Christian Christensen's wartime interaction with future freedpeople likewise revealed racial attitudes that set him apart. According to an 1865 letter from fellow officer and fervent abolitionist Brigadier General John Wolcott Phelps, Christensen's "bearing towards the negro race was peculiarly gratifying" and "indicative of a generous heart and an enlarged and liberal understanding."[23] To Fritz Rasmussen, military service under-lined the immorality of slavery. In his diary post from July 23, 1865, Rasmussen wrote about the wealthy planters' "arrogance" that led to war and added his thoughts on abolition:

What joy I felt the other day when "the provisional Governors Proclamation" was brought into the tent and Ed. Daskam, among other, read: "There is no more a slave in Alabama." Yes, what indignation I feel every time something catches my eye related to the depravity of slavery. This afternoon I went to church in a big negro church, as it is called here, and precious and beloved, relatives and friends, the feelings I suffered or went through there are impossible for me to describe.[24]

Expression of admiration and sympathy for the formerly enslaved, how-ever, seldom translated into concrete action or enthusiasm when

[21] "Fra Helena, Arkansas Oktober 1863," *Hemlandet*, November 11, 1863.
[22] O. O. Stedje, "Fra En Norsk Frivillig i Cumberland-Armeen [From a Norwegian Volunteer in the Army of the Cumberland]," *Emigranten*, April 25, 1864.
[23] Christian Thomsen Christensen, "Provost Marshals Office. April 22d 1862," in *Papers of Christian T. Christensen. Christensen (Christian Thomsen) Collection. 1862–1876. Box 1* (San Marino, CA: Huntington Library, 1862). See also John Wolcott Phelps, "Brattleboro, Vermont. June 19, 1865," in *Papers of Christian T. Christensen. Christensen (Christian Thomsen) Collection. 1862–1876. Box 1* (San Marino, CA: Huntington Library, 1865). Phelps, "Brattleboro, Vermont. June 19, 1865."
[24] Rasmussen, "Camp at Montgomery, Ala. Juli Den 23de 1865."

Scandinavian immigrants later debated or acted on the question of freed-people's civil rights. For every Stedje, Christensen, and Rasmussen, there were Danielsons, Winslöws, and Hegs who used the phrase "niggers" even while expressing some support of abolitionism.[25]

Important clues to understanding the ambiguity of equality expressed in the soldiers' letters, diaries, and memoirs are found in the Scandinavian-American press. The issue of land redistribution was for example broached in *Emigranten* on April 10, 1865, when General William Sherman's Special Field Order No. 15 was described in positive, yet prejudiced, terms:[26]

At a previous occasion, "Emigraten" has reported on an order from General Sherman which concerns setting aside islands and a part of the coast line in South Carolina, Georgia and Florida for the freed slaves' disposal. There they could build a home, manage cotton growth, agriculture or all together such operations as they from their youth are trained to do and understand ... The government has chosen a good and completely comprehensive plan to provide for "Sambo" and his colored family ... It is hereby demonstrated that the Negro can provide for himself as soon as he is put to work and this is all one can require.[27]

The expectation of freedpeople providing for themselves through agricul-tural work as soon as possible was a common refrain in the Scandinavian-American press. Still, when President Andrew Johnson by September 1865 directed the commissioner of the Freedmen's Bureau, General Oliver O. Howard, in Eric Foner's words, to order "the restoration to pardoned owners of all land except the small amount that had already been sold under a court decree," the issue was no longer at the forefront of Scandinavian immigrant newspapers, whose pages were filled with local election coverage with almost no discussion of racial issues.[28]

---

[25] Christiansen, En Pioneers Historie (Erindringer Fra Krigen Mellem Nord- Og Sydstaterne) [A Pioneer's Story: Memoirs from the War between North and South], 73–74. See also Mathilda Cassel Peterson Danielson, "Helena, Arkansas November 5, 1862"; Ferdinand Sophus Winsløw, "Pacific, Mo. 15 January 1862," in *Ferdinand Sophus Winslow letters, September 1861–February 1862* (Iowa City: University of Iowa, Special Collections Department, 1862); Theodore C. Blegen, ed., The Civil War Letters of Colonel Hans Christian Heg (Northfield, MN: Norwegian-American Historical Association, 1936), 57.

[26] Eric Foner, *Reconstruction: America's Unfinished Revolution, 1863–1877* (New York: Harper & Row, 1988), 70.

[27] Carl Fredrik Solberg, "Emigranten. Madison, 7de April 1865," *Emigranten*, April 10, 1865. See also Foner, *Reconstruction: America's Unfinished Revolution, 1863–1877*, 70.

[28] Foner, *Reconstruction: America's Unfinished Revolution, 1863–1877*, 159–160. See, for example, "Fædrelandet. Thorsdag 20de September 1865," *Fædrelandet*, September 21, 1865.

In November 1865, for example, "Wisconsin was among the first of fifteen states and territories where white men had the opportunity to enfranchise their black counterparts" and, as Alison Clark Efford reminds us, "declined to do so."[29] Scandinavian immigrants, who often professed to have come to the United States because of liberty and equality, were likely on the side that declined.

Despite the opportunity to advocate for extending the right to vote (with its implied connection to citizenship), no letters to the editor appeared in the main Scandinavian newspapers, and discussions of race were also almost completely absent from the editorial page. On the eve of the election, *Emigranten* did, however, in a longer piece manage to squeeze in one sentence criticizing the Democratic gubernatorial candidate's complete opposition to freedpeople's rights when it pointed out that "Union men grant each other the right to be for or against giving the Negroes the vote in Wisconsin," but the Scandinavian paper did not elaborate on its own position.[30] *Fædrelandet* also spent very little ink on the election but was a little clearer than *Emigranten* on November 16 when it noted the Union Party's "splendid victory" and also the "rejection" of the suffrage proposal.[31] On the question of Black men's right to vote, *Fædrelandet* added:

The time is probably not right either to answer this question in the affirmative, but we hope that the time is not distant when any friend of freedom and human rights will say: "now the time has come, now the negro is worthy of admittance as citizen."[32]

Though it is difficult to assess opinions on the ground in Scandinavian enclaves, Susannah Ural's point that "editors could not stay in business if they failed to address the interest of their communities" does at the very least indicate a split even among Republican-leaning Scandinavian voters on the Black suffrage question.[33] Among German immigrants in

---

[29] Alison Clark Efford, "The Appeal of Racial Neutrality in the Civil War-Era North: German Americans and the Democratic New Departure," *Journal of the Civil War Era* 5, no. 1 (2015): 69.

[30] "Harrison C. Hobart, 'Demokratiets' Guvernørkandidat i Wisconsin [Harrison C. Hobart, 'Democracy's' Gubernatorial Candidate in Wisconsin]," *Emigranten*, November 6, 1865; "Afvigte Tirsdag Den 7de Var Valgdag [Last Tuesday the 7th Was Election Day]," *Emigranten*, November 13, 1865. *Emigranten* omitted any mention of Black men's suffrage when describing the Union Party's victory a week later.

[31] "Fædrelandet," *Fædrelandet*, November 16, 1865.   [32] Ibid.

[33] Susannah J. Ural, ed., *Civil War Citizens: Race, Ethnicity and Identity in America's Bloodiest Conflict* (New York: New York University Press, 2010), 9.

Wisconsin, the split was likely even more pronounced. As Efford has demonstrated, "German Republican leaders in Wisconsin were firm on suffrage," but the German leaders' position differed from the position of most German-born "Wisconsinites, the majority of whom voted Democratic," and it was also more forward-thinking than was the case for Scandinavian-born editors.[34]

In a Republican Party that, according to Richard White's assessment, was the party of "nationalism, economic improvement, personal independence, and more tentatively, universal rights," the Scandinavian press generally sided with the (white) nationalism and economic improvement faction.[35] The question of citizenship, and by extension suffrage, was central to the struggle among Republican factions, and the central arena was Washington, DC.

As such, Lyman Trumbull, still chairman of the Senate Judiciary Committee, was questioned about citizenship and skin color in early 1866. Would the proposed 14th amendment guarantee citizenship for "persons born in the United States ... without distinction of color?" Democratic Senator James Guthrie of Kentucky and Republican Senator Jacob Howard of Michigan asked.[36] The answer, Trumbull explained, was yes and no: mostly "no" for Indians ("We deal with them by treaty"), but mostly "yes" for everyone else.[37] Trumbull's answer, which included "the children of Chinese and Gypsies" as potential citizens, surprised Republican Senator Edgar Cowan, who argued that an immigration influx from China could "overwhelm our race and wrest from them the dominion of that country."[38]

The use of the phrases "our race" and "dominion of that country" was telling, and Cowan in his next comment denied that children of Chinese immigrants could be considered citizens as of right now. This led Trumbull to ask, is "not the child born in this country of German parents a citizen?" To which Cowan replied: "The children of German parents are citizens; but Germans are not Chinese; Germans are not Australians, nor

---

[34] Alison Clark Efford, *German Immigrants, Race, and Citizenship in the Civil War Era* (Washington, DC: Cambridge University Press, 2013), 121.

[35] White, *The Republic for Which It Stands: The United States During Reconstruction and the Gilded Age, 1865–1896*, 24.

[36] I am grateful to Stephen Kantrowitz for bringing this debate to my attention; J. Rives and F. Rives, eds., *The Congressional Globe: Containing the Debates and Proceedings of the First Session of the Thirty-Ninth Congress* (Washington, DC: Congressional Globe Office, 1866), 498–499.

[37] Ibid., 498.   [38] Ibid., 498–499.

Hottentots, nor anything of the kind. That is the fallacy of his argument."[39] To this reply, Trumbull simply stated, "The law makes no such distinction."[40]

Scandinavians also were not Germans, but in the discussion over citizenship, the Norwegian, Swedish, and Danish ethnic elite actually considered themselves superior to competing European ethnic group such as the Germans – and even more so in relation to nonwhites. As an example, a mixed news and opinion piece, likely penned by Solberg, in *Emigranten* on August 13, 1866, asked: "Who is white?"

The question, the writer pointed out, had caused considerable trouble in Michigan, as it was "suspected" that someone "having a mix of 'black' blood in his veins," had voted.[41] Yet, the blood, according to the *Emigranten* editor, distinguished "us free Americans" from other groups:

African blood is "black," European "white" and if a man wants to be somebody, there cannot be a trace of "black" blood in his veins. Enthusiastic about the idea about freedom and equality, we Norsemen did indeed protest slavery's monstrous motto that "the Black man has no rights which the white man is bound to respect," but what was simply meant by this protest was the right to not be a slave against one's will.[42]

In short, while the editor explicitly distanced himself – and Scandinavians more broadly – from the wording of the 1857 Dred Scott decision in a case revolving around a Black man's freedom from bondage, the ideas behind the decision, that Black people where inherently inferior and could neither be equal nor citizens seemed acceptable.[43] In terms of political citizenship, only "fullblooded" Europeans, who "stood as high above anyone with mixed blood in the veins as the pure thoroughbred over the simple draft animal," should have the right to vote in the United States, *Emigranten* argued.[44]

Thus, even as Scandinavian immigrants professed their admiration for American ideals and wrote home about "the principle of equality" being "completely recognized and entirely implemented," as one Norwegian correspondent did to an Old World newspaper on September 28, 1866, the principle of equality was still far from recognized or implemented on

---

[39] Ibid., 498.   [40] Ibid.
[41] "Hvem Er Hvid Og Hvem Er Ikke Hvid? [Who Is White and Who Is Not White?]," *Emigranten*, August 13, 1866.
[42] Ibid.
[43] Manisha Sinha, *The Slave's Cause: A History of Abolition* (New Haven, CT: Yale University Press, 2016), 566–573.
[44] "Hvem Er Hvid Og Hvem Er Ikke Hvid? [Who Is White and Who Is Not White?]."

the question of suffrage extended to nonwhites and, as we shall see, women.[45]

In rural Scandinavian immigrant enclaves, gender roles by 1865 were still very much tied to Old World perceptions and practices. As Jon Gjerde has argued, paternalist European family patterns "based on Scripture and 'correct' behavior" often "informed the relationship between husband and wife," as well as that "between parent and child."[46]

Yet returning veterans, some physically or mentally ill, came home to communities where women had run the households for months if not years. Thus, the Civil War's end ushered in a transition period where traditional roles within and outside the home by necessity were in flux and at least implicitly forced community members to reassess and renegotiate gender roles.

For most of 1865, Fritz Rasmussen's wife Sidsel worked so hard at the farm in New Denmark, while raising three little girls, that she could hardly find time or energy to write in the evening. Still, Sidsel sent regular letters to her husband.[47] On June 12, Sidsel wrote about the difficulty of collecting her thoughts given the demands of childcare but still dutifully described events on the farm and also engaged Fritz Rasmussen's apparent criticism (his letter to her has not been preserved) that she had not overseen farm work closely enough.[48]

Ten days later, Sidsel noted that Union soldiers were slowly starting to return ("two Germans came the other day") and added that "Olsen and Christen 'Carpenter' would follow in a few days."[49] These returning soldiers gave reason for optimism that Fritz Rasmussen also would soon return home, and Sidsel therefore decided, contrary to her husband's request, that it did not make sense to send the money south.[50]

---

[45] While the writer specifically referenced the 1866 "killings in Memphis and New Orleans," he or she made no reference to the freedpeople victims or the white supremacist ideology behind the violence. See "From Faribault, Minnesota, 1866 [*Aftenbladet*, September 28, 1866]," in *America Letters and Articles, 1860–1890. P435.* Box 2 (Northfield, MN: Norwegian-American Historical Association, 1866).

[46] Jon Gjerde, *The Minds of the West: Ethnocultural Evolution in the Rural Middle West 1830–1917* (Chapel Hill: University of North Carolina Press, 1997), 177.

[47] Sidsel Rasmussen, "Mai Den 29," in *Fritz William Rasmussen Papers. Correspondence, 1834–1942. Green Bay Mss 4. Box no. 1* (Green Bay: Wisconsin Historical Society, 1865).

[48] "Juni Den 12 1865," in *Fritz William Rasmussen Papers. Correspondence, 1834–1942. Green Bay Mss 4. Box no. 1* (Green Bay: Wisconsin Historical Society, 1865).

[49] Sidsel Rasmussen, "Juni Den 22," in *Fritz William Rasmussen Papers. Correspondence, 1834–1942. Green Bay Mss 4. Box no. 1* (Green Bay: Wisconsin Historical Society, 1865).

[50] Ibid.

Sidsel's letters in the summer of 1865 expressed hope that his return would lead to a happy long-term family life; they also revealed the amount of labor she was doing. "It is high time to get out and milk and do the chores," Sidsel concluded her June 22 letter; her letter of June 29 noted that it was difficult to write as "little Gusta also wants to join."[51]

By July 23, Rasmus "Sailor" as well as Anton and Johan Hartman had returned home; added Sidsel: "I should so wish that you could also come tiptoeing home to us."[52] As the soldiers started returning, however, it was also clear to the community's civilians that the veterans often were physically weakened. Norwegian-born John Arvesen, who had served in the 50th Wisconsin Infantry, "came back from the hospital in Madison" so ill that the doctor, according to Fritz's father, did not expect him to live.[53] Arvesen died shortly thereafter; and Marcus Pedersen, who was drafted in the fall of 1864 with Fritz Rasmussen, also passed away soon after returning home to New Denmark.[54]

With Pedersen's death, Sidsel's thoughts immediately turned to his widow. "I can hardly hold back the tears at the moment thinking of what Markus' poor wife has gone through," Sidsel wrote. "[He] was lying there in the greatest misery imaginable. He had almost decayed before he let go of this life."[55]

And in New Denmark the story of illness, exacerbated by persistent outbreaks of smallpox, continued throughout the summer and regularly

---

[51] Ibid.; Sidsel Rasmussen, "Juni Den 29," in *Fritz William Rasmussen Papers. Correspondence, 1834–1942. Green Bay Mss 4. Box no. 1* (Green Bay: Wisconsin Historical Society, 1865). As an example of the physical and emotional toll of separation, Sidsel wrote about receiving a photo from Fritz in which he likely wore a uniform and showing it to their six-year-old daughter Rasmine, who responded, "Papa, it looks like Papa's face, but it does not look like Papa's coat." See "Juli Den 12," in *Fritz William Rasmussen Papers. Correspondence, 1834–1942. Green Bay Mss 4. Box no. 1* (Green Bay: Wisconsin Historical Society, 1865).

[52] "Juli Den 23," in *Fritz William Rasmussen Papers. Correspondence, 1834–1942. Green Bay Mss 4. Box no. 1* (Green Bay: Wisconsin Historical Society, 1865).

[53] Edward Rasmussen, "New Denmark 25 Juni Brown Co. Wis. 1865," ibid.

[54] "New Denmark Den 25 July 65," in *Fritz William Rasmussen Papers. Correspondence, 1834–1942. Green Bay Mss 4. Box no. 1* (Green Bay: Wisconsin Historical Society, 1865). See also Rasmussen, "Record! Of Skandinavians, Who Have Been Settled and Lived in the Town of New Denmark." According to a later account by Fritz Rasmussen, for Pedersen – a "good, honest man," had contracted chronic diarrhea in the service and been hospitalized just one week before the Confederates surrendered at Appomattox.

[55] Sidsel Rasmussen, "Søndag Den 31 Juli," in *Fritz William Rasmussen Papers. Correspondence, 1834–1942. Green Bay Mss 4. Box no. 1* (Green Bay: Wisconsin Historical Society, 1865).

left women the healthiest and strongest in the household. "Most of the enlisted have been ill, Cillius and Rasmus 'Carpenter' have been very sick but are now improving," Sidsel wrote.[56] Fritz's brother James added on August 27 that "cousin Rasmus" had come home with the "fever," which was a common sight: "most of the discharged soldiers become ill or indisposed when they return."[57] James attributed the health issues to the changing climate, but Fritz in his reply on September 14 seemingly also alluded to a mental health aspect: "I am not surprised that the returning soldiers are a little out of balance when they return home. I myself expect my share of indisposition if I ever see the home again," Rasmussen wrote from Alabama.[58]

Yet, just as Sidsel had hoped, her husband came home and surprised the family on Tuesday, October 24, 1865. "About 9 Oclock P.M. I tapped at my own door & immediately fondly & reverentially greeted my dear & beloved Wife," Rasmussen wrote.[59] Seeing his children was equally powerful. "The emotions I felt of hearing my little Daughter prattling Papa! Papa!! were even nearer to overcome [my] selfpos[s]ession."[60] Such a meeting was unforgettable. "Home! Home! Home!! Home!!!" he wrote and noted that in this exact moment he could have died a happy man.[61] But instead of death, Fritz's return brought life. A little over nine months later, July 19, 1866, the couple's fourth child and first son, Edwin, arrived and filled Rasmussen's diary with bliss:

Happy day for Me! A Day that I have long anticipated with sore forebodings; but, Thanks thanks! to Thee oh Lord! For undeserved mercy & blessings! ... I have this day been blessed with a new Subject for my own individual family-circle; and, not that one Sex; would [not] be as Kindly received as another, I do declare, that, it did turn a variety this time, from the usual run, so that the first I know of, was the exclamation from both of the old Ladies: "Oh! It is a – – – Boy! A Boy!!" Yes! It is a Boy! My Boy.[62]

---

[56] "August Den 20," in *Fritz William Rasmussen Papers. Correspondence, 1834–1942. Green Bay Mss 4. Box no. 1* (Green Bay: Wisconsin Historical Society, 1865).

[57] James J. Rasmussen, "New Denmark T. O. Brown Co. Wis. August 27th/65," in *Fritz William Rasmussen Papers. Correspondence, 1834–1942. Green Bay Mss 4. Box no. 1* (Green Bay: Wisconsin Historical Society, 1865).

[58] Fritz W. Rasmussen, "Camp at Mobile, Ala: September the 14' 1865 6 Oclock P.M.," ibid.

[59] "The 12" 1865 [November]," in *Rasmussen, Fritz. Additions, 1860–1918. Green Bay Mss 4. Box 9* (Green Bay: Wisconsin Historical Society, 1865).

[60] Ibid.   [61] Ibid.

[62] Fritz W. Rasmussen, "The 19th Thursday [July]," in *Fritz William Rasmussen Papers. Diaries, 1856–1876. Green Bay Mss 4. Box 8* (Green Bay: Wisconsin Historical Society, 1866).

Yet the joy of homecoming was mixed with the complexity of homecoming. Rasmussen's delight at finding the family in good health, the farm in good condition, and the harvest better than expected turned to concern toward the end of 1865. Sidsel had for some time not been feeling well, and her illness seemed "more and more suspicious."[63] The recently returned veteran had hoped that the couple's wartime separation would have helped their relationship, but on December 22, 1865, likely not knowing about Sidsel's pregnancy and the significant discomfort it caused her, he wrote that he felt his wife's "coolness" toward him acutely.[64]

Sidsel was so ill that for several days leading up to Christmas she could not get out of bed to take care of the household chores her husband expected. Childcare thus became one of Fritz's responsibilities, a task he found boring and felt ill-equipped to carry out ("I am no 'woman-man' [*qvindeman*]," Rasmussen had written in 1864).[65] In his own words, proof of Rasmussen's lack of domestic ability came on Christmas morning, when it turned out that he had forgotten to prepare gifts for his three daughters and thereby significantly disappointed the family's youngest.[66]

During his military service, Rasmussen harbored "elysian dreams" about what life would be like if only he survived, but the realities of marriage, fatherhood, and community life proved harder to handle.[67] In addition to the economy, family demands created tension in Fritz and Sidsel's marriage. Sidsel experienced physical discomfort during pregnancies to such an extent that, when she found out in late 1862 that she was pregnant with the couple's third child, she was "bathed in tears" and, to her husband's dismay, attempted to "contradict nature" by requesting a remedy for an abortion.[68]

---

[63] "Den 25de Mandag [December]," in *Fritz William Rasmussen Papers. Diaries, 1856–1876. GB Mss 4. Box 8* (Green Bay: Wisconsin Historical Society, 1865).

[64] Fritz W. Rasmussen, "Den 25de Mandag [December]," in *Fritz William Rasmussen Papers. Diaries, 1856–1876. GB Mss 4. Box 8* (Green Bay: Wisconsin Historical Society, 1865).

[65] "Den 27de Søndag [November]," in *Fritz William Rasmussen Papers. Diaries, 1857–1876; Account Books, 1856–1909; "Record of Skandinavians Who Have Been Settled and Lived in the Town of New Denmark, Brown county, Wisconsin." Box no. 8* (Green Bay: Wisconsin Historical Society, 1864).

[66] "Den 24de Søndag," in *Fritz William Rasmussen Papers. Diaries, 1856–1876. Green Bay Mss 4. Box 8* (Green Bay: Wisconsin Historical Society, 1865).

[67] Rasmussen, "Den 25de Mandag [December]," in *Fritz William Rasmussen Papers. Diaries, 1856–1876. GB Mss 4. Box 8* (Green Bay: Wisconsin Historical Society, 1865).

[68] Fritz W. Rasmussen, "The 18. Thursday [December]," in *Fritz William Rasmussen Papers. Diaries, 1856–1876. Green Bay Mss 4. Box 8* (Wisconsin Historical Society,

A baby girl, Augusta, arrived on August 11, 1863, but the tension between Fritz and Sidsel during the pregnancy, and the continued domestic and reproductive expectations put on Sidsel, spoke to women's roles in rural Scandinavian enclaves and larger society. "The family itself," as Stephanie McCurry reminds us, was a "realm of governance."[69] Despite Fritz Rasmussen's assertion that "one Sex" would be "as Kindly received as another," boys were valued more than girls from birth, as evidenced by Rasmussen's description of his first son's arrival ("A Boy!! Yes! It is a Boy! My Boy"), in contrast to the more measured acknowledgment of the arrival of his first child, Rasmine, on November 29, 1858 ("a beautiful little girl and daughter").[70] Twenty years and seven children later, Sidsel would eventually lose her life at the age of forty, a few weeks after having given birth to a baby boy, Sidselius, on April 4, 1878 ("that it is a boy is for us doubly satisfactory," Fritz Rasmussen noted immediately after the baby's arrival).[71]

Before then, despite their frequent expressions of affection for each other, Rasmussen also regularly described heated arguments with Sidsel. On July 26, 1867, after a conflict over farm work, in which Fritz had declined Sidsel's offer to help as he thought it would be too hard on her, she remarked, "That is a new thing, if you would always exempt me so, it would be pleasant!"[72] The exchange, which according to Fritz was also tied to Sidsel's desire for more material comfort, and the fact that Sidsel had demonstrably started working in the field anyway led Fritz to dejectedly write:

Such is the world: Some living through it easy and comfortable; others simi-slaves [sic], in indigency and want; Some basking in Sublimest loves blisfullness [sic] and content, others in a Simi-hell [sic]. But where is the alternative, when providence or

---

1862). Rasmussen wrote, "When I came home, I found Wife bathed in tears, which, after that I found the cause, I both, pitied and dispised [sic]."

[69] Stephanie McCurry, *Women's War: Fighting and Surviving the American Civil War* (Cambridge, MA: Harvard University Press, 2019), 11–14.

[70] "The 19th Thursday [July]." Also "Novbr 29 Mandag," in *Fritz William Rasmussen Papers. Diaries, 1856–1876. Green Bay Mss 4. Box 8* (Green Bay: Wisconsin Historical Society, 1858).

[71] "Den 24de Onsdag Formid Kl: 9 [April]," in *Fritz William Rasmussen Papers, 1834–1943. Green Bay mss 4. Box 2* (Green Bay: Wisconsin Historical Society, 1878); "Record! Of Skandinavians, Who Have Been Settled and Lived in the Town of New Denmark." After her first son's arrival in 1866, Sidsel became pregnant twice with three-year intervals before passing away shortly after having given birth to her seventh child in 1878.

[72] Fritz W. Rasmussen, "The 26th Friday [July]," in *Fritz William Rasmussen Papers. Diaries, 1856–1876. Green Bay Mss 4. Box 8* (Green Bay: Wisconsin Historical Society, 1867).

FIGURE 11.2 After his wife's death in 1878, Fritz Rasmussen named their newborn son Sidselius and lived the rest of his life in and around New Denmark surrounded by his children. Courtesy Wisconsin Historical Society.

predestination so ordains ... if it was not, that it [writing] seemingly helps to dispell my troubled thoughts ... then, I say, that I should rather fling both paper and pen into the fire – and, often in mind, to follow myself.[73]

Sidsel's insistence on grasping moments of autonomy, possibly shaped in part by her wartime experience of running the farm and resistance to Fritz's insistence that she limit work outside the home, challenged the Northern European Old World gender roles that many rural Scandinavians and also Germans in America modeled their households after. As Efford has noted, the "dominant constructions of ethnicity

[73] Ibid.

suggested that women's rights would undermine the immigrant community and endanger pluralism," and the "fear that politics would distract women from their domestic role" was prevalent.[74] Similar tropes about women's sole fitness for domestic duties appeared regularly in the Scandinavian-American press. For example, *Hemlandet* on May 15, 1866, ran a piece under the title "On the Woman's Emancipation" that cautioned against a movement for expanded women's rights in Sweden.[75] In the following years, the Scandinavian press regularly critiqued women who wanted to "forsake family life for public life," and one anonymous correspondent compared women to hens, insinuating that they had lighter brains and were happiest when they "hurried home to bring order to the household."[76]

These articles pointed to the uneasy relationship that existed between Scandinavian immigrants' profession of liberty and equality and issues of economic inequality, gender, and race in postwar American society.[77] Even the few articles and editorials that did advocate for women's rights revealed fault lines of class and race when attempting to bridge gender divides. For example, *Skandinaven* ran a piece on October 5, 1869, that argued women were just as well suited to voting as men and that they understood political issues as well as "the masses of white voters," given that most white women, the writer implied, "in intellectual and moral advancement stand above Negroes, Indians, and the Chinese."[78]

In short, Scandinavian editors' positions, as well as the letter writers they admitted into their newspapers, were generally conservative on questions of racial and gender equality. The Scandinavian-American press leaned more toward a return to a perceived economic and rural antebellum stability, now that abolition had been achieved, rather than

[74] Efford, *German Immigrants, Race, and Citizenship in the Civil War Era*, 48.

[75] "Om Qwinnans Emancipation [on the Woman's Emancipation]," *Hemlandet*, May 15, 1866; "Sweriges Presterskab Och Sändebudet [Sweden's Clergy and The Messenger]," *Hemlandet*, May 1, 1866.

[76] The quote "forsake family life for public life" appears in Arlow William Andersen, *The Immigrant Takes His Stand: The Norwegian-American Press and Public Affairs, 1847–1872* (Northfield, MN: Norwegian-American Historical Association, 1953), 123. See also En Rebel, "Kvindens Stemmeret [The Woman's Right to Vote]," *Skandinaven*, March 3, 1869.

[77] As a case in point, *Hemlandet* by April 20, 1869, ran a laudatory piece on J. D. Fulton's *The True Woman*, which argued against women's right to vote based on the Bible and recommended that all its female readers read it. See "The True Woman," *Hemlandet*, April 20, 1869.

[78] D. S., "Kvindens Stemmeret [The Woman's Right to Vote]," *Skandinaven*, October 5, 1869.

using the Civil War as a stepping stone to reinventing and extending citizenship rights to freedpeople, Native people, and women.

Such positions became increasingly apparent as Scandinavian-born leaders enthusiastically embraced the Republican Party's laissez-faire arguments in the post-war moment and simultaneously silenced voices arguing for a broader definition of equality within American borders.

12

Shades of Citizenship

When Hans Mattson rose to speak to fellow Civil War veterans in St. Paul on March 6, 1889, the former officer emphasized the apparent ease with which white Union men and their white rebel counterparts had agreed to "bury the past" in order to shake hands over the war's "bloody chasm" and together work for a better future.

As commander of a Union force in Arkansas, Mattson was tasked with protecting the local population, overseeing Confederate soldiers' parole, and enabling the transition to freedom for thousands of formerly enslaved in the state.[1] However, the Swedish-born officer, who in 1861 defined the Civil War as a conflict between "freedom and tyranny," twenty-four years later spent little energy discussing the plight of freedpeople and instead underlined how the federal military from the beginning had encouraged a laissez-faire approach to economic reconstruction in a region devastated by four years of war.[2]

"You must like free and independent citizens, place yourself by industrious labor, as soon as possible, beyond the necessity of federal support," Mattson instructed farmers around Batesville on May 22, 1865.[3] On the

---

[1] Donald J. Simon, "The Third Minnesota Regiment in Arkansas, 1863–1865," *Minnesota History*, no. Summer (1967): 281–292. According to Simon, Mattson was responsible for "appointing loyal civil officials, establishing local militia companies, supervising the paroling of six thousand Confederate soldiers, and feeding the population when necessary."

[2] H. Mattson, "Til Skandinaverna i Minnesota [To the Scandinavians in Minnesota]," *Hemlandet*, September 11, 1861.

[3] Hans Mattson, "Early Days of Reconstruction in Northeastern Arkansas" (Saint Paul: Pioneer Press Company, 1889), 7. Mattson's remarks here echoed the American Freedmen's Inquiry Commission's 1863 recommendation that "freedpeople should 'stand alone' as soon as possible." See Amy Dru Stanley, *From Bondage to Contract:*

transition to a free labor economy in the South, the Swedish veteran went on to claim that in the early years of reconstruction, the inhabitants of Arkansas generally "made fair contracts with the liberated slaves and strictly and carefully observed them."[4] Yet, even if Mattson's recollection is to be trusted, fair contracts carefully observed were not always the norm, and attempts to maintain an antebellum racial hierarchy were numerous.[5] Toward the end of his speech, Mattson's memory allowed for as much as he related "one incident of many" that underscored the prevalence of "old slave thinking" in the post-war South.[6]

"One day, a very tidy negro woman came and reported that her late master had recently killed her husband," Mattson recalled. "I sent for the former master. He was a leading physician, a man of fine address and culture, who lived in an elegant mansion near the city. He sat down and told me the story, nearly word for word as the woman did."[7] Mattson's speech, as it has been preserved, recounted the incident as follows:

Tom, the negro, had been [the planter's] body servant since both were children, and since his freedom still remained in the same service. Tom had a boy about eight years old. This boy had done some mischief and I (said the doctor) called him in and gave him a good flogging. Tom was outside and heard the boy scream, and after a while he pushed open the door and took the boy from me, telling me that I had whipped him enough. He brought the boy into his own cabin and then started for town. I took my gun and ran after him. When he saw me coming he started on a run, and I shot him, of course. ["]Wouldn't you have done the same?" he asked me with an injured look. The killing of his negro for such an offense seemed so right and natural that he was perfectly astonished when I informed him that he would have to answer to the charge of murder before a military commission at Little Rock, where he was at once sent for trial.[8]

Wage Labor, Marriage, and the Market in the Age of Slave Emancipation (Cambridge: Cambridge University Press, 1998), 35, 122–124. As Stanley notes, "emancipation brought Yankee ideals face to face with the aspirations of freed slaves as well as with the interests of former masters."

[4] Mattson, "Early Days of Reconstruction in Northeastern Arkansas," 7.
[5] Eric Foner, *Reconstruction: America's Unfinished Revolution, 1863–1877* (New York: Harper & Row, 1988), 119–123.
[6] Mattson, "Early Days of Reconstruction in Northeastern Arkansas," 12–13. See also Anders Bo Rasmussen, "'On Liberty and Equality': Race and Reconstruction among Scandinavian Immigrants, 1864–1868," in Nordic Whiteness and Migration to the USA: A Historical Exploration of Identity, edited by Jana Sverdljuk, Terje Joranger, Erika K. Jackson and Peter Kivisto (New York: Routledge, 2020).
[7] Mattson, "Early Days of Reconstruction in Northeastern Arkansas," 12.
[8] Ibid., 12–13.

Mattson, true to ideals about equality before the law, sided with the freedwoman; but his comment about her appearance, "a very tidy negro woman," also showed preconceptions, common among white men, against freedpeople themselves.[9] Implicit in Mattson's story was the fact that not all newly freed Black women were perceived as "very tidy."[10] As such, the structure of Mattson's 1889 address to local veterans reflected the fact that many Scandinavian immigrants immediately after the war were primarily concerned with economic betterment, personally and collectively, in a free market economy, but it also implicitly demonstrated the sense of white superiority that continued to inform life in the United States.[11] Less than a year before Mattson's speech in Minnesota, two Swedish settlers in Texas, Carl and Fred Landelius, wrote to their sister Hanna in Sweden about cotton growth in Travis County and their belief in a racial hierarchy:

At the moment we are very busy with cotton picking. Naturally we cannot pick all our cotton but we have 5 negroes (and negresses) hired. Don't you think that it would be strange to be where we are among so many foreign people? The negro is, I think, of the lowest race. His is very slow by nature, actually weak-willed [*viljelös*], and lives in the moment. Seldom does one see a negro who is well-off.[12]

The roots of freedpeople's poverty received little attention in the Scandinavian enclaves.[13] Neither did the associated paradox between free labor ideology and government redistribution of land to mainly

---

[9] For other examples from 1865 of prejudice based on skin color, see Kate Masur, "Color Was a Bar to the Entrance: African American Activism and the Question of Social Equality in Lincoln's White House," *American Quarterly* 69, no. 1 (2017). For ideals about "equal protection of the law," see Stanley, *From Bondage to Contract: Wage Labor, Marriage, and the Market in the Age of Slave Emancipation*, 35.

[10] Mattson, "Early Days of Reconstruction in Northeastern Arkansas," 12.

[11] Ibid. As Hannah Rosen has shown, "the social groups excluded from citizenship" in antebellum Arkansas "represented many of those who labored within the households of free white male citizens and under their control." See Hannah Rosen, *Terror in the Heart of Freedom: Citizenship, Sexual Violence, and the Meaning of Race in the Postemancipation South* (Chapel Hill: University of North Carolina Press, 2009), 94. Mattson's address thereby helped support German-born General Carl Schurz's prediction from the summer of 1865 that white southerners were "unquestionably thinking of subjecting the negroes to some kind of slavery again" and demonstrated the continuation of 'old slave' thinking" in the postwar moment. Schurz quoted in Martha Hodes, *Mourning Lincoln* (New Haven, CT: Yale University Press, 2015), 245.

[12] Quoted in Otto Rob Landelius, ed. *Amerikabreven* (Stockholm: Natur och Kultur, 1957), 127–128.

[13] For a discussion of the importance of access to land in the post-war South, see Jay R. Mandle, *The Roots of Black Poverty: The Southern Plantation Economy after the Civil War* (Durham, NC: Duke University Press, 1978), 16–27.

white citizens, what Keri Leigh Merritt has deemed part of "the most comprehensive form of wealth redistribution" in American history.[14] But both free labor ideology and homestead policy were used as arguments for continued Republican support. To well-educated Scandinavian immigrants, equality was attained through free labor on one's own land. The equality envisioned, however, was more economic than racial and social.[15]

In the early years of reconstruction, there seemed to be clear limits to how far Scandinavian ethnic leaders could envision freedom and justice extending. It was, however, increasingly important for Scandinavian leaders to situate Norwegian, Swedish, and Danish immigrants positively in a postbellum national narrative where the effort to gain political influence only increased. Hans Mattson, for example, wrote specifically about Scandinavian immigrants' love of liberty, Republican support, and zeal for Civil War service in his English-language memoirs.[16]

Indeed, the experience of Civil War did seem to strengthen support for the Republican Party, not least its economic policy, among Scandinavian immigrants and thereby also strengthen ethnic leaders' claim to political positions. On April 13, 1868, a brief front-page piece signed "many Scandinavians" appeared in the *Chicago Tribune* that touted Abraham Lincoln as "the representative and apostle of liberty to the downtrodden and oppressed of every nation on earth," and it advocated, in essence, a Scandinavian ethnic holiday by "abstaining from ordinary work and festivities" on April 15.[17] The *Tribune* piece was one among numerous indications of Scandinavian support for the Republican Party – and its Civil War–era leaders – in the years immediately after 1865. Among the Civil War veterans, support was especially pronounced. On January 1, 1867, for example, a reunion for the 15th Wisconsin regiment was held at

---

[14] Keri Leigh Merritt, *Masterless Men: Poor Whites and Slavery in the Antebellum South* (Cambridge: Cambridge University Press, 2017), 38.

[15] In an attack on the antebellum "despotism and absolute monarchy" that characterized the slave-based economy, *Skandinaven*, in the lead-up to the 1866 midterm election, proclaimed that "the Norseman's heart" had always beaten warmly "for freedom and justice," but it did not discuss racial equality. "Om Valgene [On the Elections]," *Skandinaven*, October 11, 1866.

[16] Hans Mattson, *Reminiscences: The Story of an Emigrant* (Saint Paul: D. D. Merrill Company, 1891), 57–58.

[17] Many Scandinavians, "Abraham Lincoln," *Chicago Tribune*, April 13, 1868; Många Skandinaver, "Lincolns Dödsdag [Day of Lincoln's Death]," *Hemlandet*, April 14, 1868.

the hall of "The Republican Gymnastic Association" in Madison, with speeches praising the party in power.[18]

In addition, *Hemlandet* on March 17, 1868, reported on "Grant Clubs" springing up "all across the country" and encouraged Swedes to attend meetings in Chicago's 15th Ward.[19] *Skandinaven* on October 7, 1868, reported the organization of a "Scandinavian Grant Club" in Racine County among "the Scandinavians in the towns of Norway and Raymond," in which everyone pledged to vote for the former Union general in the upcoming election.[20]

Republican loyalty and military experience, in turn, offered post-war opportunities, and numerous ethnic leaders took advantage.[21] Hans Mattson was elected secretary of state for the Republican Party in Minnesota in 1869, Norwegian-born veteran Knute Nelson became a Republican state senator in Minnesota in 1874 and later a US senator, and his countryman and fellow veteran Hans B. Warner served as Wisconsin's Republican secretary of state from 1878 to 1882.[22] Fritz Rasmussen, like Mattson, Nelson, Warner, and others, also continued his

---

[18] Johnson, "Forhandlinger Og Beslutninger, Vedtagne Af Det 15de Wisconsin-Regiment under Dets Gjenforening 1ste Januar 1867 [Negotiations and Resolutions Enacted by the 15th Wisconsin Regiment at Its Reunion January 1, 1867]."

[19] "Chicago. Grantklubb [Chicago. Grant Club]," *Hemlandet*, March 17, 1868. For a different example of Republican support, see "Misslyckandet Af Impeachment [The Failed Impeachment]," *Hemlandet*, May 26, 1868.

[20] "Skandinavisk Grant-Klub [Scandinavian Grant-Klub]," *Skandinaven*, October 7, 1868.

[21] Hundreds, if not thousands, of Scandinavian veterans received a Civil War pension as did more than 300,000 fellow soldiers and family members by the late 1880s. See, for instance, Ole P. Hansen Balling, "Declaration for an Original Invalid Pension," in *Pension Records. Invalid Pension Application 1166591* (Washington, DC: National Archives, 1899); Gjertrud Marie Hansen, "Declaration and Affidavit (Continuation)," in *Pension Records. Mother's Pension Application 424.662* (Washington, DC: National Archives, 1892). See also Theda Skocpol, *Protecting Soldiers and Mothers: The Political Origins of Social Policy in the United States* (Cambridge: Belknap Press of Harvard University Press, 1992), 102–103. Regularly, however, the application process for pensions was time-consuming and frustrating. For Norwegian-born Ole Steensland's difficulty in procuring a pension despite his experience as an Andersonville prisoner, see Brian Matthew Jordan, *Marching Home: Union Veterans and Their Unending Civil War* (New York: Liveright Publishing Corporation, 2014), 156, 276.

[22] Mattson, *Reminiscences: The Story of an Emigrant*, 115–16; Jørn Brøndal, *Ethnic Leadership and Midwestern Politics: Scandinavian Americans and the Progressive Movement in Wisconsin, 1890–1914* (Chicago: University of Illinois Press, 2004), 116; Millard L. Gieske and Steven J. Keillor, *Norwegian Yankee: Knute Nelson and the Failure of American Politics, 1860–1923* (Northfield, MN: Norwegian-American Historical Association, 1995), 48. Moreover, Danish-born Christian Christensen voted Republican while quickly rising through the post-war economic ranks in New York to manage J. P. Morgan's burgeoning financial empire by 1880. See Christian Thomsen

FIGURE 12.1 Ulysses S. Grant in the trenches before Vicksburg in 1863. Painting by Ole Balling who spent several weeks with the Union commander in the fall of 1864. Photo by Fine Art / Corbis Historical / Getty Images.

support for the Republican Party. Despite Rasmussen's reluctance to serve in the military, and the health problems it later caused him, his wartime experience became a source of pride and a motivation for continued Republican allegiance. Thus, on a clear and pleasant morning, November 3, 1868, Fritz Rasmussen went down to New Denmark's "townhouse" and gave his "Vote for the High – or General Election," adding "this time it certainly was 'electing a General,' and a Grant too."[23] In the following

Christensen, "Address by General C. T. Christensen at a Meeting Held at Germania Hall, New York, by the Independent Scandinavian Cleveland & Hendricks Campaign Club" (Brooklyn: Eagle Book and Job Printing Department, 1884). By 1884, however, Christensen claimed to have become disillusioned with what he saw as the Republican Party's blind pursuit of capitalism mixed with corruption. See also Anders Bo Rasmussen, "'Drawn Together in a Blood Brotherhood': Civic Nationalism Amongst Scandinavian Immigrants in the American Civil War Crucible," *American Studies in Scandinavia* 48, no. 2 (2016): 7–31.

[23] Rasmussen, "The 3rd Tuesday [November]."

years, Rasmussen held several positions of trust in the community and regularly lauded American government principles for being "better, than any [that has] yet existed upon earth."[24]

In this sense, the Scandinavian experience mirrored that of the German veterans, Carl Schurz most prominent among them, who, in Mischa Honeck's words, understood that "courage in combat and a noble role in victory were important bargaining chips" for "going into business or entering government service."[25] Yet, contrary to German Republican leaders in 1868, among whom "radicalism was ascendant," no forceful principled arguments for Black suffrage appeared in the Scandinavian public sphere.[26] Instead, Scandinavian immigrants who challenged the Scandinavian-American nonradical Republican orthodoxy during the early years of Reconstruction faced swift backlash.[27]

While still in its infancy, socialist-inspired agitation among Scandinavian immigrants – embodied by the Norwegian-born 1848 revolutionary Marcus Thrane – appeared in the public sphere in 1866. In the opening issue of *Marcus Thrane's Norske Amerikaner* (Marcus Thrane's Norwegian American) on May 25, 1866, Thrane laid forward a "program" that argued for active engagement on behalf of fundamental human rights, not least "every man's right to vote."[28] Without explicitly

---

[24] Fritz W. Rasmussen, "[Likely October 31]," in *Fritz William Rasmussen Papers. Diaries, 1856–1876. Green Bay Mss 4. Box 8* (Green Bay: Wisconsin Historical Society, 1876); "Record! Of Skandinavians, Who Have Been Settled and Lived in the Town of New Denmark."

[25] Mischa Honeck, "Men of Principle: Gender and the German American War for the Union," *Journal of the Civil War Era* 5, no. 1 (2015): 59.

[26] Alison Clark Efford, *German Immigrants, Race, and Citizenship in the Civil War Era* (Washington, DC: Cambridge University Press, 2013), 137–139.

[27] Demonstrating the Republican, not abolitionist, mindset in the Scandinavian press, *Fremad*'s explicit white supremacist viewpoints and warnings that "we, who stand at the forefront of civilization, in arts and sciences" could be supplanted by "fanatics" and "fall into black barbarism" were attacked frequently by its Republican-leaning competitors and proved shortlived. By 1869 *Fremad* had been taken over and shifted its editorial focus toward the Republican Party under its new editor Sophus Beder (financed by the Civil War veteran turned post-war Chicago banker Ferdinand Winslöw). Expressions of Scandinavian ethnic superiority continued to find its way into the Scandinavian news outlets regularly, however. See "'Fremad!' [Forward!]," *Fremad*, May 7, 1868. Also Arlow William Andersen, *The Immigrant Takes His Stand: The Norwegian-American Press and Public Affairs, 1847–1872* (Northfield, MN: Norwegian-American Historical Association, 1953), 12–13; Odd Sverre Lovoll, *Norwegian Newspapers in America: Connecting Norway and the New Land* (Saint Paul: Minnesota Historical Society, 2010), 73.

[28] Thrane, "Program [Program]."

connecting his editorial to freedmen's right to vote, Thrane praised the principle of equality in the Declaration of Independence and argued that slavery had always been "inreconcilable with the Republican principle."[29] Thrane also stressed women's central role in the fight for these foundational human rights and tied it concretely to the abolitionist cause.[30]

From Thrane's perspective, among the most prominent "women and men" who had shaped public opinion against the antithesis of republican government, namely slavery, and helped save this basically "flawless" republican experiment from "failure," was first and foremost Harriet Beecher Stowe. To Thrane, Stowe was followed by her younger brother Henry Ward Beecher, Charles Sumner, and Abraham Lincoln ("just mentioning his name makes the hearts beat").[31]

Thrane's program – not least his implied socialist ideas (the present danger, Thrane wrote, "is the deep divide" between "wealth and poverty, enlightenment and ignorance") and his fight for freedom, for Black people's humanity, and for recognition of women's central role in the public sphere – seemed increasingly important.[32] Enlightenment, according to Thrane, was the key issue, as it would ideally lead to the recognition of everyone's equality regardless of skin color: "Could a Negro work as a carpenter?" Thrane asked and, pointing to the lack of social equality in the post-war North, answered, "There is scarcely a shop where a laborer would continue to work if a Negro should also work there."[33] Change through enlightenment was needed, the editor argued.

Thrane's ideas, however, also included critique of religion and caused enough concern among Scandinavian ethnic leaders that both *Kirkelig Maanedstidende* and *Emigranten* published an anonymous rebuttal titled "A warning for all Christians" against Thrane's newspaper, despite its alleged small readership.[34] The letter, as well as the dissemination through the main religious and secular Scandinavian-American publications, testified to a sense of urgency in setting the agenda regarding notions of (economic) equality and morality – and, by extension, notions of American citizenship in post-war American society. In this sense, given

---

[29] Ibid.
[30] Ibid. Moreover, in America the worker was offered a "high daily wage for 10 hours of daily" which, Thrane optimistically noted, might soon be changed to eight hours, if enlightened people, not least the Norwegians, were willing to fight for it.
[31] Ibid.   [32] Ibid.   [33] Ibid.
[34] "Advarsel Til Alle Kristne Mod Markus Thranes 'Norske Amerikaner' [Warning for All Christians against Markus Thrane's 'Norske Amerikaner']," *Emigranten*, August 20, 1866.

Thrane's admiration for Charles Sumner, the radical wing of the Republican Party received little, if any, support within Scandinavian publications.[35] Instead the Scandinavian editors' policy positions aligned closely with those of the former Civil War general Benjamin Butler who, in 1869, addressed southern Republicans and stated: "Now you must help yourself."[36] In other words, there could be no long-term governmental help for supporters of freedmen and freedwomen (e.g. opportunities for landownership or legal protection in contractual disputes) in the racialized post-war free market economy.[37]

Among Scandinavian immigrants, not least editors and clergymen, there was little urge to use the Civil War as a stepping-stone to reinvent and extend citizenship rights to the formerly enslaved and to women. Instead, the Scandinavian-American press and clergy devoted space to a multitude of other issues, not least whether slavery was inherently sinful. By debating "last year's war," the Scandinavian-born elite essentially made it more difficult to start a conversation about future struggles over the meaning of equality and citizenship.

Any lingering doubt about whether Old World elites, as represented by Old World state churches, attempted to wield a conservative influence over Scandinavian communities in the New World vanished after the Civil War. *Marcus Thrane's Norske Amerikaner*, as Terje Leiren has shown, "survived only four months, largely because Thrane's social and anticlerical views precipitated a bitter feud with the clergy and its supporters."[38] Similarly, the 15th Wisconsin regiment's former chaplain, Claus Clausen, was essentially forced out of the Norwegian Synod when discussions over slavery's sinfulness erupted anew.[39]

[35] When Congress adjourned for the summer in 1868, *Emigranten*, then still under Solberg's editorship, focused mainly on the economy, including the "good" budget, government expenditures, tax, industry, the purchase of Alaska, and the Burlingame treaty with China. See "Kongressen [Congress]," *Emigranten*, August 3, 1868.

[36] Quoted in Abbott, *The Republican Party and the South, 1855–1877* (Chapel Hill: University of North Carolina Press, 1986), 204.

[37] Butler underlined his self-help philosophy, emphasizing individual agency over structural inequalities, in late 1875 when he stated that Black people could not expect government assistance against white terrorists and should themselves take up arms. Ibid., 229.

[38] Terje Leiren, "Lost Utopia? The Changing Image of America in the Writings of Marcus Thrane," *Scandinavian Studies* 60, no. 4 (1988): 470–471.

[39] The Kingdom of Sweden and Norway abolished slavery on October 7, 1847, the Danish authorities reluctantly followed suit in the West Indies on July 3, 1848, and the United States definitively outlawed slavery with the 13th Amendment on December 6, 1865, but

This schism within the Norwegian community had been evident since 1861, when Claus Clausen retracted his statement that slavery was not "in and of itself a sin," and it reemerged after July 4, 1864, when J. A. Johnson, who had been instrumental in raising the 15th Wisconsin Regiment, sided with the regiment's former chaplain.[40] By 1865, the Synod leadership was publicly known to view Clausen's interpretation as "diabolical" and rejected attempts to compromise.[41]

Throughout the 1860s, the slavery debate raged between conservative Norwegian Synod clergymen with ties to education in the Old World state church and Claus Clausen's faction who generally stuck to the 1861 statement that slavery was indeed sinful.[42] While the Norwegian Synod seemingly won the theological debate, Claus Clausen won considerable support in Scandinavian-American communities as well. *Skandinaven*, for example, pointed to Clausen's popularity in 1867. During a visit to Chicago, Clausen had attracted one of the "largest gathering of Skandinavians [sic] that has ever attended a religious service in America," *Skandinaven* reported on January 31, 1867:

It is probably especially of the strife and optimism he has shown in regard to slavery as a debatable question within the Lutheran Church that he has come to the front, so to speak, for the public and, not least, because of the harsh unforgiveable and unchristian judgement his enemies have spread against him that he [to a great extent], receives the sympathy and is held in high esteem by the public. The following Sunday morning he preached in Vor Frelsers Kirke [Church of Our Savior] in Chicago, again for an overflowing audience.[43]

still the discussion over whether the Bible sanctioned slavery continued for years in the Scandinavian immigrant communities. See Ernst Ekman, "Sweden, the Slave Trade and Slavery, 1784–1847," *Revue française d'histoire d'outre-mer* 62, no. 266–227 (1975): 228–229. See also Niklas Thode Jensen and Olsen Poul Erik, "Frihed under Tvang Og Nedgang 1848–78 [Coercion in Freedom During Downturns 1848–78]," in *Vestindien: St. Croix, St. Thomas Og St. Jan [The West Indies: St. Croix, St. Thomas, and St. Jan]*, ed. Poul Erik Olsen (Copenhagen: Gads Forlag, 2017). See also "Frie Skoler," *Emigranten*, September 24, 1866.

[40] "[W]e may if we choose to so far forget the sacred rights of humanity even believe that slavery is right and just and proper, and insult the Almighty by asserting that slavery is one of his ordained institutions, but let us agree that the will of the majority, constitutionally expressed must and shall be obeyed." See Johnson, "88 Years Ago to Day the Immortal Continental Congress," 36.

[41] Claus L. Clausen, *Gjenmæle Mod Kirkeraadet for Den Norske Synode [Response to the Church Council for the Norwegian Synod]* (Chicago, IL: 1869), 64.

[42] Clausen, "Tilbagekaldelse [Retraction]."

[43] "Pastor C. L. Clausen," *Skandinaven*, January 31, 1867.

The extent to which *Skandinaven* actually spoke for a Scandinavian "public" is difficult to assess, but the account is supported by a correspondent, identified as a former schoolteacher from Hedemarken in Norway, who wrote home from Primrose, Wisconsin, on February 4, 1868. In his description of the religious conflict, the writer stated that the people had "demonstrated common sense and distanced themselves from the clergy's arguments."[44] Only pastor Claus Clausen, according to the letter writer, represented "defense of truth and freedom."[45]

This postbellum slavery debate in the Norwegian Synod, and its leadership's insistence that slavery "in and of itself" was not sinful, was one of several examples of racial conservatism among Scandinavian-born opinion makers and helped legitimize opposition to equality and thereby citizenship rights for nonwhites.[46] In post-emancipation Scandinavian and American society, the view that white men of Nordic heritage were naturally superior to other ethnic groups, not least Black people previously held in bondage and American Indians, was common and, as we have seen, had found alleged religious and "scientific" support in the Old World for more than a century.[47]

---

[44] "An America Letter, February 4, 1868 [*Verdens Gang*, April 29, May 13, 27, 1868]," in *America Letters and Articles, 1860–1890. P435. Box 2* (Northfield, MN: Norwegian-American Historical Association, 1868).

[45] Ibid. On the more conservative Norwegian clergy, the letter writer hinted at German and Catholic influence. "Should there appear more bulls about this case or cases like it from the Missouri's papal holy see, whereto the Wisconsin Synod belongs, then one must likely assume that the Norwegian people will treat the bull like the giant Luther treated the papal bull in 1520."

[46] As Haraldsø has argued, the Norwegian Synod's conservatism was partly tied to an Old World political emphasis on authority and "support for a hierarchically constructed societal model." See Brynjar Haraldsø, *Slaveridebatten i Den Norske Synode: En Undersøkelse Av Slaveridebatten i Den Norske Synode i USA i 1860-Årene Med Særlig Vekt På Debattens Kirkelig-Teologiske Aspekter* [*The Slavery Debate in the Norwegian Synod: A Study of the Slavery Debate in the Norwegian Synod in the United States During the 1860 Emphasizing the Debate's Church-Theological Aspects*] (Oslo: Solum Forlag, 1988), 366; Engebret A. Lie, "Ossian Iowa Juli 20th 1869," in *America Letters. Papers. P0435* (Northfield, MN: Norwegian-American Historical Association, 1869). Writing to a Norwegian pastor, Engebret A. Lie on July 20, 1869, argued that the Norwegian Synod won the theological debate.

[47] See, for example, Fredrika Bremer, *The Homes of the New World: Impressions of America* (New York: Harper & Brothers, 1853), 20, 351. Also Jørn Brøndal, "An Early American Dilemma? Scandinavian Travel Writers' Reflections on the Founding Ideals of the United States and the Condition of African Americans, Ca. 1850–1900," in *Les Constitutions: Des Révolutions À L'épreuve Du Temps Aux Etats-Unis Et En Europe/ Constitutions: On-Going Revolutions in Europe and the United States*, edited by Marie-Elisabeth Baudoin and Marie Bolton (Paris, 2016), 143–144, 55.

FIGURE 12.2 Claus Clausen maintained his theological anti-slavery conviction after the Civil War and was consequently thrown out of the Norwegian Synod, again. Courtesy Vesterheim Norwegian-American Museum Archives.

Whether through religion or "science," these racist views were regularly on display in the Scandinavian-American public sphere, and the connection between Scandinavian religious conservatism and reluctance to embrace nonwhites as equal citizens in the United States was made clear in opinion pieces such as the one that appeared in *Emigranten* on March 16, 1868 linking interpretations of the Bible to racial superiority.

In a piece titled, "Is the Negro an animal or does he have a soul?" an admitted Democrat argued that the differences between white and Black people were so great that the latter could not possibly be a descendent of Adam, whom God had breathed life into, and went on to say that if "the Negro was in [Noah's] ark (and we believe he was there), he entered as an animal and is an animal to this day." Moreover, the Norwegian-born writer argued that any mixing of the Black and white race would categorize the offspring as Black and "therefore we believe that only Adam and his descendants have souls and that Negroes are not descendants of Adam."[48]

This line of argument resonated with *Emigranten*'s editor, who noted that this opinion had been sent to him by an "esteemed" fellow Norwegian and that it did not seem to make sense to do missionary work among people of African descent, for if Black people were just "soulless donkeys or, at best, enlightened mules, then it is after all too much to make them Christian."[49]

Clausen, on the other hand, continued to stress a greater sense of equality ("no Christian could be pro-slavery") and resigned from the Norwegian Synod on June 28, 1868, when its leadership insisted on different theological interpretations.[50] Along with Clausen, "a dozen or more congregations of the Synod similarly broke away or were split in two."[51] The Synod, with some merit, accused Clausen of holding theologically inconsistent views in a lengthy account published in 1868.[52] Clausen's eighty-six-page rebuttal reiterated his anti-slavery position and contained unmistakable references to Grundtvig before he "laid down his pen."[53]

With failing health, partly due to his Civil War service, Clausen instead set his sights on landownership in the South and helped spearhead an ill-fated immigrant colony scheme in Virginia.[54] The colony was partly

---

[48] [A Norwegian Democrat], "Er Negeren Et Dyr Eller Har Han En Sjæl? [Is the Negro an Animal or Does He Have a Soul?]," *Emigranten*, March 16, 1868.

[49] Ibid.

[50] Theodore C. Blegen, *Norwegian Migration to America: The American Transition* (Northfield, MN: Norwegian-American Historical Association, 1931), 447–448; Claus L. Clausen, *Gjenmæle Mod Kirkeraadet for Den Norske Synode [Response to the Church Council for the Norwegian Synod]* (Chicago, IL: 1869), 6–8.

[51] Blegen, *Norwegian Migration to America: The American Transition*, 447–48.

[52] Rasmus Andersen, *Pastor Claus Laurits Clausen – Banebryder for Den Norske Og Danske Kirke i Amerika. Første Skandinavisk Feltpræst [Pastor Claus Laurits Clausen: Trailblazer for the Norwegian and Danish Church in America. First Scandinavian Chaplain]* (Blair, NE: Danish Lutheran Publishing House, 1921), 156–157.

[53] Clausen, *Gjenmæle Mod Kirkeraadet for Den Norske Synode [Response to the Church Council for the Norwegian Synod]*; Andersen, *Pastor Claus Laurits Clausen – Banebryder for Den Norske Og Danske Kirke i Amerika. Første Skandinavisk Feltpræst [Pastor Claus Laurits Clausen: Trailblazer for the Norwegian and Danish Church in America. First Scandinavian Chaplain]*, 156–58. Also Anders Bo Rasmussen, *I Krig for Lincoln [To War for Lincoln]* (Copenhagen: Informations Forlag, 2014), 288–294; J. R. Christianson, ed., "Clausens on the Move: Chicago, St. Ansgar, Virginia, 1870–1873," The Bridge VI, no. 2 (1984): 28–29.

[54] Andersen, *Pastor Claus Laurits Clausen – Banebryder for Den Norske Og Danske Kirke i Amerika. Første Skandinavisk Feltpræst [Pastor Claus Laurits Clausen: Trailblazer for the Norwegian and Danish Church in America. First Scandinavian Chaplain]*, 225–229;

doomed by the financial crisis of 1873 but did exemplify Scandinavian immigrants' continued preoccupation with land in the post-war years. Most Norwegians, Swedes, and Danes, however, set their sights west.

Exemplifying Scandinavian immigrant concern with social mobility through landownership and an expanding American empire on the continent, Danish-born Laurence Grönlund, whose writings in time would inspire Edward Bellamy and Eugene Debs, published a piece on the Homestead Act in *Fremad* (Forward) on April 23, 1868, shortly after his arrival to the United States.[55]

Grönlund criticized American politicians for being too focused on "corporations and monopolies" at the expense of the "great mass which produce what the legislators consume."[56] One notable exemption to the pattern, "an oasis in the desert," was the Homestead Act, which Grönlund a few weeks later called a politically mandated leveller that allowed poor Old World immigrants to finally enjoy "life, liberty, and the pursuit of happiness."[57] Impressed with the speed by which "liberal ideas" had spread in the United States to protect poor people against the powerful, Grönlund argued that the nation's moral character had been elevated, as the people could now enjoy the fruits of their own labor by "sitting under one's own grapewine and fig tree."[58] To Grönlund, landownership yielded an almost "holy satisfaction."[59] What is "life worth," Grönlund asked, "if robbed of all convenience and comfort to the point where life consists of misery, degradation, and poverty"?[60] Entirely missing from Grönlund's lengthy texts, however, were questions of Native people's religious connection, and right, to the land. Such omissions, conscious or not, continued among Scandinavians for decades and helped settlers justify land appropriation.[61]

C. T. Christensen, "Danish Consulate and Legation, Pro. Tem. New York April 4th 1872," in *Papers of Claus Clausen. RG 15. Box 1. Correspondence 1871–1876* (Decorah, IA: Luther College Archives, 1872).

[55] P. E. Maher, "Laurence Gronlund: Contributions to American Socialism," *Western Political Quarterly* 15, no. 4 (1962): 620.

[56] L. A. Grönlund, "Hjemstedslovene [The Homestead Acts]," *Fremad*, April 23, 1868.

[57] Ibid; L. A. Grönlund, "Hjemmestedslovene [The Homestead Acts]," *Fremad*, May 21, 1868.

[58] Ibid.   [59] Ibid.   [60] Ibid.

[61] Karen V. Hansen, *Encounter on the Great Plains: Scandinavian Settlers and Dispossession of Dakota Indians, 1890–1930* (Oxford: Oxford University Press, 2013), 5. Hansen highlights "historian Jean M. O'Brien" who "astutely observes, [that] denying the Native presence made land taking seem justifiable." See also Louis Pio, "The Sioux War in 1862," *Scandinavia*, March, 1884.

To a greater degree than other foreign-born groups such as the German and Irish, Scandinavian immigrants settled predominantly in rural areas (see Figure 12.3).[62] For this reason, the Homestead Act, predicated on population growth and territorial expansion, was central to Scandinavian immigrants' visions of an American self-sufficient, moral citizenship and remained so for years. Conversely, high-level political attempts at territorial expansion into the Caribbean, where few Norwegian, Swedish, or Danish farmers imagined themselves settling, received much less attention.

To Scandinavian settlers, and many Americans, a contiguous American empire was the aim. Scandinavian immigrants' support was of such scale

FIGURE 12.3 "Norsk Hotel" (Norwegian hotel) reads the sign above the entrance where four unidentified people are standing in an otherwise rural Iowa setting. The photo thereby exemplifies Norwegian immigrants' continued attachment to Old World language and culture in rural America, what Jon Gjerde has called "complementary identity." Courtesy Vesterheim Norwegian-American Museum Archives.

---

[62] Torben Grøngaard Jeppesen, *Danske i USA 1850–2000. En Demografisk, Social Og Kulturgeografisk Undersøgelse Af De Danske Immigranter Og Deres Efterkommere* [*Danes in the United States 1850–2000. A Demographic, Social and Cultural Geographic Study of the Danish Immigrants and Their Descendants*] (Odense: University Press of Southern Denmark, 2005), 160–165.

that "several questions" regarding the Homestead Act arrived at the *Skandinaven* offices in Wisconsin within just one week in 1868. The queries prompted *Skandinaven*'s editors, who knew that this law was one of the "most important for the Norwegian settlers," to, once again, publish answers to these frequently asked questions.[63]

Notably, Scandinavian immigrants after the Civil War started casting their gaze even further west. A Norwegian-born settler wrote from Minnesota in early 1868 that "3 ½ years ago there was not a white man in sight. Wild Indians and deer were the only living creatures," but now numerous Norwegian, Swedish, and American settlements were part of the immediate surroundings.[64] Just a few months later, the Swedish-born pastor Sven Gustaf Larson relayed news of a small but increasing Swedish community in Jewell County, Kansas, where more than twenty-five countrymen each had laid claim to 160 homestead acres. As an indication of these Scandinavian settlers' mindset, Larson recounted a conversation with the land commissioner in Junction City who had promised that there would be enough Homestead land for half of Sweden, to which the pastor in his letter to *Hemlandet* remarked, "Why not say all of Sweden's population if one takes Nebraska and other western states into consideration."[65] That the remaining valuable Native land in Kansas would soon be available for purchase "for the usual government price" was taken for granted by Larson in a subsequent dispatch.[66] The same argument – free land formerly inhabited by American Indians, soon to be available through the Homestead Act or for sale at $1.25 an acre – appeared time and again in the Scandinavian-American texts.[67]

As far back as 1838, Ole Rynning had noted how "the Indians have now been moved far west away from" the borders of Illinois, and by early

---

[63] "Atter Om Homesteadloven [Once Again on the Homestead Act]," *Skandinaven*, March 5, 1868. In the same issue, a lengthy piece about the contours of European immigration, using "settlement-formation" and "colonization" interchangeably, ran on the front page. See "Kolonisationen [The Colonization]," *Skandinaven*, March 5, 1868.

[64] T. Olsen Hougem, "Til Fædrelandets Redaktion. Red Rock, Minn., D. 6te Febr. 1868," *Fædrelandet*, March 5, 1868; "Adopted Citizens and Expansion," *Skandinaven*, January 11, 1899.

[65] S. G. Larson, "Från Pastor Larssons Resa [from Pastor Larson's Travels]," *Hemlandet*, May 12, 1868.

[66] S. G. Larsson, "Ännu Liten Från Kansas [A Little More from Kansas]," ibid.

[67] Karen V. Hansen notes that "Scandinavian settlers privileged agriculture and therefore saw uncultivated land as unused." See Hansen, *Encounter on the Great Plains: Scandinavian Settlers and Dispossession of Dakota Indians, 1890–1930*, 5.

1869 a Swedish correspondent reported home about potential landtaking on "[so-called] Osage-Indian land" in southern Kansas but warned against taking land in western Kansas "as long as the bloodthirsty Indians there frequently make their greetings."[68]

Further north, despite an anonymous correspondent in 1864 imploring *Fædrelandet*'s readers to recognize the immense "suffering" inflicted on Native people following their removal from Minnesota, the dispossession continued in the Dakotas.[69] Karen V. Hansen explains:

These lands in the public domain of the United States had recently been ceded by Indian peoples negotiating as sovereign powers. From the perspective of American Indians, therefore, the Homestead Act amounted to a wholesale scheme for further encroachment, violating the terms of the treaties they had recently signed protecting their land. In reaction to the continuing advance by white settlers, Dakota Chief Waanatan, attending a peace commision in July 1868, said, "I see them swarming all over my country . . . Take all the white and your soldiers away and all will be well."[70]

Despite Chief Waanatan's plea, white settlers, Scandinavians among them, continued to move onto American Indian land and within decades came to occupy much of the land around Spirit Lake that had otherwise been set aside for Dakota bands following the 1862 war in Minnesota.[71] White supremacy was, as Barbara Fields reminds us, "a set of political programs," among other things, and the Homestead Act, with its requirement for citizenship or stated intent to naturalize, was one such example.[72] Many Scandinavian-Americans saw landownership or opportunities for upward social mobility, along with political participation, as a right that came along with their understanding of American citizenship.[73] In the process, Scandinavian immigrants often supported

---

[68] Blegen, *Ole Rynning's True Account of America* (Minneapolis, MN: Norwegian-American Historical Society, 1921), 50; A. Ahlqvist, "Utdrag Ur Ett Bref Från Kansas [Excerpt of a Letter from Kansas]," *Svenska Amerikanaren*, January 5, 1869.

[69] Pro Bono Publico, "Dakota. Blue Earth Winnebagoerne," *Fædrelandet*, April 28 1864.

[70] Hansen, *Encounter on the Great Plains: Scandinavian Settlers and Dispossession of Dakota Indians, 1890–1930*, 10.

[71] Ibid., 10–14, 36–45.

[72] Barbara J. Fields, "Ideology and Race in American History," in *Region, Race, and Reconstruction: Essays in Honor of C. Vann Woodward*, ed. J. Morgan Kousser and James M. McPherson (New York: Oxford University Press, 1982), 143, 56. "The determination to keep the United States a white man's country," Fields points out, "has been a central theme of American, not just Southern, history. Racism has been America's tragic flaw."

[73] For examples of the Homestead issue's continued appeal, see "Wigtigt För "Homesteadsettlare" i Minnesota [Important for Homestead Settlers in Minnesota]";

a social hierarchy where American Indians and nonwhite people were deemed inferior. Still, in 1864, *Fædrelandet*'s anonymous correspondent described Native people in the Dakota territory as "sick, naked, about to die of hunger, and defenseless"; and several descriptions of "suffering poor" freedpeople, who, in Frederick Douglass' words, were "literally turned loose, naked, hungry, and destitute, to the open sky" after the Civil War, also appeared in the Scandinavian-American public sphere.[74] Initiatives to help alleviate nonwhite poverty, organized by Scandinavian-born immigrants, however, remained rare. Instead, Scandinavian community leaders, when advocating economic assistance to groups in precarious circumstances, prioritized resources to local Scandinavian-American aid societies or collections on behalf of Old World communities suffering from starvation or deep poverty.

While Scandinavian immigrants generally subscribed to the "free labor" ideology underlying their idea of "liberty and equality," these ethnic mutual aid initiatives also testified to immigrants' awareness of the market revolution's potential fallibility.[75] White skin, a Protestant upbringing, and a relatively high educational level due to Old World compulsory education enabled many Scandinavian immigrants to steer clear of the most "exploitative class relationships," but hard work did not always yield economic success.[76]

This realization had, in part, led three Scandinavians in New York to form an association in the summer of 1844 to socialize and provide help in

"Skatten Paa Homesteadland i Minnesota [The Tax on Homestead Land in Minnesota]," *Hemlandet*, May 26, 1868.

[74] Publico, "Dakota. Blue Earth Winnebagoerne." Frederick Douglass is quoted in Susan Opotow, "'Not So Much as Place to Lay Our Head … ': Moral Inclusion and Exclusion in the American Civil War Reconstruction," *Social Justice Research* 21, no. 1 (2008): 30. *Fædrelandet* published an appeal from General Rufus Saxton to send blankets and other supplies to South Carolina ahead of winter to "alleviate the want" among freedpeople. And *Hemlandet* reported on the death among the children of Black Union soldiers and published a call for "help" from "Mrs. Josephine S. Griffin," but similar initiatives did not originate within the Scandinavian community. See "Stor Nöd Bland Friade [Great Want among the Freed]," *Hemlandet*, November 15, 1865; "Trængende Negre [Destitute Negroes]," *Fædrelandet*, November 9, 1865.

[75] Winslow, "Det Skandinaviske Selskab i New-York [The Scandinavian Association in New York]."

[76] Ibid. See also Brøndal, "An Early American Dilemma? Scandinavian Travel Writers' Reflections on the Founding Ideals of the United States and the Condition of African Americans, Ca. 1850–1900," 139–140. For a discussion of whiteness and exploitation, see David R. Roediger, *The Wages of Whiteness: Race and the Making of the American Working Class* (London: Verso, 1991), 13.

case a fellow countryman fell on hard times.[77] This Scandinavian Association established in a small house on Cherry Street on Manhattan's Lower East Side had the added purpose, according to a later travel writer, of bringing Scandinavians together to counterbalance "German, Irish, and all the other foreign nations who already have societies here."[78] The Scandinavian Association's minutes – and its underlying mutual aid idea, which inspired similar associations in the Midwest – was a reminder that Norwegian, Swedish, and Danish immigrants regularly needed a helping hand to stay afloat in the American labor market.[79]

Scandinavian immigrants in Wisconsin and Illinois also set up several mutual aid societies in 1868 as hunger in Norway became a factor that increasingly pushed people in the Old World toward the Midwest. The Swedish association Swea and "the Emigrant Aid Association" worked both separately and collaboratively to establish a shelter in Chicago.[80] Moreover, John A. Johnson in Wisconsin organized a collection of funds for needy immigrants to be sent to *Fædrelandet*'s editor or distributed through aid societies and pastors in Chicago or Milwaukee.[81]

The Scandinavian immigrant elite, however, who specifically advocated American landownership as a means for achieving equality and liberty when leaving the Old World, were conspicuously silent on the topic of land- (and by extension wealth-) redistribution in the wake of the Civil War and by 1868 were more interested in white ethnic economic issues than in national aid initiatives on behalf of nonwhites. In short, Scandinavian-Americans in the post-war moment proved more interested in organizing help for their former fellow citizens from the Old World

---

[77] "Love for Skandinavisk Forening Af 1844 [Statutes for Scandinavian Association of 1844]," in *IEP Skandinavisk Forening af 1844. Love* ... (New York: New York Public Library, 1898). See also Winslow, "Det Skandinaviske Selskab i New-York [The Scandinavian Association in New York]."

[78] Axel Felix, *Langt Fra Danmark 1–10: Skitser Og Scener Fra De Forenede Stater i Nordamerika. Bind 1* (Forlaget Danmark, 1985), 59. Felix claims that the society was organized on a Sunday but puts the date at June 27, while A. N. Rygg, writing in 1941, puts the date at July 9, 1844. See Rygg, *Norwegians in New York 1825–1925* (New York: Norwegian News Company, 1941), 9–10.

[79] Winslow, "Det Skandinaviske Selskab i New-York [The Scandinavian Association in New York]"; Clifford E. Clark Jr., "The Changing Nature of Protestantism in Mid-Nineteenth Century America: Henry Ward Beecher's Seven Lectures to Young Men," *Journal of American History* 57, no. 4 (1971): 832–846.

[80] "Till 'Emigrantens' Redaktion [for 'Emigrantens' Editorial Office]," *Hemlandet*, May 14, 1868.

[81] J. A. Johnson, "Christeligsindede Medborgere! [Christian-Minded Fellow Citizens!]," *Emigranten*, May 30, 1868.

than they were in helping American Indians, on whose lands they often settled, or in helping the newly emancipated, and soon to be fellow, American citizens navigate the structural pitfalls of a free labor economy.[82]

By 1868 the work to ensure political and civil rights for freedpeople seemed finished in the eyes of the Scandinavian-American editors. The former Confederate States were slowly adopting the rewritten Constitution that formally ended slavery within the United States, and now financial matters could again occupy the minds and newspaper pages in Scandinavian communities. The economic opportunities that had led the Civil War–era Scandinavian immigrants to the United States in the first place were now to be utilized, Homestead Act in hand, with freedpeople's and American Indians' rights taking a back seat to the renewed focus on agricultural and industrial growth.

Yet, even as Scandinavian-American communities pushed issues of reconstruction into the background, continued discussions over citizenship rights in Washington, DC, turned out to have important implications for the attainment of contiguous and noncontiguous American empire

---

[82] Ferd S. Winslow, "Til Skandinaverne i Chicago! [To the Scandinavians in Chicago]," *Hemlandet*, April 28, 1868; Johnson, "Christeligsindede Medborgere! [Christian-Minded Fellow Citizens!]."

13

Dollars and Dominion

"The harbour is a great basin, capacious enough for a small navy; and its entrance, though safe and easy, is through a narrow strait, which even the diminutive forts and antiquated ordnance of the Danes are able to defend."[1] Thus wrote William Seward's son Frederick, alluding to the fact that the secretary of state's 1866 trip to the Caribbean had a dual purpose, part recuperation and part reconnaissance. To achieve an American toehold in the Caribbean, Seward, travelling on the steamer USS *De Soto*, had decided to dip his own toe in first. When the Seward family arrived at St. Thomas on January 9, 1866, they found conditions favorable, though dated, for strategic and economic purposes. "It has as peculiar advantages for a naval station as it has for commercial support," Frederic Seward wrote.[2] From an American perspective, it was lucky that this island had fallen into Denmark's "possession" as the Northern European nation was "strong enough to keep it, but not aggressive enough to use it as a base for warfare."[3] By 1866, however, Denmark was in decline, and the islands' revitalization through American strength and energy, Seward believed, would be an advantage for all involved.[4]

---

[1] Frederick W. Seward, *Reminiscences of a War-Time Statesman and Diplomat, 1830–1915* (New York: G. P. Putnam's Sons, 1916), 263, 301–302.

[2] Ibid.   [3] Ibid., 301.

[4] Kristin L. Hoganson, *Fighting for American Manhood: How Gender Politics Provoked the Spanish-American and Philippine-American Wars* (New Haven, CT: Yale University Press, 1998), 22. Frederick Seward's emphasis on strength and aggression lends support to Hoganson argument that the "Civil War intensified the emphasis on manhood in U.S. politics" and that the "postwar era was a time of mass male politicial participation." In myriad ways, these years were years of national revitalization. Reunion, the constitutional abolition of slavery, and the

After his personal inspection and visit to other Caribbean localities, Seward was therefore well-prepared to make a concrete offer when he returned to the United States on January 28, 1866.[5] Equally importantly, Danish politicians were willing to listen.

American strength and Danish weakness, along with timing, were key variables as the negotiations moved forward. By the late summer of 1865, Seward had recovered enough from the April assassination attempt to resume negotiations, and Raaslöff, realizing Denmark's *Kleinstaat* status, kept advising Danish politicians to engage in negotiations.[6] Raaslöff by late 1865 acknowledged that the domestic situation in the United States was deteriorating but nonetheless said he "expected that there would be considerable patriotic support for a policy of strengthening the country militarily and strategically through annexation of the Danish islands."[7] Raaslöff's initial optimism was not unfounded. The American government, authorized by President Lincoln, had initiated negotiations, Seward was personally invested, and the American secretary of the navy, Gideon Welles, during the Civil War described St. Thomas as a potentially "desirable acquisition as a coaling station and central point in the West Indies."[8]

However, by March 30, 1866, Welles was already starting to think more critically about spending millions of dollars on an island group that could, essentially, just be taken by force:

Mr. Seward brought up in the Cabinet to-day, the subject of the purchase of the Danish islands in the West Indies, particularly St. Thomas … He proposes to offer ten millions for all the Danish islands. I think it a large sum. At least double what I would have offered when the islands were wanted, and three times as much as I am willing the Government should give now. In fact I doubt if Congress would purchase for three millions, and I must see Seward and tell him my opinion.[9]

In the preceding months, however, Raaslöff was assured that the American interest remained intact. Through dinner parties with Assistant Secretary of the Navy Gustavus Vasa Fox (at which Raaslöff also urged the US government to resume Caribbean slave patrols and revive the 1862 colonization agreement) Raaslöff got a feel for the

14th Amendment, tying representation to "eligible male voters" and thereby for the first time "putting the word *male* into the U.S. Constitution."

[5] Erik Overgaard Pedersen, *The Attempted Sale of the Danish West Indies to the United States of America, 1865–1870* (Frankfurt am Main: Haag + Herchen, 1997), 23–25.
[6] Charles Callan Tansill, *The Purchase of the Danish West Indies*, reprint ed. (New York: Greenwood Press, 1968), 14.
[7] See also ibid., 20.   [8] Quoted in Tansill, *The Purchase of the Danish West Indies*, 19.
[9] Quoted in Tansill, *The Purchase of the Danish West Indies*, 19, 28.

American political climate, and a Danish cabinet change moved the negotiations concretely forward.[10] On November 6, 1865, the large Danish
landholder Count Christian E. Frijs assumed power and worked closely
with Raaslöff on foreign policy hereafter.[11] By December 1865 Raaslöff
could finally notify the American government that Denmark was ready to
sell St. Thomas, St. Croix, and St. John if the price was right.[12]

Finding the right time and the right price, however, proved challenging.
William Seward's return to political life in 1865 saw him increasingly tied to
Abraham Lincoln's successor, Andrew Johnson; though the new president
generally supported expansion into the Caribbean, he also urged that
"negotiations rest a short while" to avoid a too direct connection, in the
public's eye, between Seward's St. Thomas visit and concrete discussions.[13]
Moreover, Johnson was becoming increasingly involved in a struggle over
Abraham Lincoln's legacy with the Republican-controlled Congress after it
convened in December 1865.[14]

Raaslöff, who stressed that Denmark needed a sizable offer to overcome domestic diplomatic doubts about the sale, reported home on
February 8, 1866, that he had suggested $20 million as a minimum
amount.[15] But crucial leverage was missing. As Erik Overgaard Pedersen
has noted, "Danish possession of the islands had become insecure," and if
the United States, England, or France went to war there was a sense that
the islands might well be taken by force.[16] American negotiators shared
the same view.

---

[10] "[S]hould any of our vessels succeed in making captures of the character indicated, it may
be practicable to secure the object which you so much desire," wrote Fox, but no such
occurrence ever materialized. See Gustavus Vasa Fox, "June 24, 5. [Col. Wm Raasloff],"
in *Gustavus Vasa Fox Collection 1823–1919 (bulk 1860–1889). Letters sent* (New York:
New York Historical Society, 1865). See also Waldemar Raaslöff, "Col. De Raasloff
Requests the Pleasure of the Honb. Capt. Fox's Company at Dinner on Tuesday Next 19th
at Six O' Clock P.M.," in *Gustavus Vasa Fox Collection 1823–1919 (bulk 1860–1889).
Letters received* (New York: New York Historical Society, 1865). See also Pedersen, *The
Attempted Sale of the Danish West Indies to the United States of America, 1865–1870*, 20.
[11] Pedersen, *The Attempted Sale of the Danish West Indies to the United States of America,
1865–1870*, 22.
[12] Tansill, *The Purchase of the Danish West Indies*, 17–18.
[13] Quoted in Tansill, *The Purchase of the Danish West Indies*, 21.
[14] Richard White, *The Republic for Which It Stands: The United States During
Reconstruction and the Gilded Age, 1865–1896* (New York: Oxford University Press,
2017), 36–37.
[15] Ibid., 24–25.
[16] Pedersen, *The Attempted Sale of the Danish West Indies to the United States of America,
1865–1870*, 19.

After several months of meetings between Raaslöff and Seward, the latter, on July 17, 1866, finally offered a concrete sum of $5 million, which was in line with American military officers' assessments. Brevet Major-General Richard Delafield took Denmark's vulnerable geostrategic position into account when stating that $5 million would be more than the Danish government could expect by "holding a prize that can be taken from him at any moment he become at war with a strong maritime nation."[17]

Between Seward's and Raaslöff's conversation in early 1865 and 1868, the prospect of a Danish-American treaty for the sale and purchase of St. Thomas, St. John, and possibly the agriculturally based island of St. Croix waxed and waned, but talks were generally considered promising by both parties.[18] Yet, as Pedersen has succinctly noted, the negotiations hinged on balancing domestic and international politics on both sides of the Atlantic.

Seward had tactically declined to make an offer owing to the conflict with the Radical Republicans and the division in the Cabinet on the issue. Only when it had become evident that Denmark, hoping for French support in the Schleswig Question, was definitely refusing to make an offer, was Seward finally moved to make a definite offer to buy the three islands.[19]

Raaslöff, on his part, likely believed that the personal relationships he had cultivated in Washington, DC, during his appointment as charge d'affaires and minister resident allowed him to gauge the American political climate well enough to secure a favorable outcome in the negotiations. As it turned out, Raaslöff's good relationship with William Seward and Charles Sumner (who in 1861 had described Raaslöff as "a most agreeable and accomplished gentleman") proved much less important than the two Republican leaders' own clashes over ideas of territorial expansion from 1865 and forward.[20]

By January 1867, Seward was urging the United States minister in Denmark, George H. Yeaman, to speed up negotiations, and the

---

[17] William H. Seward, "(Confidential) Department of State. Washington July 17th 1866," in *Collection 0002. Udenrigsministeriet. 1856–1909 Samlede sager. Vestindien 1865–1909. Box 771* (Copenhagen: Rigsarkivet, 1866). Also Tansill, *The Purchase of the Danish West Indies*, 38–39.

[18] Eric T. L. Love, *Race over Empire: Racism and U.S. Imperialism, 1865–1900* (Chapel Hill: University of North Carolina Press, 2004), 27–30.

[19] Pedersen, *The Attempted Sale of the Danish West Indies to the United States of America, 1865–1870*, 38.

[20] Jessie Ames Marshall, ed., *Gen. Benjamin F. Butler During the Period of the Civil War*, 5 vols., vol. 1 (Norwood, MA: Plimpton Press, 1917), 159.

American ambassador, according to Pedersen, shortly thereafter "assured Raasl[ö]ff that the President could request the Senate to remain in session and that it was unthinkable that Congress would refuse to appropriate the necessary money."[21] In the following months, Seward's ability to get congressional approval of the Alaska treaty, which was negotiated on March 30, 1867, and the territorial transfer from Russia finalized by October 11 helped support Yeaman's argument.[22]

On May 17, 1867, Frijs and Raaslöff met with Yeaman and made a concrete offer: "the two islands St. Thomas and St. John for ten millions and Santa Cruz for five millions, with the option of taking the two former and rejecting the latter."[23] Seemingly encouraged, Seward within a week formulated a draft for a treaty, predicated on Danish ratification before August 4, 1867, and American approval by May 1868, and an offer of $7.5 million for all three islands.[24]

Since France had originally sold St. Croix to Denmark in 1733, with an option to purchase the island again if offered for sale, it was necessary for the Danish authorities to consult the original colonizers before finalizing a treaty. Yet the idea of parting with additional territory in the wake of 1864 again sparked debate. On the Danish side, the main opposition to a sale was tied to the threshold principle. The Danish king, Christian IX, and minister of the navy, Carl van Dockum, both believed that Denmark, at least theoretically, would be better served strategically and internationally by holding on to the islands, but realpolitik weakened their position.[25] A handful of other politicians and powerful public servants also indirectly opposed the sale through delays, but Prime Minister Frijs and Raaslöff continued to push negotiations forward.[26]

Importantly, the Danish government's insistence on a referendum on the islands was accepted by Seward on October 5, 1867, as Denmark's

---

[21] Ibid., 45.
[22] Ibid., 3, 68. Also Love, *Race over Empire: Racism and U.S. Imperialism, 1865–1900*, 32–33.
[23] Pedersen, *The Attempted Sale of the Danish West Indies to the United States of America, 1865–1870*, 49–50.
[24] Ibid.
[25] Ibid., 63–64. As Pedersen has shown, "Admiral van Dockum was the only member who opposed the transaction outright. He could not accept the cession of territory and an important naval base after the losses of the recent War of 1864." The Danish king "shared van Dockum's feelings about the cession, but he also attached great weight to the argument that Denmark would probably be unable to uphold the neutrality of this islands in a war and, indeed, might lose them without compensation."
[26] Ibid., 60–68.

hope of, and strategy for, reclaiming northern Schleswig by the late 1860s rested on the possibility of an internationally recognized referendum. For such a claim to be internationally plausible, Danish politicians believed they needed to give the voting-age West Indian population an opportunity to determine whether the islands should be Danish or American.[27]

Thus, on October 24, 1867, the American diplomatic representative in Copenhagen, George H. Yeoman, met with Prime Minister Frijs a little past noon and signed the treaty which would transfer the islands of St. Thomas and St. Jan to the United States in exchange for $7.5 million in gold.[28] To the main negotiators, the treaty seemed to benefit both sides. Raaslöff privately noted in a letter to Seward on October 27, 1867: "Your interests and ours in this matter were not only not incompatible, but on the contrary, in all essential points identical or nearly so."[29] The question was, would Congress agree?

The ratification of Seward's Alaska Purchase set an important example in terms of the negotiation and ratification process, and Senator Charles Sumner's approval was especially critical. Sumner's importance in the ratification process was underscored by Danish diplomats such as Franz Bille, who succeeded Raaslöff in late 1866 and sent home an "extract" of Sumner's April 9, 1867, speech regarding the Alaska treaty.[30] The summary stressed Sumner's point that "it is with nations as with individuals a bargain once made must be kept" but also foreshadowed political conflict.[31]

The problem, from an American constitutional perspective, was the fact that the Senate expected its role to "advice and consent" would be honored, and Sumner expressed the wish that the Alaska purchase – where a treaty had been negotiated without Senate content – would not set "a

---

[27] Tansill, *The Purchase of the Danish West Indies*, 97; Pedersen, *The Attempted Sale of the Danish West Indies to the United States of America, 1865–1870*, 53, 60–61.

[28] Geo. H. Yeoman, "24. October 1867," in *Collection 0002. Udenrigsministeriet. 1856–1909 Samlede sager. Vestindien 1865–1909. Box 771* (Copenhagen: Rigsarkivet, 1867).

[29] Quoted in Pedersen, *The Attempted Sale of the Danish West Indies to the United States of America, 1865–1870*, 68.

[30] "Extract of a Speech of Hon. Charles Sumner on the Cession of Russian America to the United States. Shall the Treaty Be Ratified?," ibid. (undated); Edward Lillie Pierce, *A Diplomatic Episode: The Rejected Treaty for St. Thomas* (Boston, MA: 1889), 4. See also Pedersen, *The Attempted Sale of the Danish West Indies to the United States of America, 1865–1870*, 44–45.

[31] "Extract of a Speech of Hon. Charles Sumner on the Cession of Russian America to the United States. Shall the Treaty Be Ratified?"

precedent."[32] Moreover, in the extract Bille or a recipient in Denmark underlined part of Sumner's concluding remark, "I would save to the Senate <u>an important power</u> that justly belongs to it."[33]

As Eric T. L. Love has shown, the Alaska treaty was relatively easily ratified due to geography (continental "expansion" rarely needed justification) and widely accepted Old and New World scientific racism ("the temperate zone was the one proper field on which to raise an empire of Anglo-Saxon peoples").[34] Lastly, the international respect a geopolitical rival such as Russia commanded, likely combined with bribes to American officials, prompted Senate ratification in 1867.[35]

For all the same reasons, Caribbean expansion proved more challenging. The Danish West Indies were noncontiguous, the climate deemed less "congenial" to Anglo-Americans, and the stakes of ratification much lower with a less powerful treaty partner (who was disinclined to pay bribes). Seward seems to have realized some of the challenges, as he wrote to Yeaman in Copenhagen in September of 1867 that hesitation by Danish politicians could be costly:

The delays which have attended the negotiation, notwithstanding our urgency, have contributed to still further alleviate the national desire for enlargement of territory. In short, we have already come to value dollars more and dominion less.[36]

---

[32] Ibid.   [33] Ibid., emphasis in original.

[34] The scientific racism that helped undergird the Alaska purchase was tied to some of the Old World research networks that Scandinavians, such as Anders Retzius, were also part of. Swiss-born Jean Louis Agassiz wrote specifically to Sumner in 1867 to persuade him of Alaska's attraction due to the connection between climate and potential "settlement by our race." Love, *Race over Empire: Racism and U.S. Imperialism, 1865–1900*, 31. For the connection between Retzius and Agassiz, see Alan Mann, "The Origins of American Physical Anthropology in Philadelphia," *Yearbook of Physical Anthropology* 52 (2009): 160–161. See also Alan Levine, "Scientific Racism in Antebellum America," in *The Political Thought of the Civil War*, edited by Alan Levine, Thomas W. Merrill, and James R. Stoner Jr. (Lawrence: University Press of Kansas, 2018), 98.

[35] Love, *Race over Empire: Racism and U.S. Imperialism, 1865–1900*, 14; Lee A. Farrow, *Seward's Folly: A New Look at the Alaska Purchase* (Fairbanks: University of Alaska Press, 2016), 114–117. Charles Sumner biographer Edward L. Pierce also makes the argument that "continental" versus "extra-continental" location of territory was of importance in the ratification process, a perspective supported by some members of the Senate Committee on Foreign Relations such as James W. Patterson. See Pierce, *A Diplomatic Episode: The Rejected Treaty for St. Thomas*, 3; Pedersen, *The Attempted Sale of the Danish West Indies to the United States of America, 1865–1870*, 170–171.

[36] William Seward quoted in Pierce, *A Diplomatic Episode: The Rejected Treaty for St. Thomas*, 30.

Despite Seward's worries, and Sumner's warning not to negotiate a treaty without the Senate's involvement, the secretary of state agreed to the treaty with Denmark in late October 1867. Underlining the importance of personal relations to the treaty's initial completion and eventual ratification, Raaslöff on November 2, 1867, wrote directly to Charles Sumner, introducing his successor and urging the senator to help move the West Indies sale forward:[37]

I have told Mr de Bille that as the Representation of Denmark he might Count upon you as a friend, and I beg of you that you will Kindly ratify that apportion of mine, and be as good and valuable a friend to him as you were to me.[38]

Domestic politics in the United States, however, far outweighed any personal relationships that Raaslöff had cultivated, though initially the transfer proceeded according to plan. As a first step in the successful acquisition of the West Indian islands, Secretary Seward on October 26, 1867, sent the New York Reverend Charles Hawley to the West Indies as an election commissioner and instructed Rear Admiral Palmer, in command of the North Atlantic Squadron, to proceed with the flagship *Susquehannah* to oversee the election (and help ensure a favorable outcome).[39] After the Civil War, Seward had abandoned any practical support of colonization, but the secretary of state's instructions revealed his continued emphasis on territorial expansion and population growth that, in the case of the United States, was accompanied by seemingly ever-increasing military and economic might, while the opposite, Seward intimated, was true of the Danish Kingdom. Writing to Hawley before the referendum, Seward pointed to the explicit advantages the islands' white and nonwhite population would gain from being part of an expanding nation-state:

The market of this country, even now, is an eligible one for their products. It must become much more so in the event of their annexation. As one of the purposes of this Government in the acquisition, is to secure a naval station, the inhabitants of

[37] Yeaman quoted in Tansill, *The Purchase of the Danish West Indies*, 77. On Raaslöff's role in the 1867 negotiations, the American minister to Denmark, George Yeaman, wrote that his "moderation, activity and quickness of perception" had "undoubtly very greatly aided the progress of the business" and added that he doubted the October 24 treaty "could have been completed" without Raaslöff.

[38] W. Raaslöff, "Copenhagen, November 2, 1867," in *Charles Sumner Correspondence 1829–1874* (Cambridge, MA: Houghton Library, Harvard University, 1867).

[39] William H. Seward, "Department of State. Washington, 26th Oct. 1867," ibid.; Pedersen, *The Attempted Sale of the Danish West Indies to the United States of America, 1865–1870*, 48–61.

the Islands will derive benefits from that, which it is needless to expatiate upon. If, too, they should become a part of the domain of the United States, they and their property will have the same right to protection by a powerful Government in war, and to those advantages in time of peace which are enjoyed by other citizens.[40]

The referendum, which excluded a large swath of freedmen living on the Danish West Indies, underlined the Danish authorities' general disregard for "subjects" of African descent. White men from Europe and North America constituted the bulk of the voters when the referendum was held on January 9, 1868, and had at least some say in the islands' future.[41] Out of a population numbering approximately 38,000 on the three islands combined, only 2,000 to 4,000 were white, and people born in Denmark were actually a minority compared to the relatively large number of Americans, Englishmen, Germans, and people from other parts of Europe, and voters left no doubt about their preferences.[42]

In a telegram sent from Washington, DC, on January 17, 1868, the Danish diplomat Frantz Bille concisely summed up the decisive results of the St. Thomas referendum. Based on information received in a dispatch from Havana, Bille wrote that there were "twelve hundred forty four in favor [and] twenty two against" cession.[43]

This result – overwhelming support for American takeover – was followed by extensive celebrations, music, songs, and speeches in the streets of St. Thomas, which underscored the lack of enthusiasm for Danish colonial rule and the optimism associated with future prospects under American jurisdiction, not least increased political participation.[44]

The referendum thereby demonstrated at least two things in relation to citizenship and American empire. First, the Scandinavian-born elite in both the Old and the New World were generally not concerned with freedpeople's rights or opinions in post-emancipation societies, whether

---

[40] Seward, "Department of State. Washington, 26th Oct. 1867."

[41] Pedersen, *The Attempted Sale of the Danish West Indies to the United States of America, 1865–1870*, vii. As Pedersen notes, "suffrage was extended to any male citizen of 25 with certain residential, property, and income restrictions, which actually disenfranchised most of the blacks."

[42] Ibid.

[43] [Frantz] Bille, "Telegram No. 2683. Indleveret i Washington Den 17 Januar 1868 7t42 Formiddag," in *Collection 0002. Udenrigsministeriet. 1856–1909 Samlede sager. Vestindien 1865–1909. Box 771* (Copenhagen: Rigsarkivet, 1868), 97; Tansill, *The Purchase of the Danish West Indies*, 97.

[44] "Nyeste Postefterretninger," *Aarhus Stifts-Tidende*, January 22, 1868. See also "Salget Af De Vestindiske Øer [the Sale of the West Indian Islands]," *Folkets Avis*, January 31, 1868. See also Isaac Dookhan, "Changing Patterns of Local Reaction to the United States Acquisition of the Virgin Islands, 1865–1917," *Caribbean Studies* 15 (1975): 57–58.

in the Caribbean or the United States. And, second, the margins by which the inhabitants on St. Thomas and St. Jan voted for the sale demonstrated the woeful legacy left behind by the Danish government in pre- or post-emancipation matters.

In the end, however, American acquisition of the islands would not be decided through local votes or Danish politicians but hinged entirely on Seward's relationship to Johnson – and Johnson's relationship to Congress.

President Andrew Johnson spoke warmly for the West Indian acquisition in his third annual address to Congress on December 3, 1867. In the recent Civil War, "there was then a universal feeling of the want of an advanced naval outpost between the Atlantic coast and Europe," Johnson argued and added:

A good and convenient port and harbor, capable of easy defense, will supply that want. With the possession of such a station by the United States, neither we nor any other American nation need longer apprehend injury or offense from any transatlantic enemy. I agree with our early statesmen that the West Indies naturally gravitate to, and may be expected ultimately to be absorbed by, the continental States, including our own. I agree with them also that it is wise to leave the question of such absorption to this process of natural political gravitation. The islands of St. Thomas and St. John, which constitute a part of the group called the Virgin Islands, seemed to offer us advantages immediately desirable, while their acquisition could be secured in harmony with the principles to which I have alluded. A treaty has therefore been concluded with the King of Denmark for the cession of those islands, and will be submitted to the Senate for consideration.[45]

Less than a month later, Raaslöff's successor in Washington, Frantz Bille, alluded to the potential ratification trouble brewing when he sent his first report home. The treaty, which had been sent to the Senate for ratification in October 1867, was now held up in the Senate Foreign Relations Committee chaired by Sumner. Ratification of the treaty, Bille assessed, was therefore "subject to influence of several special circumstances, several of whom are unknown."[46] The uncertainty, Bille added, was tied to the domestic political situation's volatility.

Domestic political tension was heightened in Washington, DC, in 1868. On February 21, 1868, three days before the deadline for ratifying

---

[45] Andrew Johnson, "Third Annual Message" (online by Gerhard Peters and John T. Woolley, The American Presidency Project, www.presidency.ucsb.edu/ws/index.php?pid=29508, 1867).

[46] F. Bille, "Kongeligt Dansk Gesandtskab. Washington. D.C. Den 31te December 1867," in *Collection 0002. Udenrigsministeriet. 1856–1909 Samlede sager. Vestindien 1865–1909. Box 771* (Copenhagen: Rigsarkivet, 1867).

the St. Thomas treaty passed, President Johnson removed Secretary of War Edwin Stanton from office. Shortly thereafter, between February 29 and March 3, 1868, the United States House of Representatives reviewed and – for the first time in American history – adopted Articles of Impeachment against a sitting president. The resulting impeachment trial, as Bille alluded to in a dispatch dated April 7, 1868, swallowed all domestic political energy until the middle of May and left little, if any, room for discussions of the Danish American treaty.

"I have had a conversation about the St. Thomas treaty's present status with Senator Charles Sumner," Bille wrote, "I fear that Mr. Sumner's opinion on this matter must be attributed an almost critical importance."[47] The formal Articles of Impeachment, written by such prominent Republicans as Thaddeus Stevens, George Julian, and Hamilton Ward broadly charged President Andrew Johnson with neglect of the "high duties of his office, of his oath of office, and of the requirements of the Constitution that he should take care that the laws be faithfully executed."[48] Specifically, the trial centered on President Johnson's violation of the Tenure of Office Act, which passed in early March 1867 over the president's veto, stipulating that the Senate was to give permission to remove any official it had previously confirmed.[49]

In the Scandinavian press, the proceedings in Washington were met with a sense of sensation. "A court of impeachment, already a rarity in the country's history, have never before been brought against the highest executive authority, the President," wrote *Hemlandet* in Chicago. *Fædrelandet* from Wisconsin noted: "Not since the news of the first shot fired against Fort Sumter, has all of America, to a man, been as desirous of news as now." And a few weeks later, *Emigranten*, in an editorial, called the trial "the most important question of the day."[50]

---

[47] "Washington Den 7de April 1868. No. 21. (Confidentielt)," in *Collection 0002. Udenrigsministeriet. 1856–1909 Samlede sager. Vestindien 1865–1909. Box 771* (Copenhagen: Rigsarkivet, 1868). Bille's analysis was based on an expected "change in government this month as a result of the impeachment process against the president."

[48] Donald E Heidenreich Jr., *Articles of Impeachment against Andrew Johnson*, Defining Documents: Reconstruction Era (History Reference Center, EBSCOhost [accessed April 7, 2017], 2014), 105–114. See also Anders Bo Rasmussen, "'The States' Readmission Puts an End to All Civil and Political Questions': Scandinavian Immigrants and Debates over Racial Equality during the Impeachment of President Andrew Johnson," *Swedish-American Historical Quarterly* 68, no. 4 (2017): 202–217.

[49] Ibid., 113.

[50] "Presidentens Anklagande [The President's Trial]," *Hemlandet*, March 3, 1868. Also "Præsident Johnson Sat under Tiltale [President Johnson Indicted]," *Fædrelandet*, March 5, 1868. Also "Madison, 28de Marts 1868," *Emigranten*, March 30, 1868.

The Reconstruction contest between the Republican Congress and the president, a former War Democrat, had been a regular topic in the Scandinavian press at least since the congressional election of 1866. Here the editor of the Chicago paper *Skandinaven*, Knud Langeland, predicted that the president's "dismissal of Republican officials" and attempts to defeat the 14th Amendment, which had established birthright citizenship and legal protection for "life, liberty, and property," would come back to haunt him in the 1868 presidential election.[51]

To *Fædrelandet*, Andrew Johnson's unilateral appointment and removal of officials reminded the editors of the absolutist and monarchical actions they had all experienced in the Old World.[52] As such, the trial only magnified the issues and divisions that had come into sharper focus since the end of the Civil War and the 1866 midterm elections. The Scandinavian-American press coverage of the trial revealed the fact that all attention was directed at domestic politics, with foreign relations pushed into the background. The connection between the Johnson administration and Caribbean expansion largely went unreported, but Scandinavian editors' opposition to the sitting president's obstinate style would have made it difficult for them to simultaneously advocate for the Johnson administration's policy of noncontiguous expansion.

With an eye to describing the proceedings for a Swedish-American audience in *Hemlandet*, Pastor Eric Norelius made his way to the United States Capitol a little past noon on Friday, April 3, 1868. Norelius, aided by his local representative, managed to get into Congress and follow the impeachment trial, witnessing a high-level legal battle that most involved knew served as a proxy for deep underlying political divisions. Norelius' observations in April led him to confidently predict that President Andrew Johnson, seemingly guilty of a "high misdemeanor in office," would have to resign in the face of the Republican Senate majority.[53] Yet the reality of the trial, and the machinations of American politics, proved to be more complex. In Congress, the Republican Party's different factions had by 1868 increasingly united in opposition to President Johnson's approach to Reconstruction, but it was unclear if moderates and radicals would eventually vote united.[54]

---

[51] Arlow W. Anderson, "Knud Langeland: Pioneer Editor," Norwegian-American Studies 14 (1944): 122–138. See also David Herbert Donald, Jean H. Baker, and Michael F. Holt, *The Civil War and Reconstruction* (New York: W. W. Norton, 2001), 544–549.

[52] "Washington," *Fædrelandet*, April 9, 1868.

[53] Heidenreich Jr., *Articles of Impeachment against Andrew Johnson*, 112.

[54] Eric Foner, *Forever Free: The Story of Emancipation and Reconstruction* (New York: Alfred A. Knopf, 2005), 112–114.

E. NORELIUS OCH HUSTRU 1855.

FIGURE 13.1   Before embarking on an Old World visit from New York City, Pastor Eric Norelius, here with his wife Inga, found time to visit Washington D.C. and reported frequently back to *Hemlandet*, mixing commentary on religion with observations related to social and political issues. Courtesy of Gustavus Adolphus College.

Herein lay the seeds for political conflict at the highest level. The Republican Party attempted to maintain a coalition of business interests and Midwestern farmers and simultaneously to protect freedpeople against post-war vigilantism in the form of southern paramilitary groups such as the Ku Klux Klan. At the same time, the president, elected by the Republican-backed National Union Party, seemed intent on restoring and protecting former rebels' political rights, to a greater extent than was the case for the party that had helped secure his vice-presidential nomination in 1864.[55]

Consequently, between the midterm elections of 1866 (the starting point of so-called Radical Reconstruction) and the spring of 1868, American politics was defined by a power struggle between the executive and legislative branch that culminated in impeachment.[56]

[55] "National Union Convention," *New York Times*, June 8, 1864.
[56] Heidenreich Jr., *Articles of Impeachment against Andrew Johnson*, 105–114.

The Scandinavian-American press followed the case closely, and the coverage revealed that the Scandinavian-American editors took the impeachment of Andrew Johnson as a sign that the Republican-led Congress was finally bringing a perceived Southern sympathizer to heel and thereby imposing terms for reconstruction on the former Confederacy, which they argued might enable the nation to move forward on matters of more direct pressing economic interest.

The coverage of Andrew Johnson's impeachment trial therefore served a snapshot of how and why the Scandinavian elite's commitment to racial equality was overshadowed by economic concerns. Scandinavian editors (as was the case for most middle-class white Midwesterners) proved to be Republicans, not abolitionists.[57]

By the time slavery was abolished within American borders, the Scandinavian-American elite interpreted Republican ideology as free land (exemplified by the Homestead Act) and free labor (understood as compensated employment but not reparations) that would lead to free men (meaning social mobility through property-owning independence). Such views were at the forefront of the newspaper pages at the expense of foreign policy and expressions of racial equality in both heart and mind.[58]

In short, to the Scandinavian press, the proceedings in Washington had powerful implications in terms of racialized understandings of citizenship, not least in terms of voting. During the impeachment trial, the more "established" Scandinavian press outlets *Emigranten*, *Fædrelandet*, and *Hemlandet* adopted the main talking points of nonradical Republican congressmen and a conservative undercurrent in relation to racial equality generally ran through the newspaper pages.

Hemlandet implicitly questioned freedmen's right to serve in Congress as it reminded readers that the Constitution required representatives to have been citizens for seven years and senators to have held citizenship for nine. The question was, *Hemlandet* wrote, "when did a colored man become a citizen?"[59] At a time when the 14th Amendment had not been ratified nationally, *Hemlandet*'s lingering answer, while not directly stated, implied that freedmen had only been citizens for such a short period, if at all, that they should not yet serve in Congress.

---

[57] Stephen Kantrowitz, *More Than Freedom: Fighting for Black Citizenship in a White Republic, 1829–1889* (New York: Penguin Press, 2012), 230.

[58] Eric Foner, *Free Soil, Free Labor, Free Men: The Ideology of the Republican Party before the Civil War* (New York: Oxford University Press, 1995), 27, 61.

[59] "Kunna Negrer För Närwarande Blifwa Kongressmän? [Could Negroes Presently Become Congressmen?]," *Hemlandet*, March 31, 1868.

Hemlandet's position on Black people's fitness for political office tied into a longer debate in the Scandinavian press about Black people's intellectual abilities that seemed to overlook several decades of important writings from Black abolitionists such as Frederick Douglass, Martin Delany, Harriet Tubman, Sojourner Truth, and John S. Rock, among others.[60] Also, an opinion piece published in *Emigranten* in early 1867 claimed that "freed negroes" should not presently be allowed to enjoy citizenship rights such as voting.[61] Since Black Americans' "intellectual faculties" had remained "dormant" during slavery, as education was denied the enslaved, the anonymous correspondent – who claimed to have spent nineteen years in a slave state – argued that educational level alone should keep Black people from voting in the "first 5 to 10 years."[62]

In short, what was suggested in the Scandinavian-American press – and what became increasingly clear as the impeachment trial was covered in the newspapers' weekly play-by-play format – was the fact that questions of racial equality took a back seat to issues of economic opportunity for Scandinavian immigrants. Or put in another way, while Scandinavian editors were generally supportive of slavery's abolition, they were far more guarded in their support for freedmen's civil and political rights. Moreover, the Scandinavian-American editors proved to be contiguous settlers and colonists, not Caribbean expansionists.

Either through editorial decisions of exclusion or through genuine lack of subscriber interest, almost all the letters to the editor published in the Scandinavian newspapers in the first half of 1868 dealt with issues of landownership, the Homestead Act, and religious issues, while issues of race and Caribbean acquisition were almost entirely absent from the newspaper pages.[63]

---

[60] See for example, Benjamin Fagan, "*The North Star* and the Atlantic 1848," *African American Review* 47, no. 1 (2014): 51–67; Beverly C. Tomek, *Colonization and Its Discontents: Emancipation, Emigration, and Antislavery in Antebellum Pennsylvania* (New York: New York University Press, 2011), 245; John S. Rock, "Speech of John S. Rock, Esq., at the Annual Meeting of the Massachusetts Anti-Slavery Society, Thursday Evening, Jan. 23."

[61] "Bør De Frigivne Negere Have Stemmeret? [Should the Freed Negroes Have the Vote?]," *Emigranten*, January 28, 1867.

[62] Ibid.

[63] See, for example, "Atter Om Homesteadloven [Once Again on the Homestead Act]"; "Wigtigt För 'Homesteadsettlare' i Minnesota [Important for Homestead Settlers in Minnesota]"; Sando, "Til Fædrelandets Redaktion"; Ole Engebrigtsen, "Til

The newly emerged Scandinavian-American Democratic press, however, complicated the prevalent public-sphere narrative by exposing the discrepancy between rhetorical equality and racial practice. *Fremad*, published out of staunchly Democratic (and heavily German) Milwaukee, was the first Democratic newspaper launched in the Midwest since 1860.[64]

The press debates between *Fremad* and the Republican-leaning Scandinavian-American press testified to the sharp political divisions between Democrats and Republicans and the disdain held for the Democratic Party's constituency by the more established Scandinavian editors. *Hemlandet* reminded its readers that the Democratic Party had written derogatorily about Scandinavian settlers in Minnesota, and the newspaper's editor added an appeal to Scandinavians to avoid degrading themselves by voting with German saloon-keepers and uneducated Irishmen as well as former slave-owners and slave drivers.[65] Additionally, the Republican-leaning Scandinavian papers moved quickly to portray themselves as independent guardians of the ethnic and national interest, while the newly arrived *Fremad* was depicted as completely beholden to the Democratic Party.[66] As it turned out, *Fremad*'s emergence laid bare the fact that the zeal of the Scandinavian press in advocating abolition, which was achieved with the 13th Amendment's de jure abolition of slavery, did not translate into the same commitment to de

Fædrelandets Redaktion. Medo Tp., Blue Earth Co.," *Fædrelandet* May 14, 1868; H. Borchsenius, "Fra H. Borchsenius [From H. Borchsenius]," *Emigranten*, June 8, 1868.

[64] Borchsenius, "Cirkulære Til Nordstjernens Abonnenter [Circular to the North Star's Subscribers]"; Robert Booth Fowler, *Wisconsin Votes: An Electoral History* (Madison: University of Wisconsin Press, 2008), 36–37. Abraham Lincoln, who won Wisconsin with 56 percent in the 1864 presidential election, received less than 40 percent of the vote in Milwaukee.

[65] "Demokraterne Lägga an På Att Wärfwa Skandinaverne För Sitt Parti [Democrats Aiming to Recruit the Scandinavians for Their Party]," *Hemlandet*, May 5, 1868.

[66] These charges were probably not unfounded, as *Fremad*'s editor Just M. Caen, a Danish immigrant of Jewish descent, took time and space on the front page of his May 14, 1868, issue to note: "We are obliged for the kind support we have received from all the English and German Democratic Newspapers throughout the West, and we take this opportunity to return our best thanks, and hope that the 'Fremad' hand in hand with its many friends shall do its part of the great work of enlightening the people of the true course of American liberty." See The Editor, "To the American and German Democratic Press," *Fremad*, May 14, 1868.

facto equal rights for freedpeople, despite the promises of the 14th Amendment, ratified in Wisconsin, Minnesota, and Illinois in 1867. Where discussions of race were at times hidden between the lines in the mainstream Scandinavian newspapers, they almost jumped off the page in *Fremad*.

In its first issue, published on April 23, 1868, *Fremad* took the position that "to stay in power, [the Republican Party] will give complete voting and civil rights to the newly freed Negroes in the South."[67] Going forward, *Fremad* promised, among other things, to fight for a "reasonable arrangement of the freed negroes' circumstances, so that these could be trained as useful citizens in our society, without simultaneously making slaves of our white brothers."[68] In the weeks to come, *Fremad* continued its attacks on the Republican Party and on Scandinavian press support of the Republican Party. On May 7, 1868, *Fremad* accused the Scandinavian press, not wholly without merit, of being elitist.[69]

While *Fremad* was clearly exaggerating the Republican Party's past, present, and proposed policies, the Republican-leaning *Fædrelandet* seemed to sum up the Scandinavian immigrant elite's feelings toward Reconstruction by late April 1868. On April 30, 1868, *Fædrelandet* argued that, for as long as Andrew Johnson was given free rein, reconstruction of the Southern states had proceeded (too) slowly.[70] What was left unwritten was the fact that *Fædrelandet*, while supporting Reconstruction, saw the readmission of the former Confederate States by their acceptance of the United States Constitution with its new and proposed amendments as the natural end to the government's efforts on behalf of securing freedpeople's rights.

As such, the Scandinavian ethnic elite's public retreat from Reconstruction predated that of its German-born counterparts. As Alison Clark Efford has shown, German Republicans' support for Reconstruction mainly waned after 1870, when Old World exclusionary ideas of a German *Volk* impacted New World interethnic ideology.[71]

---

[67] "Vor Politiske Trosbekendelse [Our Political Creed]," ibid., April 23, 1868.   [68] Ibid.

[69] "Washington-Nyheder [Washington News]," *Fremad*, May 7, 1868. In bold letters, *Fremad* reported that "the latest news suggests that President Johnson will be acquitted, Senator Fessenden will vote with the Democrats" and ended with a question for fellow Scandinavian editors: "How are you [feeling now]?"

[70] "Rekonstruktionen [The Reconstruction]," *Fædrelandet*, April 30, 1868.

[71] Alison Clark Efford, *German Immigrants, Race, and Citizenship in the Civil War Era* (Washington, DC: Cambridge University Press, 2013), 143–146. For a Scandinavian immigrant perspective, see also Anders Bo Rasmussen, "'On Liberty and Equality': Race and Reconstruction among Scandinavian Immigrants, 1864–1868," in *Nordic*

Fædrelandet's position, as expressed on May 14, 1868, less than a week before the impeachment trial for all intents and purposes came to a close, seemed to encompass a larger Scandinavian reconstruction story.[72] Republican resolve in regard to the former Confederate States had forced these states to adopt the United States Constitution with its newly added provisions for slavery's abolition and birthright citizenship and signified a "crowning achievement" of Reconstruction:

The states' readmission puts an end to all civil and political questions that people are now quarreling over. It will end military rule and let civil authorities regain control. It averts people's attention from rebellion and lawlessness and lets them consider the necessity of commerce, agriculture, and production.[73]

Fædrelandet thereby established a link between congressional Republicans' hard line toward the president and the former rebels and the fact that Southern states were now beginning to formally accept the reconstruction demands imposed upon them.[74]

In other words, *Fædrelandet* argued that Southern paramilitary violence, such as murders of "union men and negroes" by the Ku Klux Klan, would be curtailed now that Republicans, through their resolve against President Johnson, had forced the former rebel states to accept congressional reconstruction by adopting new state constitutions.[75] Now, former Confederates, rededicated to national loyalty, would win political representation, and the country could leave violence behind while reawakening industrial and agricultural production, which in turn would greatly benefit Scandinavian immigrants in the Midwest, *Fædrelandet* argued.

This line of reasoning, a return to free labor with emancipation without compensation, instead of expressions of racial equality, was a departure from *Fædrelandet*'s March 10, 1864 editorial where it was pointed out that "negroes everywhere" were supportive of the North and in numerous cases had helped Union soldiers escape Southern prisons during the war. In that same editorial, *Fædrelandet* called it "foolish prejudice" to voice opinions against "the poor negroes, who in chains, that is against their

Whiteness and Migration to the USA: A Historical Exploration of Identity, edited by Jana Sverdljuk, Terje Joranger, Erika K. Jackson, and Peter Kivisto (New York: Routledge, 2020).

[72] "De Rekonstruerede Staters Gjenoptagelse i Unionen [The Reconstructed States' Readmission to the Union," *Fædrelandet*, May 14, 1868.

[73] Ibid.   [74] Ibid.

[75] "Rekonstruktionen [The Reconstruction]," *Fædrelandet*, April 30, 1868.

will, were brought to America and whose greatest crime consists of the creator having given them black skin color."[76]

The inconsistency between the Scandinavian press's attack on "foolish prejudice" as well as support for the universal rights embodied in the 13th and 14th Amendments and their regular advocacy for a return to "normalcy," which, in the final analysis, meant pulling federal troops out of Southern cities and leaving freedpeople with little political, economic, or legal support, did not go unnoticed by *Fremad*'s editor, whose editorial page succinctly pointed out the hypocrisy between the Republican press's anti-slavery and pro-amendment stance and their actual actions.

In an editorial, *Fremad* detailed its view on issues of race and reconstruction and tied these views closely to the Democratic Party's politics ahead of the 1868 election while drawing a clear distinction between a perceived self-reliant Scandinavian-American "we" and a dependent freedpeople "other."

"Our Scandinavian farmers and artisans are not under the slightest obligation to work for the Negroes while these [Black people] only have to work on election day by voting the Republican ticket," *Fremad* wrote:

> [If Scandinavian-American editors] personally want to wash the negroes' children's clothes and affectionately place them on their laps and feed them gruel and sweets, then it is something these noble and empathetic souls should do on their own account and not force it upon their subscribers and readers to emulate.[77]

While the Republican-leaning editors, as opposed to *Fremad*'s, did not specifically advocate returning freedpeople to plantation and servant work, they also did not get to work personally feeding the formerly enslaved or even organize aid initiatives.[78] On the contrary, as *Hemlandet* revealed on May 19, 1868, just three days after Andrew Johnson had been saved from impeachment by a single vote (35–19 with 7 Republicans voting against impeachment), there was still significant skepticism regarding freedpeople's ability to manage the rights of citizenship after the Civil War.[79]

---

[76] "Negernes Opførsel [The Negroes' Behavior]," *Fædrelandet*, March 10 1864.

[77] "Hvad Vil Det Demokratiske Parti Gjøre for Negerne? [What Will the Democratic Party Do for the Negroes?]," *Fremad*, May 14, 1868.

[78] Ibid. According to *Fremad*, freedmen would need to "learn to read and write and remember their own name" in order to become self-sufficient without the Freedmen's Bureau "stealing immense sums annually" instead of the present situation where "4 million ignorant, unlearned, and raw creatures" were alleged to hold the United States' welfare in their hands by exercising their newly acquired franchise.

[79] "Rekonstruktionswerkets Framgång [The Progress of Reconstruction]," *Hemlandet*, May 19, 1868; Donald E Heidenreich Jr., *Articles of Impeachment against Andrew*

After South Carolina adopted a state constitution recognizing Black people's right to freedom and electoral equality on April 16, *Hemlandet* essentially argued that, if the former Confederates had been more sensible in defeat, electoral politics could have returned to "normal" more quickly – meaning white men voting without freedmen's political representation.[80] President Johnson's policy had emboldened "the once conquered rebels," and if that had not been the case, "a majority in Congress would not have had to declare themselves in favor of the Negro's right to vote in order to overcome the rebel element."[81]

Thus, the Scandinavian-American press opposed President Johnson's leniency toward former Confederates but also, time and again, failed to recognize freedpeople as equally deserving fellow citizens. While the relationship between foreign policy and the conflict over freedpeople's position in post-war America received less attention in the Scandinavian-American public sphere, Andrew Johnson's policies had important ramifications for the signed Danish-American treaty as well. Among the thirty-five senators who voted for Johnson's impeachment was Charles Sumner.

When Henrik Cavling, a famous Danish journalist, traveled through the United States and the West Indies in the 1890s, he became interested in the attempted sale of the Danish colonies in the 1860s. Why, Cavling wondered, had the sale not been concluded? After all, Seward's interest in St. Thomas led to a signed treaty on October 24, 1867. Based on interviews and letters, not least from Christian T. Christensen (the Civil War officer who had later served as Danish consul), Cavling in the end suggested that the sales treaty was never ratified because Denmark did not bribe American politicians like the Russians had done during the 1867 Alaska sale. Cavling's conclusion was likely based on Christensen's assessment in 1894:

I know rather certainly that Russia in the Alaska Sale paid a half million dollars as private commission to distribute in places where it would have good effect and I also know that the Danish treaty could have been pushed through on similar conditions but General Raaslöff would not enter into those.[82]

Johnson, Defining Documents: Reconstruction Era (History Reference Center, EBSCOhost [accessed April 7, 2017], 2014), 104.
[80] "Rekonstruktionswerkets Framgång [The Progress of Reconstruction]."   [81] Ibid.
[82] C. T. Christensen, "Brooklyn Trust Co. Brooklyn, N.Y. D. 31te August 1894," in *Dansk pressemuseum og arkiv. Håndskriftsamlingen. NSA2-A04990. Acc. 1989/174. Box 46* (Copenhagen: Det Kongelige Bibliotek, 1894).

Since Cavling, scholars relying less on information gathered decades after the negotiations have chalked the failed treaty ratification up to lack of domestic American popular support for territorial expansion, Danish diplomatic naivety, and the political struggle between the White House and Congress.[83] Of all the factors, the most important issue, as Erik Overgaard Pedersen reminds us, was the Johnson administration's continued expansionist vision having "no possibility of winning support in the Senate Foreign Relations Committee" after 1867.[84]

Yet, in Seward's office, it was hoped, at least officially, that Johnson's survival of the impeachment proceedings would provide new opportunities for American expansion.[85] As Bille reported home to the Danish Ministry of Foreign Affairs on May 18, 1868, he had visited Secretary Seward in the evening two days earlier to congratulate him on the impeachment trial's expected outcome. Seward, according to Bille, used the occasion "to express that he now had renewed hope to soon process the treaty regarding the cession of St. Thomas."[86]

Still, Seward's alleged hopefulness may have been more about diplomatic courtesy than realpolitik-based optimism. Edward Pierce, at least, who wrote a biography of Charles Sumner, argued in his *A Diplomatic Episode* in 1889 that the treaty was "dead" by the time "Mr. Seward handed it to the Senate, as he well knew at the time."[87] In addition to Sumner's April 1867 warning and Seward's correspondence with Yeaman, Pierce based his argument on a November 25, 1867, House resolution introduced by Wisconsin representative C. C. Washburn

---

[83] Henrik Cavling, *Det Danske Vestindien [The Danish West Indies]* (Copenhagen: Det Reitzelske Forlag, 1894), 148–149. See also Pedersen, *The Attempted Sale of the Danish West Indies to the United States of America, 1865–1870*, 199–201. See also Tansill, *The Purchase of the Danish West Indies*, 149–151. Tansill rejects the idea that the treaty failed because of personal quarrels between President Johnson and congressmen like Charles Sumner and claims that the "real reason for the rejection of the Danish treaty was the evident disinclination of the American public to follow Seward in his schemes for colonial domination."

[84] Pedersen, *The Attempted Sale of the Danish West Indies to the United States of America, 1865–1870*, 140.

[85] F. Bille, "Washington, D.C., Den 18de Mai 1868," in *Collection 0002. Udenrigsministeriet. 1856–1909 Samlede sager. Vestindien 1865–1909. Box 771* (Copenhagen: Rigsarkivet, 1868).

[86] Ibid.

[87] United States Congress, ed. *The Congressional Globe: Containing the Debates and Proceedings of the First Session Fortieth Congress; Also Special Session of the Senate* (Washington, DC: 1867). See also Pierce, *A Diplomatic Episode: The Rejected Treaty for St. Thomas*, 9–10.

resolving that "in the present financial condition of the country any further purchases of territory" were "inexpedient" and that the House would refuse to "pay for any such purchase" unless conditions changed.[88]

To this, Nathaniel Banks, former speaker of the House, objected, as he wanted an explanation of Washburn's understanding of "further," to which the Wisconsin politician replied that he did not "intend the resolution to apply to the purchase of Walrussia" as it had already taken place:

But it is rumored in the papers – whether it is true or not I cannot say – that the Secretary of State has been making another purchase without consulting with any one, in the absence of any public sentiment requiring it, or of any demand from any quarter. I intend that that action shall be covered by the resolution. I intend to serve notice upon the kingdom of Denmark that this House will not pay for that purchase.[89]

Still, Danish politicians and diplomats held out hope for ratification, in part, based on the optimism expressed by Seward to Bille on May 16, 1868, and also because high-level interest in the Caribbean was on full display during the latter half of the 1860s despite opposition in the Sumner-led Senate Committee on Foreign Relations.

The Danish West Indies, Santo Domingo, and even Cuba were part of American expansion discussions after 1865, and Caribbean communities at times also sought to "influence annexationist initiatives," as Christopher Wilkins has demonstrated.[90] In short, the attempt to build expansionist support in Congress occupied a great amount of diplomatic energy between 1868 and 1870, and Danish envoys worked hard to get the United States Senate ratification process going.

---

[88] United States Congress, *The Congressional Globe: Containing the Debates and Proceedings of the First Session Fortieth Congress; Also Special Session of the Senate*, 792–793.

[89] Ibid.

[90] Dominican president José Maria Cabral, who had proposed leasing "Samaná to the United States in exchange for weapons and funding," was overthrowh by Buenaventura Baéz in early January 1868, but the change in power did little to interrupt dealings with the United States. Baez "promptly began his own negotiations with Seward and in late 1868 proposed the admission of Santo Domingo in to the Union. Seward agreed to Báez's proposal but left office in March 1869, before he could attempt to build sufficient support for annexation in Congress." See Christopher Wilkins, "'They Had Heard of Emancipation and the Enfranchisement of Their Race': The African American Colonists of Samaná, Reconstruction, and the State of Santo Domingo," in *The Civil War as Global Conflict*, edited by David T. Gleeson and Simon Lewis (Columbia: University of South Carolina Press, 2014), 214–218. See also Gregory P. Downs, *The Second American Revolution: The Civil War-Era Struggle over Cuba and the Rebirth of the American Republic* (Chapel Hill: University of North Carolina Press, 2019), 112–118.

On May 24, 1868, Waldemar Raaslöff wrote to his friend Gustavus Fox, the assistant secretary of the navy, to say that he has received a parcel "containing diplomatic Correspondence, with your compliments," and added: "My thoughts are very often in the U.S."[91]

As the presidential election of 1868 drew nearer, Danish diplomats and politicians tried to spur ratification by entreating American politicians and officials personally. In Denmark, the St. Thomas treaty was perceived as a badly needed foreign policy success in the wake of the disastrous 1864 war and the even more disastrous peace negotiations conducted in London that summer. Raaslöff explained what was at stake for his government and himself in a "Private & confidential" letter to Gustavus Fox on September 14, 1868, which perhaps also suggested that Fox was the inspiration for Lincoln and Seward's interest in the Danish West Indies in the first place:

[I was most happy to see] that you were not hopeless in regard to a satisfactory arrangement of the St. Thomas affair. As you have started the idea of the purchase it is quite natural that you should feel a considerable interest in the accomplishment of it, but I was nevertheless extremely glad to see from your letter that you continue to identify yourself with the measure, and that you will give it attention, and labor for it with all your well-known energy. I need not say how much I and the Danish Government will appreciate your most valuable assistance in this matter.[92]

Toward the end of the letter, Raaslöff added that he would have to resign if the treaty was not ratified by the United States, as he had staked his political career in Denmark on ensuring its passage. Given Denmark's *Kleinstaat* status, however, little changed, as Washington, DC, was – not surprisingly – mostly concerned with the 1868 presidential election and its domestic consequences.

In a last-ditch attempt to keep options open, Denmark on October 15, 1868, agreed to extend the ratification deadline by one year and shortly thereafter sent Raaslöff to the United States hoping that he could draw on personal connections, not least his relationship to Charles Sumner.[93] On

---

[91] Waldemar Raaslöff, "Copenhagen May 24. 1868," in *Gustavus Vasa Fox Collection 1823–1919 (bulk 1860–1889). Letters received* (New York: New York Historical Society, 1868). Also F. Bille, "Washington Den 7de April 1868. No. 21. (Confidentielt)."

[92] Waldemar Raaslöff, "Private & Confidential. Copenhagen Septbr. 15. 1868," in *Gustavus Vasa Fox Collection 1823–1919 (bulk 1860–1889). Letters received* (New York: New York Historical Society, 1868).

[93] Pedersen, *The Attempted Sale of the Danish West Indies to the United States of America, 1865–1870*, 97–100.

Thursday, December 17, 1868, Raaslöff wired the following message
to Fox from New York indicating increased desperation on the
Danish government's part: "Just arrived. Leave Friday night for
Washington."[94]

Using all his diplomatic experience, Raaslöff pulled every possible
political string he could find until his departure in April 1869. The
frequency of Raaslöff's correspondence after his arrival in
Washington, DC, at least thirty letters sent to Fox between
January 3 and March 21, 1869, along with more than twenty to
Sumner, testify to the Danish minister's urgency.[95] Between
February 15 and March 20, 1869, Raaslöff, with the help of
Christian T. Christensen, even commissioned writer James Parton to
make the case for the treaty's ratification. The resulting book – *The
Danish Islands: Are We Bound in Honor to Pay for Them?* – opened
with Lincoln and Seward initiating negotiations to purchase the
Danish West Indies and thus made the only argument still believed
by the Danes to be convincing: American politicians had wanted to
buy, Denmark had reluctantly sold, and now the only honorable
course of action was ratification of a signed treaty.[96]

Raaslöff sensed that the honor argument resonated personally with
Sumner, which also fit well with the senator's 1867 point that "a bargain
once made must be kept" even if the foreign relations chairman had also
emphasized a need for the Senate to maintain the "important power" to
ratify treaties.[97] Trying to appeal to a sense of American obligation,
Raaslöff therefore met personally with several high-ranking American
administration officials such as William Seward, Gustavus Vasa Fox,
and Hamilton Fish and continued to send numerous letters to key congressional figures such as Sumner and Banks.

[94] *A Nineteenth Century Diplomat at Work: W. R. Raasloeff's Letters to Gustavus Vasa
Fox, 1866–1873*, 32.
[95] W. Raaslöff, "181 G Street. Sunday January 31," in *The Papers of Nathaniel Banks.
Box 44* (Washington, DC: Library of Congress, 1869). See also Waldemar Raaslöff,
"Private & Confidential. Washington March 8th 1869," in *Gustavus Vasa Fox
Collection 1823–1919 (bulk 1860–1889). Letters received* (New York: New York
Historical Society, 1869). See also James Parton, *The Danish Islands: Are We Bound in
Honor to Pay for Them?* (Boston, MA: Fields, Osgood, & Co., 1869).
[96] Parton, *The Danish Islands: Are We Bound in Honor to Pay for Them?*
[97] "Extract of a Speech of Hon. Charles Sumner on the Cession of Russian America to the
United States. Shall the Treaty Be Ratified?"

In the end, however, despite his considerable effort to save the treaty and his own political career, Raaslöff realized the futility of his mission. After the election of Ulysses S. Grant in 1868, there was no longer any incentive for Congress to ratify the treaty. Raaslöff's efforts in some ways culminated with two appearances before the Senate's Foreign Relations Committee on January 26 and January 28, 1869, but the tension between the executive branch, which had negotiated the treaty, and the legislative committee he tried to convince was too deep to overcome.

A similar impression, one of a deep divide between two crucial branches of government, was given to Scandinavian-American readers in the Midwest when *Hemlandet,* in one of its rare articles on the topic, matter-of-factly observed that Sumner's committee considered the treaty a solely nonbinding "piece of paper" until it was ratified.[98] The lack of Scandinavian-American editorial energy regarding territorial expansion into the Caribbean stood in stark contrast to the emphasis in the ethnic press on westward expansion through Indian removal on the continent. Scandinavian-American editors and their readers strongly supported contiguous American empire but took a guarded approach, which stretched back to Even Heg in 1848, against incorporating territory south of the current border into the United States.[99]

When William Seward retired as Secretary of State on March 4, 1869, it proved to be the end of Danish hopes to sell their West Indian "possessions." Seward had worked relatively closely with Raaslöff for almost a decade, but by 1869, Seward's influence, due to his relationship with the outgoing president, Andrew Johnson, was negligible.

After Ulysses S. Grant took office, the White House was occupied by yet another president sympathetic to American expansion. But where Johnson had specifically talked about the importance of St. Thomas,

---

[98] "Washington. Kongressen [Washington. Congress]," *Hemlandet,* February 9, 1869.

[99] Quoted in Arlow William Andersen, *The Immigrant Takes His Stand: The Norwegian-American Press and Public Affairs, 1847–1872* (Northfield, MA: Norwegian-American Historical Association, 1953), 34. Since American Indians were not deemed sufficiently civilized to be incorporated into the United States either, Scandinavian editors and correspondents, as we have seen, took it for granted that they would be removed outside of current borders, and one correspondent in 1863 even suggested removing all native people within Minnesota to "a big island in Lake Superior" where they could learn "agriculture" and "acquire Christianity and civilization." See N. "Til Red. Af Hemlandet [To the Editor of Hemlandet]."

Grant focused his energy on Santo Domingo.[100] According to Pierce, Grant took the position that the St. Thomas treaty was "a scheme of Seward's and he would have nothing to do with it."[101]

At this time, Raaslöff had likely also given up hope. By March 28, 1869, Hamilton Fish, recently appointed secretary of state, wrote to Sumner: "Raasl[ö]ff does not wish any action on his treaty" knowing it would fail in a Senate vote.[102] Due to the poor prospects for ratification, Sumner delayed reporting the treaty to the Senate for ratification.[103]

Seen from Copenhagen, the lack of ratification was a sign of the international immaturity of the United States. As *Dagbladet* (The Daily) editorialized, it would have been "honorable" and "justifiable" for the Americans to officially have said no, but, by letting the "matter go by default," the young nation's politicians showed a lack of international etiquette.[104] Where President Johnson "could not" do anything to further the ratification process, it seemed to *Dagbladet* that President Grant "would not" do anything.[105]

An editorial in the *New York Times*, however, summed up the American perspective: *Dagbladet*, and Danes in general, had forgotten that there were "new ideas working on the American mind," and the main idea now was that "we can annex[,] protect, or 'take' all we want of the Western hemisphere, without the trouble and cost of purchase."[106]

---

[100] David W. Blight, *Frederick Douglass: Profet of Freedom* (New York: Simon & Schuster, 2018), 536.

[101] Pierce, *A Diplomatic Episode: The Rejected Treaty for St. Thomas*, 15. Trying to overcome opposition to expansion, and once again appealing to American honor, Raaslöff wrote to Nathaniel Banks on March 27, 1869, and implored the former general to help rally support for the Danish West Indies treaty. "I had a long conversation with the Secy of State – last night. He expected to see you to-day and will ask you whether – the treaty being ratified – the appropriation could pass the house. I trust you will encourage him ... The members of the Administration are as far as I can find more or less convinced [that] the honor of the country is at stake, and I think prompt action can be brought about if those who wish the thing to be done will show some decision & determination." See W. Raaslöff, "Saturday Morning [March 27]," in *The Papers of Nathaniel Banks. Box 45* (Washington, DC: Library of Congress, 1869).

[102] Pierce, *A Diplomatic Episode: The Rejected Treaty for St. Thomas*, 12.

[103] According to Pedersen, Raaslöff in his own assessment "felt that the Committee was well-disposed towards him personally, but overtly hostile to Seward." See Pedersen, *The Attempted Sale of the Danish West Indies to the United States of America, 1865–1870*, 121.

[104] "Kjøbenhavn, Den 24de April [Copenhagen April 24]," *Dagbladet*, April 24, 1869.

[105] Ibid.   [106] "St. Thomas," *New York Times*, May 26, 1869.

In other words, the Danish government did not have enough influence on the international stage to make an emerging great power respect a mutually agreed-upon treaty, even one initiated by the stronger power.[107] Where Sumner in April 1867 had difficulty seeing how the Alaska treaty could possibly be refused without putting "to hazard the friendly relations" existing between the United States and Russia, there were few such fears in dealing with Denmark.[108]

Danish politicians officially held out hope until 1870, but lobbying efforts had run their course. The aftermath of Charles Sumner's closed Senate Foreign Relations committee meeting on March 24, 1870, formally concluded the matter. According to newspaper reports of the meeting, and the memory of Nevada Senator William Stewart, Sumner argued against the imperialism that was inherent in the St. Domingo scheme (and indirectly in the St. Thomas scheme) as "the proposed annexation would probably encourage further American acquisitions of Caribbean territory."[109] After the meeting, Sumner reported the St. Thomas treaty "adversely" to the Senate and officially put an end to the process as "the Senate declined to ratify it."[110] The St. Domingo treaty suffered the same fate in June 1870.[111]

---

[107] Isaac Dookhan aptly pointed out in his study of local reactions in the Danish West Indies to the prospect of American annexation: "The reasons for the sale of the islands by Denmark and their purchase by the United States were varied and complex, but they turned upon the question of imperialism – declining in the case of Denmark and increasing on the part of the United States." See Isaac Dookhan, "Changing Patterns of Local Reaction to the United States Acquisition of the Virgin Islands, 1865–1917," *Caribbean Studies* 15 (1975): 50. See also Theodore Clarke Smith, "Expansion after the Civil War, 1865–71," *Political Science Quarterly* 16, no. 3 (1901): 412–413.

[108] "Extract of a Speech of Hon. Charles Sumner on the Cession of Russian America to the United States. Shall the Treaty Be Ratified?," in *Collection 0002. Udenrigsministeriet. 1856–1909 Samlede sager. Vestindien 1865–1909. Box 771* (Copenhagen: Rigsarkivet, undated).

[109] Quoted in Charles Callan Tansill, *The United States and Santo Domingo, 1798–1873: A Chapter in Caribbean Diplomacy*, reprint ed. (Gloucester, MA: Peter Smith, 1967), 406.

[110] *64th Congress, 2d Session. House of Representatives. Report No. 1505. Cession of Danish West Indies* (Washington, DC: Government Printing Office, 1917), 2.

[111] Tansill, *The United States and Santo Domingo, 1798–1873: A Chapter in Caribbean Diplomacy*, 407. As Frymer notes, Sumner again used race and climate as part of his reason for not supporting ratification: Sumner "ended with 'one other consideration, vast in importance and conclusive in character, to which I allude only, and that is all. The island of San Domingo, situated in tropical waters and occupied by another race, never can become a permanent possession of the United States.'" See Paul Frymer, *Building an American Empire: The Era of Territorial and Political Expansion* (Princeton, NJ: Princeton University Press, 2017), 214.

As we have seen, however, Sumner's opposition to expansion was most forceful in relation to noncontiguous expansion. On the American continent, the Republican Party's support for territorial growth remained strong, and in the following years its policy of landtaking only attracted Scandinavian immigrants in ever-increasing numbers.[112]

[112] Jørn Brøndal, *Ethnic Leadership and Midwestern Politics: Scandinavian Americans and the Progressive Movement in Wisconsin, 1890–1914* (Chicago: University of Illinois Press, 2004), 22–29; Karen V. Hansen, Encounter on the Great Plains: Scandinavian Settlers and Dispossession of Dakota Indians, 1890–1930 (Oxford: Oxford University Press, 2013), 2–7; Erika K. Jackson, *Scandinavians in Chicago: The Origins of White Privilege in Modern America* (Urbana: University of Illinois Press, 2019), 41–46.

Conclusion

Scandinavian immigration floodgates opened into the Midwest after 1870. Over the next half-century, more than two million Norwegians, Swedes, and Danes came to the United States and changed the ethnic makeup of burgeoning cities such as Chicago, Saint Paul, and Milwaukee. For agricultural and industrial workers, Norway, Sweden, and Denmark were undesirable places to live in the nineteenth century, as evidenced by the emigration of more than 10 percent of each country's population, and America, with its growing territory and population, was perceived as an ideal destination. What many Scandinavian settlers had in common were visions of America as a place with opportunities for land-ownership, social mobility, and central citizenship rights such as voting.

As Erika Jackson has demonstrated, Scandinavian immigrants soon became established near the top of a racial hierarchy in the Midwest due to Anglo-Americans regarding them as "pious," Protestant, property-owning businessmen – and not least white.[1] This Anglo-American acceptance aided countless Scandinavian newcomers in attaining property and a sense of belonging. In time, a number of these immigrants helped shape American debates over landownership, labor, and progressivism.

In 1860, however, fewer than 100,000 Scandinavian-born settlers lived within American borders, and only approximately 10,000 Scandinavian

---

[1] Erika K. Jackson, *Scandinavians in Chicago: The Origins of White Privilege in Modern America* (Urbana: University of Illinois Press, 2019), 41. Describing Scandinavian immigrants, the *Chicago Tribune* in 1886 claimed that "no other nationality assimilates with the American more rapidly." See "Our Scandinavian Citizens," *Chicago Daily Tribune*, June 6, 1886.

men served in the Union army. The contribution of Scandinavians to the overall Union war effort was therefore marginal, but the ones that did serve established important toeholds in mainstream American society. The Civil War connections, in a relatively short time span, elevated Scandinavian veterans such as Knute Nelson, Hans B. Warner, Hans Mattson, Christian T. Christensen, and Hans Borchsenius to leadership positions of greater regional significance, and the political views that they established in the Civil War era left important imprints on Midwestern politics and eastern business/philanthropy in the years after the Civil War. Many Scandinavian-born leaders and voters, however, pushed their antebellum advocacy for racial justice and (to a lesser extent) gender equality to the margins of political discourse in the postwar era. Consequently, continued engagement with these early immigrants' understandings of citizenship and American empire, and the echoes of what George Lipsitz calls "the complexity and contradictions of whiteness," remains critical to constructing well-informed contemporary conversations.[2]

Among Scandinavian and American historians, the past decades have witnessed a wealth of important scholarship that engages the questions, and structural factors, surrounding Norwegian, Swedish, and Danish immigrants' socioeconomic experience in an American ethnic hierarchy. As an example, Torben Grøngaard Jensen, in a recent study offers settlement patterns, occupation, marriage, and religion as variables that explain Scandinavian immigrants' relative success in the United States.[3] Such explanations, however, must be accompanied by an increased understanding of the historical factors related to citizenship and American empire, such as skin color, territorial expansion, and landownership opportunities that Scandinavian immigrants, implicitly or explicitly, benefited from.

In the Civil War era, Scandinavian immigrant men's dreams of citizenship rights, liberty, and equality were often attainable almost upon arrival to the United States due to their Northern European, Protestant background, but from 1862 and forward the prospect of forced military service

---

[2] George Lipsitz, *The Possessive Investment in Whiteness: How White People Profit from Identity Politics* (Philadelphia, PA: Temple University Press, 2006), 213.
[3] Torben Grøngaard Jeppesen, *Fra Skandinavisk Immigrant Til Amerikaner* [*From Scandinavian Immigrant to American*] (Odense: Syddansk Universitetsforlag, 2017), 8, 14–15.

led an increasing number of Norwegians, Swedes, and Danes to oppose the citizenship duties of military service.

Scandinavian immigrants resisted the draft, even in the face of broadening citizenship definitions by the federal government, to such an extent that ethnic leaders feared a Civil War scenario where lack of willingness to serve in the United States military would be perceptible to larger American society. Thus, the draft issue was front and center in the Scandinavian press until late in the war, but dissent was quickly forgotten after the conflict.

When Scandinavian immigrants did fight after the end of hostilities in 1865, they increasingly engaged in a predominantly white (working) class struggle for economic equality. As such, the Norwegian, Swedish, and Danish immigrant community played a significant role in the rise of Robert LaFollette, whose strand of socially and economically progressive Midwestern politics paid little attention to the plight of nonwhites.[4]

Thus, Scandinavian immigrants after the Civil War proved hesitant to fight for universal equality. This limited sense of interracial and gender equality, as we have seen in previous chapters, had roots stretching back to the Old World. Scandinavian immigrants' support for Homestead legislation, due to the importance of landownership, led to tension and at times outright violent conflict with American Indians, as evidenced by the 1862 US–Dakota War. In this era, immigrants from Norway, Sweden, and Denmark supported an American imperial project premised on white settlement and expansion west across the American continent but were less interested in noncontiguous expansion into the Caribbean.

Still, at the political level, prominent Republican politicians within the Lincoln and Johnson administrations continually took steps to increase American empire, and their overtures regarding the Danish West Indies were generally well-received by Danish politicians who had little concern for freedpeople's wishes. As it happened, however, Danish policy converged almost entirely with the islands' populations wishes, as Denmark had by the late 1860s become a *Kleinstaat* while the United States was an expanding nation of increasing international significance and perceived economic opportunity.

---

[4] Jørn Brøndal, Ethnic Leadership and Midwestern Politics: Scandinavian Americans and the Progressive Movement in Wisconsin, 1890–1914, 6–10. See also Jørn Brøndal, "The Ethnic and Racial Side of Robert M. La Follette Sr," *Journal of the Gilded Age and Progressive Era* 10, no. 3 (2011): 342.

This change in the international balance of power between Denmark and the United States, which made the latter more attractive to the islands' population, also complicated annexation. Denmark lost one-third of its territory after the Second Schleswig War in 1864, and, when Old World hostilities broke out between Prussia-led German troops and France in 1870, the Danish fear of being incorporated into the German Confederation reached a climax. In Denmark, there was a real sense that the declining nation might be annexed by an expanding German *Grossstaat*. An annihilated Denmark then might have to be reborn culturally and physically on "American soil," a Danish-American consul in Wisconsin suggested.[5] Such Danish fears never fully materialized, but the concrete ramifications of *Kleinstaat* diplomacy and psychology time and again showed their importance in an age of expanding empires.

The United States, conversely, reincorporated the seceded Southern states and purchased Alaska in 1867. The end of the Civil War thereby solidified American *Grossstaat* status, which was a contributing factor to the United States Senate in 1870 declining to ratify a treaty signed with Denmark three years earlier. In this diplomatic struggle between a *Kleinstaat* and a *Grossstaat* over the purchase of the Danish West Indies, there was little the former could do.

It would be several decades before American politicians were ready to revisit a treaty centered on the Danish West Indies, but on March 31, 1917, the islands were finally transferred and became the US Virgin Islands. By then important new questions of citizenship and American empire had emerged. Yet, many remained the same.

---

[5] Quoted in Torben Grøngaard Jeppesen, *Dannebrog På Den Amerikanske Prærie* [*Dannebrog on the American Prarie*] (Odense: Odense University Press, 2000), 10.

Bibliography

ARCHIVAL COLLECTIONS

Augustana College (Rock Island, IL)
Collection of Augustana Synod letters, 1853–1908. SSIRC MSS P: 342.
Eric Norelius papers, 1851–1916.
Jønsson (Johnson), Erik and Erickson, Ingar papers 1863; n.d. SSIRC SAC P: 81.
Mathilda Cassel Peterson Danielson (1834–). SSIRC Mss P: 55.
Sven August Johnson Papers, 1831–1921. SSIRC Mss P: 9.
Williamson family papers 1854–1950. Mss 122.
Det Danske Udvandrerarkiv (Aalborg, Denmark)
Afskrift af 22 breve til Frederik Nielsen, Herlev DK fra A.F. Wilmington Ill. og
West Denmark og Neenah Wisc. (1847–1872).
Det Kongelige Bibliotek (Copenhagen)
Karl Larsen's Collection, Unused Material. Wilhelm Adolf Leopold Wermuth,
USA. (Soldat, guldgraver, mine-ejer.)
Harvard University. Houghton Library (Cambridge, MA)
Charles Sumner Correspondence 1829–1874
Huntington Library (San Marino, CA)
Papers of Christian T. Christensen.
Samuel R. Curtis Papers.
Illinois State Archives (Springfield, IL)
Civil War Records. 82nd Infantry Regiment. Misc. Letters and Telegrams.
Civil War Records. 82nd Infantry Regiment. Misc. Orders & Reports.
Library of Congress (Washington, DC)
The Papers of Nathaniel Banks.
Louisiana State University Libraries (Baton Rouge, LA)
Ambrose Dudley Mann letters, 1850–1889. Microfilm Edition.
Christian D. Koch and Family Papers.
Minnesota Historical Society (Saint Paul, MN)
Hans Mattson and Family Papers.

National Archives (Washington, DC)
Court-Martial Case Files 1809–1894.
Letters Received by the Commission Branch of the Adjutant General's Office, 1863–1870.
Pension Records.
Records of the Provost Marshal General's Bureau (Civil War).
National Archives (College Park, MD)
M-52. Notes from the Danish Legation in the U.S. to the Dept. of State, 1801–1906. Roll T3.
M-60. Notes from the Swedish Legation in the U.S. to the Dept. of State, 1813–1906.
RG 59. General Records of the Department of State. Civil War Papers, 1861–1865. Case Files on Drafted Aliens. 1862–64. Entry 970.
RG 59 Records of the Department of State. Despatches from U.S. Consuls in Gothenburg, Sweden 1800–1906.
New York Historical Society (New York)
Gustavus Vasa Fox Collection 1823–1919 (bulk 1860–1889). Letters received.
Norwegian-American Historical Association (Northfield, MN)
America Letters. Papers. P0435.
Civil War Diary. Gunvold Johnsrud, 1841–1923. P468.
Clausen, Claus L. (1820–1892). P59.
John A. Johnson Papers. P691.
Local history: Minnesota – Jackson County. P1523
Pacific Lutheran University. Archives and Special Collections/Library Services (Tacoma, WA)
Carl Fredrik Solberg Papers.
Rigsarkivet (Copenhagen)
Collection 0002. Udenrigsministeriet. 1856–1909 Samlede sager. Konsulatet New York.
Collection 691. St. Croix Borgerråd. 1814–1865 Forhandlings- og referatprotokoller.
Collection 1175. Koloniernes centralbestyrelse kolonialkontoret. 1855–1918.
Udenrigsministeriet. 1856–1909 Samlede sager. Vestindien 1865–1909.
Washington, DC, diplomatisk repræsentation. 1854–1909 Korrespondancesager (aflev. 1918).
Politisk Korrespondance 1864–1868.
Sadovnikoff Family Private Collection (Warwick, RI)
Ferdinand Winslöw Letters.
Stanford University Libraries, Department of Special Collections (Stanford, CA)
General Frederick Steele Papers.
State Historical Society of Iowa (Des Moines)
Samuel R. Curtis Papers.
University of Iowa, Special Collections Department (Iowa City)
Ferdinand Sophus Winslow Letters.
University of Rochester, Department of Rare Books, Special Collections and Preservation (Rochester, NY)
William Henry Seward Papers. Microform Edition.
Wisconsin Historical Society (WHS, Green Bay)
Fritz William Rasmussen Papers, 1834–1942.

Wisconsin Historical Society (Madison)
  Adjutant General. Draftee Substitutes (c.1861–1865), Camp Washburn. Series 1137.
  Archives Division. Wisconsin. Executive Department. Military Correspondence. Series 49.
  County Clerk. Civil War Draft Records, 1862. Dane Series 42.
  Hans Christian Heg Letters
  Johnson, John A., *1861–1866*, Wis Mss 237s
  Letters Madison 1862. Volume 5. Series 33 of Governors Correspondence General, 1838–1926.
  Manuscript Collection. Reminiscences. Wis Mss 102S.
  Stephen Vaughn Shipman, Diary, 1865, Transcription.
  Wisconsin. Governor Military Votes, 1862–1865. Series 60.
  Wisconsin. Adjutant General. Draft Records, 1862–1865. Series 1137. Reel 1.

NEWSPAPERS AND PERIODICALS

Aarhus Stiftstidende (Aarhus, Denmark).
Alexandria Gazette (Alexandria, VA).
British and Foreign Anti-Slavery Reporter (London, England).
Brooklyn Daily Eagle (New York, NY).
Chicago Tribune (Chicago, IL).
Den Norske Amerikaner (Madison, WI).
Den Norske Rigstidende (Christiania (Oslo), Norway).
Emigranten (Madison, WI).
Fædrelandet (La Crosse, WI).
Flyveposten (Odense, Denmark).
Fremad (Milwaukee, WI).
Fyns Stifts (Copenhagen, Denmark).
Green Bay Advocate (Green Bay, WI).
Harper's Weekly (New York, NY).
Hemlandet (Chicago, IL).
Illustreret Tidende (Copenhagen, Denmark).
Kirkelig Maanedstidende (Inmansville, WI).
Lolland-Falsters Stiftstidende (Nyköbing Falster, Denmark).
Marcus Thrane's Norske Amerikaner (Chicago, IL)
Morgenbladet (Christiania (Oslo), Norway).
New York Herald (New York, NY).
New York Times (New York, NY).
Nordlyset (Norway, WI).
Prescott Journal (Prescott, WI).
Silkeborg Avis (Silkeborg, Denmark).
Skandinaven (Chicago, IL).
Star Tribune (Minneapolis, MN).
Svenska Amerikaneran (Chicago, IL).
The Liberator (Boston, MA).
Tilskueren (Copenhagen, Denmark).

PUBLISHED PRIMARY AND SECONDARY SOURCES

Abbott, Richard H. *The Republican Party and the South, 1855–1877.* Chapel Hill: University of North Carolina Press, 1986.

Adriansen, Inge, and Jens Ole Christensen. *Første Slesvigske Krig 1848–1851: Forhistorie, Forløb Og Følger [First Schleswig War 1848–1851: Causes, Course, and Consequences].* Sønderborg: Sønderborg Slot, 2015.

Ager, Waldemar. *Oberst Heg Og Hans Gutter [Colonel Heg and His Boys].* Eau Claire, WI: Fremad Publishing Company, 1916.

Allen, Julie. *Danish, but Not Lutheran: The Impact of Mormonism on Danish Cultural Identity, 1850–1920.* Salt Lake City: University of Utah Press, 2017.

Anbinder, Tyler. "Which Poor Man's Fight? Immigrants and the Federal Conscription of 1863." *Civil War History* 52, no. 4 (2006): 344–372.

Ander, Oscar Fritiof. *T. N. Hasselquist: The Career and Influence of a Swedish-American Clergyman, Journalist and Educator.* Rock Island, IL: Augustana Historical Society, 1931.

Andersen, Arlow William. *The Immigrant Takes His Stand: The Norwegian-American Press and Public Affairs, 1847–1872.* Northfield, MN: Norwegian-American Historical Association, 1953.

"Knud Langeland: Pioneer Editor." *Norwegian-American Studies* 14 (1944): 122–138.

Andersen, Bent Knie. *Sukker Og Guld [Sugar and Gold].* Copenhagen: National Museum of Denmark, 2015.

Andersen, Hans Christian. *Mulatten [The Mulatto].* Copenhagen: Bianco Luno's Bogtrykkeri, 1840.

Andersen, Rasmus. *Pastor Claus Laurits Clausen – Banebryder for Den Norske Og Danske Kirke i Amerika. Første Skandinavisk Feltpræst [Pastor Claus Laurits Clausen: Trailblazer for the Norwegian and Danish Church in America. First Scandinavian Chaplain].* Blair, NE: Danish Lutheran Publishing House, 1921.

Anderson, Gary Clayton. *Kinsmen of Another Kind: Dakota-White Relations in the Upper Mississippi Valley, 1650–1862.* Lincoln: University of Nebraska Press, 1984.

"Myrick's Insult: A Fresh Look at Myth and Reality." *Minnesota History,* Spring (1983): 198–206.

Anderson, Gary Clayton, and Alan R. Woolworth, eds. *Through Dakota Eyes: Narrative Accounts of the Minnesota Indian War of 1862.* Saint Paul: Minnesota Historical Society Press, 1988.

Anderson, Kristen Layne. *Abolitionizing Missouri: German Immigrants and Racial Ideology in Nineteenth-Century America.* Baton Rouge: Louisiana State University Press, 2016.

Anderson, Rasmus B. *The First Chapter of Norwegian Migration, Its Causes and Results.* Second ed. Madison, WI: Published by the author, 1896.

Anderson, William J., and William A. Anderson, eds. *The Wisconsin Blue Book.* Madison, WI: Democrat Printing Company, 1929.

Andræ, Poul. *De Dansk-Vestindiske Øer Nærmest Med Hensyn Til Deres Nuværende Politiske Og Finantsielle Forhold [The Danish West Indian*

Islands Regarding Their Present Political and Financial Conditions].
Copenhagen: C. A. Reitzel, 1875.

Andrews, Christopher Columbus. *History of the Campaign of Mobile; Including the Cooperative Operations of Gen. Wilson's Cavalry in Alabama (1867)*. New York: D. Van Nostrand, 1867.

Applegate, Debby. *The Most Famous Man in America: The Biography of Henry Ward Beecher*. New York: Doubleday, 2006.

Armitage, David, Thomas Bender, Leslie Butler, Don H. Doyle, Susan-Mary Grant, Charles S. Maier, Jörn Naigler, Paul Quigley, and Jay Sexton. "Interchange: Nationalism and Internationalism in the Era of the Civil War." *Journal of American History* 98, no. 2 (2011): 455–489.

Baker, George E., ed. *The Works of William H. Seward*. Vol. 4. Boston, MA: Houghton, Mifflin, 1884.

Balling, O. P. Hansen. *Erindringer Fra Et Langt Liv* [*Memories from a Long Life*]. Kristiania: S. & Jul Sørensens Bogtrykkeri, 1905.

Barton, Albert O. "The Most Historic Norwegian Colony." *Wisconsin Magazine of History* 21, no. 2 (1937): 129–138.

"Reminiscences of a Pioneer Editor." *NAHA Studies and Records* 1 (1926): 134–144.

Basler, Roy P., ed. *Collected Works of Abraham Lincoln*. Vol. 3. New Brunswick, NJ: Rutgers University Press, 1953.

ed. *Collected Works of Abraham Lincoln*. Vol. 4. New Brunswick, NJ: Rutgers University Press, 1953.

Beckert, Sven. *Empire of Cotton: A Global History*. New York: Alfred A. Knopf, 2014.

Benjaminson, Eric. "A Regiment of Immigrants: The 82nd Illinois Volunteer Infantry and the Letters of Captain Rudolph Mueller." *Journal of the Illinois State Historical Society* 94, Summer (2001): 137–180.

Bergius, Olof Erik. *Om Westindien* [*About The West Indies*]. Stockholm: A. Gadelius, 1819.

Bergland, Betty. "Norwegian Immigrants and 'Indianerne' in the Landtaking, 1838–1862." *Norwegian-American Studies* 35 (2000): 319–350.

Betænkning Afgiven Af Den i Henhold Til Lov Nr. 294 Af 30. September 1916 Nedsatte Rigsdagskommission Angaaende De Dansk Vestindiske Øer [*Report Submitted by the Parliamentary Commission Appointed under Act of September 30, 1916, Regarding the Danish West Indian Islands*]. Copenhagen: J. H. Schultz A/S, 1916.

Bjørn, Klaus. *1848: Borgerkrig Og Revolution* [*1848: Civil War and Revolution*]. Copenhagen: Gyldendal, 1998.

Blanck, Dag. *The Creation of an Ethnic Identity: Being Swedish American in the Augustana Synod, 1860–1917*. Carbondale: Southern Illinois University Press, 2006.

Blegen, Theodore C., ed. *The Civil War Letters of Colonel Hans Christian Heg*. Northfield, MN: Norwegian-American Historical Association, 1936.

"Cleng Peerson and Norwegian Immigration." *Mississippi Valley Historical Review* 7, no. 4 (1921): 303–331.

"Colonel Hans Christian Heg." *Wisconsin Magazine of History* 4, no. 2 (1920): 140–165.

Norwegian Migration to America 1825–1860. Northfield, MN: Norwegian-American Historical Association, 1931.

Norwegian Migration to America: The American Transition. New York: Haskell House Publishers, 1940.

ed. *Ole Rynning's True Account of America*. Minneapolis, MN: Norwegian-American Historical Society, 1921.

Blight, David W. *Frederick Douglass: Prophet of Freedom*. New York: Simon & Schuster, 2018.

Bregnsbo, Michael. "Danmark 1848 – Systemskifte Og Borgerkrig [Denmark 1848 – Political Change and Civil War]." *Fortid og Nutid* (December 1998): 251–269.

Breidbach, Olaf, and Michael T. Ghiselin. "Lorenz Oken and 'Naturphilosophie' in Jena, Paris and London." *History and Philosophy of the Life Sciences* 27, no. 2 (2002): 219–247.

Bremer, Fredrika. *The Homes of the New World: Impressions of America*. New York: Harper & Brothers, 1853.

Brøndal, Jørn. "An Early American Dilemma? Scandinavian Travel Writers' Reflections on the Founding Ideals of the United States and the Condition of African Americans, Ca. 1850–1900." In *Les Constitutions: Des Révolutions À L'épreuve Du Temps Aux Etats-Unis Et En Europe/Constitutions: On-Going Revolutions in Europe and the United States*, edited by Marie-Elisabeth Baudoin and Marie Bolton. Paris: Clermont-Ferrand: École de droit, UDA Université d'Auvergne, [Issy-les-Moulineaux], 2017.

"The Ethnic and Racial Side of Robert M. La Follette Sr." *Journal of the Gilded Age and Progressive Era* 10, no. 3 (2011): 340–353.

Ethnic Leadership and Midwestern Politics: Scandinavian Americans and the Progressive Movement in Wisconsin, 1890–1914. Chicago: University of Illinois Press, 2004.

"'The Fairest among the So-Called White Races': Portrayals of Scandinavian Americans in the Filiopietistic and Nativist Literature of the Late Nineteenth and Early Twentieth Centuries." *Journal of American Ethnic History* 33, no. 3 (2014): 5–33.

Brøndal, Jørn, and Dag Blanck. "The Concept of Being Scandinavian-American." *American Studies in Scandinavia* 34, no. 2 (2002): 1–31.

Bruce, Susannah Ural. *The Harp and The Eagle: Irish-American Volunteers and the Union Army, 1861–1865*. New York: New York University Press, 2006.

Bugge, K. E. "Grundtvig and the Abolition of Slavery." *Grundtvig-Studier* 56, no. 1 (2005): 160–191.

Grundtvig Og Slavesagen [Grundtvig and the Slavery Cause]. Aarhus: Aarhus Universitetsforlag, 2003.

Buk-Swienty, Tom. *1864: The Forgotten War That Shaped Modern Europe*. London: Profile Books, 2015.

Burke, Peter. "History of Events and the Revival of Narrative." In *New Perspectives on Historical Writing*, edited by Peter Burke, pp. 283–300. University Park: Pennsylvania State University Press, 2001.

Burton, William. *Melting Pot Soldiers: The Union's Ethnic Regiments.* 2nd ed. New York: Fordham University Press, 1998.

Buslett, Ole A. *Det Femtende Regiment Wisconsin Frivillige [The Fifteenth Regiment Wisconsin Volunteers].* Decorah, IA: B. Anundsen, 1894.

Cavling, Henrik. *Det Danske Vestindien [The Danish West Indies].* Copenhagen: Det Reitzelske Forlag, 1894.

Fra Amerika, vol. II. Copenhagen: Gyldendalske Boghandels Forlag, 1897.

Check, Earl D., and Emeroy Johnson (translator). "Civil War Letters to New Sweden, Iowa." *Swedish-American Historical Quarterly* 36, no. 1 (1985): 3–25.

The Chief Clerks of the Senate and Assembly in the Year 1863. *The Legislative Manual of the State of Wisconsin.* Madison: Atwood & Rublee, 1863.

Childs, George W., ed. *The National Almanac and Annual Record for the Year 1863.* Philadelphia: George W. Childs, 1863.

Chomsky, Carol. "The United States-Dakota War Trials: A Study in Military Injustice." *Stanford Law Review* 43, no. 13 (1990): 13–98.

Christensen, Christian Thomsen. "Address by General C. T. Christensen at a Meeting Held at Germania Hall, New York, by the Independent Scandinavian Cleveland & Hendricks Campaign Club." Brooklyn, NY: Eagle Book and Job Printing Department, 1884.

Christensen, Thomas P. "A German Forty-Eighter in Iowa." *Annals of Iowa* 26, no. 4 (1945): 245–253.

Christiansen, Celius. *En Pioneers Historie (Erindringer Fra Krigen Mellem Nord- Og Sydstaterne) [A Pioneer's Story: Memoirs from the War between North and South].* Aalborg: Eget forlag, 1909.

Christianson, J. R., ed. "Clausens on the Move: Chicago, St. Ansgar, Virginia, 1870–1873." *The Bridge* VI, no. 2 (1984): 28–29.

Clark, Christopher. *The Roots of Rural Capitalism: Western Massachusetts, 1780–1860.* Ithaca, NY: Cornell University Press, 1990.

Clark Jr., Clifford E. "The Changing Nature of Protestantism in Mid-Nineteenth Century America: Henry Ward Beecher's Seven Lectures to Young Men." *Journal of American History* 57, no. 4 (1971): 832–846.

Clausen, Clarence A., and Andreas Elviken, eds. *The Chronicle of Old Muskego: The Diary of Søren Bache, 1839–1847.* Northfield, MN: Norwegian-American Historical Association, 1951.

Clausen, Clarence A., and Derwood Johnson. "Norwegian Soldiers in the Confederate Forces." *Norwegian-American Studies* 25 (1972): 105–141.

Clausen, Claus L. *Gjenmæle Mod Kirkeraadet for Den Norske Synode [Response to the Church Council for the Norwegian Synod].* Chicago, IL: Skandinavens Bog- og Accidents-Trykkeri, 1869.

Crane, L. D. H. *A Manual of Customs, Precedents and Forms, in the Use in the Assembly of Wisconsin.* Madison: E. A. Calkins & Co., 1861.

Current, Richard N. *The History of Wisconsin. Volume II. The Civil War Era, 1848–1873.* Madison: State Historical Society of Wisconsin, 1976.

Dalhoff-Nielsen, Sven. *Nordiske Frivillige [Nordic Volunteers].* Graasten: Nordisk Institut, 1944.

Daniels, George H. "Immigrant Vote in the 1860 Election: The Case of Iowa." In *Ethnic Voters and the Election of Lincoln*, edited by Frederick C. Luebke, pp. 146–162. Lincoln: University of Nebraska Press, 1971.

Dew, Charles B. *Apostles of Disunion: Southern Secession Commissioners and the Causes of the Civil War*. Charlottesville: University Press of Virginia, 2001.

Dietrichson, Johannes W. C. *Pastor J.W.C. Dietrichsons Reise Blandt De Norske Emigranter i "De Forenede Nordamerikanske Fristater." Paany Udgiven Af Rasmus B. Anderson [Pastor J. W. C. Dietrichson's Travels among the Norwegian Emigrants in "the United North American States." Reprinted by Rasmus B. Anderson]*. Madison: Amerika's Bogtrykkeri, 1896.

Dookhan, Isaac. "Changing Patterns of Local Reaction to the United States Acquisition of the Virgin Islands, 1865–1917." *Caribbean Studies* 15 (1975): 54–59.

Douma, Michael J., and Anders Bo Rasmussen. "The Danish St Croix Project: Revisiting the Lincoln Colonization Program with Foreign-Language Sources." *American Nineteenth Century History* 15, no. 3 (2014): 311–342.

Douma, Michael J., Anders Bo Rasmussen, and Robert O. Faith. "The Impressment of Foreign-Born Soldiers in the Union Army." *Journal of American Ethnic History* 38, no. 3 (2019): 76–106.

Downs, Gregory P. *The Second American Revolution: The Civil War-Era Struggle over Cuba and the Rebirth of the American Republic*. Chapel Hill: University of North Carolina Press, 2019.

Downs, Gregory P., and Kate Masur. "Echoes of War: Rethinking Post-Civil War Governance and Politics." In *The World the Civil War Made*, edited by Gregory P. Downs and Kate Masur, pp. 1–21. Chapel Hill: The University of North Carolina Press, 2015.

Downs, Jim. *Sick from Freedom: African-American Illness and Suffering During the Civil War and Reconstruction*. New York: Oxford University Press, 2012.

Doyle, Don H. *Cause of All Nations: An International History of the American Civil War*. New York: Basic Books, 2013.

Drevland, Petter Strøm. "Norwegian Immigrants in the American Civil War: Reasons for Enlistment According to the America Letters." M.A. Thesis: Universitetet i Oslo, 2013.

Efford, Alison Clark. "The Appeal of Racial Neutrality in the Civil War-Era North: German Americans and the Democratic New Departure." *Journal of the Civil War Era* 5, no. 1 (2015): 68–96.

"Civil War–Era Immigration and the Imperial United States." *Journal of the Civil War Era* 10, no. 2 (2020): 233–253.

German Immigrants, Race, and Citizenship in the Civil War Era. Washington, DC: Cambridge University Press, 2013.

Emberton, Carole. *Beyond Redemption: Race, Violence, and the American South after the Civil War*. Chicago, IL: University of Chicago Press, 2013.

Evans, William McKee. "Native Americans in the Civil War: Three Experiences." In *Civil War Citizens: Race, Ethnicity, and Identity in America's Bloodiest Conflict*, edited by Susannah J. Ural, pp. 187–212. New York: New York University Press, 2010.

Fagan, Benjamin. "*The North Star* and the Atlantic 1848." *African American Review* 47, no. 1 (2014): 51–67.

Farrow, Lee A. *Seward's Folly: A New Look at the Alaska Purchase*. Fairbanks: University of Alaska Press, 2016.

Felix, Axel. *Langt Fra Danmark 1–10: Skitser Og Scener Fra De Forenede Stater i Nordamerika. Bind 1*.: Forlaget Danmark, 1985. Langt fra Danmark 1–10. Udkom første gang i perioden 1852–1855 på Andr. Fred Høsts forlag.

Fett, Sharla M. *Recaptured Africans: Surviving Slave Ships, Detention, and Dislocation in the Final Years of the Slave Trade*. Chapel Hill: University of North Carolina Press, 2017.

Fevold, Eugene F. "The Norwegian Immigrant and His Church." *Norwegian-American Studies* 23 (1967): 3–16.

Fields, Barbara J. "Ideology and Race in American History." In *Region, Race, and Reconstruction: Essays in Honor of C. Vann Woodward*, edited by J. Morgan Kousser and James M. McPherson, pp. 143–177. New York: Oxford University Press, 1982.

Fitch, John. *Annals of the Army of the Cumberland: Comprising Biographies, Descriptions of Departments, Accounts of Expeditions, Skirmishes, and Battles*. Philadelphia, PA: J. B. Lippincott & Co., 1864.

Foner, Eric. *The Fiery Trial: Abraham Lincoln and American Slavery*. New York: W. W. Norton, 2010.

Forever Free: The Story of Emancipation and Reconstruction. New York: Alfred A. Knopf, 2005.

Free Soil, Free Labor, Free Men: The Ideology of the Republican Party before the Civil War. New York: Oxford University Press, 1995.

"Lincoln and Colonization." In *Our Lincoln*, edited by Eric Foner, pp. 135–166. New York: W. W. Norton, 2008.

Reconstruction: America's Unfinished Revolution, 1863–1877. New York: Harper & Row, 1988.

Fribert, L. J. *Haandbog for Emigranter Til Amerikas Vest [Handbook for Emigrants to America's West]*. Christiania (Oslo): Forlaget af Johan Dahl, 1847.

"From Hon. Charles Sumner to General Butler. Washington, June 24th, 1861." In Benjamin F. Butler, *Private and Official Correspondence of Gen. Benjamin F. Butler During the Period of the Civil War*, pp. 159. Norwood, MA: Plimpton Press, 1917.

Frymer, Paul. *Building an American Empire: The Era of Territorial and Political Expansion*. Princeton, NJ: Princeton University Press, 2017.

Fur, Gunlög. "Indians and Immigrants – Entangled Histories." *Journal of American Ethnic History* 33, no. 3 (2014): 55–76.

Gallman, J. Matthew. *Defining Duty in the Civil War: Personal Choice, Popular Culture, and the Union Home Front*. Chapel Hill: University of North Carolina Press, 2015.

Gaylord, August. *Annual Report of the Adjutant General of the State of Wisconsin for the Year 1862*. Madison, WI: Atwood & Rublee, State Printers, 1863.

Geary, James W. *We Need Men: The Union Draft in the Civil War*. DeKalb: Northern Illinois University Press, 1991.

Geertz, Clifford. "'From the Native's Point of View': On the Nature of Anthropological Understanding." *Bulletin of the American Academy of Arts and Sciences* 28, no. 1 (1974): 26–45.

Generalstaben [General Staff]. *Den Dansk-Tydske Krig i Aarene 1848–1850* [*The Danish-German War between 1848 and 1850*]. Copenhagen: J. H. Schultz's Bogtrykkeri, 1867.

Genovese, Eugene D. *Roll, Jordan, Roll: The World the Slaves Made*. New York: Vintage Books, 1974.

Giardino, Marco, and Russell Guerin. *Mississippi's No-Man's Land: An Echo of the Koch Family Letters*. Denver, CO: Outskirts Press, 2006.

Gieske, Millard L., and Steven J. Keillor. *Norwegian Yankee: Knute Nelson and the Failure of American Politics, 1860–1923*. Northfield, MN: Norwegian-American Historical Association, 1995.

Ginzburg, Carlo. "Checking the Evidence: The Judge and the Historian." *Critical Inquiry* 18, no. 1 (1991): 79–92.

The Cheese and the Worms: The Cosmos of a Sixteenth-Century Miller. New York: Penguin Books, 1982.

"Microhistory: Two or Three Things That I Know About It." *Critical Inquiry* 20, no. 1 (Autumn 1993): 10–35.

Ginzburg, Carlo, and Anna Davin. "Morelli, Freud and Sherlock Holmes: Clues and Scientific Method." *History Workshop* 9 (Spring 1980): 5–36.

Gjerde, Jon. "Conflict and Community: A Case Study of the Immigrant Church in the United States." *Journal of Social History* 19, no. 4 (1986): 681–697.

"'Here in America There Is Neither King nor Tyrant': European Encounters with Race, 'Freedom,' and Their European Pasts." *Journal of the Early Republic* 19, no. 4 (1999): 673–690.

The Minds of the West: Ethnocultural Evolution in the Rural Middle West 1830–1917. Chapel Hill: The University of North Carolina Press, 1997.

Gleeson, David T. *The Green and the Gray: The Irish in the Confederate States of America*. Chapel Hill: University of North Carolina Press, 2013.

The Irish in the South, 1815–1877. Chapel Hill: The University of North Carolina Press, 2001.

Gleeson, David T., and Simon Lewis, eds. *The Civil War as Global Conflict: The Transnational Meanings of the American Civil War*. Columbia: University of South Carolina Press, 2014.

"Introduction." In *The Civil War as Global Conflict: Transnational Meanings of the American Civil War*, edited by David T. Gleeson and Simon Lewis, pp. 1–13. Columbia: University of South Carolina Press, 2014.

Glenthøj, Rasmus. *1864: Sønner Af De Slagne* [*1864: Descendants of the Defeated*]. Copenhagen: Gads Forlag, 2014.

"Adskillelsen: Hvorfor Denmark Og Norge Blev Skilt i 1814 [The Partition: Why Denmark and Norway Were Separated in 1814]." In *Mellem Brødre: Dansk-Norsk Samliv i 600 År* [*Between Brothers: Danish-Norwegian Co-Existence over 600 Years*], edited by Rasmus Glenthøj, pp. 92–107. Copenhagen: Gads Forlag, 2016.

"Pan-Scandinavism and the Threshold Principle?" In *A History of the European Restorations: Governments, States and Monarchy*, edited by Michael Broers and Ambrogio Caiani, pp. 245–255. London: Bloomsbury Academic, 2019.

"Skandinavismen Som En Politisk Nødvendighed [Scandinavism as a Political Necessity]." In *Skandinavismen: Vision Og Virkning [Scandinavism: Vision and Effect]*, edited by Ruth Hemstad, Jes Fabricius Møller, and Dag Thorkildsen, pp. 227–255. Odense: Syddansk Universitetsforlag, 2018.

Glenthøj, Rasmus, and Morten Nordhagen Ottosen. *Union Eller Undergang: Kampen for Et Forenet Skandinavien [Union or Ruin: The Struggle for a United Scandinavia]*. Copenhagen: Gads Forlag, 2021.

Graber, Jennifer. "Mighty Upheaval on the Minnesota Frontier: Violence, War, and Death in Dakota and Missionary Christianity." *Church History* 80, no. 1 (2011): 76–108.

Guldi, Jo, and David Armitage. *The History Manifesto*. Cambridge: Cambridge University Press, 2014.

Hacker, J. David. "New Estimates of Census Coverage in the United States, 1850–1930." *Social Science History* 37, no. 1 (2013): 71–101.

Hahn, Steven. *A Nation without Borders: The United States and Its World in an Age of Civil Wars, 1830–1910*. New York: Viking, 2016.

Hale, Frederick. "The Americanization of a Danish Immigrant in Wisconsin 1847–1872." *Wisconsin Magazine of History* 64, no. 3 (1981): 202–215.

Hansen, Blaine. "The Norwegians of Luther Valley." *Wisconsin Magazine of History* 28, no. 4 (1945): 422–430.

Hansen, Carl. "Pressen Til Borgerkrigens Slutning [The Press until the Civil War's End]." In *Norsk-Amerikanernes Festskrift 1914*, edited by Johannes B. Wist, pp. 9–40. Decorah, IA: Symra Company, 1914.

Hansen, Karen V. *Encounter on the Great Plains: Scandinavian Settlers and Dispossession of Dakota Indians, 1890–1930*. Oxford: Oxford University Press, 2013.

Haraldsø, Brynjar. *Slaveridebatten i Den Norske Synode: En Undersøkelse Av Slaveridebatten i Den Norske Synode i USA i 1860-Årene Med Særlig Vekt På Debattens Kirkelig-Teologiske Aspekter [The Slavery Debate in the Norwegian Synod: A Study of the Slavery Debate in the Norwegian Synod in the United States During the 1860s Emphasizing the Debate's Church-Theological Aspects]*. Oslo: Solum Forlag, 1988.

Heard, Isaac V. D. *History of the Sioux War and Massacres of 1862 and 1863*. New York: Harper & Brothers, Publishers, 1865.

Heg, James E., ed. *The Blue Book of the State of Wisconsin*. Madison, WI: Democrat Printing Co., 1885.

Heidenreich Jr., Donald E. *Articles of Impeachment against Andrew Johnson*. Defining Documents: Reconstruction Era. History Reference Center, EBSCOhost (accessed April 7, 2017). 2014.

Hobsbawm, Eric J. *Nations and Nationalism since 1780: Programme, Myth, Reality*. Cambridge: Cambridge University Press, 1992.

Hodes, Martha. *Mourning Lincoln*. New Haven, CT: Yale University Press, 2015.

Hoganson, Kristin L. *Fighting for American Manhood: How Gender Politics Provoked in Spanish-American and Philippine-American Wars*. New Haven, CT: Yale University Press, 1998.

Hokanson, Nels. *Swedish Immigrants in Lincoln's Time*. Scandinavians in America. Reprint ed. New York: Arno Press, 1979.

Holm, Jette, and Elisabeth A. Glenthøj, eds. *Grundtvig: Prædikener i Vartov, 1842–43* [*Grundtvig: Sermons in Vartov, 1842–43*]. Vol. 5. Copenhagen: Forlaget Vartov, 2007.

Holmberg, Åke. *Skandinavismen i Sverige, Vid 1800-Talets Mitt* [*Scandinavianism in Sweden, by the Middle of the 1800s*]. Göteborg: Elanders, 1946.

Holzer, Harold. *Lincoln and the Power of the Press: The War for Public Opinion*. New York: Simon & Schuster Paperbacks, 2015.

Honeck, Mischa. "Men of Principle: Gender and the German American War for the Union." *Journal of the Civil War Era* 5, no. 1 (2015): 38–67.

Hornby, Ove. *Kolonierne i Vestindien* [*The West Indian Colonies*]. Edited by Svend Ellehøj and Kristoff Glamann. Copenhagen: Politikens Forlag, 1980.

Horton, Russell. "Unwanted in a White Man's War: The Civil War Service of the Green Bay Tribes." *Wisconsin Magazine of History* 88, no. 2 (2004): 18–27.

Howe, Daniel Walker. *What Hath God Wrought: The Transformation of America, 1815–1848*. Oxford: Oxford University Press, 2007.

Howes, David., ed. *The Sixth Sense Reader*. New York: Berg, 2009.

Hvidt, Kristian. *Flugten Til Amerika, Eller Drivkræfter i Masseudvandringen Fra Danmark 1868–1914* [*Flight to America or Driving Forces in the Mass Emigration from Denmark 1868–1914*]. Aarhus: Universitetsforlaget i Aarhus, 1971.

Immerman, Richard H. *Empire for Liberty: A History of American Imperialism from Benjamin Franklin to Paul Wolfowitz*. Princeton, NJ: Princeton University Press, 2012.

Ipsen, Pernille. *Daughters of the Trade: Atlantic Slavers and Interracial Marriage on the Gold Coast*. Philadelphia: University of Pennsylvania Press, 2015.

———. "'Plant Ikke Upas-Træet Om Vor Bolig': Colonial Haunting, Race, and Interracial Marriage in Hans Christian Andersen's *Mulatten* (1840)." *Scandinavian Studies* 88, no. 2 (2016): 129–158.

Ipsen, Pernille, and Gunlög Fur. "Scandinavian Colonialism: Introduction." *Itenerario* 33, no. 2 (2009): 7–16.

Jackson, Erika K. *Scandinavians in Chicago: The Origins of White Privilege in Modern America*. Urbana: University of Illinois Press, 2019.

Jensen, Niklas Thode, Gunvor Simonsen, and Poul Erik Olsen. "Reform Eller Revolution 1803–48 [Reform or Revolution 1803–48]." In *Vestindien: St. Croix, St. Thomas Og St. Jan*, edited by Poul Erik Olsen., pp. 212–281. Copenhagen: Gads Forlag, 2017.

Jensen, Peter Hoxcer. *From Serfdom to Fireburn and Strike: The History of Black Labor in the Danish West Indies, 1848–1916*. Christiansted, St. Croix: Antilles Press, 1998.

Jeppesen, Torben Grøngaard. *Dannebrog På Den Amerikanske Prærie* [*Dannebrog on the American Prarie*]. Odense: Odense University Press, 2000.

——— *Danske i USA 1850–2000. En Demografisk, Social Og Kulturgeografisk Undersøgelse Af De Danske Immigranter Og Deres Efterkommere* [*Danes in the United States 1850–2000: A Demographic, Social and Cultural Geographic Study of The Danish Immigrants and Their Descendants*]. Odense: University Press of Southern Denmark, 2005.

——— *Fra Skandinavisk Immigrant Til Amerikaner* [*From Scandinavian Immigrant to American*]. Odense: Syddansk Universitetsforlag, 2017.

——— *Skandinaviske Efterkommere i USA* [*Scandinavian Descendants in America*]. Odense: Odense Bys Museer, 2010.

Johnson, Andrew. "Third Annual Message." Online by Gerhard Peters and John T. Woolley, The American Presidency Project. www.presidency.ucsb.edu/ws/index.php?pid=29508, 1867.

Johnson, J. A., ed. *Det Skandinaviske Regiments Historie* [*The Scandinavian Regiment's History*]. La Crosse: Fædrelandet og Emigrantens Trykkeri, 1869.

Johnson, Walter. *Soul by Soul: Life inside the Antebellum Slave Market*. Fourth printing. Cambridge, MA: Harvard University Press, 2000.

Jones, Martha S. *Birthright Citizens: A History of Race and Rights in Antebellum America*. Cambridge: Cambridge University Press, 2018.

Jordan, Brian Matthew. *Marching Home: Union Veterans and Their Unending Civil War*. New York: Liveright Publishing Corporation, 2014.

Jörgensen, Lars. *Amerika og De Danskes Liv Herovre* [*America and the Danes' Existence over Here*]. Copenhagen: Louis Kleins Bogtrykkeri, 1865.

Joy, Natalie. "The Indian's Cause: Abolitionists and Native American Rights." *Journal of the Civil War Era* 8, no. 2 (2018): 215–242.

Jung, Moon-Ho. *Coolies and Cane: Race, Labor, and Sugar in the Age of Emancipation*. Baltimore, MD: Johns Hopkins University Press, 2006.

Kalm, Pehr. *En Resa Til Norra America* [*Travels to North America*]. Stockholm: Lars Salvii, 1756.

Kamphoefner, Walter D., and Wolfgang Helbich, eds. *Germans in the Civil War: The Letters They Wrote Home*. Chapel Hill: University of North Carolina Press, 2006.

Kantrowitz, Stephen. *More Than Freedom: Fighting for Black Citizenship in a White Republic, 1829–1889*. New York: Penguin Press, 2012.

——— "'Not Quite Constitutionalized': The Meaning of 'Civilization' and the Limits of Native American Citizenship." In *The World the Civil War Made*, edited by Gregory P. Downs and Kate Masur, pp. 75–105. Chapel Hill: University of North Carolina Press, 2015.

——— "White Supremacy, Settler Colonialism, and the Two Citizenships of the Fourteenth Amendment." *Journal of the Civil War Era* 10, no. 1 (2020): 29–53.

Keating, Ryan W. *Shades of Green: Irish Regiments, American Soldiers, and Local Communities in the Civil War Era*. New York: Fordham University Press, 2017.

Kendi, Ibram X. *Stamped from the Beginning: The Definitive History of Racist Ideas in America.* New York: Nation Books, 2016.

Kennedy, Joseph C. G., ed. *Population of the United States in 1860.* Washington, DC: Government Printing Office, 1864.

Kerber, Linda K. "The Meanings of Citizenship." *Journal of American History* 84, no. 3 (1997): 833–854.

Klement, Frank. "The Soldier Vote in Wisconsin During the Civil War." *Wisconsin Magazine of History* 28, no. 1 (1944): 37–47.

Koht, Halvdan. "The Origin of Seward's Plan to Purchase the Danish West Indies." *American Historical Review* 50, no. 4 (1945): 762–767.

Kolchin, Peter. "Whiteness Studies: The New History of Race in America." *Journal of American History* 89, no. 1 (2002): 154–173.

Krall, Lisi. "Thomas Jefferson's Agrarian Vision and the Changing Nature of Property." *Journal of Economic Issues* 36, no. 1 (2002): 131–150.

Krick, Robert. *Civil War Weather in Virginia.* Tuscaloosa: University of Alabama Press, 2007.

Kvist, Roger. *For Adoptivlandets Och Mänsklighetens Sak: Svenskarna i Illinois Och Det Amerikanska Inbördeskriget* [*For Adopted Country and Humanity's Sake: The Swedes in Illinois and the American Civil War*]. Umeå: Norrlands Universitetsförlag, 2003.

Landelius, Otto Rob, ed. *Amerikabreven.* Stockholm: Natur och Kultur, 1957.

Lawson, Victor E., Martin E. Tew, and J. Emil Nelson. *The Illustrated History of Kandiyohi County, Minnesota.* Saint Paul, Mn: The Pioneer Press Manufacturing Departments, 1905.

Leiren, Terje. "Lost Utopia? The Changing Image of America in the Writings of Marcus Thrane." *Scandinavian Studies* 60, no. 4 (1988): 465–479.

Levi, Giovanni. "On Microhistory." In *New Perspectives on Historical Writing*, edited by Peter Burke, pp. 93–113. Cambridge: Polity Press, 1991.

Levine, Alan. "Scientific Racism in Antebellum America." In *The Political Thought of the Civil War*, edited by Alan Levine, Thomas W. Merrill, and James R. Stoner Jr., pp. 98–132. Lawrence: University Press of Kansas, 2018.

Lincoln, Abraham. "First Annual Message." Online by Gerhard Peters and John T. Woolley, The American Presidency Project. www.presidency.ucsb.edu/documents/first-annual-message-9, 1861.

Lipsitz, George. *The Possessive Investment in Whiteness: How White People Profit from Identity Politics.* Philadelphia, PA: Temple University Press, 2006.

Lonn, Ella. *Foreigners in the Union Army and Navy.* Baton Rouge: Louisiana State University Press, 1951.

Love, Eric T. L. *Race over Empire: Racism and U.S. Imperialism, 1865–1900.* Chapel Hill: University of North Carolina Press, 2004.

"Love for Skandinavisk Forening Af 1844 [Statutes for Scandinavian Association of 1844]." In *IEP Skandinavisk Forening af 1844. Love* ... New York Public Library, 1898.

Lovoll, Odd Sverre. *Norwegian Newspapers in America: Connecting Norway and the New Land.* Saint Paul: Minnesota Historical Society, 2010.

Luebke, Frederick C., ed. *Ethnic Voters and the Election of Lincoln.* Lincoln: University of Nebraska Press, 1971.

Lütken, P. C. "Noticer Vedkommende Agerdyrkningsvæsenet Og Landboforholdene i Territoriet Wiscounsin i Nord-Amerika [Notices Regarding Agriculture and Farming in the Wisconsin Territory in North America]." *Tidsskrift for Landoekonomie* 9 (1848): 394–427.

Mackey, Thomas C., ed. *A Documentary History of the Civil War Era: Legislative Achievements*, vol. 1. Knoxville: University of Tennessee Press, 2012.

Magness, Phillip W., and Sebastian N. Page. *Colonization after Emancipation: Lincoln and the Movement for Black Resettlement.* Columbia: University of Missouri Press, 2011.

Maher, P. E. "Laurence Gronlund: Contributions to American Socialism." *Western Political Quarterly* 15, no. 4 (1962): 618–624.

Mahin, Dean. *The Blessed Place of Freedom: Europeans in Civil War America.* Washington, DC: Brassey's Incorporated, 2002.

Malcolm, Corey. "Transporting African Refugees from Key West to Liberia." *Florida Keys Sea Heritage Journal* 19, no. 2 (Winter 2008/2009): 1–4.

Malmin, Gunnar, ed. *America in the Forties: The Letters of Ole Munch Ræder.* Minneapolis: University of Minnesota Press, 1929.

Mandle, Jay R. *The Roots of Black Poverty: The Southern Plantation Economy after the Civil War.* Durham, NC: Duke University Press, 1978.

Mann, Alan. "The Origins of American Physical Anthropology in Philadelphia." *Yearbook of Physical Anthropology* 52 (2009): 155–163.

Maris-Wolf, Ted. "'Of Blood and Treasure': Recaptive Africans and the Politics of Slave Trade Suppression." *Journal of the Civil War Era* 4, no. 1 (2014): 53–83.

Masur, Kate, *An Example for All the Land: Emancipation and the Struggle over Equality in Washington.* Chapel Hill: University of North Carolina Press, 2010.

——— "Color Was a Bar to the Entrance: African American Activism and the Question of Social Equality in Lincoln's White House." *American Quarterly* 69, no. 1 (2017): 1–22.

Matteson, John Gotlieb. *Matteson Liv Og Adventbevægelsens Begyndelse Blandt Skadinaverne – En Selvbiografi [Matteson's Life and the Adventist Movement's Origin among the Scandinavians – an Autobiography].* College View: International Publishing Association, 1908.

Mattson, Hans. *Early Days of Reconstruction in Northeastern Arkansas.* St. Paul, MN: Pioneer Press Company, 1889.

——— *Reminiscences: The Story of an Emigrant.* Saint Paul, MN: D. D. Merrill Company, 1891.

May, Robert E. *Slavery, Race, and Conquest in the Tropics.* New York: Cambridge University Press, 2013.

McCurry, Stephanie. *Women's War: Fighting and Surviving the American Civil War.* Cambridge, MA: Harvard University Press, 2019.

McPherson, James M. *Abraham Lincoln.* New York: Oxford University Press, 2009.

——— *Battle Cry of Freedom: The Civil War Era.* New York: Oxford University Press, 1988.

——— *Crossroads of Freedom: Antietam.* New York: Oxford University Press, 2002.

——— *For Cause and Comrades: Why Men Fought in the Civil War.* New York: Oxford University Press, 1997.

"'Two Irreconcilable Peoples'? Ethnic Nationalism in the Confederacy." In *The Civil War as Global Conflict: Transnational Meanings of the American Civil War*, edited by David T. Gleeson and Simon Lewis, pp. 85–97. Columbia: University of South Carolina Press, 2014.

Medford, Edna Greene. *Lincoln and Emancipation*. Carbondale: Southern Illinois University Press, 2015.

Medick, Hans. "Weaving and Surviving in Laichingen, 1650–1900: Micro-Historyas History and as Research Experience." In *Agrarian Studies: Synthetic Work at the Cutting Edge*, edited by James C. Scott and Nina Bhatt, pp. 283–296. New Haven, CT: Yale University Press, 2001.

Merritt, Keri Leigh. *Masterless Men: Poor Whites and Slavery in the Antebellum South*. Cambridge: Cambridge University Press, 2017.

Miller, Hunter, ed. *Treaties and Other International Acts of the United States of America*. Vol. 8. Documents 201–240: 1858–1863. Washington, DC: Government Printing Office, 1948.

Mitchell, James. *Report on Colonization and Emigration Made to the Secretary of the Interior by the Agent of Emigration*. Washington, DC: Government Printing Office, 1862.

Moberg, Wilhelm. *Sista Brevet Till Sverige [The Last Letter Home]*. Reprint ed. Stockholm: Alb. Bonniers boktryckeri, 1968.

Mollenhoff, David V. *Madison: A History of the Formative Years*. Madison: University of Wisconsin Press, 2003.

Moneyhon, Carl H. "From Slave to Free Labor: The Federal Plantation Experiment in Arkansas." In *Civil War Arkansas: Beyond Battles and Leaders*, edited by Anne J. Bailey and Daniel E. Sutherland, pp. 177–193. Fayetteville: University of Arkansas Press, 2000.

Mortensen, Enok. *The Danish Lutheran Church in America*. Philadelphia: Board of Publication, Lutheran Church in America, 1967.

Muir, Edward, and Guido Ruggiero. "Afterword: Crime and the Writing of History." In *History from Crime*, edited by Edward Muir and Guido Ruggiero, pp. 226–236. Baltimore, MD: Johns Hopkins University Press, 1994.

Munch, Peter A. *The Strange American Way: Letters of Caja Munch from Wiota, Wisconsin, 1855–1859. With an American Adventure Excerpts from "Vita Mea" an Autobiography Written in 1903 for His Children by Johan Storm Munch – Translated by Helene Munch and Peter A. Munch with an Essay Social Class and Acculturation by Peter A. Munch*. Carbondale: Southern Illinois University Press, 1970.

Munslow, Alun. *Narrative and History*. New York: Palgrave Macmillan, 2007.

Müller-Wille, Stefan. "Race and History: Comments from an Epistemological Point of View." *Science, Technology & Human Values* 39, no. 4 (2014): 597–606.

Nelson, Olof Nickolaus. *History of the Scandinavians and Successful Scandinavians in the United States*. Vol. I. Minneapolis: O. N. Nelson & Company, 1900.

Norelius, E. "Dr Andrew Jackson." In *Korsbanneret*, edited by J. G. Dahlberg and A. O. Bersell, pp. 160–199. Rock Island, IL: Lutheran Augustana Book Concern, 1902.

Notz, William. "Frederick List in America." *American Economic Review* 16, no. 2 (1926): 249–265.

Novak, William J. "The Legal Transformation of Citizenship in Nineteenth-Century America." In *The Democratic Experiment: New Directions in American Political History*, edited by Meg Jacobs, William J. Novak, and Julian E. Zelizer, pp. 89–91. Princeton, NJ: Princeton University Press, 2003.

Oakes, James. *Freedom National: The Destruction of Slavery in the United States, 1861–1865*. New York: W. W. Norton, 2013.

"Om Fremme Af Jespersens Og Wilkens Indbragte Forslag [On Furthering Jespersen's and Wilkens' Motion]." In *Rigsdagstidende*, 1852.

Orr, William J. "Rasmus Sørensen and the Beginning of Danish Settlement in Wisconsin." *Wisconsin Magazine of History* 65, no. 3 (1982): 195–210.

Otteson, James R., ed. *Adam Smith: Selected Philosophical Writings*. Exeter: Imprint Academic, 2004.

Ottosen, Morten Nordhagen. "Folkenes Vår: De Europeiske Revolusjonene 1848–1851 [The People's Spring: The European Revolutions 1848–1851]." In *Demokratiet: Historien Og Ideerne*, edited by Raino Malnes and Dag Einar Thorsen, pp. 218–233. Oslo: Dreyers Forlag, 2014.

Page, Sebastian N. *Black Resettlement and the American Civil War*. Cambridge: Cambridge University Press, 2021.

———. "'A Knife Sharp Enough to Divide Us': William H. Seward, Abraham Lincoln, and Black Colonization." *Diplomatic History* 41, no. 2 (2017).

Pearson, Charles E. "Captain Charles Stevens and the Antebellum Georgia Coasting Trade." *Georgia Historical Quarterly* 75, no. 3 (1991): 485–506.

Pedersen, Erik Helmer. *Drømmen Om America [The Dream of America]*. Politikens Danmarkshistorie. Copenhagen: Politikens Forlag, 1985.

Pedersen, Erik Overgaard. *The Attempted Sale of the Danish West Indies to the United States of America, 1865–1870*. Frankfurt am Main: Haag + Herchen, 1997.

Pierce, Edward Lillie. *A Diplomatic Episode: The Rejected Treaty for St. Thomas*. Boston, MA: 1889.

Pierson, Michael D. *Mutiny at Fort Jackson: The Untold Story of the Fall of New Orleans*. Chapel Hill: University of North Carolina Press, 2008.

Pio, Louis. "The Sioux War in 1862." *Scandinavia*, March, 1884.

Pleasant, Alyssa Mt., and Stephen Kantrowitz. "Campuses, Colonialism, and Land Grabs before Morrill." *Native American and Indigenous Studies* 8, no. 1 (2021): 151–156.

Polk, James K. "Inaugural Address." Online by Gerhard Peters and John T. Woolley, The American Presidency Project. www.presidency.ucsb.edu/documents/inaugural-address-30, 1845.

Pålsson, Ale. *Our Side of the Water: Political Culture in the Swedish Colony of St Barthélemy 1800–1825*. Stockholm: Stockholm University, Faculty of Humanities, Department of History, 2016. http://su.diva-portal.org/smash/record.jsf?pid=diva2%3A967510&dswid=-7542.

Quarstein, John V. *Big Bethel: The First Battle*. Charleston, SC: History Press, 2011.

Quigley, Paul, ed. *The Civil War and the Transformation of American Citizenship*. Baton Rouge: Louisiana State University, 2018.

"Civil War Conscription and the International Boundaries of Citizenship." *Journal of the Civil War Era* 4, no. 3 (2014): 373–397.

Quiner, E. B. *Military History of Wisconsin*. Chicago, IL: Clarke & Co., 1866.

Rashford, R. M., ed. *The Legislative Manual of the State of Wisconsin*. Madison, WI: E. B. Bolens, State Printer, 1877.

Rasmussen, Anders Bo. "'Drawn Together in a Blood Brotherhood': Civic Nationalism Amongst Scandinavian Immigrants in the American Civil War Crucible." *American Studies in Scandinavia* 48, no. 2 (2016): 7–31.

I Krig for Lincoln [*To War for Lincoln*]. Copenhagen: Informations Forlag, 2014.

"'I Long to Hear from You': The Hardship of Civil War Soldiering on Danish Immigrant Families." *The Bridge* 37, no. 1 (2014): 11–40.

"'On Liberty and Equality': Race and Reconstruction among Scandinavian Immigrants, 1864–1868." In *Nordic Whiteness and Migration to the USA: A Historical Exploration of Identity*, edited by Jana Sverdljuk, Terje Joranger, Erika K. Jackson, and Peter Kivisto. New York: Routledge, 2020.

"The Spoils of the Victors: Captain Ferdinand Winslow and the 1863 Curtis Court of Inquiry." *Annals of Iowa* 76, no. 2 (2017): 161–179.

Rasmussen, Mathilde. *Martha Rasmussen*. Little Library of Lutheran Biography, 1945.

Rathbun, Mary Yeater, ed. *The Historic Perry Norwegian Settlement*. Daleyville, WI: Perry Historical Center, 1994.

Reierson, Johan Reymert. *Veiviser for Norske Emigranter Til De Forenede Nordamerikanske Stater Og Texas* [*Guide for Norwegian Emigrants to the North American States and Texas*]. Christiania (Oslo): G. Reiersens Forlag, 1844.

Rives, John C., ed. *The Congressional Globe: Containing the Debates and Proceedings of the Second Session of the Thirty-Sixth Congress*. Washington, DC: Congressional Globe Office, 1861.

ed. *The Congressional Globe: Containing the Debates and Proceedings of the Second Session of the Thirty-Seventh Congress*. Washington, DC: Congressional Globe Office, 1862.

Rives, J., and F. Rives, eds. *The Congressional Globe: Containing the Debates and Proceedings of the First Session of the Thirty-Ninth Congress*. Washington, DC: Congressional Globe Office, 1866.

Roediger, David R. *The Wages of Whiteness: Race and the Making of the American Working Class*. London: Verso, 1991.

Rogers, Jr., William Warren. *Confederate Home Front: Montgomery During the Civil War*. Tuscaloosa: University of Alabama Press, 1999.

Roopnarine, Lomarsh. "The First and Only Crossing: Indian Indentured Servitude on Danish St. Croix, 1863–1868." *South Asian Diaspora* 1, no. 2 (2009): 113–140.

Rosen, Hannah. *Terror in the Heart of Freedom: Citizenship, Sexual Violence, and the Meaning of Race in the Postemancipation South*. Chapel Hill: University of North Carolina Press, 2009.

Rosenstand, Ph. "Fra Guvernør Birchs Dage [From Governor Birch's Days]." In *Tilskueren*, edited by M. Galschiøt, pp. 373–394. Copenhagen: Det Nordiske Forlag, 1900.

Rosholt, Jerry. *Ole Goes to War: Men from Norway Who Fought in America's Civil War*. Decorah: IA: Vesterheim Norwegian-American Museum, 2003.

Rossel, Sven H. "The Image of the United States in Danish Literature: A Survey with Scandinavian Perspectives." In *Images of America in Scandinavia*, edited by Poul Houe and Sven Hakon Rossel, pp. 1–23. Amsterdam: Rodopi, 1998.

Rygg, A. N. *Norwegians in New York 1825–1925*. New York: Norwegian News Company, 1941.

Samito, Christian G. *Becoming American under Fire: Irish Americans, African Americans, and the Politics of Citizenship During the Civil War Era*. Ithaca, NY: Cornell University Press, 2009.

Schloss, Rebecca Hartkopf. *Sweet Liberty: The Final Days of Slavery in Martinique*. Philadelphia: University of Pennsylvania Press, 2009.

Schwalm, Leslie A. *Emancipation's Diaspora: Race and Reconstruction in the Upper Midwest*. Chapel Hill: University of North Carolina Press, 2009.

The Seventh Census of the United States: 1850. Washington, DC: Robert Armstrong, Public Printer, 1853.

Severin, Ernest, Alf L. Scott, T. J. Westerberg, and J. M. Öjerholm. *Svenskarne i Texas i Ord Och Bild, 1838–1918 [The Swedes in Texas in Text and Images, 1838–1918]*. Vol. I. Austin, TX: E. L. Steck, 1919.

Seward, Frederick W. *Reminiscences of a War-Time Statesman and Diplomat, 1830–1915*. New York: G. P. Putnam's Sons, 1916.

Shuffelton, Frank. "Circumstantial Accounts, Dangerous Art: Recognizing African-American Culture Intravelers' Narratives." *Eighteenth-Century Studies* 27, no. 4 (1994): 589–603.

Siemann, Wolfram. *The German Revolution of 1848–49*. Translated by Christiane Banerji. New York: St. Martin's Press, 1998.

Simon, Donald J. "The Third Minnesota Regiment in Arkansas, 1863–1865." *Minnesota History*, no. Summer (1967): 281–292.

Simonsen, Asger Th. *Husmandskår Og Husmandspolitik i 1840erne [Smallholder Conditions and Smallholder Politics in the 1840s]*. Copenhagen: Landbohistorisk Selskab, 1977.

Simpson, Brooks D., Stephen W. Sears, and Aaron Sheehan-Dean, eds. *The Civil War: The First Year Told by Those Who Lived It*. New York: Library of America, 2011.

Sinha, Manisha. *The Slave's Cause: A History of Abolition*. New Haven, CT: Yale University Press, 2016.

Skarstein, Karl Jakob. *The War with the Sioux*. Digital Press Book, 2015. https://commons.und.edu/cgi/viewcontent.cgi?article=1004&context=press-books.

Skocpol, Theda. *Protecting Soldiers and Mothers: The Political Origins of Social Policy in the United States*. Cambridge, MA: Belknap Press of Harvard University Press, 1992.

Skrubbeltrang, Fridlev. *Dansk Vestindien 1848–1880: Politiske Brydninger Og Social Uro [Danish West Indies 1848–1880: Political Conflict and Social*

Unrest]. Vore Gamle Tropekolonier, edited by Johannes Brøndsted. Second ed. 8 vols., vol. 3, Copenhagen: Fremad, 1967.

Smith, Anders Madsen. *En Omvandrende Danskers Tildragelser Paa Jagt Efter Lykken [A Wandering Dane's Pursuit of Happiness]*. Minneapolis, MN, 1891.

Smith, Henry Nash. *Virgin Land: The American West as Symbol and Myth*. First Vintage ed. New York: Vintage Books, 1957.

Smith, Theodore Clarke. "Expansion after the Civil War, 1865–71." *Political Science Quarterly* 16, no. 3 (1901): 412–36.

Sollors, Werner. "How Americans Became White: Three Examples." In *Multiamerica: Essays on Cultural Wars and Cultural Peace*, edited by Ishmael Reed, pp. 3–16. New York: Penguin, 1998.

Sommer, M. A. *Nogle Bemærkninger Til Det Skandinaviske Folk Angaaende Udvandring Til Amerika Især Til Den Store Engelske Provinds Canada Samt Oplysning Om Befordring Til Australien, Ny Seland Og Nord Amerika [Some Remarks to the Scandinavian People Regarding Emigration to America Espeically the Large English Province Canada as Well as Information About Transportation to Australia, New Zeeland and North America]*. Copenhagen: J. Cohens Bogtrykkeri, 1864.

Sperber, Jonathan. *The European Revolutions, 1848–1851*. Cambridge: Cambridge University Press, 1994.

Stahr, Walter. *Seward: Lincoln's Indispensable Man*. New York: Simon & Schuster, 2012.

Stanley, Amy Dru. *From Bondage to Contract: Wage Labor, Marriage, and the Market in the Age of Slave Emancipation*. Cambridge: Cambridge University Press, 1998.

Stiles, T. J. *Jesse James: Last Rebel of the Civil War*. New York: Alfred A. Knopf, 2002.

Stollman, Jennifer A. *Daughters of Israel, Daughters of the South: Southern Jewish Women and Identity in the Antebellum and Civil War South*. Boston, MA: Academic Studies Press, 2013.

Stone, Lawrence. "The Revival of Narrative: Reflections on a New Old History." *Past & Present* 85 (1979): 3–24.

Swanson, Alan. "The Civil War Letters of Olof Liljegren." *Swedish Pioneeer Historical Quarterly* 31, no. 2 (1980): 86–121.

Sørensen, Rasmus. *Er Det for Tiden Nu Bedre for Danske Udvandrere at Søge Arbeidsfortjeneste Og Jordkjøb i Canada, End i Wisconsin Eller i Nogen Anden Af De Vestlige Fristater i Nord-Amerika? [Is It Now Better for Danish Emigrants to Seek Profit and Land in Canada Than Wisconsin or Any Other of the Western Freestates in North America?]* Copenhagen: Græbes Bogtrykkeri, 1863.

Om De Udvandrede Nordmaends Tilstand i Nordamerika: Og Hvorfor Det Vilde Vaere Gavnligt, Om Endeel Danske Bønder Og Handvaerker Udvandrede Ligeledes, Og Bosatte Sig Sammesteds [On the Condition of Emigrated Norwegians in North America: And Why it Would be Beneficial if Some Danish Peasants and Artisans Emigrated and Settled There as Well]. Copenhagen: Niskenske Bogtrykkeri, 1847.

Tansill, Charles Callan. *The Purchase of the Danish West Indies*. Reprint ed. New York: Greenwood Press, Publishers, 1968.

The United States and Santo Domingo, 1798–1873: A Chapter in Caribbean Diplomacy. Reprint ed. Gloucester, MA: Peter Smith, 1967.

Thum, Gregor. "Seapower and Frontier Settlement: Friedrich List's American Vision for Germany." In *German and United States Colonialism in a Connected World: Entangled Empires*, edited by Janne Lahti, pp. 17–39. London: Palgrave Macmillan, 2021.

Tolo, Harold M. "The Political Position of Emigranten in the Election of 1852: A Documentary Article." *Norwegian-American Studies* 8 (1934): 92–111.

Tomek, Beverly C. *Colonization and Its Discontents: Emancipation, Emigration, and Antislavery in Antebellum Pennsylvania*. New York: New York University Press, 2011.

Tyler-McGraw, Marie. *An African Republic: Black and White Virginians in the Making of Liberia*. Chapel Hill: University of North Carolina Press, 2007.

United States Department of State. *Employment of Laborers of African Extraction in the Island of St. Croix. Correspondence between the State Department of the United States and the Chargé D'affaires of Denmark, in Relation to the Advantages Offered by the Island of St. Croix for the Employment of Laborers of African Extraction*. Washington, DC: Government Printing Office, 1862.

United States War Department. *The War of the Rebellion: a Compilation of the Official Records of the Union and Confederate Armies*. Series 3. Vol. 2, Washington, DC: Government Printing Office, 1899.

Unonius, Gustaf. *Minnen Från En Sjuttonårig Vistelse i Nordvestra Amerika I–II* [*Memories from a Seventeen Year Long Stay in the American Northwest I–II*]. Uppsala: W. Schultz's förlag, 1862.

Ural, Susannah J., ed. *Civil War Citizens: Race, Ethnicity and Identity in America's Bloodiest Conflict*. New York: New York University Press, 2010.

Vammen, Hans. "Anmeldelse Af Betænkninger Fra Christian VIII's Tid Om Styrelsen Af Det Danske Monarki [Review of Deliberations from Christian VIII's Reign on Ruling the Danish Monarchy]." *Historisk Tidsskrift* 13, no. 2 (1975): 352–357.

Van Eyck, William O. "The Story of the Propeller Phoenix." *Wisconsin Magazine of History* 7, no. 3 (1924): 281–300.

Vig, Peter Sørensen. *Danske i Amerika* [*Danes in America*]. 2 vols., vol. 1, Minneapolis, MN: C. Rasmussen Company, 1907.

Danske i Krig i Og for Amerika [*Danes Fighting in and for America*]. Omaha, NE: Axel H. Andersen, 1917.

Viscor, Pia. "Danish Immigration to Racine County, Wisconsin: A Case Study of the Pull Effect in Nineteenth-Century Migration." *The Bridge* 31, no. 2 (2008): 9–57.

Waite, Kevin. "Jefferson Davis and Proslavery Visions of Empire in the Far West." *Journal of the Civil War Era* 6, no. 4 (2016): 536–565.

Watt, Robert. *Hinsides Atlanterhavet: Skildringer Fra Amerika* [*Beyond the Atlantic: Accounts from America*]. 3 vols., vol. 2. Copenhagen: P. Bloch, 1872.

White, Richard. *The Republic for Which It Stands: The United States During Reconstruction and the Gilded Age, 1865–1896.* Oxford: Oxford University Press, 2017.

Widen, Carl T. "Texas Swedish Pioneers and the Confederacy." *Swedish Pioneer Historical Society* 12, no. 3 (1961): 100–107.

Wilkins, Christopher. "'They Had Heard of Emancipation and the Enfranchisement of Their Race': The African American Colonists of Samaná, Reconstruction, and the State of Santo Domingo." In *The Civil War as Global Conflict*, edited by David T. Gleeson and Simon Lewis, pp. 211–234. Columbia: University of South Carolina Press, 2014.

Willey, Norman L. "Wergeland and Emigration to America." *Scandinavian Studies and Notes* 16, no. 4 (1940): 121–127.

Winslow, Ferdinand S. "Henry Ward Beechers Prædikener Om Negerne i Amerika [Henry Ward Beecher's Sermons on the Negros in America]." In *Kirkelig Maanedstidende* [*Church Monthly*], edited by Kirkens præster i Amerika, pp. 343–352. Inmansville, WI: Den Skandinaviske Presseforening, 1857.

Wisconsin Constitutional Convention. *Constitution of the State of Wisconsin.* Madison, WI: Beriah Brown, 1848. Online facsimile at www.wisconsinhistory .org/turningpoints/search.asp?id=1627.

Wolfe, Patrick. "Settler Colonialism and the Elimination of the Native." *Journal of Genocide Research* 8, no. 4 (2006): 387–409.

Woodworth, Steven E., ed. *The Loyal, True, and Brave: America's Civil War Soldiers.* Wilmington, DE: Scholarly Resources, 2002.

Manifest Destinies: America's Westward Expansion and the Road to Civil War. New York: Knopf, 2010.

Yinger, Milton J. "Ethnicity." *Annual Review of Sociology* 11 (1985): 151–180.

Zimmermann, Andrew. "From the Rhine to the Mississippi." *Journal of the Civil War Era* 5, no. 1 (2015): 3–37.

Index

CPSIA information can be obtained
at www.ICGtesting.com
Printed in the USA
LVHW110826130922
728238LV00003B/67